Lecture Notes in Computer Science　　9181

Commenced Publication in 1973
Founding and Former Series Editors:
Gerhard Goos, Juris Hartmanis, and Jan van Leeuwen

Editorial Board

More information about this series at http://www.springer.com/series/7409

P.L. Patrick Rau (Ed.)

Cross-Cultural Design

Applications in Mobile Interaction, Education, Health, Transport and Cultural Heritage

7th International Conference, CCD 2015
Held as Part of HCI International 2015
Los Angeles, CA, USA, August 2–7, 2015
Proceedings, Part II

 Springer

Editor
P.L. Patrick Rau
Department of Industrial Engineering
Tsinghua University
Beijing
P.R. China

ISSN 0302-9743   ISSN 1611-3349   (electronic)
Lecture Notes in Computer Science
ISBN 978-3-319-20933-3   ISBN 978-3-319-20934-0   (eBook)
DOI 10.1007/978-3-319-20934-0

Library of Congress Control Number: 2015943044

LNCS Sublibrary: SL3 – Information Systems and Applications, incl. Internet/Web, and HCI

Springer Cham Heidelberg New York Dordrecht London

Printed on acid-free paper

Springer International Publishing AG Switzerland is part of Springer Science+Business Media
(www.springer.com)

Foreword

The 17th International Conference on Human-Computer Interaction, HCI International 2015, was held in Los Angeles, CA, USA, during 2–7 August 2015. The event incorporated the 15 conferences/thematic areas listed on the following page.

A total of 4843 individuals from academia, research institutes, industry, and governmental agencies from 73 countries submitted contributions, and 1462 papers and 246 posters have been included in the proceedings. These papers address the latest research and development efforts and highlight the human aspects of design and use of computing systems. The papers thoroughly cover the entire field of Human-Computer Interaction, addressing major advances in knowledge and effective use of computers in a variety of application areas. The volumes constituting the full 28-volume set of the conference proceedings are listed on pages VII and VIII.

I would like to thank the Program Board Chairs and the members of the Program Boards of all thematic areas and affiliated conferences for their contribution to the highest scientific quality and the overall success of the HCI International 2015 conference.

This conference could not have been possible without the continuous and unwavering support and advice of the founder, Conference General Chair Emeritus and Conference Scientific Advisor, Prof. Gavriel Salvendy. For their outstanding efforts, I would like to express my appreciation to the Communications Chair and Editor of HCI International News, Dr. Abbas Moallem, and the Student Volunteer Chair, Prof. Kim-Phuong L. Vu. Finally, for their dedicated contribution towards the smooth organization of HCI International 2015, I would like to express my gratitude to Maria Pitsoulaki and George Paparoulis, General Chair Assistants.

May 2015

Constantine Stephanidis
General Chair, HCI International 2015

HCI International 2015 Thematic Areas and Affiliated Conferences

Thematic areas:

- Human-Computer Interaction (HCI 2015)
- Human Interface and the Management of Information (HIMI 2015)

Affiliated conferences:

- 12th International Conference on Engineering Psychology and Cognitive Ergonomics (EPCE 2015)
- 9th International Conference on Universal Access in Human-Computer Interaction (UAHCI 2015)
- 7th International Conference on Virtual, Augmented and Mixed Reality (VAMR 2015)
- 7th International Conference on Cross-Cultural Design (CCD 2015)
- 7th International Conference on Social Computing and Social Media (SCSM 2015)
- 9th International Conference on Augmented Cognition (AC 2015)
- 6th International Conference on Digital Human Modeling and Applications in Health, Safety, Ergonomics and Risk Management (DHM 2015)
- 4th International Conference on Design, User Experience and Usability (DUXU 2015)
- 3rd International Conference on Distributed, Ambient and Pervasive Interactions (DAPI 2015)
- 3rd International Conference on Human Aspects of Information Security, Privacy and Trust (HAS 2015)
- 2nd International Conference on HCI in Business (HCIB 2015)
- 2nd International Conference on Learning and Collaboration Technologies (LCT 2015)
- 1st International Conference on Human Aspects of IT for the Aged Population (ITAP 2015)

Conference Proceedings Volumes Full List

1. LNCS 9169, Human-Computer Interaction: Design and Evaluation (Part I), edited by Masaaki Kurosu
2. LNCS 9170, Human-Computer Interaction: Interaction Technologies (Part II), edited by Masaaki Kurosu
3. LNCS 9171, Human-Computer Interaction: Users and Contexts (Part III), edited by Masaaki Kurosu
4. LNCS 9172, Human Interface and the Management of Information: Information and Knowledge Design (Part I), edited by Sakae Yamamoto
5. LNCS 9173, Human Interface and the Management of Information: Information and Knowledge in Context (Part II), edited by Sakae Yamamoto
6. LNAI 9174, Engineering Psychology and Cognitive Ergonomics, edited by Don Harris
7. LNCS 9175, Universal Access in Human-Computer Interaction: Access to Today's Technologies (Part I), edited by Margherita Antona and Constantine Stephanidis
8. LNCS 9176, Universal Access in Human-Computer Interaction: Access to Interaction (Part II), edited by Margherita Antona and Constantine Stephanidis
9. LNCS 9177, Universal Access in Human-Computer Interaction: Access to Learning, Health and Well-Being (Part III), edited by Margherita Antona and Constantine Stephanidis
10. LNCS 9178, Universal Access in Human-Computer Interaction: Access to the Human Environment and Culture (Part IV), edited by Margherita Antona and Constantine Stephanidis
11. LNCS 9179, Virtual, Augmented and Mixed Reality, edited by Randall Shumaker and Stephanie Lackey
12. LNCS 9180, Cross-Cultural Design: Methods, Practice and Impact (Part I), edited by P.L. Patrick Rau
13. LNCS 9181, Cross-Cultural Design: Applications in Mobile Interaction, Education, Health, Transport and Cultural Heritage (Part II), edited by P.L. Patrick Rau
14. LNCS 9182, Social Computing and Social Media, edited by Gabriele Meiselwitz
15. LNAI 9183, Foundations of Augmented Cognition, edited by Dylan D. Schmorrow and Cali M. Fidopiastis
16. LNCS 9184, Digital Human Modeling and Applications in Health, Safety, Ergonomics and Risk Management: Human Modeling (Part I), edited by Vincent G. Duffy
17. LNCS 9185, Digital Human Modeling and Applications in Health, Safety, Ergonomics and Risk Management: Ergonomics and Health (Part II), edited by Vincent G. Duffy
18. LNCS 9186, Design, User Experience, and Usability: Design Discourse (Part I), edited by Aaron Marcus
19. LNCS 9187, Design, User Experience, and Usability: Users and Interactions (Part II), edited by Aaron Marcus
20. LNCS 9188, Design, User Experience, and Usability: Interactive Experience Design (Part III), edited by Aaron Marcus

Cross-Cultural Design

Program Board Chair: P.L. Patrick Rau, P.R. China

The full list with the Program Board Chairs and the members of the Program Boards of all thematic areas and affiliated conferences is available online at:

http://www.hci.international/2015/

HCI International 2016

The 18th International Conference on Human-Computer Interaction, HCI International 2016, will be held jointly with the affiliated conferences in Toronto, Canada, at the Westin Harbour Castle Hotel, 17–22 July 2016. It will cover a broad spectrum of themes related to Human-Computer Interaction, including theoretical issues, methods, tools, processes, and case studies in HCI design, as well as novel interaction techniques, interfaces, and applications. The proceedings will be published by Springer. More information will be available on the conference website: http://2016.hci.international/.

General Chair
Prof. Constantine Stephanidis
University of Crete and ICS-FORTH
Heraklion, Crete, Greece
Email: general_chair@hcii2016.org

http://2016.hci.international/

Contents – Part II

Culture for Health, Learning and Games

Contents – Part I

Cross-Cultural Design Methods and Case Studies

Design, Innovation, Social Development and Sustainability

Cultural Aspects of Social Media and Mobile Services

Culturally Appropriate Design of Mobile Learning Applications in the Malaysian Context

Shamsul Arrieya Ariffin[1](✉) and Laurel Evelyn Dyson[2]

[1] Faculty of Art, Computing and Creative Industry, University Pendidikan
Sultan Idris, Tanjung Malim, Perak, Malaysia
shamsul@fskik.upsi.edu.my
[2] Faculty of Engineering and Information Technology,
University of Technology, Sydney, Australia

Abstract. Many developing countries lack culturally appropriate design guidelines to inform the development of m-learning applications suitable for local use. This study presents the findings from a heuristic evaluation by academics and students at public universities in Malaysia for three locally produced mobile learning applications. The local cultural content and aesthetic values of the applications found a high level of acceptance with the participants. As a result, four principles were identified to support the design of culturally appropriate interfaces for mobile learning applications for the Malaysian context. These were: suitable local cultural content; aesthetic value according to local culture, including appropriate choice of color, and traditional designs and motifs derived largely from local flora and fauna; local language or bilingual communication; and local philosophical values embedded in the content and design.

Keywords: Culturally appropriate interface design · Mobile learning · Usability

1 Introduction

According to Hussin (2011), students at Malaysian universities are ready for mobile learning (m-learning) due to their high rate of ownership of mobile devices. However, to date, there are no national policies on m-learning in Malaysia (So, 2012). In developing countries, such as Malaysia, there is a lack of local content for use in m-learning and a shortage of local digital multimedia learning resources, including local online resources that students might access from their mobile devices (So, 2012). The dominance of mobile content and applications ("apps") from overseas, particularly from English-speaking countries, such as the USA and the UK, contributes to this situation. Faced with this competition and given the relatively small market in which Malaysian mobile developers are operating, there is little financial incentive for the production of content for mobile use for m-learning, either generally or specifically (Ariffin, 2014). In addition, there is a lack of culturally appropriate design guidelines

© Springer International Publishing Switzerland 2015
P.L.P. Rau (Ed.): CCD 2015, Part II, LNCS 9181, pp. 3–14, 2015.
DOI: 10.1007/978-3-319-20934-0_1

to inform developers who might wish to create m-learning content and applications for local use. Meanwhile, Kukulska-Hulme (2008) notes that usability issues have often been ignored in m-learning, while Sharples, Taylor and Vavoula (2007) emphasize the significance of usability in improving m-learning effectiveness. Having user interfaces for m-learning purposes designed with local culture in mind can facilitate learning by representing students' own cultural values and engender a greater sense of belonging (Young, 2008). In the same way that students are more motivated when elements of their own culture are included in traditional learning materials (Abdullah & Chandran, 2009), local culture can motivate students in m-learning. Studies have been conducted for implementing African American and American Indian (Eglash et al., 2006), and Chinese culture (Sun, 2012) for a culturally appropriate technology design. However, this study focuses on a culturally appropriate design that can reduce the usability challenges for students employing new mobile applications in Malaysia with the inclusion of the Malay culture.

This paper reports on an investigation of a culturally appropriate interface design for m-learning applications for use in public educational institutions in Malaysia. Despite the cultural plurality of Malaysia, many aspects of culture are shared by all ethnic groups in the country; for example, everyone learns the national language, Bahasa Malaysia, and Islam is the national religion, and, thus, informs government policy on behavioral norms for digital content (SKMM Guidelines, 2012). In order to develop the principles of culturally appropriate interface designs, academics and students at two public universities were asked to take part in a heuristic evaluation of three Malaysian m-learning applications, during and after which they provided their perspectives on culturally appropriate designs and usability. The tool for obtaining their input and stimulating discussion on this issue was a set of usability principles or heuristics based largely on those of Nielsen (Nielsen, 1993; Nielsen, & Mack, 1994), and the mobile adaptations of Nielsen by Bertini, Gabrielli and Kimani (2006), but with the addition of Malay cultural dimensions.

This research does not focus on classifying cultures using the abstract dimensions that are widely used by Hofstede (1984). Hofstede's dimensions focus on the hidden parts of a culture, and, therefore, are not suitable for cultural analysis or "*the inspection of the tangible artefacts produced by that culture*" (Jones & Marsden, 2006, p. 324). Thus, this research proposes and applies a pragmatic approach (Ariffin, 2011) for evaluating the tangible products, such as the m-learning application's user interface for culturally appropriate design principles for the Malaysian context.

We begin by presenting the literature on the role of culture in the usability of m-learning applications, especially in the Malaysian context. A description of our research methods outlines the procedure for the heuristic evaluation by academics and students, and the interviews and focus group discussions that followed. The results of the research include insights into those aspects of Malaysian culture that are perceived by users to be important in the design of m-learning applications, centering around four principles: suitable local cultural content, aesthetic value according to local culture, local language or bilingual communication, and local philosophical values. It is hoped that the understanding developed through this process will lead to the production of better m-learning resources for Malaysian students and stimulate other countries to develop their own guidelines that are appropriate to their own cultures. Most importantly, we believe that this research will stimulate more discussion of the significant role of culture in human computer interaction, and, specifically, in interface design for m-learning.

1.1   Culture and the Usability of Malaysian M-Learning Applications

Nielsen (1990, p. 39) emphasizes the importance of culture in interface design and the resulting lack of transferability of usability testing from one culture to another. Yeo (1996) stresses the need for cultural considerations of user interfaces for Asian cultures. Specifically, in the Malaysian context, Yeo et al. (2011) indicate that there is a lack of research in the area of interface usability and local culture. Existing usability design guidelines, such as those of Nielsen (1993), do not consider cultural aspects. The importance of culture applies equally to the design of user interfaces for m-learning. Young (2008) highlights one of the important challenges for m-learning as coming from the lack of guidelines for acknowledging local culture in the design of m-learning applications. The inclusion of cultural differences in the design of mobile user interfaces is for the benefit of m-learning application users, such as students and teachers. One of the few studies undertaken in Malaysia is that of Seong (2006), which focuses on the design of a Malaysian m-learning portal. The study proposes usability guidelines for a web portal to facilitate learning using mobile phones. The guidelines cover user analysis, interaction and m-learning interface design. He highlights nationality and language as part of the user analysis but provides no further details on how these might be incorporated. Neither does his study provide information on culturally appropriate design guidelines specifically for the Malay culture. The 1Malaysia studies by Zaibon and Shiratuddin (2010), though culturally focused, dealt with intercultural issues of the Malays, Chinese and Indians rather than Malay cultural appropriateness. In fact, there have been limited qualitative studies of m-learning that focus solely on Malay cultural appropriateness in the Malaysian context.

The cultural design principles are largely inspired by the national cultural policy and Malay cultural literature, which, in the Malaysian context, pertains to Bahasa Malaysia (local language), Malay and Islamic philosophical values, local aesthetic elements (e.g. local motifs from flora and fauna; and local color preferences), and local cultural content (e.g. art and craft traditions).

- **Local Language (Bahasa Malaysia).** Language plays an important role in the Malay society (Mastor, Jin, & Cooper, 2000). Bahasa Malaysia is the official language, and, together with English, is widely spoken, whether in formal educational institutions, such as universities, or outside of these institutions. Therefore, for m-learning applications, Bahasa Malaysia, or bilingual Bahasa Malaysia and English, represent the obvious languages of choice wherever titles, captions, spoken language, etc. are needed. Linked to Bahasa Malaysia is Jawi, an old writing script for the Malay language based on the Arabic script, which dates back to the fifteenth-century (Diah, Ismail, Hami, & Ahmad, 2011). Although it has been replaced by the Western alphabet in most practical situations, it is still studied and used in Malaysia.

- **Local Philosophy (Malay and Islamic).** The Malay philosophy of life is related to nature and Islamic philosophy (Hussin, 2010; Jamal, 1992; Mastor, Jin, & Cooper, 2000). This includes the Malay attitudes and moral values embedded in m-learning applications. Local moral values are reflected in the Content Code of the Malaysian Communications and Multimedia Commission (SKMM Guidelines, 2012), which specifies the content to be avoided, such as content that is indecent, obscene, violent, menacing, contains offensive language, makes false claims, is unsafe for children, or which neglects family values. The Content Code applies to any digital content developed locally, and thus, includes Malaysian m-learning applications. Thus, m-learning applications need to portray characters in a dignified way, and avoid bad language and violence, which might be imitated by children.
- **Local Aesthetic Values (Flora and Fauna) and local colors (from Nature).** The Malay culture is closely related to nature, in as much as the country has its own distinctive flora and fauna. Most of the environmental elements, even people's lifestyle in the "kampongs" or villages, influence the Malay local art and design. This includes plants and flowers, as well as the philosophy that lies beneath. For example, the motifs and designs in Malay culture are reflected in the design of traditional clothes made from Batik and Songket textiles (Bahauddin & Abdullah, 2003; Hussin, 2010; Ismail, 2010; Jamal, 1992; Jamil, Sembok, & Bakar, 2012). In Malaysian Batik, the motifs and designs are derived from the flora and the universe, instead of from animals and human figures, the representation of which is discouraged by the Islamic religion (Hussin, 2010). On the other hand, colors also influence the life of the Malay people, for example, black represents bad luck, white represents purity and yellow represents royalty. The Malay usage of color is rarely bright unless it is used for festivals, such as "Aidilfitri" at the end of Ramadan or for weddings. Local aesthetic values must fit with local philosophical values (Malay and Islamic).
- **Local Cultural Content.** The Malay culture highlights the importance of art and craft. Typical examples include woodcraft, musical instruments and textiles like Batik (patterned cloth produced by a process of waxing and dying) and Songket (gold and silver hand-woven brocades) (Asiapac Editorial, 2010; Bahauddin & Abdullah, 2003). Malay crafts are inextricably linked to Malay aesthetics and philosophical values, representing the Malay people's attitudes: tolerance of one another, and, despite their differences, respect for everyone living in the community, (Ahmadi, 2004). For example, woodcraft includes concepts, such as "growing from a source", "growing without piercing a friend", "climbing without clinging to a rival", and "intertwining with grace and friendliness" (Ahmadi, 2004, p. 67; Othman, 2005, p. 102). The incorporation of these four elements of local culture into the design of m-learning applications in the Malaysian context would appear to be one way of ensuring culturally appropriate interfaces.

2 Research Methods

The academics and students who took part in this study came from the Faculties of Music and Performing Arts, Art and Design, Technical and Vocational Education, Education and Human Development, Human Sciences, Computing and Creative Industries, Management and Economics, and Science and Mathematics at two public Malaysian universities. Firstly, three Malaysian m-learning applications were chosen for a heuristic evaluation. The applications focused on learning about three of the traditional forms of Malaysian culture described above: Batik, Songket and Jawi. The language used in the applications was mostly English. The number of participants was as follows: 10 academics and 51 students evaluated the Batik application; 10 academics and 46 students evaluated the Songket application; and 9 academics and 39 students evaluated the Jawi application. The applications were evaluated on mobile phones provided by the researchers, which included a variety of devices with large screen formats operating on Windows, Android and Symbian operating systems. The duration of the evaluation lasted about 15 to 30 min for each participant, with academics undertaking their evaluation individually, and two or three students undertaking their evaluations simultaneously, but with one phone per participant. During the evaluations, one of the researchers acted as an observer and assisted the participants if they were having trouble using the mobile applications, for example, if they did not know how to start the application. The participants responded to a series of statements based on heuristic principles, rating each according to a 5-point Likert scale. This provided an overall quantitative measure of how the applications measured up against the usability criteria. In addition, there were two open-ended questions: What are the advantages of the mobile applications? And, what can be improved through these applications? The answers to these two questions provided qualitative data and rich insights into the views of the participants on the usability of the applications, particularly with respect to their cultural appropriateness.

A battery of statements was devised using principles modified from the Nielsen Heuristic Evaluation User Interface Design Guidelines (Nielsen & Mack, 1994), as adapted by Bertini et al. (2006) to mobile applications. A summative evaluation was undertaken since the applications were all finished products (Nielsen, 1993). The statements probed the views of the participants concerning accessibility, consistency, good ergonomic and minimalist user interface design, readability and ease of recall, efficiency and flexibility, and realistic error management. The first heuristic of Nielsen and Mack (1994), and Bertini et al. (2006) – "visibility of system status" – was replaced by accessibility as this was believed to be more important in m-learning: "*Before students can engage in any m-learning activity, they must be able to effectively access and interact*" with the mobile application on the device (Rainger, 2005, p. 58). In addition, the evaluation was extended with heuristics about the Malay culture: suitable local cultural content, and aesthetic value according to the local culture. The heuristic "suitable local cultural content" was adapted from the second heuristic of Nielsen and Mack (1994), and Bertini et al. (2006) – "match between system and the real world" – following the principle that "The system should speak the user's lan-guage" (Nielsen & Mack, 1994, p. 13). In the Malaysian context, this was interpreted to mean that the cultural content should be familiar to students at Malaysian public universities, who are predominantly from a Malay background. The heuristic "aesthetic value according to the local culture" was adapted from Bertini et al.'s (2006) "aesthetics, privacy and social conventions" in which our adaptation takes into account local cultural aesthetic preferences, for example, colors and visual elements.

Following the heuristic evaluation, the opinions of the participants concerning culturally appropriate user interface design for m-learning applications were collected via interviews and focus groups. Fifteen academics were involved in individual semi-structured interviews, and 127, mostly Malay students, took part in 15 focus groups. Focus group discussions were selected as an appropriate method for data collection from the students, as Malaysian students are more responsive when they discuss in groups, rather than being asked questions individually. The interviews and focus groups were part of a wider study to gain an understanding of academic and student perspectives towards m-learning, particularly in the context of local culture. The researcher's methodology in examining the data from the interviews and focus groups discussions was through thematic analysis (Braun & Clarke 2006). The researcher handled, gathered and arranged the data by utilizing NVivo.

2.1   Results of the Heuristic Evaluation

We present the participants' responses to all the user interface design principles since they have a bearing on how Malaysian m-learning applications should be designed. However, the two principles that focus on local cultural content and aesthetic values are the most interesting from a cultural point of view. The rankings for each statement for both academics and students have been averaged to provide an overall evaluation of whether or not the participants agree with the statements. It can be seen that, on average, the participants ranked the three applications highly, including the cultural heuristics regarding local content and local aesthetic value. The greatest problems were experienced with touch screen interaction, navigation and error management, nevertheless, even these scored only slightly below 4.0 on the Likert scale of 1-5. The aesthetics of the audio files associated with the applications received the lowest ranking of the cultural heuristics, scoring 3.92 for the Batik and 3.89 for the Songket applications (Ariffin, 2014).

Good Ergonomic and Minimalist User Interface Design. Apart from some issues with the design of the mobile phones on which the applications were being tested, the participants responded well to the applications from the point of view of ergonomic and minimalist design. The interface of the Batik application, in particular, was viewed as simple, easy to understand, and brief but informative.

Readability and Ease of Recall. The participants wanted a readable user interface, but, by contrast, most encountered difficulties. However, one academic noted that *"The Batik pictures look real. The interface is readable"*, all other academics concurred with *"a need to enlarge the size of the visual, which is small and it needs to be clearer."* Likewise, students requested *"that the text be enlarged for Batik and Songket local mobile applications ... The Jawi mobile application needs to increase the size of the* *text ... The buttons and hyperlinks should be more visible.*" From this evaluation, the importance of the readability of m-learning applications is emphasized.

Efficiency and Flexibility. Academics indicated that they wanted efficiency when using the m-learning applications. They wanted a mobile application that was fast to access for immediate use. However, most academics commented on having difficulty with slow speeds using the applications: comments included *"The application should be faster for the Batik and Songket applications"*; *"The Songket application has problems with exiting because it is very slow."* Students also had issues with the speed of using the m-learning applications.

Realistic Error Management. Both academics and students voiced their concerns over the lack of a 'Help' function for providing users with instructions on how to utilize the applications. Students noted that the Batik application *"can be improved by having clear information with pictures as instructions."* In addition, the greatest impact on usability was with the Jawi application: *"With the Jawi mobile application, the only drawback is that there is no help or instruction on how to play the games".* Because of the lack of a Help function, or, as one academic suggested *"the use of icons and symbols embedded into the Jawi application"*, most users did not know how to use it properly.

Suitable Local Cultural Content. The academics and students agreed that the m-learning application content was mostly suitable to the local culture. In addition, they found that the local content was useful and informative for learning about the Malay culture. On the other hand, both groups demanded greater availability of mobile applications with local content, and greater and more detailed cultural content in the three applications that were tested. One issue noted by a number of students, but overlooked by the academics, was the issue of the Malay language. All three applications were in the English language, apart from odd words like 'batik' and some terms for particular motifs or patterns. Students expressed a wish for the applications to be created *"in our local Malay language too."* However, one academic noted how the Jawi application answered a need for representation of the local language, not so much as a means of communication, but as an icon of Malay culture: *"For me Jawi portrays an example of Islam identity".*

Aesthetic Value according to the Local Culture. The participants responded fairly positively to the aesthetic values of the m-learning application interfaces, particularly with respect to the Batik application and Jawi software, which were seen to be in accord with local culture: *"... beautiful graphics design color."* These findings indicate the importance for the user interface of the m-learning applications used in Malaysia to comply with the aesthetic values that have their roots in local culture.

2.2   Results of the Academic Interviews and Student Focus Groups

Following the heuristic evaluation, academics were interviewed and focus groups conducted to gain their perspectives on an appropriate user interface design for m-learning applications. Many academics cited general usability principles that had nothing to do with culture. For example, ease of use, speed and efficiency were all priorities, with some academics quoting their BlackBerry, iPhone or tablet PC as being efficient for achieving their tasks or for their students to use. For several academics, the simplicity of presentation of local content was important, as mobile content that was dense with images could be difficult to view. The themes generated are: Need more local content, help to facilitate learning local culture better, mobile application limitations, potential for incorporating local philosophical values, local aesthetic values in design, and fusion of new ideas.

Need More Local Content. Academics worry about how 'overseas' cultures, such as the USA, have influenced the minds of the younger generation, such as students. One of them pointed out that the younger generation idolized overseas content, such as from 'Disney' cartoons compared to their own local cultural heritage icon story: *"There is so much Western content, such as embedded characters of 'Snow White' and all other sorts of Disney cartoons."* Students expressed a desire for applications that conveyed their own culture, complaining about the predominance of applications from overseas: *"... Why do we not have an application for our own culture on mobile phones?"*

Help to Facilitate Learning Local Culture Better. However, there were also academics who valued the fact that the cultural content from the mobile applications could improve the learning of their students: *"From the mobile application we can study the relation between motifs in Batik now with motifs from crafts in the Stone Age..."* The m-learning applications were rated very highly. Typical comments from academics include: *"I like the Batik and Songket applications for learning. The Jawi application also facilitates the learning process and is a fun learning culture source."* Students noted that m-learning was an ideal way of learning about their culture, including the diverse cultures that make up the states of Malaysia: *"We hope there will be mobile application software available for other states."* The students also rated the applications very highly from an educational and usability point of view and obviously found them very engaging: *"The Batik application is interesting and easy to understand for the students. The Songket application can introduce the motifs that are rarely seen."*

Mobile Application Limitations. On the other hand, one academic noted the limitations of conveying local content via mobile applications: *"It is a good start for learners."* One student suggested that the applications should be brief with simple information and interactivity, such as a combination of information and games: *"combine the concept of Jawi games, and information of the Batik apps..."*

Local Philosophical Values. A number of academics also appreciated the potential for Malay philosophical values to be embedded with local design motifs in mobile application interfaces. They saw this as adding local aesthetic value and reflecting the local cultural identity. One interviewee highlighted that Japanese people are proud of their own local design motifs that are widely utilized in their lives, including mobile applications. Another academic preferred local colors, which reflected the Malay culture instead of adopting those from other cultures, and saw the possibility of transferring local design elements used on local artefacts to the mobile application user interface: *"...promote our own Batik".*

Local Aesthetic Values in Design. In addition, academics noted the relation between learning content and the aesthetic design in which that content was embedded, and that learning is much more interesting using a mobile application because of this: *"The visuals in Batik and Songket applications are very beautiful."* However, there were many negative comments about color from both academics and students. Although some liked the Songket application and found its interface aesthetically pleasing, it also incurred the most negative comments: *"...looks dull ...has less of a chance to attract the kids... orange looks 'Indianish'."* Many students in the focus groups expressed a desire for the use of local motifs, designs and colors in the user interfaces of mobile applications. Batik motifs were specifically mentioned. In addition, designs derived from local flora and fauna were particularly popular, and brown and green were seen as culturally appropriate colors because they were linked to the flora and fauna.

Fusion of New Ideas. An academic preferred more vibrant colours, as this could attract learners to use the mobile application: *"Use brighter colour, such as red, black and orange for Islamic applications."* However, some students preferred more vibrant colours, and saw these as a way of enhancing local cultural elements by creating a fusion of new ideas with traditional design: *"User Interface must be vibrant to attract the attention."*

3 Discussion

This exploration of a culturally appropriate interface design for m-learning in Malaysia has demonstrated that in the opinion of our participants, culture is a consideration that must be taken into account when designing m-learning applications. Both academics and students responded very positively to the inclusion of local cultural content and to the Malay aesthetic values used on the application interfaces, such as color and traditional designs and motifs. This was seen as motivating for students' learning and a way of engaging them in their studies. Malay and Islamic philosophical values, on the other hand, were seen as being embedded in the local content and aesthetic values, and were less often mentioned as a separate entity. However, they are part of the Content Code to which all mobile developers in Malaysia must adhere (SKMM Guidelines, 2012).

Language was one aspect of the interface design that students emphasized but which our heuristics failed to highlight, despite its importance in Malaysian culture. It is curious that all three applications, despite being developed in Malaysia, chose English as their mode of communication, perhaps following the convention established by the mobile content imported from overseas, which dominates the market. In addition, the use of a Jawi transcript, without having a Bahasa Malaysia translation in the user interface instructions, could discourage novices who did not know how to read Jawi. This study shows that language needs to be defined by a separate heuristic in order to encourage developers to choose either the local language, Bahasa Malaysia, or a bilingual interface. As a result of the findings of this research, we propose four principles for a culturally appropriate interface design for m-learning applications for the Malaysian context, in no specific order of importance: Suitable local cultural content; Aesthetic value according to local culture; Local language or bilingual communication; and local philosophical values embedded in content and design.

We note that keeping to traditional cultural norms may not always be appropriate as some participants expressed a desire for a fusion of the traditional with the modern, which may be a way of attracting young people to m-learning. Further research is needed on this point. However, our research also shows that it is insufficient to focus solely on culture. General usability principles are also viewed as important, for example, consistency, minimalist design, efficiency, flexibility and error management. Failure with respect to these heuristics in the trial of the m-learning applications evoked criticism from both academics and students. For example, the lack of a help function to provide users with instructions on how to utilize the applications was of concern to most participants, particularly with the Jawi game. The slow speed of the applications also resulted in negative feedback with respect to the heuristic of efficiency. The evaluation further shows that m-learning applications need to consider the smaller size of the interface, particularly when mobile phones are the device being used. Thus, the heuristic of readability included in the model by Bertini et al. (2006) has been demonstrated to be extremely important; most academics and students voiced their concern over the small size of text, images, buttons or hyperlinks for all three applications. There is possibly a higher level of difficulty in achieving this with interfaces that include Malay cultural content and aesthetics since many of the traditional designs and motifs are highly intricate. This requires further investigation, which is beyond the current study.

4 Conclusion

Overall, the m-learning applications were rated very highly by the academics and students who took part in this study, as measured quantitatively by means of a Likert scale as well as qualitatively by analyzing the comments of the participants. Moreover, the cultural content and local aesthetics were widely appreciated. Even participants who were not associated with cultural studies courses valued the way in which the applications reflected local culture. M-learning applications that acknowledge local culture may be a way of improving usability and keeping the Malaysian culture alive and thus avoiding the pressure of the globalizing forces of overseas mobile content.

The study resulted in the identification of four principles for a culturally appropriate design for m-learning applications in the Malaysian context: suitable local cultural content; aesthetic value according to local culture, including appropriate choice of color, and traditional designs and motifs; local language or bilingual communication; and local philosophical values embedded in content and design. Further research is needed to order the principles in this list according to their importance, and to validate their impact on usability, even though the literature supports the view that culture has a role in improving usability (Young, 2008). In addition, there is a need to investigate further the interplay between the cultural factors and the more general usability principles that this research confirms must be satisfied in order to produce application interfaces that users find acceptable. It would also be of benefit to extend this work to m-learning applications that incorporate cultural aspects but for which the main purpose is not cultural learning. While acknowledging the limitations of the research, it is expected that these findings will lead to a more culturally appropriate interface design for m-learning applications in Malaysia. It is also hoped that the principles put forward here will form the basis for other countries, especially those in the developing world, to develop guidelines to satisfy the requirements of their own cultural traditions.

References

Abdullah, N., Chandran, S. K.: Cultural elements in a Malaysian English language textbook (2009) viewed 27 August 2013, <http://ddms.usim.edu.my/handle/123456789/713>

Ahmadi, A.R.: Tamadun rumpun budaya Melayu (Malay Culture Community Civilization). Kementerian Kebudayaan, Kesenian dan Warisan Malaysia (2004)

Ariffin, S. A.: The Contribution of mLearning to the Study of Local Culture in the Malaysian University Context (Doctoral thesis, UTS, Sydney, Australia) (2014)

Ariffin, S.A.: Mobile learning in the institution of higher learning for Malaysia students: Culture perspectives. IJASEIT 3, 283–288 (2011)

Editorial, Asiapac: Gateway to Malay Culture, 5th edn. Asiapac Books, Singapore (2010)

Bahauddin, A., Abdullah, A.: The songkct motifs: between reality and belief. Paper presented at the Tourism, Histories and Representations Conference at the University of Central Lancashire, Preston England (2003). http://citeseerx.ist.psu.edu/viewdoc/download?doi=10.1.1.200.5688&rep=rep1&type=pdf

Bertini, E., Gabrielli, S., Kimani, S.: .Appropriating and assessing heuristics for mobile computing. In: Proceedings of the Working Conference on Advanced Visual Interfaces pp. 119–26. ACM, Venice, Italy (2006)

Braun, V., Clarke, V.: Using thematic analysis in psychology. Qual. Res. Psychol. 3(2), 77–101 (2006)

Diah, N.M., Ismail, M., Hami, P.M.A., Ahmad, S.: Assisted Jawi-writing (AJaW) software for children. In: 2011 IEEE Conference Open Systems (ICOS), pp. 322–326, Langkawi, Malaysia (2011)

Eglash, R., Bennett, A., Casey, D., Jennings, S., Cintorino, M.: Culturally situated design tools: ethnocomputing from field site to classroom. Am. Anthropol. 108(2), 347–362 (2006)

Hofstede, G.: Culture's consequences: International differences in work-related values, vol. 5 Sage (1984)

Hussin, H.: Nature motifs in Malay batik and songket. DBP, KL, Malaysia (2010)

Hussin, S.: Mobile learning readiness among Malaysian students at higher learning institutes. APAC MLearning 2011, pp. 1–11, Bandung, Indonesia (2011)

Ismail, S.Z.: 100 Malay proverbs: Pepatah petitih Melayu. 1st edn. KL, Malaysia: Institut Terjemahan Negara Malaysia Berhad (2010)

Jamal, S.A.: Rupa dan jiwa (Appearance and soul). 1st edn. KL, Malaysia: DBP (1992)

Jamil, N., Sembok, T.M.T., Bakar, Z.A.: Digital Archiving of Traditional Songket Motifs using Image Processing Tool. In: Niola, V., Ng, K.-L. (eds.) Recent Researches in Chemistry, Biology, Environment and Culture, pp. 33–39. WSEAS Press, Montreux Switzerland (2012)

Jones, M., Marsden, G.: Mobile Interaction Design. Wiley & Sons, England (2006)

Kukulska-Hulme, A.: Human factors and innovation with mobile devices. In: Hansson, T. (ed.) Handbook of Research on Digital Information Technologies: Innovations, Methods and Ethical Issues, pp. 392–403. IGI Global, Hershey, PA (2008)

Mastor, K.A., Jin, P., Cooper, M.: Malay culture and personality. Am. Behav. Sci. 44(1), 95–111 (2000)

Nielsen, J.: Usability testing of international interfaces. In: Nielsen, J. (ed.) Designing User Interfaces for International Use, pp. 39–44. Elsevier Science Pub. Ltd, Essex (1990)

Nielsen, J.: Usability engineering. Morgan Kaufmann, San Diego, CA (1993)

Nielsen, J., Mack, R.L.: Usability inspection methods. Wiley & Sons, USA (1994)

Othman, R.: The language of the Langkasukan motif. Indonesia & the Malay World **33**(96), 97–111 (2005)

Rainger, P.: Accessibility and mobile learning. In: Kukulska-Hulme, A. Traxler, J. (eds.), Mobile learning: a handbook for educators and trainers, pp. 57–69. Routledge, London & New York (2005)

Seong, D.S.K.:.Usability guidelines for designing mobile learning portals. In: Proceedings of the 3rd International Conference on Mobile Technology, Applications & Systems, pp. 1–8. ACM, Bangkok, Thailand (2006)

Sharples, M., Taylor, J., Vavoula, G.: A Theory of Learning for the Mobile Age. In: Andrews, R., Haythornthwaite, C. (eds.) The Sage Handbook of Elearning Research, pp. 221–247. Sage, London (2007)

SKMM Guidelines. Content code, SKMM, Malaysia (2012). Retrieved 2 January 2013. http://www.skmm.gov.my/Resources/Guidelines/Content-Code.aspx

So, H.-J.: Turning on mobile learning in Asia: Illustrative initiatives and policy implications, pp. 1–32, vol. 1. UNESCO, Paris (2012)

Sun, H.: Cross-cultural technology design: Creating culture-sensitive technology for local users. Oxford University Press, New York (2012)

Yeo, A.W.: Cultural User Interfaces: A Silver Lining in Cultural Diversity, pp. 4–7. SIGCHI Bulletin New York (1996)

Yeo, A.W., Chiu, P.-C., Lim, T.-Y., Tan, P.-P., Lim, T., Hussein, I.: Usability in Malaysia. In: Douglas, I., Liu, Z. (eds.) Global Usability, pp. 211–222. Springer, London (2011)

Young, P.A.: Integrating culture in the design of ICTs. British J. Educational Tech. **39**(1), 6–17 (2008)

Zaibon, S.B., Shiratuddin, N.: Heuristics evaluation strategy for mobile game-based learning. In: the 6th IEEE International Conference on Wireless, Mobile, and Ubiquitous Technologies in Education, pp. 127–31, Taiwan (2010)

How Online Social Network and Wearable Devices Enhance Exercise Well-Being of Chinese Females?

Hao Chen, Ting-Yu Tony Lin, Qiaochu Mu,
and Pei-Luen Patrick Rau[(⊠)]

Institute of Human Factors and Ergonomics,
Department of Industrial Engineering, Tsinghua University,
Beijing 100084, China
{c-hl4, lintyl3, mqcl3}@mails.tsinghua.edu.cn,
rpl@mail.tsinghua.edu.cn

Abstract. Firstly, in the context of exercise, the current study explored the effects of online social network and wearable devices in the enhancement of Chinese females' subjective well-being. An in situ 2*2 experiment design was conducted. Result showed that online social network was significantly related to positive affects. Wearable devices didn't show significance due to problems of accessibility. Secondly, this study explored the potential linguistic variables that could predict Chinese females' emotional well-being according to exercise-based online tweets. Regression model was applied to explore the relation between potential variables and participants' self-reported emotional states. Positive additional activities and number of likes were two important variables that could be referred for further analysis.

Keywords: Exercise · Subjective well-being · Social network · Wearable devices

1 Introduction

1.1 Enhancement of Subjective Well-Being

In recent years, exercise has become an important activity for Chinese people than ever before. According to a national survey [1], more than 49 % of the population participated in exercise, and the number is continuously rising. However, doing exercise for women is often not as enjoyable as for men due to motivational difference. Men are often driven by self-determined goals like competence, enjoyment and social interaction, while women often endorse weight and body-related reasons for exercise [2, 3]. It is reported that, under those external motivations, women experience body dissatisfaction and poor emotional well-being [4]. The bad exercise experience is associated with lack of autonomy and body dissatisfaction, making it difficult to fully benefit from exercise.

On the other point of view, improving women's exercise experience would help them gain more from the activity. For example, research showed that higher enjoyment

© Springer International Publishing Switzerland 2015
P.L.P. Rau (Ed.): CCD 2015, Part II, LNCS 9181, pp. 15–21, 2015.
DOI: 10.1007/978-3-319-20934-0_2

and mood enhancement could bring greater body satisfaction and self-esteem [5], and contribute to exercise adherence [6]. Therefore, to help enhance the cognitive level of exercise experience is crucial for women to get involved in the activity.

Subjective well-being (SWB) represents the self-perceived level of enjoyment based on two measurements: emotions and satisfaction with life. [7]. Two solutions were examined to improve SWB of exercise: online social network and wearable devices. Exploring their effects forms the first contribution of the present study.

Chinese females tend to express their experiences on social network sites (SNSs) after exercise. SNSs give them a platform for self-disclosure and communication. It is shown that these two functions of SNSs have positive effects on well-being. For example, study showed that the amount of self-disclosure on SNSs was positively related to affective balance and satisfaction with life [8]. Positive feedback from SNSs friends helped enhance self-presented SWB and psychological well-being through social support [9]. Moreover, SNSs remind users of their social connections and increase their self-esteem [10], which in turn, have positive effect on well-being.

Wearable devices have developed rapidly in China and exercise monitoring is the most important usage for customers. Some kinds of wearable devices can track physiological parameters (e.g., burnt calories, number of steps, distances) and provide performance feedback or exercise suggestions to users. Researches in this field now focus mainly on wearable technologies and applications. Our goal is to see if wearable devices have influences on SWB in the context of exercise.

1.2 Prediction of Emotional Well-Being

For some health-related organizations or companies, they show great interests in the general conditions of public exercise, such as collective exercise performance, public emotive trends, public opinions, etc. For example, government may be interested in the opinions towards public exercise facilities or wearable devices companies may concern users' emotional reaction of certain coaching plans. With the intervention of online social network, it is now possible for them to access exercise participants' emotional feedback based on online tweets.

Sentiment analysis is often used to evaluate users' opinion or affective state. Researchers have successfully showed the consistency of collective online sentiment and real-life contextual information [11, 12] Due to technological challenges, sentiment analysis now mainly focused on emotional words. For example, Dodds [13] looked at variation in emotional used in tweets and Facebook.

In the present study, we concentrate on the potential linguistic variables in online tweets, give a more complete linguistic analysis to the text than emotional words alone provide. Instead of mining millions of tweets by program, linguistic variables was manually recognized and classified by researchers in a small sample size. We considered that firstly, for some contextual linguistic variables, it was really challenging to find an effective way to implement the AI program and secondly, our goal here was not to try all possible candidate variables, but explore the potential variables that have not been tested ever, to better understand the components that contribute to the prediction. That was the second contribution of the study.

The results would be helpful to further sentiment analysis job when we seek for more independent variables to analyze the tweets of exercise.

2 Methodology

An in situ assessment was conducted to evaluate the main effects of online social network and wearable devices in the enhancement of subjective well-being. Online tweets were collected for the phase of sentiment analysis.

2.1 Participants

Twenty-eight Chinese female students from Tsinghua University participated in the experiment. Participants ranged in age from 19 to 26. Nearly 18 % exercise less than 30 min/week, 71 % between 30 min/week and 90 min/week, and 11 % exercise more than 90 min/week. All of them use SNS. 50 % use it more than 1 h/day, 14 % less than 0.5 h/day. Only 21 % of them have the experience of using a wearable device.

2.2 Measurement

Positive/Negative Affects Schedule [14] is a 12-item scale that is used to assess participants' emotional states. Six items represent the positive affect (pleasure, affection, joy, gratefulness, cheer, pride) and the other 6 items represent the negative affect (anger, shame, envy, anxiety, compunction, sadness).

The Satisfaction with Life Scale (SWLS) is a 5-item scale that was used to evaluate participants' cognitive judgment of satisfaction of life [15]. Both of the two schedules were answered on a 7-scale Likert form.

2.3 Procedure

All participants were asked to do the recommended level of exercise: jogging in the gymnasium no less than 30 min per time, 3 times per week and 3 weeks during a month. They were divided into 4 groups: with/without wearable devices and with/without online sharing. Participants in online sharing groups were asked to publish an online tweet on Wechat, currently the most popular SNS in China, in the context of exercise. It could be pure text, or text with emoticon, or with pictures, etc. Participants in wearing wearable device group were provided with Gudong's smart loop 2 and they were asked to use the device while doing exercise.

Self-reported emotional states were collected on the day when they did exercise. Satisfaction with life was obtained by SWLS at the beginning and the end of the experiment. Finally, participants were asked to take a 30 min interview individually with researchers. The interviews aimed at figuring out how social network and wearable devices influenced their self-reproted SWB.

2.4   Sentiment Analysis: Recognition of Potential Variables

The online tweets published in the experiment were collected and there were 99 validate samples. 13 potential linguistic variables were defined as *Number of positive/negative emotional lexicons* (The classification of the emotional words refers to *Hownet Sentiment Dictionary* [16]), *Number of positive/negative emoticons, Number of positive/negative physiological feeling lexicons, Number of exercise process words, Number of positive/negative additional activities* (topics, except exercise, mentioned in the tweet), *Number of exercise related pictures, Occurrence of self-portrait picture, Number of likes,* and *Number of replies.* The group of researchers manually recognized all the variables. Multiple linear regression model was applied to explore the relation between the variables and participants' self-reported emotional status.

3   Results

3.1   Main Effects of Online Social Network and Wearable Device

Descriptively, the level of positive affect ($M = 25.366$, $SD = 2.027$) was generally higher than that of negative affect ($M = 10.104$, $SD = 1.087$). On average, the group of social network sharing ($M = 27.919$, $SD = 2.002$) and using wearable device ($M = 26.119$, $SD = 2.179$) both reported more positive emotions than control group. However, wearable devices brought more negative emotion as well, which is not as expected. Online sharing group ($M = 28.071$, $SD = 2.784$) reported higher level of satisfaction with life than the control group ($M = 25.964$, $SD = 4.359$).

Two-way repeated ANOVA was conducted to examine the main effects of online social network and wearable device for positive/negative affects and each emotional state. Results showed that social network sharing had significant influence on positive emotions such as pleasure ($p = .015$), joy ($p = .034$) and cheer ($p = .033$). Thus it was significantly related to positive affects as a whole ($p = .046$). It had also significant influence on satisfaction with life (p < .01). No significance was found for negative emotions. For wearable devices, only anxiety showed significance ($p = .042$). Using wearable devices tended to make users more anxious.

3.2   Regression Model of Sentiment Analysis

It was shown that the number of negative emotional lexicons was significantly related to anger (p < .01), anxiety (p < .01), compunction ($p = .025$), and sadness (p < .01), while no significance was reported to positive emotional lexicons. It was interesting to note that number of positive emoticons was significantly related to anxiety ($p = .012$). The more positive emoticons a young woman use, the more chance she may suffer from anxiety.

The number of exercise process words was positively related to cheer ($p = .027$), pride ($p = .018$), and it was negatively related to anxiety (p < .01).

The number of positive additional activities was significantly related to all positive emotions: pleasure ($p = .022$), affection ($p = .019$), joy ($p = .032$), gratefulness ($p < .01$), cheer ($p = .015$), and pride ($p = .038$).

The number of likes showed significance to cheer ($p < .01$), gratefulness ($p < .01$), pleasure ($p = .038$), and joy ($p < .01$).

4 Discussion

4.1 Effects of Online Social Network & Wearable Device

The use of social network is positively related to the enhancement of positive affects and satisfaction with life. This result is consistent to existing conclusions as SNS is a platform of self-disclosure. Actually, there are two different types: honest self-presentation and positive self-presentation. Chinese females prefer the latter one because they try to maintain a positive self-portrait. According to Kim's path model [17], positive self-presentation could directly influence well-being, which emphasizes the result. It also explains that as Chinese females don't often send negative emotional expressions, it is difficult for them to relieve negative emotions through SNS.

Except for the enhancement of positive affects, the use of SNS helps to gain positive feedback and strengthens the relatedness with others. This can become one of the motivations of exercise. Intrinsic motivation based on social interaction is related to exercise adherence and intentions, especially for women [18]. Information feeding is another main function of SNS. It can make people stay motivated to exercise. Research suggested that an exercise-based SNS would give a social-supportive environment to encourage people to get involved in exercise [19].

Wearable devices showed no influence on positive affects and were significantly related to anxiety. According to participants' opinions reported in interviews, Davis's Technology Acceptance Model [20] could be useful to explain the results.

Perceived Ease of Use. The functionality of the device is not so user-friendly that 50 % of the participants reported that it was sometimes difficult to perform a task. The inconvenience made users pay great efforts and led to a decrease in autonomy. Participants felt unwilling to use it and it contributed little to the SWB.

Perceived Usefulness. Nearly 80 % of the participants reported that the tracking data (steps, distances, brunt calories) did not mean much for them. All participants complained that system errors existed while tracking data and they didn't believe that incorrect information would help them enhance exercise performance.

4.2 Prediction of Subjective Well-Being

The results of negative emotional lexicons were consistent to their polarity. As a classical variable, emotional lexicon showed its effects in many researches of sentiment analysis [13]. Positive emoticons were negatively related to gratefulness and pride, positively related to anxiety. This is due to the fact that female users have added more emotional dimensions in the expression of emoticon [21]. Participants reported that positive emoticons were used to express self-mockery in some cases. Unlike the direct textual information as lexicons and emoticons, additional topics are difficult to be recognized by algorithm. Results showed that the positive additional topic had significant influence on all dimensions of positive affects.

Further job can be conducted to explore how the additional topics in tweets can be identified, how the polarity of the topic can be judged and how it reveals users emotional states. The number of likes had significant influence on positive affects because of the fact that likes give a way to provide positive feedback in SNS and it brings social support [9]. The number of replies is not significantly related to affects but as another source of text, it can be analyzed as well.

5 Conclusion

Social networking would be an indispensable part of tomorrow's exercise by improving experience, providing social supports and information. However, wearable devices today don't show their effects as expected. Design of the functionality and the information provided should be concerned to improve the accessibility.

Besides explored variables like lexicons and emoticons, positive additional activities and number of likes were found useful in the prediction of SWB. Further studies can try to find new valuable predictors, such as punctuations, through the same manually approach, and not necessarily in the context of exercise.

Acknowledgments. This study was funded by a Natural Science Foundation China grant 71188001 and State Key Lab of Automobile Safety and Energy. The wearable devices used in experiment was sponsored by Gudong Company.

References

1. General Administration of Sport of China. http://www.sport.gov.cn
2. Anderson, C.B.: When more is better: number of motives and reasons for quitting as correlates of physical activity in women. Health Edu. Res. **18**, 525–537 (2003)
3. Markland, D., Ingledew, D.K.: The relationship between body mass and body image and relative autonomy for exercise among adolescent males and females. Psychol. Sport Exerc. **8**, 836–853 (2007)
4. Berman, E., Kerr, G., De Souza, M.J.: A qualitative examination of weight concerns, eating, and exercise behaviors in recreational exercisers. Women Sport Phys. Act. J. **14**, 24–38 (2005)
5. Strelan, P., Mehaffey, S.J., Tiggemann, M.: Self-objectification and esteem in young women: the mediating role of reasons for exercise. Sex Roles **48**, 89–95 (2003)
6. Edmunds, J., Ntoumanis, N., Duda, J.L.: Adherence and well-being in overweight and obese patients referred to an exercise on prescription scheme: a self-determination theory perspective. Psychol. Sport Exerc. **8**, 722–740 (2007)
7. Diener, E., Lucas, R.E., Oishi, S.: Subjective well-being: the science of happiness and life satisfaction. In: Snyder, C.R., Lopez, S.J. (eds.) Handbook of Positive Psychology, pp. 63–73. Oxford University Press, New York (2002)

8. Lee, G., Lee, J., Kwon, S.: Use of social-networking sites and subjective well-being: a study in South Korea. Cyberpsychol. Behav. Soc. Netw. **14**(3), 151–155 (2011)
9. Valkenburg, P., Peter, J., Schouten, A.: Friend networking sites and their relationship to adolescents' well-being and social self-esteem. CyberPsychol. Behav. **9**, 584–590 (2006)
10. Gonzales, A.L., Hancock, J.T.: Mirror, mirror on my Facebook wall: effects of exposure to Facebook on self-esteem. Cyberpsychol. Behav. Soc. Netw. **14**(1–2), 79–83 (2011)
11. Bollen, J., Pepe, A., Mao, H.: Modeling public mood and emotion: Twitter sentiment and socio-economic phenomena. arXiv preprint arXiv:0911.1583 (2009)
12. Cohn, M.A., Mehl, M.R., Pennebaker, J.W.: Linguistic markers of psychological change surrounding September 11, 2001. Psychol. Sci. **15**(10), 687–693 (2004)
13. Dodds, P.S., Harris, K.D., Kloumann, I.M., Bliss, C.A., Danforth, C.M.: Temporal patterns of happiness and information in a global social network: hedonometrics and twitter. PLoS ONE **6**(12), 26 (2011)
14. Diener, E., Suh, E.M., Lucas, R.E., Smith, H.L.: Subjective well-being: three decades of progress. Psychol. Bull. **125**(2), 276 (1999)
15. Diener, E., Emmons, R.A., Larsen, R.J., Griffin, S.: The satisfaction with life scale. J. Pers. Assess. **49**, 71–75 (1985)
16. Hownet. http://www.keenage.com
17. Kim, J., Lee, J.E.R.: The Facebook paths to happiness: effects of the number of Facebook friends and self-presentation on subjective well-being. Cyberpsychol. Behav. Soc. Netw. **14** (6), 359–364 (2011)
18. Izquierdo-Porrera, A.M., Powell, C.C., Reiner, J., Fontaine, K.R.: Correlates of exercise adherence in an African American church community. Cult. Divers. Ethn. Minor. Psychol. **8**, 389–394 (2002)
19. Mahan III, J.E., et al.: Exploring the impact of social networking sites on running involvement, running behavior, and social life satisfaction. Sport Manage. Rev. **18**, 182–192 (2014)
20. Davis, F.D.: Perceived usefulness, perceived ease of use, and user acceptance of information technology. MIS quart. **13**, 319–340 (1989)
21. Wolf, A.: Emotional expression online: Gender differences in emoticon use. CyberPsychol. Behav. **3**(5), 827–833 (2000)

Social Media Design Requirements
for the Collectivist International Students

Kanrawi Kitkhachonkunlaphat[✉] and Mihaela Vorvoreanu

Computer Graphics Technology, Purdue University,
West Lafayette, Indiana, USA
{kkitkhac,mihaela}@purdue.edu

Abstract. Major social networking sites (SNSs) are developed in the United
States, the country with the highest individualism score. Individualist cultural
values are therefore likely to be embedded in social media design. This study
aims to understand the consequence of collectivist cultural values on design
requirements for social media tools. The study used a co-design activity with the
value sensitive action-reflection model. Participants were international students
from collectivistic cultures who were enrolled at a large state university in the
United States. Inductive thematic analysis was applied to analyze themes from
design results. Four main themes emerged: media, cost, user-system interaction,
and interpersonal interaction. Then, design requirements informed by collectivist cultural values were derived from the themes using theoretical thematic
analysis. Three main design requirements emerged: the need to support strong
relationship within group, the need to support narrow relationships, and the need
for continuous relationship maintenance.

Keywords: Cross-cultural · Social media · Social networking · Collectivist ·
User experience

1 Introduction

International students are physically separated from their old friends and families.
Social networking sites (SNSs) are important tools for them in relationship maintenance with families and friends in their home countries as well as new friends with
shared ethnicity [22, 24]. Based on data from the Institute of International Education, at
least 67.23 % of the entire international student population in the academic year
2013-2014 came from countries with collectivistic culture [10, 11]. However, SNSs
designed within individualist cultures are unlikely to support efficiently the interpersonal behaviors of international students from collectivistic countries [17]. Many
popular SNSs such as Facebook and Twitter were developed in the United States, the
country with the strongest individualistic culture [10]. The goal of this study was to
understand the consequence of collectivist cultural values on design requirements for
social media tools. The study aimed to improve further designs and developments of
social media tools by increasing the awareness of the dimension of culture.

© Springer International Publishing Switzerland 2015
P.L.P. Rau (Ed.): CCD 2015, Part II, LNCS 9181, pp. 22–33, 2015.
DOI: 10.1007/978-3-319-20934-0_3

2 Relevant Literature

2.1 College Students' Social Media Usage

International students have to move into a new country for their studies. A different environmental culture and the physical separation from families and friends were found to be two important causes of loneliness, especially in their first few months. This loneliness resulted in psychosocial issues such as feelings of isolation, anxiety, and confusion [22].

In order to address loneliness resulting from migration, studies have reported that international students use SNSs. Students use SNSs to exchange information with other international students from the same ethnic group or with family members and old friends [22, 24]. Direct communication through SNSs provides the perception of a close relationship between these groups and was found to reduce the students' loneliness [3]. Managing and maintaining social capital using SNSs is one way to address international students' loneliness.

Social capital in the context of social media refers to the collection of information and resources from other people in one's network [5]. Putnam defines two types of social capital based on relationships between people: bridging and bonding. People gain social capital by "bridging" connections with acquaintances, while "bonding" comes from close relationships such as friends and family. Bridging relationships result in wide gain in social capital from a large group of people. On the other hand, people maintain intimacy via bonding relationships [16].

According to [3, 18], college students use SNSs to acquire bridging social capital and maintain distant relationships, or bonding social capital. Studies reported that Facebook specifically was an important tool for U.S. students to maintain bonding social capital [6, 23]. Facebook could be a good tool for international students as well to maintain bonding social capital. However, it is possible that SNSs designed to support individualist communication goals [13] might not be ideal for communication among members of collectivistic cultures. How would SNSs design change if it were to accommodate not only individualist, but also collectivist communication goals?

2.2 Conflict in Cultural Values in the Current SNSs

The individualist-collectivist characteristic of cultures is one of the dimensions proposed by Hofstede in his characterization of world cultures. The individualist-collectivist dimension refers to the strength of relationships among people in a culture. Individualistic cultures have weak interpersonal relationships because personal achievement is valued over the goal of the group. In contrast, collectivistic cultures have highly cohesive relationships between people and the goal of the group is prioritized over that of the individual [9, 10, 19]. Interpersonal relationships among collectivists are tighter and narrower than those among individualists. The individualist-collectivist dimension is the most popular dimension applied in cross-cultural design [19].

Individualists and collectivists adopt SNSs differently. One reason for the difference is their goal in communication [13]. Members of individualistic cultures communicate with the goal to express personal ideas, while the intention of the collectivists' words is to maintain interpersonal relationships [13]. Accordingly, it is not surprising that the two groups also have different behaviors in SNSs usage. For example, a lot of collectivists used a picture of a toy or an animal as their avatar to represent themselves on SNSs instead of their real picture, as individualists did [15].

From the perspective of SNSs developers, even if overall functions of the SNSs are the same, there are details that the individualistic and collectivistic developers design and implement differently. Marcus and Krishnamurthi pointed out that this difference could be seen in the access to a person's friend list on SNS. Making that list public is considered an implementation of individualist values, whereas collectivist values that are more relationship-oriented would restrict access to the friend list and other personal information. [15]. A study on SNS users from collectivistic cultures who commonly used both Facebook and Renren, a Chinese-developed SNS with the same functions as Facebook, even found that the collectivists felt free to share content more on Renren than Facebook. The collectivists applied some sharing features- picture tagging, link sharing, and sharing others' - significantly less on Facebook than on Renren. The reason for more sharing was because Renren allowed sharing content with specific groups, while Facebook sharing was to wider audiences [17].

The SNSs designed and developed by in individualistic cultures may not support well the values of users from collectivistic cultures because individualist values are embedded in the design. Anticoli and Toppano explained that designers always embed their cultural values into their designs, intentionally or unintentionally [1]. Their culture's values and attitudes influence designers' way of thinking and mental models of emotion expression. It is hard for designers to avoid the interference of values in design [10, 19]. Identifying design requirements for SNS from collectivistic cultures can provide specific insights on how interfaces could be altered to serve their truly international audiences. Co-design is a suitable method for exploring collectivist SNS users' preferences due to the fact that it allows users to get involved in a design process as a co-designer.

3   Methodology

This study applied co-design activities [20] with the value sensitive action-reflection model [25] to collect qualitative data from SNS users from collectivistic cultures. Co-design is a design method in the area of participatory design [20]. The main characteristic of co-design is the involvement of users as a part of the design team. The researcher plays a facilitator role to prepare, control, and communicate during the design process [21].

The value sensitive action-reflection model is a framework that adds the consideration of values to a co-design activity [25]. The model is an extension of co-design and value-sensitive design. In addition to previous methods, the model adds more consideration of human values, stakeholder and designer views, and as such is appropriate for exploring cultural values in design.

3.1 Participants

Six international students from collectivistic cultures participated in the co-design activities [10]. They were all from countries whose national individualism score was lower than 25, also known as intently collectivist. We conducted three co-design sessions. Each session consisted of the facilitator and a pair of friends with the same nationality, to ensure shared cultural and national experience between participants. The pairs of participants had a certain level of familiarity with each other to enable discussions especially on the topic related to relationship maintenance with close friends and family using SNSs.

The group of participants consisted of five graduate students and one visiting scholar, two males and four females. The participants varied in background – two English as second language students, one Educational Psychology student, two Computer Graphics Technology students, and one Geotechnical Engineering visiting scholar.

In term of nationality, two of the friend pairs were Chinese and one was Thai. Both China and Thailand are countries with an equally low score of individualism, 20 out of 100. For comparison, the United States scores 91 on the individualism-collectivism scale [10].

3.2 Environment

The facilitator hosted each co-design session in a quiet room where participants could talk freely. The facilitator prepared materials including sketching paper, different color pens, post-it notes of different sizes and colors, clips, tape, and scissors, for participants to use during the co-design activity. There was a large table with space surrounding it to enable movement. Consequently, each pair could easily grab tools to design and share the developing design with the partner.

3.3 Co-Design Activity

There were three main parts in the activity - design activity, stakeholder prompt, and designer prompt. The co-design activity started with the design activity by informing participants of the design topic "Designing a dream social media tool." The participants were encouraged to design without the limitation of platform, type of devices, or number of devices. The target users of the design were international students who are studying in the United States. The designed social media tool aimed to help the target users maintain relationship with the following groups: family members who are living in the international students' home countries and close friends who are living in the international students' home countries.

The participants were asked to list the expected key functions for their dream social media tool. Then, they expanded key features for each listed key function. After that, the participant required to create low-fidelity prototyping of their design using materials provided by the facilitator.

The second part of the co-design activity was the stakeholder prompt [25]. The purpose of the prompt was to reconsider the design from the perspective of the stakeholders. The facilitator randomly selected a user scenario from the collection, set of generated scenarios with a situation reflecting the collectivistic culture that required the use of the social media tool. The participants considered the scenario and were encouraged to revise the design as needed. After that, the facilitator asked for the explanation of how the person in the scenario could use the design.

The third step was the designer prompt [25]. The objective of the prompt was to consider designer concepts using envisioning cards [7]. The cards were developed using the concept of value criterion card [7]. The content on the cards contained concepts from area of social media or collectivistic culture. For example, some of the cards read, *"Group Opinion: A lot of people with close relationships are using social media to communicate with each other. Discussions to reach final conclusion for something are common. Feature that well support group action and group decision making will help to create great user experience.*

Brainstorm to identify one or more design feature(s) to support group decision making."

"Situation Awareness: Knowing of what other people is doing is one of the important benefits of social media. The information related to current situation of people with close relationships leads to more meaningful interactions and great user experience.

Brainstorm three design features that help users (international students) to know the current situation of their friends and families living in their home country."

The participants considered the concept on a randomly selected card. Then they were encouraged to revise the design as needed. After that, the participants clarified their design by answering the questions stated on the card.

3.4 Data Collection

The facilitator audio-recorded the conversations of all three co-design activities. During each session, the facilitator encouraged participants to talk out loud. Participants were encouraged to discuss their ideas, their experiences, and their expectations related to SNSs. When the participants created their design, the facilitator asked for clarification on unclear points in the design. The facilitator encouraged the participants to explain the underlying reasons for their design decisions. The facilitator also repeated her understanding to the participants to check if she understood correctly.

The duration of the co-design sessions ranged between 60 to 85 min with 225 min of audio record time in total. The facilitator also collected artifacts including lists of key functions, lists of key features, and finished low-fidelity prototypes, one of which is illustrated in Fig. 1.

Fig. 1. Low-fidelity prototype from a co-design session

3.5   Data Analysis

One of the authors transcribed the conversations from the design activities. Then, the data including transcriptions, list of design functions, list of design features, and low-fidelity prototypes were analyzed using inductive thematic analysis [2]. Thematic analysis is a flexible analysis method, which allows the analysis across different types of data.

Initial codes were merged into themes. Then, we analyzed the social media design requirements from the themes and subthemes using theoretical thematic analysis [2] informed by collectivist cultural values.

4   Results

Four main themes emerged from the data analysis - media, cost, user-system interaction, and interpersonal interaction. The themes represent different dimensions of needs that the collectivistic international students expected to see in social media tools. There are also subthemes which are discussed in detail in this section.

4.1   Media

The media theme related to types of the media needed in social media tools for collectivistic cultures. The participants expressed the desire to have multiple types of media especially rich media including audio chat, video chat, group video chat, and fragrance transmission. Video chat was highly mentioned to be used as the main media. A group agreed that they did not need other communication functions if the video chat would be available.

Male: *Right. I don't need fancy functions. I only need to clearly see their face, clear picture, and clear voice. Then, all problems are solved.* [comments were edited for minor grammar issues]

Even if rich media was mentioned frequently, basic text media was still required. The participants needed written communication for situations such as communication in noisy environments, sending secret information, sending detailed information, and communication when both parties were not simultaneously available.

Female A: *So, how will you communicate with your lawyer in public places?*

Female B: *Texts... Yeah... I know I have to still use it. Oh, I think text is still necessary. They can leave me text if I am not available.*

4.2   Cost

The cost theme presented the need for free or inexpensive services for social media tools. Data transmission and software installation had to be free and easy, with no additional hardware costs.

Female A: *I think that the younger people will use the kind of thing like more fancy technologies.*

Female B: *They don't have to buy extra devices. They can download plug-ins to their smartphones or any device that they have currently. They can download software like....it's an app... We can design an app.*

4.3   User-System Interaction

The third theme describes the expected interaction between users and the imagined social media tool. The participants highly recommended the use of voice command as an alternative interaction. The participants would have liked the voice command to support multiple languages - English, English with foreign accent, and multiple accents of local languages.

Female A: *How about we add the audio control? Like some old people… they can not move like young people, even my parents. So they can say "call* Female B's name*", and they can call me.*

Male: *Thai-English. The tool should be able to understand Thai-English accent.* (Laugh) *Sometime it is too hard to understand the Thai-English accent.*

Female: *It also has to support different accents. China is big, and we have different accents.*

The system should be able to display text in both English and other alphabets. The participants mentioned they would like to have a language switching function. A translation function was required for communication with foreign relatives as well as for uncommon English words. Handwriting was also needed as an alternative input method.

The participants also focused on enabling easy interaction with the system for older adults. In addition to the voice recognition function, the participants also needed a smart system that could hide all technical details, so the elderly can operate it by unassisted.

Female: ...*or we have to have writing recognition for Chinese characters. My old grandparents, they don't know how to use Pinyin.* (A phonetic system using to input Chinese characters into electronic devices)

Female: *So, how the grandparents can do it* (setup a Skype call) *without any help. So, they can do it as many time as they want. Now my grandparents can only see me only when my parents do it for them.*

4.4   Interpersonal Interaction

The interpersonal interaction theme focuses on the interactions among users that were expected to be supported by the dream social media tools. The major discussion was about time management functions. The participants expected to communicate using rich media such as video chat and audio chat; however, those media required both parties to be available at the same time. Consequently, the problem was huge time difference between countries. The participants needed the social media tools to consider the schedules of both parties and suggest appropriate time slots to call. The participants also wished to have a way to reject incoming rich media calls during the predefined "Do not disturb" period. However, the participants mentioned that text messages should be allowed during that period.

Female: *...The point is we are busy. Time difference. When she wants to call me, I am busy. When I want to call her, she is busy. So, when both of us are free, we don't know. She thinks I am busy. Maybe there is a calendar function. She inputs her schedule. I input my schedule. The phone compounds the schedule automatically and finds the time for us within a day that both of us are free. So, we can call each other.*

The participants needed a function to display the other users' status. The status included their current activities as they appear in their schedule, local time of both parties, and updated status acquired from other SNSs.

Female: *So my time...my China time is like 8am. And the time in UK is like.... I don't know. So, it shows that my grandkid is sleeping. It will be a picture of the boy sleeping in bed. Here is the blanket cover him. Let's say if my grandparents are not blind but they cannot read. Let's say they aren't educated at all, they can understand my kid is sleeping. I can't call him now.... Like that.*

A function to search for an existing friend was also required. The participants would like to search and add known friends from the existing databases. Manual search using real name as the keyword was preferable. The displayed friend list should provide at least the name and the picture of other users.

Social media tools should have clear boundaries between users with close relationship and other acquaintances. The participants divided people connected with them online into multiple groups basing on interpersonal relationships. They expected to treat and receive information from each group differently.

Female: *Yeah, this one is the mail screen when you open it. This square* (top left of the designed screen) *is for psychological need. I would like to relate to close friends and family. This square* (top right) *is for career. It is related to me. This* (top left) *is for relatedness. I would like to feel back up* (supported) *from friends and family. It is more important than work.*

For privacy and access, the participants would like to have the authority to prevent people from freely joining their group chat or group video chat as well as choices to decline or accept invitations. The participants also needed options to accept or reject media that are submitted to them before they can see the content inside.

5   Discussion

The researchers applied theoretical thematic analysis to the themes and subthemes that emerged from the data using concepts of collectivistic culture. Theoretical thematic analysis is the analysis method that allows researchers to analyze some specific aspect of qualitative data using a predefined coding frame such as concepts [2]. Collectivistic behavior in SNSs usage [4] was the coding frame used in our study. Three main design requirements for development of social media tools with the consideration of collectivistic culture were derived from the analysis.

First, social media tools have to support strong relationships within a group. The relationships among people in collectivistic cultures are often tighter than those in individualistic cultures. The media theme suggested that collectivists needed multiple types of media, especially video chat. Those media usually require synchronous communication. The requirement corresponds to findings in previous studies that people with closer relationships need multiple media to communicate [8], and video communication provides more feelings of closeness than other communications such as phone calls [14].

Moreover, the strong relationships in collectivistic cultures include cross-generational relationships. A lot of young people from collectivistic cultures wish to keep in touch with their grandparents. Social media tools with the consideration of collectivistic culture should support the communication between different generations, especially with elders. Design for aging is a challenging issue due to elders' physical and literacy limitations.

The second design requirement is the support for narrow relationships, high cohesive relationships but only within small groups [4]. The relationships among members of collectivistic cultures are often narrower than those in individualistic cultures. Our participants wanted to share personal data, but only with their own high-intimacy group. Being relationship-oriented was very important for the participants in our study, which is similar to behavior identified in other studies [15, 17]. In order to accommodate the use of collectivists, good social media tools need a content management function to show different information to different group of people based on interpersonal relationships. Multiple levels of content managements might be needed. A group close friends should be able to access different piece of information in comparison to a group of co-workers or acquaintances. Social media tools that consider cultural difference require features such as invitation and acceptance to let people make the decision for content management. Studies related to self-disclosure in collectivistic cultures support this requirement [7, 17].

As a way of supporting narrow relationships, social media tools with the consideration of collectivistic culture should accommodate local languages for both text display and voice command. In many countries, the local language comprises of multiple accents. The tools should be able to support all major accents.

The last design requirement is the support of continuous relationship maintenance. Collectivistic cultures have high in-group cohesion. They would like to have situational awareness of in-group members and to make sure that all members stay in touch [12, 13]. To take collectivistic culture into account, social media tools should be able to monitor and display users' current status to provide situational awareness clues. Then, the user can adapt their role and behavior to the behavior of other people and the situation within the group, as collectivists usually do [12].

Moreover, collectivists would like to preform actions to let people in the group know that they are paying attention to them. The actions do not necessary need to contain rich meaning, such as sending an emoticon. The purpose of the actions is to signal the receivers that the sender does care of them [13]. Social media tools with the consideration of collectivistic culture should provide features to easily transmit the sense of attention and care.

6 Conclusion

The goal of this study was to understand the consequence of collectivistic cultural values on design requirements for development of social media tools with the consideration of collectivistic culture. The focus was international students from collectivistic cultures who were enrolled at a large state university in the United States. The researchers used a co-design activity [20] with the value sensitive action-reflection model [25] to collect qualitative data. Inductive thematic analysis [2] was used to analyze themes from the conversations during the co-design activities, key functions, key features, and the low-fidelity prototypes from the design result. Then, design requirements for social media tools for collectivistic cultures were extracted from the themes using theoretical thematic analysis [2] informed by collectivistic cultural values.

Four main themes emerged from the study - media, cost, user-system interaction, and interpersonal interaction. The analysis applying collectivistic cultural values suggested three design requirements. First, social media tools for collectivists have to support strong within group relationships. The tools have to provide multiple media types especially video chat. Elders should be able to use the tools by themselves.

Second, social media tools for collectivists should support narrow relationships. The tools should support multiple levels of content management to show different information to different group of people based on interpersonal relationships. Social media tools have to support local languages including different local accents.

Third, social media tools should help continuous relationship maintenance. The tools were required to have functions to monitor and display users' current status as well as to transmit expressions of attention and care.

The design requirements developed from this study can guide further designs of social media tools to be more collectivist-friendly. It is possible that the study results could be transferrable to the maintenance of bonding capital in individualist cultures as well. However, the current study considered only cultural dimension, individualism-collectivism. Other dimensions of culture related to personal relationships, such as power distance and uncertainty avoidance, should be taken into account in future work.

References

1. Anticoli, L., Toppano, E.: The role of culture in collaborative ontology design. In: Proceedings of the 2011 International Conference on Intelligent Semantic Web-Services and Applications, p. 4. ACM (2011)
2. Braun, V., Clarke, V.: Using thematic analysis in psychology. Qual. Res. Psychol. 3(2), 77–101 (2006)
3. Burke, M., Marlow, C., Lento, T.: Social network activity and social well-being. In: Proceedings of the SIGCHI Conference on Human Factors in Computing Systems, pp. 1909–1912. ACM (2010)
4. Cho, S.E.: Cross-cultural comparison of korean and american social network sites: exploring cultural differences in social relationships and self-presentation (Doctoral dissertation, Rutgers University-Graduate School-New Brunswick) (2010)
5. Coleman, J.S.: Social capital in the creation of human capital. Am. J. sociol. 94, S95–S120 (1988)
6. Ellison, N.B., Steinfield, C., Lampe, C.: The benefits of Facebook "friends:" Social capital and college students' use of online social network sites. J. Computer-Mediated Commun. 12 (4), 1143–1168 (2007)
7. Friedman, B., Hendry, D.: The envisioning cards: a toolkit for catalyzing humanistic and technical imaginations. In: Proceedings of the 2012 ACM annual conference on Human Factors in Computing Systems, pp. 1145–1148. ACM (2012)
8. Haythornthwaite, C.: Social networks and internet connectivity effects. Inf. Commun. Soc. 8 (2), 125–147 (2005)
9. Hofstede, G.H.: Cultures and Organizations: Software of the Mind. Intercultural Cooperation and Its Importance for Survival, McGraw-Hill International, London (1991)
10. Hofstede, G.H.: Culture's consequences: Comparing values, behaviors, institutions and organizations across nations. Sage, Thousand Oaks, CA (2001)
11. Institute of International Education. Top 25 Places of Origin of International Students, 2012/13-2013/14. Open Doors Report on International Educational Exchange. (2014). Retrieved from http://www.iie.org/opendoors
12. Khaled, R., Biddle, R., Noble, J., Barr, P., Fischer, R.: Persuasive interaction for collectivist cultures. In: Proceedings of the 7th Australasian User interface conference, vol. 50, pp. 73–80. Australian Computer Society, Inc. (2006)
13. Kim, H.S., Sherman, D.K.: Express yourself: culture and the effect of self-expression on choice. J. Pers. Soc. Psychol. 92(1), 1 (2007)
14. Kirk, D. S., Sellen, A., Cao, X.: Home video communication: mediating 'closeness'. In: Proceedings of the 2010 ACM conference on Computer supported cooperative work, pp. 135–144. ACM (2010)
15. Marcus, A., Krishnamurthi, N.: Cross-Cultural Analysis of Social Network Services in Japan, Korea, and the USA. In: Aykin, N. (ed.) IDGD 2009. LNCS, vol. 5623, pp. 59–68. Springer, Heidelberg (2009)
16. Putnam, R.D.: Bowling alone: The collapse and revival of american community. Simon & Schuster, New York (2000)

17. Qiu, L., Lin, H., Leung, A.K.Y.: Cultural differences and switching of in-group sharing behavior between an American (Facebook) and a Chinese (Renren) social networking site. J. Cross Cult. Psychol. **44**(1), 106–121 (2013)
18. Raacke, J., Bonds-Raacke, J.: MySpace and Facebook: applying the uses and gratifications theory to exploring friend-networking sites. Cyberpsychology Behav. **11**(2), 169–174 (2008)
19. Salvendy, G.: Handbook of human factors and ergonomics, pp. 162–168. . John Wiley & Sons, New York (2012)
20. Sanders, E.B.N., Stappers, P.J.: Co-creation and the new landscapes of design. Co-Design **4** (1), 5–18 (2008)
21. Sanders, E.B.N., Westerlund, B.: (2011). Experiencing, exploring and experimenting in and with co-design spaces. Nordes, (4)
22. Sawir, E., Marginson, S., Deumert, A., Nyland, C., Ramia, G.: Loneliness and international students: an Australian study. J. Stud. Int. Educ. **12**(2), 148–180 (2008)
23. Vitak, J., Ellison, N.B., Steinfield, C.: The ties that bond: Re-examining the relationship between Facebook use and bonding social capital. In: 44th Hawaii International Conference on System Sciences (HICSS), 2011, pp. 1–10. IEEE (2011)
24. Ye, J.: Traditional and Online Support Networks in the Cross-Cultural Adaptation of Chinese International Students in the United States. J. Computer-Mediated Commun. **11**(3), 863–876 (2006)
25. Yoo, D., Huldtgren, A., Woelfer, J.P., Hendry, D.G., Friedman, B.: A value sensitive action-reflection model: evolving a co-design space with stakeholder and designer prompts. In: Proceedings of the SIGCHI Conference on Human Factors in Computing Systems, pp. 419–428. ACM (2013)

"Faith to Go or Devil's Work" – Social Media Acceptance in Taboo-Related Usage Contexts

Judith Leckebusch[✉], Sylvia Kowalewski, Chantal Lidynia,
and Martina Ziefle

Communication Science, RWTH Aachen University,
Campus-Boulevard 57, 52074 Aachen, Germany
{leckebusch, kowalewski, lidynia,
ziefle}@comm.rwth-aachen.de

Abstract. Beyond their ubiquity, social media have fundamentally changed the nature of social, economic, and communicative pathways in modern societies. Communication and information with digital media are present everywhere and at any time. Social media overcome physical as well as mental borders and are increasingly incorporated in our private lives. While there is a substantial body of knowledge about the usage of social media in public or working areas, yet, there are also uncovered fields. Religious applications delivered by social media are one of the unlighted areas of mobile application development within the last years. In contrast to their low publicity in research stand a high number of various applications for any number of persuasions. Using a qualitative pre-study and a quantitative survey, this study gains insights into personal perceptions of using religious applications and the acceptance by believers and non-believers.

Keywords: Mobile application · Acceptance · Religion · Social media

1 Introduction

In the last decade, the cross-media move and the media change conquered all private and professional fields. Social media and their rapid penetration in the digital media landscape in the last years have evolved to substantial communication means in many parts of business and cover a wide range of different professional contexts [1]. Recent studies are, for example, concerned with the question how knowledge and professional information exchange can be accomplished with social media [2, 3]. Also individual factors shaping the using habit were under study and the need of social media specific communication etiquettes [4]. Increasingly, social media also gained attention in sensible areas, as e.g. health monitoring [5] and care [6].

Although social media did not stop at any usage context, there remains a blind research-spot [7]. On the one hand, electronic media and the church work well together. The affiliation between church and media has been a topic of public and church internal discussions even before the introduction of TV broadcast of church services in the 1950s [8–11]. Analogously to the medial change of that time, a new one is approaching now. The rapidly progressing mobile services range from the "Pope app," which has

© Springer International Publishing Switzerland 2015
P.L.P. Rau (Ed.): CCD 2015, Part II, LNCS 9181, pp. 34–45, 2015.
DOI: 10.1007/978-3-319-20934-0_4

been officially launched by the Vatican, to various watchword and confession apps. Thus, (non-)believers can be awoken by the peal of bells of St. Peters Basilica, study the watchwords of "iLosungen" by the Moravian Church during breakfast, and use "Confession: A Roman Catholic App" in the evening to confess the sins committed that day by working through a list of questions and then receiving a penitential prayer suggested for atonement. The sinners then can use "Ramadan Times" or "iQuran" whose services offer pointers about mealtimes in different time zones. Additionally, Arabic translations of suras and their recitals are provided. A digital call commemorates the five daily prayers and gives the proper orientation. This navigation-based support also allows finding halal restaurants close by. Muslims as well as Christians can find the closest house of prayer even during vacations or business trips.

On the other hand, faith and church are a no-go for social media. Historically, churches lag behind in adopting and using novel technology. Already in the early 1950s, church officials of both Catholic and Protestant denominations questioned personal participation as well as the sensational and mysterious character of a worship service or mass during broadcasts. Social media has been no different. Though there is an impressive number of biblical apps, the walkover of electronic devices into church contexts is slow if present at all, at least in Germany. Most churches have failed to effectively integrate social media, even though they represent the most effective means to establish communities, connect persons living remotely, and provide a social backdrop which is especially important facing the demographic change that leads to increasingly more older and solitary people that need to be integrated.

2 Related Work

So far, research into the topic of religion and spirituality from the HCI-perspective has been done only sparsely, cf. [7]. There are thousands of apps available[1] that offer support or guidance to believers, non-believers, and anybody with access to such apps, i.e., smartphone or tablet users. The available apps have been summarized and/or introduced in a few works, e.g., [7, 12, 13]. This shows that these apps are of interest, even to scholars. The focus of this paper is the motivation to use and acceptance of such apps, a topic that, to our knowledge, has not yet been studied to a larger degree.

Bellar focuses on the use of religious and spiritual apps by Evangelical Christians in the US [14], but does the motivation to use these apps differ depending on type of religious affiliation? After all, there are apps for all the major religions available on iTunes, e.g., [12, 15]. What is the motivation behind using religious apps and what are possible hindrances?

According to [16], the phenomenon of "digital religion" dates back as early as the 1980s. With the emergence of the Internet and its spreading availability, discussion platforms with religious topics at their center were established [14]. This was followed in the 1990s with websites, mailing lists, and even online parishes [14, 17]. Yet it is only in recent years that the topic earned some more interest in the academic field with

---

[1] In all studies we found, the search results for available religious apps were obtained from iTunes and therefore do not necessarily include apps for android phones.

a couple of forerunners that provided comprehensive introductions into the topic, e.g., [17–20], especially concerning mobile technologies.

Although the Internet is still the basic backbone of information, the new, mobile technologies provide the opportunity to gain access virtually everywhere and at any time. But with smaller devices, the running programs have to be adapted accordingly. This is what most research into mobile applications has been about, the technical aspects of these programs [14, 15].

However, Campbell et al. [15] provide another approach to religious apps in their attempt to classify the available apps on iTunes. Expanding on [21], they offer 11 categories, for example, prayer, focus/meditation, sacred textual engagement, religious social media, or religious games that arrange religious apps based on their main purpose. On a broader scale, this leaves two groups of apps: those meant to enhance religious practice, e.g., prayer or sacred textual engagement, and those that have religious content such as games or religious social media.

In accordance with this distinction, this paper offers insight into what kind of apps someone with or without religious affiliation would use and why. Although there are many religions and considerable numbers of apps available for each [15], our study focuses on the adoption behavior and the reasons for (non)using religious apps, contrasting Christian and Muslim believers or non-believers.

3 Method

This research followed a two-step procedure by using the focus-group method and an online survey. On the base of the focus group results, items of the questionnaire were developed.

3.1 Qualitative Insights: Focus-Group Approach

In the first step, we consulted two focus-groups, one with five, the other with six participants between the ages of 21 and 56. There were seven men and four women of whom four were affiliated with and seven active participants in a religion. Of the latter, three were Christians, and four Moslems. Participants discussed their attitudes and requirements for mobile phone usage. Beside general questions, we asked for their religious affiliation, their technological expertise, and what they expect from a religious application. As general factors we observed that people participating in religion know about religious apps, but their usage is in an observation period and the believers reported to be very aloof about these kind of applications. Most importantly, for the majority religious applications should be flawless. It comes as no surprise that non-believers did not know much about religious apps and they were quite distant and reserved towards religious applications.

Summarizing, we transferred the following factors as central content into the online survey: religious affiliation, impact of religion in everyday life, participants' attitude towards technology in general, usage behavior, and the reasons and requirements for using religious applications.

3.2   Quantitative Insights: Questionnaire Approach

The questionnaire was divided into five main parts:

(1) *Demographic variables*: The first part included questions about demographic data as well as information about religious education, piety, and attendances and activities at church in the last 3 months.

(2) *Knowledge about and attitude towards religious applications*: The second part dealt with relatedness and affiliation to religion and knowledge about religious applications as well as the general attitude towards values.

(3) *Moral concepts*: The third part used Likert-scales to evaluate general value judgment.

(4) *App use*: The fourth part of the questionnaire dealt with apps in general. The participants were asked about their usage frequency as well as the number of apps they use. We inquired what kind of application the participants would like to use in the context of religion and if there are contexts or areas for which the participants cannot imagine the use of an application at all.

(5) In the last part, we investigated the participants' *control beliefs* when dealing with technology [22].

3.3   Participants

A total of N = 388 respondents participated in this survey, aged between 14 and 67 (M = 24.8; SD = 7.1). The gender distribution was quite symmetrical, with 47.9 % women (N = 186) and 52.1 % men (N = 202). The number of religious participants and atheists is almost equal with 58 % believers (N = 225) and 42 % atheists (N = 163). Among the group of religious participants (N = 225), 69.3 % were Christian (N = 156) and 24.4 % Muslim (N = 55); the remaining 6.3 % stated a different affiliation that was counted as "other" (N = 14). The ratio of men (N = 74) and women (N = 82) among the Christians was almost equal with 47.4 % male Christians and 52.6 % female. Among the Muslims, the gender ratio was not as symmetrical with 72.7 % female Muslims (N = 40) and only 27.3 % male Muslims (N = 15) participating.

4   Results

First of all, the participants were divided into three groups according to their religiousness. Thus, for further analyses, the three groups Christians, Muslims, and Non-Believers (Atheists) were distinguished.

4.1   Do "Religious Groups" Differ in Their Intent to Use Apps?

The questionnaire surveyed the intention to use a total of 26 apps. Four of them were characteristically Christian, 11 were Muslim oriented, and another 11 apps were independent of a specific religious affiliation.

In order to answer the question which of the three groups shows the highest interest in using religious apps, the 11 religion-independent apps were summed up as "intention to use-score" for each participant. One-way ANOVA with post hoc-analysis (LSD) revealed that Muslims, on average, show the highest intention to use the apps (M = 3.2; SD = 2.5). In contrast, Christian people would use, on average, 1.7 (SD = 2.3) apps whereas non-believers show the lowest intention to use (M = 1.1; SD = 2.4). Post hoc-analysis revealed that all three groups differ significantly from each other (F(2,326) = 13.5; p < 0.00). In Fig. 1 descriptive outcomes are illustrated.

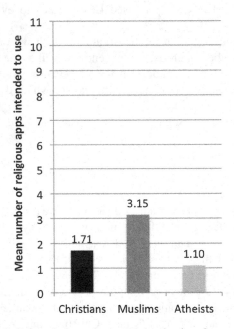

Fig. 1. Intention to use (religious-independent apps) (evaluation: 0 = certainly not; 3 = definitely yes).

4.2   What Kind of App Do the Specific Groups Use?

In a further step, we analyzed the intention to use religious apps for Christians and Muslims in more detail. Figure 2 gives a descriptive overview of the percentage of participants of the respective group who intend to use one of the specific apps. For each of the groups, the religious-specific apps are presented additionally. Thus, Fig. 2 shows 23 apps for Muslims (left side, black) and 15 for Christian people (right side, gray).

All in all, Muslims would like to use more religious and religion-independent apps than Christians. While both of them, Christians (39.3 %) and Muslims (69.2 %), would like to use apps with a holiday calendar function, there are only 3 other applications which both of them can imagine to use: "quizzes about religion" (Muslim: 45.1 %; Christians: 22.1 %), "information on religious taboos" (Muslim: 40.4 %; Christians: 24.8 %), and apps about "history of the sutra/Bible" (Muslim: 36.5 %; Christians: 27.6 %).

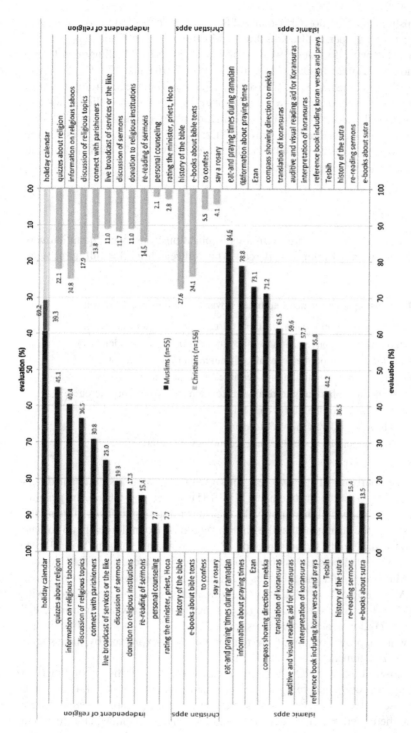

Fig. 2. Relative frequency of intention to use religious apps (in percent)

Neither Muslims (7.7 %) nor Christians (2.8 %) considered "rating the minister, priest, hoca" or to get a "personal counseling" (Muslims: 7.7 %; Christians: 2.1 %). Apps to get or exchange information were appreciated more by Muslims than Christians: "discussion of religious topics" (Muslims: 36.5 %; Christians: 17.9 %), "connect with parishioners" (Muslims: 30.8 %; Christians: 13.8 %). The specific religious apps for Muslims with the highest scores were assistance-apps, which supplied "eat- and praying-times during Ramadan" (84.6 %), "information about praying times" (78.8 %) in general, and initialized the call for praying "Ezan" (73.1 %). While Tesbih, the Muslim rosary, would be used by 44.2 % Muslims, only 4.1 % Christians could imagine to use an app for saying a rosary.

4.3   Using Motives

Participants' general attitudes towards religious application usage were quantitatively assessed, using four items (4-point Likert scale, 0 = full rejection, 3 = full agreement, see Table 1).

Table 1. Items regarding general attitudes towards religious application usage

"Yes, I would use apps based on religion... (0 = full rejection 3 = full agreement)
... because they give fast and convenient access to information about religion"
... because I am not dependent on the schedule of church and mosque times"
... because I think it's great that religion is accessible to me due to technology"
... because it gives me the opportunity to deal with religion in my own private circle"
... because I can read/listen [to] the liturgy any time"
... because I don't have to walk all the way to church"
... because the church should be up-to-date in a technology way, too"

MANOVA comparisons of the two religious groups revealed a significant difference in agreement to 6 of the 7 statements ($F(7,185) = 9.5$; $p < 0.001$). In general, Muslims, on average, show a higher approval to reasons militating in favor of using the apps than Christians; the statement that the church should be technologically up-to-date is though not rated differently by both groups. Based on a scale ranging from 0 to 3, scores higher than 1.5 can be seen as approval of a specific reason. Therefore, we can conclude that Muslims would use religious apps because they provide "fast religious information" ($M = 1.9$; $SD = 1.1$), offer the possibility to "practice religion with technology" ($M = 1.7$; $SD = 1.2$), and practice "religion in private environments" ($M = 1.8$; $SD = 1.2$) as well as "re-reading sermons" ($M = 1.5$; $SD = 1.1$). In contrast, Christians show no approval of any of the reason, which is expressed by means <1.5 for each of these 7 statements.

Having a closer look, MANOVA analyses revealed no significant findings for gender and religion group concerning all seven statements ($F(7,185) = 1.4$; n.s). For this reason, gender effects were analyzed separately in each group. Whereas in the Christian group there were no differences between men and women, Muslim men and women differed in their approval of some of the statements ($F(7,44) = 3.97$; $p < .001$).

From Fig. 3 it can be seen that Muslim women would use religious apps because they like the fact that technology makes religion feasible (M = 1.9; SD = 1.2), they prefer re-reading of sermons (M = 1.6; SD = 1.3) and practicing religion in a private environment (M = 1.8; SD = 1.2) as well as getting fast religious information (M = 2; SD = 1.1). In contrast, Muslim men mentioned only two reasons. They like practicing religion in a private environment (M = 1.7; SD = 1.1) and getting religious information fast (M = 1.7; SD = 0.9) by using religious apps.

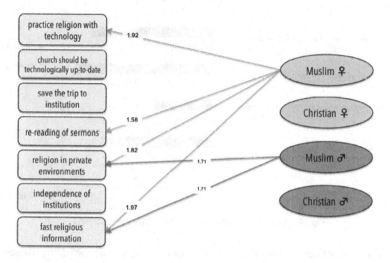

Fig. 3. Intention of use social media in different religions

4.4   Usage Barriers

Participants' general attitudes against religious application usage were quantitatively assessed, using five items (4-point Likert scale, 0 = full rejection, 3 = full agreement, Table 2).

Table 2. Items regarding general attitudes against religious application usage

No, I would not use apps based on religion... (0 = full rejection 3 = full agreement)
... because it's not possible to transmit religions through technology
... because it doesn't get you in the right mood
... because I am generally not interested in these apps
... because I cannot be sure that the information is correct
... in any case

Do Muslims and Christians differ in their reasons against using religious apps? MANOVA revealed that both religious groups have different objections to using religious apps (F(5),184) = 6; p < .001). In general, Christians show higher approval of reasons against using religious apps in 4 of the 5 statements. The only exception is the statement of possible inaccuracy of information provided by apps, which Muslims (M = 1.4; SD = 0.9) state a stronger agreement to than Christians (M = 0.9; SD = 0.9). Figure 4 shows the reasons against application usage in a religious context by religious group.

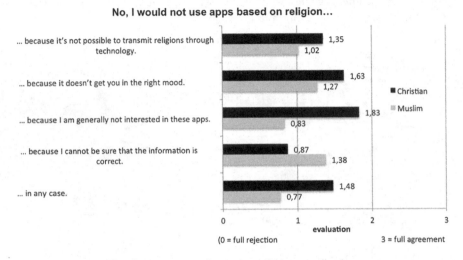

Fig. 4. Reasons against using religious applications

Christians mentioned that they are "generally not interested in these apps" (M = 1.8; SD = 1.3) and added "in any case" (M = 1.5; SD = 1.2); in their perspective it is not possible to transmit religions through technology (M = 1.4; SD = 1.1) and it would not "get you in the right mood" (M = 1.6; SD = 1.1).

5   Discussion

Due to the qualitative pre-study, the focus on the quantitative online survey was to construct a map of acceptance of social media in tabooed usage contexts, in this case between the faithful and atheists, furthermore, between Muslims and Christians. Understanding that technology acceptance is not merely "black and white," but rather an attitude towards technology that is formed by pro- and contra-using arguments we quantified the uncertainty borders of social media usage in the religious context.

More specifically, we examined the perceptions of application usage in taboo-related contexts by people of different religious affiliations. In a first step, we addressed a random sample of different religions and ages, including both, believers and non-believers, in order to reveal prevailing knowledge and attitudes towards religious applications.

Overall, 27 religious applications were selected (with religion-independent, typically Christian and typically Muslim character). The participants' intention to use the religious apps and their assumptions about the use of these specific apps were assessed.

The latter was related to the hypothesis that the faithful are more interested in religious applications than atheists.

Outcomes revealed that Muslims, Christians, and non-believers show a broad range in the intention to use those apps. On the one hand, non-believers reported to have only a marginal intention to use, followed by Christians with a slightly higher intention, but Muslims showed the highest intention to use religious applications on their smart phones.

When it comes to the evaluation, it was found that the three groups of applications (religion-independent, typically Muslim and typically Christian) related to four categories. We tested applications with information character (e.g., "information about religion," "information about religious taboos," "holiday calendar"), many with participation or interaction character ("quizzes about religion," "discussion about religious topics," "connect with parishioners"), some, especially typically Muslim application with assistance character ("eat- and praying times during Ramadan," "compass showing the direction to Mecca," "Ezan"), and a few with private interaction ("say a rosary"/"tesbih"). First of all, Christians and Muslims would use applications information as well as participation & interaction applications. Neither of them showed any intention to use private interaction applications like getting a "personal counseling" or "rating a minister, priester, hoca."

Incidentally, it is noteworthy that the Islamic religion, in contrast to the Christian religion, own structures and rules for everyday life that are very affine to mobile phone applications. By asking for motives to use such applications, there is a significant difference between Christians and Muslims. In general, Muslims show, on average, a higher approval towards the reasons for using the apps than Christians; the statement "because church should be technologically up-to-date" is not rated differently by the groups.

We can conclude that Muslims would use religious apps because they provide "fast religious information," offer the possibility to "practice religion with technology," and practice "religion in private environments" as well as facilitate the "re-reading sermons." In contrast, Christians show no approval of any of the reasons.

Additionally, in the Christian group were no differences between the evaluations by men and women, whereas Muslim men and women differed in their approval to some of the statements. Muslim women reported to be much more opened to religious social media - approving two more reasons to use religious apps than men. Furthermore, it is observable that while Muslims show a high intention to use apps, acceptance turned out to be conditional: they conceded that they would not use apps based on religion if they cannot be sure that the information they provided is correct. This is the only reason for Muslims against using religious apps. In contrast, Christians mentioned much more reasons against such applications and their use. The most important reason was that they generally are not interested in religious applications and that they do not use them in any case. The Christians supposed that this way of religious activity would not get them in the right mood for worship or prayer. Once again, this could be based on the structure of each religion and their rituals in everyday life.

In conclusion, we consider as key results that Muslims and Christians differed in their intention to use and in their reasons for or against using mobile phone applications in taboo-related contexts. Despite the high numbers of intention to use religious apps, Muslims display a lot of skepticism toward the content of religious applications.

6 Future Research

Naturally, the research here was only a first step into the understanding of how and why religious apps could be useful and accepted across different confessions. Future studies have to investigate whether these perceptions are limited to Muslims and Christians, as examined here, and to what extent these attitudes change by including other religions. Finally, future research has to find out in what ways the acceptance of religious application usage differs when the cultural upbringing and (non)believers in other countries of other countries are taken into consideration. Different from the approach here in which a random sample of participants was surveyed, another interesting approach could be to specifically form user profiles out of different extents of religious faiths that would (a) not use and (b) would use social media and to undertake ethnographic studies in which the natural usage of religious social media during the day would be captured. This would allow a more natural understanding in which situations mobile apps could be useful and accepted. Furthermore we also plan to include priests as another important group and their perspective on the usage of digital media in the religious context. On a first sight it could be assumed that religious professionals could have a reluctant attitude towards digital media as they might fear that the digital media could increasingly replace themselves, on the other hand it could be the other way round that religious professionals could strongly support digital media usage in order to bring more younger people to faith and church.

References

1. Hogan, B., Quan-Haase, A.: Persistence and change in social media. Bull. Sci. Technol. Soc. **30**(5), 309–315 (2010)
2. Schaar, A.K., Calero Valdez, A., Ziefle, M., Eraßme, D., Löcker, A.-K., Jakobs, E.-M.: Reasons for using social networks professionally. In: Meiselwitz, G. (ed.) SCSM 2014. LNCS, vol. 8531, pp. 385–396. Springer, Heidelberg (2014)
3. Schaar, A.K., Calero Valdez, A., Ziefle, M.: The impact of user diversity on the willingness to disclose personal information in social network services. In: Holzinger, A., Ziefle, M., Hitz, M., Debevc, M. (eds.) SouthCHI 2013. LNCS, vol. 7946, pp. 174–193. Springer, Heidelberg (2013)
4. Valdez, A.C., Schaar, A.K., Ziefle, M.: State of the (Net)work address developing criteria for applying social networking. Work J. Prev. Assess. Rehabil. **41**, 3459–3467 (2012). IOS Press
5. Hawn, C.: Take two aspirin and tweet me in the morning: how Twitter, Facebook, and other social media are reshaping health care. Health Aff. **28**(2), 361–368 (2009)
6. Sarasohn-Kahn, J.: The Wisdom of Patients: Health Care Meets Online Social Media. California HealthCare Foundation, Oakland (2008)
7. Buie, G., Blythe, M.: Spirituality: there's an app for that! (But not a lot of research). In: CHI 2013, Newcastle, pp. 2315–2324 (2013)
8. Buddenbaum, J.M.: Characteristics and media-related needs of the audience for religious TV. Journalism Mass Commun. Q. **58**(2), 266–272 (1981)
9. Gilles, B.: Durch das Auge der Kamera. Eine liturgietheologische Untersuchung zur Übertragung von Gottesdiensten im Fernsehen. Münster, LIT (2000)

10. Gaddy, G.D., Pritchard, D.: When watching religious TV is like attending church. J. Commun. **35**(1), 123–131 (1985)
11. Gauntlett, D., Hill, A.: TV Living: Television, Culture and Everyday Life. Routledge, London (2002)
12. Bell, G.: *No more SMS from Jesus:* Ubicomp, religion and techno-spiritual practices. In: Dourish, P., Friday, A. (eds.) UbiComp 2006. LNCS, vol. 4206, pp. 141–158. Springer, Heidelberg (2006)
13. Martin, J.: Status update. How well is the church reaching out to people in the digital age? Commun. Soc. **45**(1), 53–57 (2012)
14. Bellar, W.R.: Pocket full of Jesus: evangelical christians' use of religious iPhone applications. Media Studies - theses. Paper 9 (2012)
15. Campbell, H.A., Altenhofen, B., Bellar, W., Cho, K.J.: There's a religious app for that! A framework for studying religious mobile applications. Mob. Med. Commun. **2**(2), 154–172 (2014)
16. Gelfgren, S.: Is there such a thing as digital religion? Hum. IT **12**, 1–4 (2013)
17. Campbell, H.A.: When Religion Meets New Media. Routledge, New York (2010)
18. Campbell, H.A. (ed.): Digital Religion: Understanding Religious Practice in New Media Worlds. Routledge, New York (2013)
19. Mahan, J.H.: Media, Religion, and Culture: An Introduction. Routledge, New York (2014)
20. Granholm, K., Moberg, M., Sjö, S.: Religion, Media, and Social Change. Routledge, New York (2015)
21. Wagner, R.: You are what you install: religious authenticity and identity in mobile apps. In: Campbell, H.A. (ed.) Digital Religion: Understanding Religious Practices in New Media Worlds, pp. 199–206. Routledge, New York (2013)
22. Beier, G.: Kontrollüberzeugung im Umgang mit Technik [Control beliefs when dealing with technology]. Rep. Psychol. **9**, 684–693 (1999)

The Impact of Natural Utilization of Traditional Chinese Cultural Elements on the User Experience in Mobile Interaction Design

Tian Lei[1(✉)], Xu Liu[1], Lei Wu[1], Tianjian Chen[2], Yuhui Wang[1], Luyao Xiong[1], and Shuaili Wei[1]

[1] Department of Industrial Design,
Huazhong University of Science and Technology, Wuhan, China
andrew.tianlei@hust.edu.cn
[2] Department of Mechanical Engineering, Carnegie Mellon University,
Pittsburgh, PA, USA

Abstract. This paper, by making two experiments, studies the impact of natural culture integration on the user experiences. The results of experiment I indicate that: (1) Cloud Pattern and Ink Painting are the most likely to activate "sliding" gesture, followed by "tapping" gesture; (2) Chinese Seals and Paper-cut tend to activate "pinching" gesture, followed by "sliding" and "tapping" gestures; (3) Gu Zheng and Shadow Figures have generally same tendency to activate "tapping", "sliding" and "pinching" gestures; (4) Calligraphy tends to activate "sliding" gesture. The results of experiment II show that: (1) gesture type has very limited influence on the interaction experience; (2) task complexity affects the user experience significantly; (3) the way of integration of cultural elements has significant relationship with "Feedback Clarity", "Easy-to-use", "Satisfaction in Feedback", "Satisfaction for Culture Utilization", "Natural Degree of Culture Utilization" and "Degree of Interesting", and has very limited correlations with "Feedback Understandability" and "Memorability". Except for "Feedback Clarity", other 5 evaluations are the best in the natural integration condition and the worst in no integration condition. In brief, the two experiments indicate that the natural integration of cultural elements promoted the user experience, even though it reduced the clarity.

Keywords: Culture representation · User experience · Mobile usability

1 Background

Mobility and portability of the mobile device determine the limitation of its interface, and the diversity and the personalization of the applications also can result in the complexity. The way of interaction and feedback can affect the user experience. Good user experiences require the consistency of the feedback mode triggered by a user gesture with the user's cognitive habits, which are closely related to the user's cultural contexts and preferences.

© Springer International Publishing Switzerland 2015
P.L.P. Rau (Ed.): CCD 2015, Part II, LNCS 9181, pp. 46–56, 2015.
DOI: 10.1007/978-3-319-20934-0_5

2 Literature Review

The academia started the research of the impact of the culture on the interaction design since 1990s. For example, Mushtaha et al. found that the cultural background would influence users' feeling, choice and perception of the websites, based on the data from subjects from Malaysia, Greece, United Kingdom, Nederland, United States and Japan [1]. They used the text, page layout, colors, pictures and interaction as the independent variables, and asked the subjects with various cultural backgrounds to evaluate old and new versions of 22 websites, in which some cultural markers were integrated into the new version. The results indicated that cultural background influenced the evaluation of the websites to a large extent, and the new version of the websites had higher scores than the old version. Moreover, the conclusion drawn by Mashtaha was also verified by other researchers.

For example, Marcus et al. studied the cultural differences in Social Networking Services (SNSs) through 39 seemingly well-known SNS websites from Japan, South Korea, and the USA [2]. They used the First Page, Sign-up Page, Sign-in Page and the Home as their experiment materials, and evaluated the design components of each material based on the Hofstede's Cultural Dimensions. From the usability report and streaming data, Marcus found that the differences in users' cultural context caused the differences in understanding and choice of the information. For instance, people from the countries with high uncertainty avoidance may prefer simple, clear, and consistent UI layout when compared to people from the countries with low uncertainty avoidance [2].

Based on Hall's theory of time and space [3], Honold ct al. proposed that the effectiveness of the interaction on the internet was affected by cultural factors and personal factors because in HCI dialogs, interaction, and information presentation were strongly linked with time (interaction, communication) and space (layout, structure) as well as the mental aspects (relations, thoughts) [4].

Smith et al. used the Taguchi Method to study the difference between British and Chinese satisfactions and preferences of websites, based on Hofstede's study on the generic cultural differences [5]. This study indicated that the attitude towards e-financial websites was very different. For example, Chinese users preferred to browse the website in a more general way compared to British users. They believed this was because Chinese have more prominent long-term-oriented thinking, which was possibly resulted from the deeply rooted Confucian philosophy.

These studies showed that the cultural context indeed affected the users' cognitions and behaviors, but such results are often general and scattered, and it's difficult to guide the interaction design using these results. One of the reason is that researchers don't have agreement on the definition of "Culture", or "Culture" itself is indeed very vague. Then what is culture? Let's have a look at the famous "Iceberg Model of Culture" [6]. This theory compares the culture to the iceberg and divides it into 3 levels: superficial level (visualization and materials, such as architecture and fine arts), middle level (behaviors and habits, such as history and customs), and core level (philosophy and spirit, such as values and attitudes towards universe, nature and time). Generally, only a few can be seen and most of them are hidden under the water. Therefore, it may be difficult to understand people from different cultural contexts because of the hidden part of their cultures.

Geert Hofstede proposed another point of view on culture based on the experimental research on cultural differences [7]. He believed that culture was the collective programming of the mind that distinguished the members of one group or category of people from another, where the mind stood for thinking, feeling and acting, with consequences for beliefs, attitudes and skills. Meanwhile, he suggested that culture should be defined by 5 dimensions, which were power distance, collectivism/individualism, femininity/masculinity, uncertainty avoidance, and time orientation, and all the differences of the user's cultural contexts could correspond to one or several of them.

Edward T. Hall and Mildred Reed Hall proposed their view of cultural mode from practice. They believed culture could be defined by the following dimensions: fast and slow messages, high and low context, territoriality, personal space, and monochromic and polychromic time. Edward T. Hall also suggested that culture was a "silent language" or "hidden dimension" that steered people unconsciously [8].

Alexander Thomas believed that culture "expresses the normal, typical, and valid attributes for the majority of the members of a certain culture regarding the kinds of perception, thoughts, judgments, and actions, encompasses learning basic human abilities in the social arena, control of one's own behavior and emotions, the satisfaction of basic needs, worldview, verbal and nonverbal communication, and expectations of others as well as the understanding of one's role and scales for judgment" [9].

From the above, we know that culture is a very broad concept, which involves every aspect of society. However, not all cultural elements can influence a person in a balanced and uniform way. In a certain environment, there must be a certain type of typical culture that affects people's mind, which may be the explicit part of culture (such as some patterns, architectures or arts with some typical styles), or the hidden part (such as values and formal beauty) [4]. In this case, there will be a certain framework of the interface and interaction appearing in users' minds, which includes metaphor, mental model, navigation, interaction, and presentation. For example, Marcus suggested that the users in Confucian cultural contexts would form such a framework of the interface and interaction: traditional powerful structures, feminine colors, exact, complete, detailed input and feedback, and high context dependency [10].

Despite Marcus' conclusion still needs to be verified, he provided a good thought: if we can integrate the local cultural element into the UI design of mobile apps in a natural way, and bring the user familiarity in such aspect as metaphor, mental model, representation and interaction process, does that mean we can design a product that matches the local cultural expectation and cognitive habits?

This paper is focused on the impact of natural integration of the culture's explicit part (i.e. the visual features) on the user experiences. This study is divided into 2 parts: Experiment 1 is the correlation test of the explicit culture and interaction, and Experiment 2 is the test of influence of the naturally integrated culture elements on the users' mental and interactive experience.

3 Experiment I - Correlation Test Between Typical Explicit Culture and Interaction

The goal for this part is to select typical ones from multiple Chinese cultural elements to be candidates for the integration into mobile apps.

We invited 6 experienced specialists to choose 8 typical cultural representations with various forms, based on cultural identity, semantic and symbolic meaning, and the relationship with interaction. These representations were Embroidery, Paper-cut, Gu Zheng, Ink Painting, Shadow Figure, Calligraphy, Chinese Seal and Cloud Pattern. We used these cultural representations as the samples in Experiment I (shown in Fig. 1), and asked 20 college student aged 18–26 to evaluate these samples according to the aspects of "Typicality of Chinese Culture", "Shape-Gesture Correlation", "Semantics", "Identification", "Expected Easy-to-use", "Expected Memorability" and "Satisfaction", using 5-point scale.

| Embroidery | Paper-cut | Gu Zheng | Ink Painting |

| Shadow Figure | Calligraphy | Chinese Seal | Cloud Pattern |

Fig. 1. Chinese culture representations for experiment I

The results indicate that:

These 8 culture representations have significant differences in "Typicality of Chinese Culture", "Identification", "Expected Easy-to-use", "Expected Memorability" and "Satisfaction", with the corresponding α values smaller than the threshold 0.01 (Shown in Table 1).

Table 1. Results of one-way ANOVA

		Sum of Squares	df	Mean Square	F	Sig.
Typicality of Chinese Culture	Between Groups	46.833	7	6.690	16.611	.000
	Within Groups	25.778	64	.403		
	Total	72.611	71			
Identification	Between Groups	78.000	7	11.143	31.774	.000
	Within Groups	22.444	64	.351		
	Total	100.444	71			
Expected Easy-to-use	Between Groups	80.167	7	11.452	42.835	.000
	Within Groups	17.111	64	.267		
	Total	97.278	71			
Expected Memorablity	Between Groups	97.542	7	13.935	20.580	.000
	Within Groups	43.333	64	.677		
	Total	140.875	71			
Satisfaction	Between Groups	52.611	7	7.516	20.615	.000
	Within Groups	23.333	64	.365		
	Total	75.944	71			

Cloud patterns and ink painting are the most likely to activate "sliding" gestures, followed by "tapping". Chinese seals and paper-cut tend to activate "pinching", followed by "sliding" and "tapping". Gu Zheng and Shadow Figures have generally same tendency to activate "tapping", "sliding" and "kneading". Besides, calligraphy tends to activate "sliding"(Shown in Fig. 2).

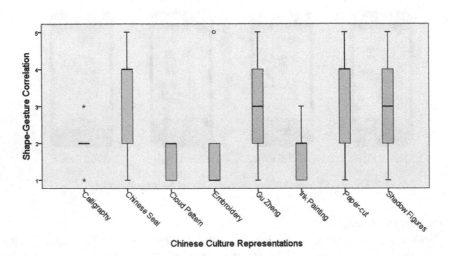

Fig. 2. Box plot of shape-gesture correlation

The cloud pattern is the most appropriate to be applied into mobile interactive design, because it has the highest scores in the "Typicality of Chinese Culture", "Identification", "Expected Easy-to-use", "Expected Memorability" and "Satisfaction". And the ink painting is in the 2nd place (shown in Fig. 3).

The possible reasons may be: (1). cloud patterns are more recognizable in life; (2). It has more features of Confucian culture; (3). similar to ink painting, the cloud patterns have the expanding tendency like ripples.

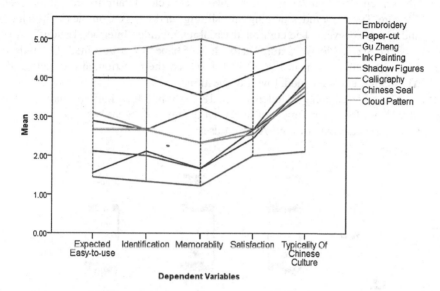

Fig. 3. Chinese culture representations' scores in dependent variables

Since the cloud pattern is significantly better according to this experiment, we used it as the elements in Experiment II.

4   Experiment II – Test on the Influence of Cultural Elements on the Interactive Feedback

The goal of the part is to explore how the ways of integration of cultural elements could affect the user experience in the mobile apps. In this study, we selected the button feedback as the main scenario to understand this integration, because the button feedback is one of the basic and important way of interaction.

In terms of the way to integrate the cultural elements, the most common one nowadays is to embed these elements into the interface by direct duplication. This method may bring intimacy and familiarity to the user, however, it may also result in abruptness and conflict with existing cognitive habit and mental model. The culture should be incorporated into the mobile apps in a natural way, which refers to the intrinsic feature, for example, the content, style, symbol and metaphor should be in accordance with the style, usage and image of the design objectives.

The independent variables in this experiment are "the Way of Integration", "Gesture Type" and "Task Complexity". We divided "the Way of Integration" into 3 conditions: "Natural Utilization", "Abrupt Utilization" and "No Utilization". "Natural Utilization" means that the cloud patterns appear on the screen gradually around the touch point, and they change from light to dark, and from vague to clear, just like a real cloud. "Abrupt Utilization" means the cloud patterns appear immediately as the finger touches the screen. "No Utilization" means there are no cloud patterns around the touch point. "Gesture Type" includes tapping and sliding, and "Task Complexity" includes simple and complex levels. The controlled variables include "Interface Layout", "Icon Colors", "Icon Size", "Icon Texture" and "Icon Shape". We designed 12 kinds of experiment materials (shown in Fig. 4) and designed the questionnaire based on the PACMAD mobile usability model with 8 questions.

The subjects are 22 college students aged 18 – 26, in which half are male and half are female, 15 are from department of industrial design, and the other 7 are from other areas. All subjects are experienced Android users.

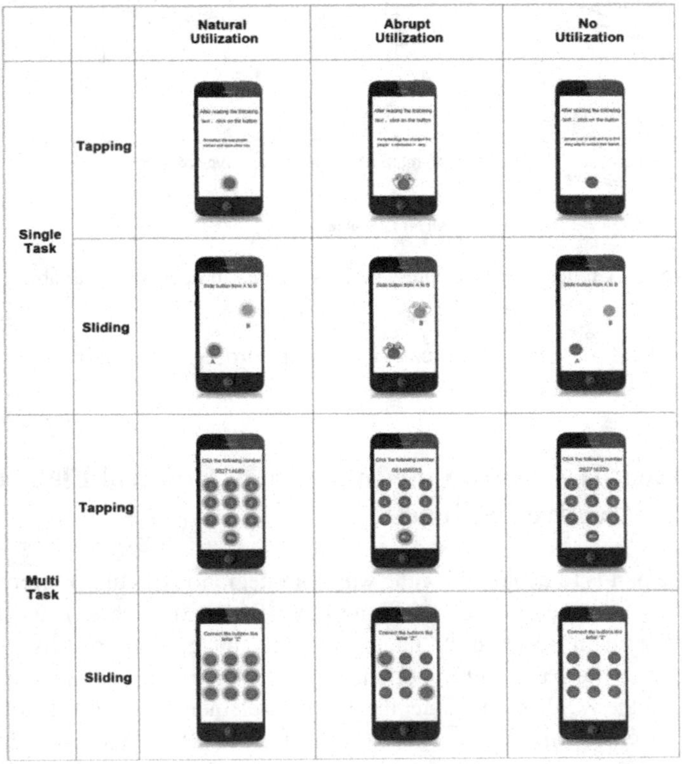

Fig. 4. Materials for experiment II

Table 2. Results of one-way ANOVA

		Sum of Squares	df	Mean Square	F	Sig.
Feedback Clarity	Between Groups	5.186	1	5.186	2.725	.100
	Within Groups	498.629	262	1.903		
	Total	503.814	263			
Feedback Understandability	Between Groups	2.182	1	2.182	1.604	.206
	Within Groups	356.348	262	1.360		
	Total	358.530	263			
Easy-to-use	Between Groups	41.761	1	41.761	31.338	.000
	Within Groups	349.144	262	1.333		
	Total	390.905	263			
Satisfaction in Feedback	Between Groups	4.125	1	4.125	2.921	.089
	Within Groups	370.023	262	1.412		
	Total	374.148	263			
Satisfaction for Culture Utilization	Between Groups	3.409	1	3.409	2.677	.103
	Within Groups	333.682	262	1.274		
	Total	337.091	263			
Memorablity	Between Groups	1.670	1	1.670	1.660	.199
	Within Groups	263.689	262	1.006		
	Total	265.360	263			
Degree of Interesting	Between Groups	35.640	1	35.640	37.866	.000
	Within Groups	246.598	262	.941		
	Total	282.239	263			

The results indicate that:

"Gesture Type" has very limited influence on the interaction experience. Only "Easy-to-use" and "Degree of Interesting" show significant relationship (shown in Table 2). This means the gesture type doesn't have much impact on the user experience with integration of cultural elements.

"Task Complexity" affects the user experience significantly. What's interesting is that the more complex the task is, the better the user experience is (shown in Fig. 5). This may be related to the interaction time.

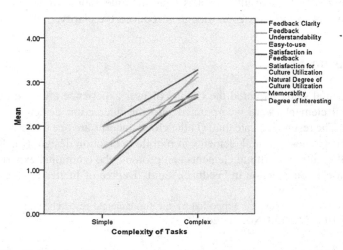

Fig. 5. Relationship between task complexity and dependent variables

Table 3. Results of one-way ANOVA

		Sum of Squares	df	Mean Square	F	Sig.
Feedback Clarity	Between Groups	17.417	2	8.708	4.673	.010
	Within Groups	486.398	261	1.864		
	Total	503.814	263			
Feedback Understandability	Between Groups	6.689	2	3.345	2.481	.086
	Within Groups	351.841	261	1.348		
	Total	358.530	263			
Easy-to-use	Between Groups	17.235	2	8.617	6.019	.003
	Within Groups	373.670	261	1.432		
	Total	390.905	263			
Satisfaction in Feedback	Between Groups	17.614	2	8.807	6.447	.002
	Within Groups	356.534	261	1.366		
	Total	374.148	263			
Satisfaction for Culture Utilization	Between Groups	26.341	2	13.170	11.062	.000
	Within Groups	310.750	261	1.191		
	Total	337.091	263			
Natural Degree of Culture Utilization	Between Groups	26.030	2	13.015	14.633	.000
	Within Groups	232.136	261	.889		
	Total	258.167	263			
Memorablity	Between Groups	4.598	2	2.299	2.301	.102
	Within Groups	260.761	261	.999		
	Total	265.360	263			
Degree of Interesting	Between Groups	19.182	2	9.591	9.516	.000
	Within Groups	263.057	261	1.008		
	Total	282.239	263			

The way of integration of cultural elements has significant relationship with "Feedback Clarity", "Easy-to-use", "Satisfaction in Feedback", "Satisfaction for Culture Utilization", "Natural Degree of Culture Utilization" and "Degree of Interesting", and has very limited correlations with "Feedback Understandability" and "Memorability" (shown in Table 3). Except for "Feedback Clarity", other 5 evaluations are the best in the natural integration condition and the worst in no integration condition (shown in Fig. 6). This result indicates that the integration of cultural elements promoted the user experience, even though it reduced the clarity.

5   Conclusion

This experimental study explored the change of user experience after the explicit and visual cultural elements were incorporated into the interaction design in the mobile environment. The results indicate that: (1).the cloud patterns are one of the most popular symbol for the Chinese cultural elements in mobile interaction design; (2). The natural integration of traditional cultural elements can promote the emotional experience, such as "Easy-to-use", "Satisfaction in Feedback" and "Degree of Interesting", etc.

Acknowledgement. This paper is supported by the fundamental research funds for the central universities of HUST (2013 QN011 & 2014 QN017).

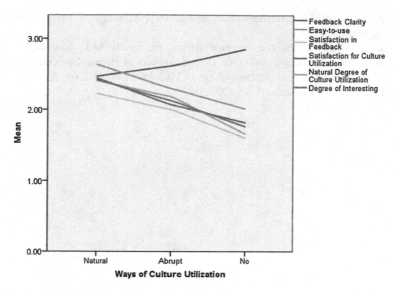

Fig. 6. Relationship between ways of culture utilization and dependent variables

References

1. Mushtaha, A., De Troyer, O.: Cross-culture and website design: cultural movements and settled cultural variables. In: Aykin, N. (ed.) IDGD 2009. LNCS, vol. 5623, pp. 69–78. Springer, Heidelberg (2009)
2. Marcus, A., Krishnamurthi, N.: Cross-cultural analysis of social network services in Japan, Korea, and the USA. In: Aykin, N. (ed.) IDGD 2009. LNCS, vol. 5623, pp. 59–68. Springer, Heidelberg (2009)
3. Hall, E.: The Silent Language. Doubleday, New York (1959)
4. Honold, P.: Interkulturelles usability engineering: Eine Untersuchung zu kulturellen Einflüssen auf die Gestaltung und Nutzung technischer Produkte [Intercultural usability engineering: An investigation of cultural influences on the design and usage of technical products]. Als Ms. gedr. ed. vol. 647. Düsseldorf, Germany : VDI Verl. (2000)
5. Smith, A., French, T., Chang, Y., McNeill, M.: eCulture: Acomparative study of eFinance web site usability for Chineseand British users. Designing for global markets. Conference (6th. 2001). In: Day, D., Duckley, L. (eds.) Proceedings of the 3rd International Workshop on Internationalisation of Products and Systems, pp. 87–100. The Open University, Buckinghamshire (2001)
6. Hoft, N.L.: Developing a cultural model. In: Del Galdo, E.M., Nielsen, J. (eds.) International Users Interface, pp. 41–73. Wiley, New York (1996)
7. Hofstede, G.: Cultures and Organisations: Software of the Mind. McGraw-Hill, New York (1991)
8. Hall, E.T., Hall, M.R.: Understanding Cultural Differ-ences: [Germans, French and Americans]. Intercultural Press, Yarmouth (2004)

9. Thomas, A.: Psychologie Interkulturellen Handelns [Psychology of intercultural acting]. Hogrefe, Göttingen (1996)
10. Marcus, A.: Cross-cultural user-interface design. In: Smith, M.J., Salvendy, G. (eds.) Systems, Social and Internationalization Design Aspects of Human-Computer Interaction, (pp. 502–505). Volume 2 of the Proceedings of HCI International 2001, pp. 5–10, August 2001, New Orleans, Louisiana, USA (2001)

Service Design Towards Sustainable Lifestyle in the Context of Mobile Internet

Xueliang Li, Miaosen Gong[✉], and Dongjuan Xiao

School of Design, Jiangnan University, No. 1800, Lihu Road, Binhu District,
Wuxi 214122, Jiangsu Province, China
1185110176@qq.com, miaosen.gong@gmail.com,
dj.xiao@yahoo.com

Abstract. Mobile internet with infrastructures and services built around develops rapidly, creating an opportunity to reflect on and overturn the traditional way dealing with economy, culture and social structure. Under such a background, service-oriented solutions have been endowed with reforming power to access the sustainable way of living and producing. With diffuse social resources and personal capabilities highly mobilized, grassroots social innovation based on mobile platform has emerged as a new trend to engage people in a collaborative activity. Through the case study and key elements analysis, a service model is put forward to define structural features and dynamic interactions within the service system.

Keywords: Service design · Mobile internet · Sustainable lifestyle · Grassroots social innovation · Mobile platform

1 Introduction

Along with the high diffusion of mobile communication technologies (MCTs), the ways we are dealing with social issues have been changed a lot. Ubiquitous network as it spreads and overwhelms every corner of our lives has influenced how we behave ourselves in different situation, integrating and transcending the spaces geographically, physically and virtually, evolving into a hybrid space, Space of Auras, which serves as a catalyst for social relation [1]. On the other hand, although we all realize the peculiar role of Internet, reflective and analytical knowledge about the impact on our behavior and social activities has not been explained clearly, and there is still some undefined space for us to exploit [2].

This paper has focused on the service with a specific value orientation or objective, i.e. sustainable lifestyle, as a subject for which the implementation and outcome would depend significantly on people's behavioral change and interactive effect. In this particular situation, mobile internet acts as both an environmental condition and a service-enabling infrastructure, whilst mobile platform is put forward to be an

The research is partially supported by Ministry of Education Humanities and Social Science Youth Fund (11YJC760018) and National Social Science Foundation-Art (13ZD03).

© Springer International Publishing Switzerland 2015
P.L.P. Rau (Ed.): CCD 2015, Part II, LNCS 9181, pp. 57–67, 2015.
DOI: 10.1007/978-3-319-20934-0_6

important medium constructing the whole system. According to the analysis of selected cases, with structural and paradigmatic concerns on the subject, dimensions such as actors, interactive relation and systematic cohesion are brought into discussion, which shed some light on the principles of how to establish and maintain the service as it is formulated. Subsequently, an ideal picture is given for the hypothetical scenario considering the social resources consumption and relational quality between the actors.

As a pilot exploration, the primary concern of this discussion is to articulate the mechanism of technologies promoting social innovation by creating the context and foundation for people gathered at a social scale, and affecting the way they interact with each other to solve the particular problem and at the same time strengthen social cohesion.

2 Service-Oriented Solutions in the Context of Mobile Internet

In recent years, service-oriented solutions are emerging as a response to the complicated aspects referring to environmental and social crisis, with a wide agreement that it's time to re-orientate the entire production and consumption system ecologically [3]. By dealing with these issues, the service-oriented solution has shown its dominance when it comes to integrating diffuse resources and connecting people regardless of physical obstacles, which has been more accessible and conducive with the utilization of mobile communication and ubiquitous network. In a social sense, we can see some characteristics and trends reflected through those phenomena, which provide a flexible foundation for service creation leading to social innovation.

2.1 Local Issues at a Social Scale

Looking deep into the social changes caused by technological development, we can still find some inherent characters existing behind the changes. To put it precisely, even though the forms of how it is taken and met differ from moment to moment, the social requirements have always come from the living experience which appear and converge at first at a local level, meaning that people would like or prefer to the services with a sense of belonging to the community, even though mobile internet has generalized it as a virtual concept. With the help of the enlarged network, the technological and social potentialities can be bridged in a new dimension connecting people who are not related in a traditional way.

Service design has a lot to do with this vision. By proposing a commonly recognized value and creating a particular scenario, issues can be managed in an organized way, in which situation people are invited or motivated to collaborate with others to achieve the positive results, reminding us of the expression creative community [4–6]. These characteristics and distinctions give us a look at the core of services built on and promoted by mobile internet, i.e. however diffuse and scattered the issues are, it is always necessary to hold people together with a positive value proposition and a social connection.

2.2   Convergence of Diffuse Resources for Personalized Requirements

In the last decades, MCTs have shown the advantage of integrating and deploying diffuse resources in the social range. The aspects are promoted with the development of Mobile Internet, leapfrogging from manufacturing of production to the era of individualization by making possible a variety of customerized services. It is gradually understood by the companies to pay more attention to "user experience", as the driving effect to the economy of the manufacturing or technology has been stagnated recently, while from the perspective of design, the focus is being diverted from the "design of products" to "design for people's purposes" [7]. With the arrival of the experience economy, diffuse knowledge and people's capacities are taken as a kind of resource, which helps reduce the cost of society being collected and utilized appropriately.

In such a circumstance, people's capability and initiative have been reinforced by the digital technology. Taking smart phone as an example, not only as a communication tool, more than this, it has been a platform with a set of functions, the particular composition of which is partially decided by users. In the form of App, surface of services are simplified and condensed into a finger's controlling area, with flow of material and information moving behind, leaving a flexible space for people to switch the activities they are taking a part in.

2.3   Collaborative Services Towards Sustainability

Different from the standard services which are based on asymmetrical interactions between active providers and passive users, collaborative services [8] found in the networks of contemporary society tend to be more symmetrical and ask for the direct and active involvement of all the interested actors [3].

Thanks to the "Internet Revolution", new forms and typologies of services have been developed to enrich the possibilities of actions. By creating a balance where users get access to the consumption passively, at the same time are free to choose what kinds of more creative experiences to engage in and how [9], mobile communication and ubiquitous network provide a new dimension as people participate in the activities with strong motivation, changing the processes and experiences of interaction in the collaborative services [10]. In view of value creation, this co-producing process features the experience and emotion feedback when people are integrated into the system with their enthusiasm, care and sense of achievement aroused. To be more precise, the users' role has evolved from "destroyer of value, to source of value, and finally to co-creator of value" [11], not only for the material and process requirement, but also for the systematic balance and the actor's self-improvement. That's why it matters a lot how we behave ourselves and interact with each other in an interconnected environment especially when it involves a social concern.

2.4   Social Cohesion in a Decentralized Structure

Since the service scenarios have been transferred, most of them, into virtual spaces, interconnection and interaction between the actors tend to depend more on the infrastructures set up by the companies or initiators, i.e. a set of rules and technological supports would be needed to build an equal and liberal environment where the identity difference is removed and status repositioned. Nevertheless, however complex and volatile the situation is, The relational quality [12] is always considered a key element and the achievement of wellbeing is still based on interpersonal encounter. Through the flat structure of communication network, services based on Mobile Internet build a new form of social tie by ensuring users a multi-dimensional communicating experience and, to make it reliable and extensible, an organizational guarantee.

Therefore, a new body of common knowledge need to be established to reorient people's learning process and reorganize the social resources from a broader perspective, with highly motivated and mobilized actors interacting with each other. To further explain this, there will be different typologies and paradigms making sense for different situation, and the final vision is built on a basis of socialized connection, which relies to a great degree on the quality of the relational network and reliability of links between the actors.

3 Case Study

Sustainable lifestyle leads to conceptual and behavioral changes, as well as reconfiguration of the social structure. To achieve this, it has been an important way to exploit the diffuse social resources and redistribute them throughout the society, in which process personal capabilities would be fully mobilized. Eventually, in some way, the innovative approaches and situations relate closely to the expression grassroots social innovation, in the context of mobile internet which would play a larger role in the field of social innovation, especially in China [13].

To get a basic acknowledgement, and continually based on which to carry out a further analysis, a set of cases were collected making a picture of what is happening in this particular situation. Finally, four cases were selected as typical ones. There is the case, Chunyu Doctor which seeks to rebuild the relationship between patients and doctors, by improving the process of health inquiry online with recording tools for daily activities related to people's physical condition; And we also focus on a service helping people to book vehicles from personal owners (non-taxi drivers), as what Yongche.com is doing; In the case of Xiaozhu.com, similar to Airbnb, it makes an agent interconnecting people with vacant apartments and the ones who need to rent a place for a short term; Gudong is an App service collecting users' data when they are taking exercises, and further than that try to build a social network based on people's common interest in outdoor sports.

Looking attentively at the cases, we can see that four aspects appear as primary concerns to form a basic impression of the services, i.e. platform utilization, actors involvement, interactive relation and systematic integrity, corresponding to the particular phases when conceiving or developing a service-oriented solution (Table 1).

Table 1. Four aspects as primary concerns

Cases	Platform utilization	Actors involvement	Interactive relation	Systematic integrity
Chunyu Doctor	App	Motivated/Related	Expert-to-Ordinary	Weak
Yongche.com	App/Web	Engaged	Haves-to-Havenots	Strong
Xiaozhu.com	App/Web	Engaged	Haves-to-Havenots	Strong
Gudong	App	Integrated	Peer-to-Peer	Strong

3.1 Platform Utilization

Considering the services we are discussing here rely mostly on mobile applications, it is widely agreed that a mobile platform is needed to make a common space for communication and to equip the actors with appropriate tools, i.e. the infrastructures built within virtual spaces to enable a particular activity to exist [4].

Personalized, participative, configurable and expansible, mobile platforms have shown a variety of elementary characteristics when applied into the social area dealing with people's diversified and immediate demands. Taking Gudong as an example, the platform is made to be a personal exercise log, a GPS tracker as well as a social network, with dynamic feedback and interaction in real time. Such situation can also be found in Chunyu Doctor, which provides users a method to record one's physiological index and living habit, composing personal health database reflecting one's health condition. With accurate calculating and systematic planning, services are formed from users' experience and made to be universal, applicable and available. Different from the production or technology driven business with strong productivity supporting, social resources driven services are created, in which process mobile platforms play an important role.

3.2 Actors Involvement

Different from the traditional way involving actors in a service issue, in which situation more attentions are paid to the practical participation and it is hard to form a long term relationship away from the service scenarios, in the context of mobile internet, online connections open up new possibilities to define how and where people are involved into the activities. It is found that there exist four stages corresponding to the particular conditions of the general users taking part in the services, considering different complexity requirements of the activity, as indicated in Fig. 1.

In the first stage, people are "motivated" by the common value or basic acknowledgement, such as Chunyu Doctor, where the communication between patients and doctors are often on a superficial level related to slight illness or minor symptoms. That is, for the present situation, users only get supported from online information without physical encounters, and it takes little effort to be a part of it. Secondly, in the next stage, users become "related" in the service, with more concern on continuous improvement and interaction with others. We can still see that in Chunyu Doctor, users

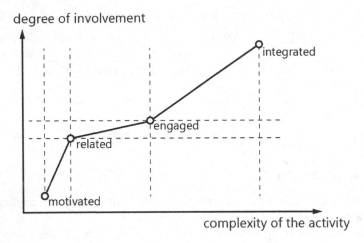

Fig. 1. Four stages of actors involvement

can get into a deeper level by establishing a long term relation with the doctors, i.e. putting them into a watchlist, or, if it's convenient and necessary, making appointments with them directly. For the third stage, the adjective "engaged" refer much more to the personal commitment and achievement based on a stable interconnection with each other which requests a trust relationship and reliable organizational support, such as Yongche.com and Xiaozhu.com. At last, as an ideal situation, actors are "integrated" as indispensable part of the system supporting the main body of the service, while mobile platform serves as basic infrastructures or enabling tools making users active subjects keeping the service running.

There are two points to be clarified as supplementary explanation: It is found that the degree of difference between every two stages varies with intensity of motivation, and to move into the next stage different level of complexity will be needed; The four stages are brought up to define a dynamic performance, by saying which it means actors involvement can be at different level even in one particular situation as the service condition or users motivation change.

3.3 Interactive Relation

Mobile communication and ubiquitous network has bought a new dimension into our view to differentiate and evaluate the role of actors and interactive relation within the system. At first, faced with the interface of services, are users from social area with their creativity and deliverability taken as a new form of resource. And there appear some different situations when it comes to the way how general users participate and interact with each other in a specific scenario. For example, in the case of Chunyu Doctor there exists a clear boundary between service providers and clients given that the supply-demand relationship is based on a highly specialized field and the doctors involved have to be qualified to give the advice, to define which we can call it as "expert-to-ordinary". While in other cases, it is difficult to distinguish between providers and clients, such as Yongche.com where people can be both the drivers (which need a simple certification process) and passengers. What makes the difference is whether one gets the applicable possession or capacity for another in a particular situation, i.e. "haves-to-havenots". Same things can be found in Xiaozhu.com. In the case of Gudong, actors' role distinction has been further eliminated, and users are treated equally as both providers and clients, getting satisfied or supported by each other, where the relationship can be defined as "peer to peer".

3.4 Systematic Integrity

Services towards sustainability in the context of mobile internet have presented a range of possibilities to reach the social needs, opening up a new model by treating general users as providers endowed with resources and specialties. And Systematic integrity is to be achieved as an ideal result, with five dimensions particularly concerned: core value, infrastructures, relational ties, network and sustainability.

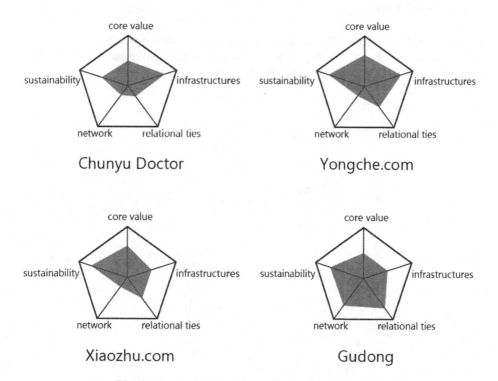

Fig. 2. Systematic integrity analysis of the four cases

It is the core value that brings people together and makes a common base to set off the activity, which often encompasses common concerns, positive objectives or benefit drivers. And infrastructures, here mostly in virtual sense, refer to digital technologies and organizational conditions that help to establish and facilitate the services and transform the common recognition into action. While relational tie highlights the fundamental basis when establishing relationship, to which such procedures as identity authentication, mutual evaluation and, if necessary, interpersonal encounters can make a difference. With socialized connection built within the system, a kind of network is being formed, i.e. social interaction based on mobile platform plays an important part in the service process, making an open and multi-dimensional communication environment. Different from all the issues mentioned above, sustainability has more to do with ecological benefits of the services, concerning the way how services are conceived and developed, not only in an environmental sense but also as a sociology category involving such factors as behavioral experience, self-achievement, relational quality, and so on.

As indicated in Fig. 2, we make an evaluation to the systematic integrity of the four cases by establishing an analysis diagram with the five dimensions placed around the pentagon at each point, and some interesting points can be found.

4   Service Model

A model is put forward (as Fig. 3) to depict an ideal picture of the dynamic system, which features the service based on mobile platform built to gather users, mobilize the interaction, and finally realize a systematic integrity.

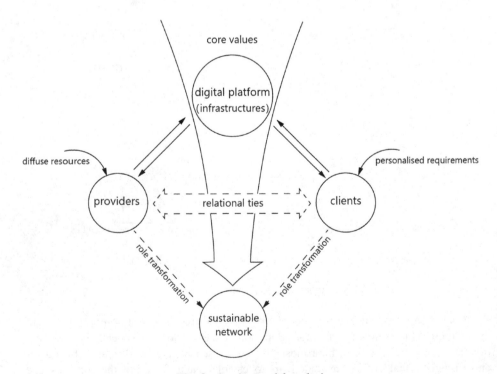

Fig. 3. Service model analysis

As we can see from Fig. 3, the mobile platform acts as a bonding agent as well as a driving force. Looking horizontally, it holds together the users with core values, while dividing them into two groups: the group of people who serve as providers by transforming idle resources or personal capacities into applicable services; and the ones acting as clients with personalized needs and requirements. By providing or being satisfied, the users are involved into a symbiotic relationship forming varieties of relational ties. And from the vertical perspective, it is found that the core values are embodied into specific infrastructures to achieve proposed objectives. Through building comprehensive scenarios and enabling users with appropriate tools, mobile platform enrich the contents of the interaction, pushing the actors involvement into a different level. That is, finally, a sustainable network is established where the users are integrated into the system as equal parts, co-producing the main body of service with their potentialities fully exploited considering personal knowledge or skill complementarity. In this way, social problems and needs are addressed by a low-cost solution where personal performance is treated as input as well as output while technology facilitates the activity fundamentally and peripherally.

5 Design Proposal: Baby Plan

Baby plan is a service proposal based on a mobile platform, defined as "an supporting network for pregnant women to deliver a healthy baby", whose purpose is to engage new mothers and the pregnant women into a collaborative community, where the new

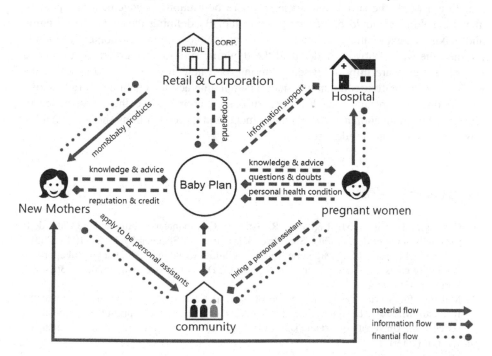

Fig. 4. System map of Baby plan

mothers are endowed with a new role: the adviser or assistant of the pregnant with their personal experience and knowledge. And as the pregnant women turn out to be new mothers, it's natural for them to switch the role (Fig. 4).

Baby plan provide a better access to the personal knowledge for young pregnant women especially who have no such experience before and normally get themselves supported through internet or directly going to hospital. It also helps to relieve their fear and anxiety when communicating with the ones who have just gone through it. By informing and supporting pregnant women, new mothers would be rewarded in form of reputation or credit, earning them a better chance to get a discount when buying mom&baby products. On the other hand, the mobile platform is established based on interpersonal links formed around the shared activity, which support registration, validation and the rules to motivate people to be engaged, with links to the periphery commercial resources. In addition, the service has also tried to build an online community where the pregnant woman can seek to establish a long term relationship with a particular mother as her personal assistant who will be paid monthly in return.

6   Conclusion

Such explorations and hypotheses help us to take a further step when considering the potentialities using latest technology to solve social problems from the perspective of design. Digital social innovation as a recent label to include and describe the activities motivated or driven by the digital technology, indicates a socialized movement in a flat structure towards the sustainable society, where both public engagement and personalized capabilities should be of significant value. By defining the particular situation and making an exploratory depiction of the service innovation in the context of mobile internet, the way of how to understand the dynamic system and further to conceive a feasible solution are fully discussed, bringing us a new angle of view to look at the ideas of collaborative community, interpersonal interaction, enabling infrastructure, and so on. As a result, what has been discussed above prove the convergence of technological innovation and social engagement, and more attentions should be paid to this field to facilitate an ideal society.

References

1. Casalegno, F., Susani, M., Tagliabue, R.: Atlas de Communication Aurale: Une Carte de la Communication et de Ses Flux. Soc. Rev. Sci. Humaines Sociales **79**(1), 89–104 (2003)
2. Valsecchi, F., Gong, M.: Design implications of digital social innovation: a playful approach to analyse cases study dataset. In: Rau, P. (ed.) CCD 2014. LNCS, vol. 8528, pp. 361–372. Springer, Heidelberg (2014)
3. Manzini, E.: Service design in the age of networks and sustainability. In: Miettinen, S., Koivisto, M. (eds.) Designing Services with Innovative Methods, pp. 44–59. Publication series of the University of Art and Design Helsinki/Savonia University of Applied Sciencies, Keuruu (2009)

4. Manzini E, DIS I: creative communities and enabling platforms. In: Taking Responsibility (2005)
5. Manzini, E., Meroni, A.: Emerging user demands for sustainable solutions. In: Michel, R. (ed.) Design Research Now, pp. 157–179. Birkhäuser, Basel (2007)
6. Meroni, A.: Creative Communities: People Inventing Sustainable Ways of Living. Edizioni Polidesign, Milano (2007)
7. Sanders, E.B.N., Stappers, P.J.: Co-creation and the new landscapes of design. J. Co-Des. **4** (1), 5–18 (2008)
8. Jegou, F., Manzini, E.: Collaborative Services: Social Innovation and Design for Sustainability. Edizioni Polidesign, Milano (2008)
9. Sanders, E.B.N.: Design serving people. J. Cumulus Work. Pap. Copenhagen **15**(5), 28–33 (2006)
10. Gong, M., Manzini, E., Casalegno, F.: Mobilized collaborative services in ubiquitous network. In: Rau, P. (ed.) IDGD 2011. LNCS, vol. 6775, pp. 504–513. Springer, Heidelberg (2011)
11. Ramirez, R., Mannervik, U.: Designing value-creating systems. J. Des. Scrv. Multi. Perspect. **35**, 1–5 (2008)
12. Cipolla, C.: Designing for interpersonal relational qualities in services: a model for service design theory and practice. Journal Unpublished Ph.D. thesis, Politecnicdo di Milano, Milano (2007)
13. Gong, M.: Service Design for Social Innovation. In: Designing Services with Innovative Methods, pp. 220–231. University of Art and Design Helsinki, Keuruu (2009)

From Technology to Design

A Case Study of Netizen's Perception
Toward Dechnology Products

Hsi-Yen Lin[✉], Wen-Zhong Su, Pei-Hua Hung, and Chi-Ying Hung

Graduate School of Creative Industry Design, National Taiwan University of
Arts, Ban Ciao District, New Taipei City 22058, Taiwan
{p3yann, orpheussu, paywhathome, yumeeiren}@gmail.com

Abstract. The purpose of this study was to explore new online communities' awareness of and preferences for technology products. By conducting questionnaire surveys on 13 dechnology (a portmanteau word of design and technology) products, this study aimed to understand the preferences and the characteristics of a specific online virtual community—the Internet and technology enthusiasts group. The study results revealed that the Internet and technology enthusiasts believed the products with more prominent utilization of technology should place more emphasis on human-centered connotations in order to earn high ratings. The results also suggested that this particular group of individuals prefer products that elaborate on human-centered concerns and needs, and even satisfy humans' inner desires. In view of the observations aforementioned, it was concluded that the products' features should be thoroughly studied beforehand. Future product designs should base on the demands of specific users, and well-integrated with appropriate technologies. The end result will more closely match the users' needs in the real market. Online communities with specific interests tend to have their own unique insights and ideas about product preferences. They pay more attention to the needs for humane care related to their lifestyles, and use them as inspirations for technology product designs.

Keywords: Dechnology · Cyber/virtual community · Community characteristic · Product preference

1 Introduction

Under the impact of information technology, by both providing functions for relationship building and knowledge sharing on cyberspace, virtual communities already affect our living standards in a certain way, wherein, individual behavior has been intensively changed (Brown 2000). Without the boundary of geography and time consuming, cyber community as a participants-driven world provides a forum engaging members to share their thoughts and interests. As virtual communities are constructed with different attributes and various objectives, interest-based community has common concerns among members and often provides information more involved in certain

© Springer International Publishing Switzerland 2015
P.L.P. Rau (Ed.): CCD 2015, Part II, LNCS 9181, pp. 68–79, 2015.
DOI: 10.1007/978-3-319-20934-0_7

aspect which would attract loyal net users plunging into. And from their continuous interactions, it would become a platform where members share consensus and trust.

Since Electronic Commerce and Mobile Commerce have emerged around whole cyber world, enterprises and companies contribute much effort on the ways to dig out their potential customers. The mass markets of previous decades have splintered into smaller market segments or niches, in which companies could focus merely on certain target groups and explore new market opportunities (Dalgic, Leeuw, 1994). Meanwhile, Kelman (1958) claimed that individuals' role and value orientations to a group —conceptually linked to compliance, identification, and internalization, it influences individual's beliefs and changes his/her attitude and intention. Based on this feature, interest-based or subject-based virtual communities with strong public consensus may therefore be an ideal target group or niche market for company, technologists and designers.

Creating a design product or high-tech product to please the whole world is impossible, thus customized-product already became the tendency toward future design. Netizens of virtual community are the group with certain common values and preferences, especially the fans of high-tech interest who are concerned as high technology acceptance. Hence, their insights toward technology and design products might provide critical information to technologists, designers, and companies.

The research objectives of this study therefore are listed as follows:

1. To explore Netizens' perception and preference toward technology + design products.
2. To investigate the relationship between virtual community characteristics and their advocators' (Netizens) preferences.

2 Virtual World and the Hidden Reality

2.1 Cyber Community/Virtual Community

Cyber community is a form of virtual human interaction. This virtual interaction transforms the way people relate to each other and being as a new virtual social relationship. Since Computer-Mediated Community (CMC) with the spatial metaphor is adopted for discourse as thinking of virtual social relations in terms of community. CMC is referred to be place centered, and the cyberspace in it as a place where community can develop and be sustained, and new social and economic relationships can be created (Fernback 1998). On the functional and technical point of view, cyber community is a technologically mediated and persistent environment which supports multiple interaction styles, capability for real-time interaction, and multi-user engagement (Ho, Schraefel and Chignell, 2000). As the term of community is addressed by Cohen (1985) as being symbolically constructed, with the unity of normative codes and values it provides community members with a sense of identity. Rheingold (1993) claimed it as creating "social aggregations that emerge from the Net when enough people carry on those public discussions long enough, with sufficient human feeling, to form webs of personal relationships in cyberspace". Likewise, virtual communities offer an engaging environment in which people connect, trust, and share real insight mutually (Carver 1999). The uniqueness of virtual communities is that most of their content is member-generated, as opposed to other Internet information which is typically provided by the site provider (Ridings & Gefen 2004; Hagel & Arnstrong, 1997).Hence, the definition of virtual community might be concluded as the community on cyberspace which can provide information and transaction within a member-generated and social relationship.

2.2 Community Characteristics and Its Present Situation

Virtual community is a real entity that is given meaning by its participants (Baym 1995). Since the content of communication is based upon the self-categorization process and associated perceptions of shared social category membership (Turner 1991), virtual communities have been widely created on different attributes based on intention varieties. Figallo (1998) also described that virtual communities are those where members feel part of a social group, sense a connection with other members, have common values, and have lasting relationships with others (Ridings & Gefen 2004). Namely, perceptions of shared social identity not only can provide members with multiple motivations for communicating but also with a shared cognitive framework that allows the communication to be mutually beneficial and productive (Postmes 2003). Since the content or concerns of virtual communities are driven by the participants, community characteristics therefore could be classified as: interest, relationship, fantasy (entertainment), and transaction (Hagel & Armstrong 1997; Carver 1999; Jones & Rafaeli 2000).

According to the report of "The Analysis of Virtual Communities' Present Situation" employed by the Marketing Intelligence & Consulting Institute (MIC, Taiwan) (mic.iii.org.tw/index.asp), it revealed that the frequency of usage among internet users achieved 92 % high on "Social Relationship" communities, and 35.1 % on advocating "Interests" communities in 2014. Furthermore, some social media trends forecasted in the coming future commonly include: (1) the physical and virtual/media worlds will be more highly connected; (2) major social networks/communities will battle harder for our wallet than before; (3) commercial transactions on social media/online will increasing strongly; (4) Information on the cyberspace will become customized to our needs (Noff 2011; Holmes 2014).

2.3 Product Preference and the Opportunity
of E-Commerce/M-Commerce

MIC (2014) indicated 81 % of internet users would research product reputation on cyberspace and the sequence of the ranking are "Social Relationship" communities (45.8 %), communities with "Discussion Forum" (44.7 %) and "Blog" communities (33.1 %). And to the analysis focused on ages, under 19-year-old internet users (53.2 %) and above 40-year-of-age internet consumers (46.6 %) would research the product reputation mainly relied on "Social Relationship" communities. The users among 20-29 years-of-age (50.2 %) and 30-39 years-of-age (52.2 %) would prefer the information provided from "Discussion Forum". Meanwhile, it also indicated that 82.7 % internet users always search 3C products and home appliances (36 %) on virtual communities. E-commerce and Mobile commerce indeed exists on the relations between virtual communities and their advocators and the influence is believed getting tremendous.

Since online commerce is becoming more related with our daily life, enterprises pay more concerns focusing on the connection and relationship between virtual communities and their potential customers. Customers however are not blind, they search commends or feedbacks from the experienced user online. Products designed or invented with the purpose of involving technology into human daily life, but they sometimes be found are not acceptable properly to the public. Since preferences could be conceived of as an individual's attitude towards a set of objects, typically reflected in an explicit decision-making process (Lichtenstein & Slovic 2006), knowing the needs and preferences of certain group is becoming essential to technologists and designers today. "Lead Users" termed by Hippel (1986) are users whose present strong needs will become general in a market place in the future. They are familiar with conditions which lie in the future for most others and can serve as a need-forecasting laboratory for marketing research, and also provide new product concept and design data as well. With this notion, releasing technology and design products to a certain group, especially the group of high-tech acceptance as the lead users, is convinced that can provide practical comments to the deisgn + technology field.

3 Methodologies

In "Dechnology 2014 New Collection," the Industrial Technology Research Institute (ITRI) attempted to incorporate technology into everyday lives. It divided 41 design products into 12 categories that are closely related to people's daily lives: life, cook, appliance, detect, home, fitting, assist, traffic, information, leisure, medical, and alert. The ITRI further believed that these 12 categories will continue to play a part in our future lives. The word "dechnology" is a portmanteau word of "design" and "technology." It was created in hopes of generating more values for technology by utilizing the abundant creative energy of Taiwanese designers (Hung & Huang, 2012). Regarding the development of Taiwan's design industry, Lin (2009) suggested that the industry is currently enhancing its design energy and values while moving toward the emotional technology design that emphasizes "aesthetic experiences." This study aimed to investigate whether all of the design products (created by using various resources) presented in the "Dechnology project" were in accordance with the project's spirit—creating more values for technology by utilizing the abundant creative energy of Taiwanese designers. The characteristics of the design products were examined by three attributes: "the application of forward-looking technologies," "the demonstration of aesthetic designs," and "the expression of humane care."

To further explore the relationship between the proportions of the three product attributes provided by a specific online community and their preferences for the products, the more representative and preferable items were prescreened. The study was conducted in three stages.

Stage one: The 20 products that received the highest ratings and preferences on the expert questionnaires for "Dechnology 2014 New Collection" were used as control samples for comparison with the online community's preferences.

Stage two: A second questionnaire survey was administered using the three attributes (ABC)—"the application of forward-looking technologies" (A), "the demonstration of aesthetic designs" (B), and "the expression of humane care" (C). Ratings on the ABC attributes of all products were obtained through the second survey. They served as the references for the distribution of the products' attributes.

Stage three: Based on the analytical results of the data obtained in the previous two stages, 11 products were chosen as study objects by two criteria—1) having two attributes that ranked in the top 20 on the ABC survey while also being selected as the top 20 on the experts' questionnaire survey, and 2) having one attribute that ranked in the top 20 on the ABC survey while also being selected as the top 10 on the experts' questionnaire survey. The items of a commercialized product (as presented in Q2) and a worst product selected by the experts (as presented in Q4) were also included to validate the accuracy of the retrieved questionnaires. A total of 13 products (as listed in Table 1) were used on the Google forms for online questionnaire survey.

Table 1. The 13 design products used in the questionnaires

| Q1 | Q2 | Q3 | Q4 | Q5 | Q6 | Q7 |

| Q8 | Q9 | Q10 | Q11 | Q12 | Q13 |

This questionnaire survey targeted netizens who were familiar with the use of technology and possessed specific preferences as research subjects. Other than animation games and model toys, most of the netizens who participated in the survey also had a strong interest and passion for forward-looking technologies. In addition, these netizens responded and reacted enthusiastically to technology-related information shared on the Facebook fan pages. Hence, this study targeted these netizens as research subjects in order to understand the feelings and preferences of the Internet and technology enthusiasts for Dechnology design products.

This study conducted frequency distribution analysis on the ABC attribute ratings and the product preference ratings of the 13 products retrieved from the survey subjects' questionnaires. The ABC attributes were also used for the regression analysis on product preferences, in order to understand the relationship between the Internet technology enthusiasts' preferences and the products' attributes.

4 Results

A total of 127 subjects participated in the Internet questionnaire for the 13 products. There were 120 copies of valid questionnaires. Fifty-five percent of the research subjects were under the age of 25 and another 34 % were between the ages of 26 to 35 years. In regard to the gender ratio, 86 % of the subjects were male, which reflected that the Internet technology enthusiasts' community was mainly composed of male members. The majority of the community's core members were under 35 years of age.

The questionnaire divided the subjects' interests and hobbies into nine attributes—technology knowledge, aesthetics and arts, humane care, animation games, political issues, film and television, sports, leisure and travel, and model toys. On average, the participants were interested in the attributes shown in Fig. 1. The majority of the participants favored model toys, animation, and technology. This corresponded to the originally targeted population of Internet and technology enthusiasts who were familiar to technology and products. Judging from the three attributes of technology knowledge, aesthetics and arts, and humane care, the results revealed this age group to be most concerned about technology knowledge. Next to that were aesthetics and arts as well as humane care.

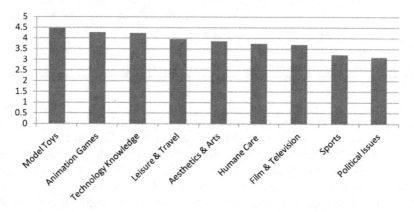

Fig. 1. The distribution of research subjects' nine attributes

This study targeted netizens who were interested in science fiction comics, animations, and model toys as research subjects, because a certain percentage of them were also Internet and technology enthusiasts. As the authors of this study began managing science fiction blogs that shared related reviews and information since 2008, and established the Pihiko Studio Facebook fan page in 2013, a number of loyal netizens who shared common interests and hobbies have gathered together. They continued to participate in the discussion and information exchange, and they turn out to be the core members of this study who actively participated in filling out the questionnaires.

4.1 The Comparison of the Design Products' Attribute Ratings

As shown in Table 2, product Q13 (Medical HMD) received the highest score in terms of attribute A, which was "the application of forward-looking technologies." This product was highly praised in the category of forward-looking technologies by the research subjects as it demonstrated virtual reality technology and was perceived as a high-tech product by the online community. The product that earned the lowest ratings on attribute A was Q2 (Sheathing Fabric Pot). While being a commercialized product, Q2 earned low ratings due to a lack of direct associations with the research subjects' lives as well as a lack of room for imagination. On the contrary, product Q13 had more connections with the science fiction plots that exist in video games.

Table 2. The ranking of the three attributes and the preferences

RANK	1	2	3	4	5	6	7	8	9	10	11	12	13
A Ratings	4.22	4.13	4.13	4.12	4.09	4.02	4.01	3.93	3.89	3.89	3.83	3.7	3.7
A Products	Q13	Q7	Q10	Q12	Q5	Q6	Q11	Q8	Q4	Q9	Q3	Q1	Q2
B Ratings	4.01	3.97	3.94	3.86	3.78	3.71	3.65	3.61	3.41	3.3	3.3	3.28	3.28
B Products	Q6	Q10	Q8	Q7	Q1	Q3	Q11	Q12	Q13	Q4	Q9	Q2	Q5
C Ratings	4.32	4.27	4.23	4.13	4.13	4.12	4.11	4.08	4.01	3.91	3.64	3.56	3.34
C Products	Q11	Q8	Q7	Q4	Q10	Q5	Q13	Q12	Q6	Q9	Q3	Q2	Q1
Preferences (%)	11.52	11.28	10.09	9.40	8.48	8.18	7.86	7.80	5.45	5.36	5.36	4.94	4.29
Preferred Products	Q8	Q7	Q6	Q10	Q11	Q3	Q4	Q2	Q1	Q12	Q13	Q5	Q9

Having received the highest ratings on attribute B, "the demonstration of aesthetic designs," product Q6 (Portal) was merely ranked as the 19th on the experts' questionnaire survey. This result suggested that while the research subjects were often regarded as geeks who only care about technologies, they were actually concerned about the atmosphere of the interior space and the quality of living life as they spend a lot of time indoor working on computers. This explained their high ratings of product Q6. The product that ranked lowest on attribute B was Q5 (Dual Ray Desk Lamp)—a wearable high-tech caring device. It received unfavorable reviews as its design was unable to highlight the high-tech feel.

In regard to attribute C, "the expression of humane care," product Q11 (Health Travel Band) won top stop. The reason might be that the subjects felt especially warm and considerate after understanding its assistive functions for outdoor travels. The product paid extra attention to the online community's inner feelings. Most of the general public regards Internet and technology enthusiasts as "loners" who live or spend time alone. In reality, this particular online community still had the need for humane care. What set them apart from the ordinary people was that they needed more assistance and caring from making connections with the public. The product that earned the lowest rating on attribute C was Q1 (Chinese Cake Steamer). Having little connection with the research subjects' lives, the product's main appeal—suitable for families of two to four people—in turn highlighted the life experiences that the online community was unfamiliar with. The product turned out as something that the Internet and technology enthusiasts' community found to be the most insensitive and even heartbreaking product.

4.2   The Comparison of Preferences

The questionnaire showed that the product with the highest level of preference was Q8 (Siproperly; sit properly). Based on the ABC attribute results, it was revealed that the product ranked second on attribute C, third on attribute B, and relatively lower as the eighth on attribute A. In addition, the technology of Q8 was not the most advanced among all products. Typically, chairs are regarded as an object that is closest to people's everyday life. Furthermore, what an Internet and technology enthusiast needs when he/she uses a computer every day is a comfortable chair. As a result, Q8 became the Dechnology product with the highest level of preference in this study. To the research subjects, the product with higher preferences must meet their intuitive desires and provide them with the comfort and sense of belonging needed in their daily lives.

Interestingly, the product with the lowest level of preference—Q9 (IRB; UNFLIP IRB)—ranked fourth on the experts' questionnaire survey. The product's overall ABC attribute rankings appeared to be mediocre at best. The low ratings might be due to the lack of association between the product's appeals and the research subjects' demands and preferences. The indifferent styling and high-tech feel also contributed to the product's low level of preference. On the other hand, Q7 (Urban Traveler Personal Water Purification Bag) that ranked second on the preference survey and Q11 which earned highest ratings on attribute B were both outdoor travel related products. This explained that the Internet and technology enthusiasts do not only participate in indoor activities. They might simply feel uncertain about the outside world due to their cautious nature, which in turn contributed to their positive evaluation of the products that care about their inner needs.

After reviewing the retrieved questionnaires, it was revealed that over half of the research subjects were young people under 25 years of age who were familiar with the use of Internet. Their choices of products were very different from those of the older experts. As the research subjects were unable to actually use these products and make the judgments, the products' ability to arouse the subjects' interests can be observed from the disparate opinions of the experts and the research subjects. Product Q4 (Touch Handlebar) that was rated by the experts as the worst product did not receive the lowest rating on the subjects' questionnaires. On the other hand, product Q9 (IRB; UNFLIP IRB) which earned expert praise bored the subjects and received poor preferences. In the book *Emotional design*, author Donald A. Norman suggested that the consumers would be delighted to use a product—even if it's not the best of its kind—as long as the product can generate pleasurable feelings. This explains that the Internet and technology enthusiasts, owing to their preferences for Gundam models with strong styling and technological knowledge, relied on their instincts and preferred styling as references when making judgments about the products. Comparing with the experts' preferential evaluations, the online community placed a greater emphasis on the depth and the taste of designs.

4.3   The Comparison of Preferences and Design Attributes

This study further analyzed and discussed the relationships between the netizens' levels of preferences, forward-looking technologies, aesthetics designs, and humane care. All four items showed significant positive correlations (p < 0.001) with each other and the correlation coefficient reached 0.77. Using the level of preference as a dependent variable and forward-looking technologies, aesthetics designs, and humane care as independent variables, the regression model of the level of preference constructed by multiple regression analysis is as follows:

Preference = − 0.020−0.154 (forward-looking technologies) + 0.091 (aesthetics designs) + 0.095 (humane care)

Adj. $R^2 = 0.69$,P < 0.01

From the correlation coefficient of the ABC attributes and the level of preference, it was concluded that there was significant correlation between attribute A and C—the r value reached 0.771, suggesting the two attributes were highly correlated). This regression equation can be explained as people who gave attribute A high ratings also provided high credits to attribute C. The influence of attribute A in the regression equation appeared to be negative. The possible reason was not because A represented a technology with negative influence; rather, it was more likely that the significant correlation between A and C influenced the preference together. The F test in the analysis of variance (ANOVA) has reached a significant level (F = 6.4527) and the R Square reached 0.685. This suggested that when using the ABC attributes to estimate the preference, the explained variation reached 68.5 % —a relatively high level. It was then concluded that to the Internet and technology enthusiasts' community, technology is not the most critical influential factor when judging the preference for a certain product. Instead, the subjects would appreciate a product if its technology can connect with the subjects' needs—or even satisfy their inner desires—and is of stylish appearance. This can be confirmed by the high preference ratings for the chair, which was associated with the subjects' life experiences. Most online community members spend a significant amount of time in front of the computer and long for a beautiful and comfortable computer chair, which is a distinctive and reasonable choice. On the other hand, the experts' selection focused on the depth and the taste of the design concept. In the study result, it was suggested that the Dechnology products should not only have intimate connections with human lives but also pay more attention to the demands of the certain users.

After comparing the design products with the regression equation obtained in this study, it was found that Q7 was the product that fit the regression equation the most. Consequently, by reviewing all of the Dechnology products with the regression equation, it was discovered that the products considered to have more extensive utilization of technology also received higher ratings on the level of humane care. On the other hand, the products that only placed an emphasis on technology earned relatively lower ratings on the preferences, which can be most well-demonstrated by the differences between the products of Q7 and Q13. This illustrated how technology must be human-centered in order to exert its potentials. As Lin (2014) suggested, the more advanced technology becomes, the more emphasis should be placed on humane cares. The goal of all new century designers is to eliminate the gap between users and high-tech products by "embracing new technologies and incorporating human factors." From this study, the needs of the Internet and technology enthusiasts can be understood. The Dechnology products, while being created based on the idea of demonstrating new technologies, revealed the characteristics shown by the different user communities. The sooners the users' demands are incorporated into the designs the more feedbacks and accolades can be received from the users, resulting in more popular products being created.

5 Conclusion and Suggestion

To understand the characteristics of the Internet and technology enthusiasts' community, the research subjects of this study were mostly young online community members under 35 years of age. Other than liking the themed model toys in the blogs established by the researcher of this study, most of these subjects were interested in animation, video games, and technological knowledge. In regard to the three attributes—technology knowledge, aesthetics and arts, and humane care—it was revealed that the subjects placed the greatest emphasis on technology knowledge, followed by aesthetics and arts and humane care. From the results of the questionnaires, the subjects' preferences for the Dechnology products were obtained and analyzed for regression equations. It was revealed that the subjects cared the most about how technology can be utilized in human lives—especially the parts that are most relevant to themselves. If the products were able to deliver the senses of comfort and belonging that the subjects needed in their daily lives, they will provide positive feedback and show their preference for the products—even when the subjects were animation, comics, and technology enthusiasts. The result confirmed that all designs are created for human-centered demands; as technology becomes more advanced, more attention should be placed on the values of human beings, and more emphasis should be placed on humane care (Lin, 2014).

From the regression equation analyzed in this study, it was concluded that technology is not the most critical influential factor when the Internet and technology enthusiasts' community judged their preferences for a particular product. Instead, the subjects would appreciate a product if its technology can connect with the subjects' needs—or even care about their inner desires—and supplemented by stylish appearance. When designing products, in addition to utilizing technological advantages and introducing aesthetic design elements, designers should also create products that consider human needs. Depending on the level of how close the products' humane care attributes are to the users' needs, the ratings of user preferences might be significantly varied. It was suggested that the Dechnology products should not only have closer connections with human lives, but also pay more attention to the demands of specific user populations. The greatest advantage of Dechnology product was to establish close relationships between technology and users.

In the ITRI data, the 41 Dechnology products were divided into 12 categories that were closely related to people's daily lives. The present study results discovered that there were no significant relationships between the preferences for the product and these 12 categories. On the contrary, the preferences reflected the characteristics of the research subjects. In the book *Democratizing Innovation* by Eric von Hippel (2005), it was suggested that user' demands for customization will increase in the long run. Future product designs will be based on the demands of particular users and integrated with the appropriate technologies. The end result will more closely resemble the needs of real users in real markets. It is recommended to incorporate users' or potential customers' opinions into the design process during the early stage of design. Their demands should be understood so that the required technologies can be applied to the design, resulting in the increase of users' preferences for the products and the designs' advantages.

Owing to the limits of both time and subjects, this study was unable to conduct a more comprehensive analysis research. As the subjects of this study were Internet and technology enthusiasts' community, the result suggested that online community with specific hobbies have their own opinions and demands regarding the product preferences. The product design, therefore, should focus on humane care and needs while incorporating technology and aesthetics approaches—to serve as recommendations for technology product design. As the manufacturing methods change over time, consumers no longer solely pursue products that are inexpensive and produced in mass quantities. They want products that are custom-made and satisfy the individual's unique demands. The progress of the Internet has resulted in more online users and online communities with different characteristics. In this study, the research subjects were limited to followers of the blogs established by the researcher. If big data can be incorporated and analyzed in the future, more online communities' user experiences can be understood and products that fit the specific users' characteristics can be designed. This is the future goal for designers who create innovative product designs in this new era.

Acknowledgements. The authors gratefully acknowledge the support for this research provided by the Ministry of Science and Technology under Grant No. MOSY-103-2410-H-144-003 and MOST-103-2221-E-144-001. The authors also wish to thank Prof. Jhon. G. Kreifeldt and Po-Hsien Lin, especially, Prof. Rungtai Lin.

References

Baym, N.K.: The emergence of community in computer-mediated communication. In: Jones, S.G. (ed.) Cybersociety: Computer-Mediated Communication and Community, pp. 138–163. Sage, London (1995)

Brown, J.S.: Growing up digital: how the Web changes work, education, and the ways people learn. Change **32**, 10–20 (2000)

Carver, C.: Building a virtual community for tale-learning environment. IEEE Commun. Mag. **37** (3), 114–118 (1999)

Cohen, A.P.: The Symbolic Construction of Community. Ellis Horwood, Chichester (1985)

Dalgic, T., Leeuw, M.: Niche marketing revisited: concept, applications and some european cases. Eur. J. Mark. **28**(4), 39–55 (1994)

Fernback, J.: Notes toward a definition of cybercommunity. In: Jones, S. (ed.) Doing Internet Research Critical Issues and Methods for Examining the Net, p. 203. Sage publication, California (1998)

Hagel, J., Armstrong, A.: Net Gain: Expanding Markets through Virtual Communities. Harvard Business School Press, Mass (1997)

Von Hippel, E.: Lead users: a source of novel product concepts. Manage. Sci. **32**(7), 791–805 (1986)

Ho, J., Schraefel, M.C., Cingnell, M.: Towards an evaluation methodology for the development of research-oriented virtual communities. In: Proceedings of the 9th International Workshops on Enabling Technologies: Infrastructure for Collaborative Enterprises (WET ICE 2000), Gaithersburg, Maryland (2000)

Holmes, R.: What comes next? 5 social media trends for 2015 (2014) http://thenextweb.com/socialmedia/2011/06/14/whats-next-in-social-media/

Hung, W.K., Huang, W.: Creating value for technology by design: a case study of dechnology project. J. Des. **18**(1), 41–64 (2013)

Jones, Q., Rafaeli, S.: Time to split, virtually: 'discourse architecture' and 'community building' as means to creating vibrant virtual metropolises. Int. J. Electron. Commer. Bus. Media **10**(4), 214–223 (2000)

Kelman, H.C.: Compliance, identification, and internalization: Three processes of attitude change. J. Conflict Resolut. **2**, 51–60 (1958)

Lee, F.S., Vogel, D., Limayem, M.: Virtual community informatics: a review and research agenda. J. Inf. Technol. Theory Appl. (JITTA) **5**(1), 5 (2003)

Lin, R.: From Dechnology to Humart in Taiwan Design Development. Research Project Supported by Taiwan National Science Council (2012)

Lin, R., Lin, C.L.: From digital archives to E-business: a case study on turning "art" into "business". In: Proceedings of the 2010 International Conference on E-Business (ICE-B), pp. 1–8. EEE, July 2010

Lin, R., Yen, C.-C., Chen, R.: From adaptive design to adaptive city-design in motion for taipei city. In: Rau, P. (ed.) CCD 2014. LNCS, vol. 8528, pp. 643–649. Springer, Heidelberg (2014)

Marketing Intelligence & Consulting Institute, MIC, Taiwan. http://mic.iii.org.tw/index.asp

Noff, A.: What's next in social media?, The Next Web (2011).http://thenextweb.com/socialmedia/2011/06/14/whats-next-in-social-media/

Norman, D.A.: Emotional design: Why We Love (or Hate) Everyday Things. Basic books, New York (2004)

Postmes, T.: A social identity approach to communication in organizations. In: Haslam, A., van Knippenberg, D., Platow, M.J., Ellemers, N. (eds.) Social Identity at Work: Developing Theory for Organizational Practice, vol. 81, pp. 191–203. Phychology press, Philadelphia (2003)

Rheingold, H.: The virtual community: Homesteading on the electronic frontier. Addison-Wesley Publishing Company, Reading (1993)

Ridings, C.M., Gefen, D.: Virtual community attraction: why people hang out online. J. Comput.-Med. Commun. **10**, 00 (2004). doi:10.1111/j.1083-6101.2004.tb00229.x

Lichtenstein, S., Slovic, P.: The Construction of Preference. Cambridge University Press, New York (2006)

Turner, J.C.: Social Influence. Open University Press, Milton Keyes (1991)

Von Hippel, E.: Democratizing Innovation. MIT Press, Cambridge (2005)

Yang, C.F., Wu, C.S., Gong, Y., Sung, T.J.: Transformative service design: from technology to dechnology. In: Advances in The Human Side of Service Engineering, vol. 1, p. 210 (2014)

From Customer Satisfaction to Customer Experience: Online Customer Satisfaction Practice in International E-commerce

Yanyang Liuqu[✉], Xinheng Fan, and Paul L. Fu

International UED, Alibaba Group, No. 969,
West Wenyi Road, 311121 Hangzhou, China
{Yanyang.lqyy,paulfu}@alibaba-inc.com,
dujie@taobao.com

Abstract. By focusing on online international shopping, this study investigates customer satisfaction measured by applying the mainstream research model and satisfaction metrics. Net promoter score, continuous purchase intention, product satisfaction, and the pros and cons of each of the metrics are discussed. The paper advocates understanding customer from a more comprehensive view than mere satisfaction. A new customer experience model is introduced.

Keywords: Customer satisfaction · Loyalty · NPS · Continuous purchase intention · Customer experience · Online shopping

1 Background and Research Objectives

1.1 Significance of Customer Satisfaction

In the past year, international giants in e-commerce has almost invariably expedited their market strategy globally. Internet shopping (IS) has extended customer's physical limit. Customers from Beijing can taste the newly picked cherry from Chile, while ladies from Ukraine can enjoy the most up-to-date fashion in China. As smart phone becomes more affordable worldwide, it is a matter of a click to purchase products from anywhere in the world at any time. According to eMarketer, nearly one-quarter of the world's total population uses smartphone [1]. The consumption urge for more product selection together with technology availability boost IS' expansion.

Even in the booming stage of international IS, customer experience is and needs to be a core part in the strategic planning of IS websites rather than something nice to have. Compared to in-store shopping, it is much less controllable for online sellers to persuade a purchase. Online shopping offers more opportunities for interactive and personalized marketing [2], enabling customers to compare hundreds of alternatives at one time. The cost of retrieval or withdrawal when shopping online is very subtle compared with in-store shopping. Meanwhile, given the risk and uncertain nature of online shopping, online customer tends to be less rational. Emotions and feelings at the moment of clicking are more involved in the occasions of online shopping. From all the choices and browses online customers engaged, they look for value [3]. However, there

© Springer International Publishing Switzerland 2015
P.L.P. Rau (Ed.): CCD 2015, Part II, LNCS 9181, pp. 80–89, 2015.
DOI: 10.1007/978-3-319-20934-0_8

is no practice yet which is able to anatomize the value clearly. On the contrary, value brings stronger competition among e-commerce websites than ever in the battle of winning customers. Hence, understanding and improving customer satisfaction is vital for players in B2C (business to customer) e-commerce market.

1.2   Conceptualizing Customer Satisfaction

Before thinking of how to measuring customer satisfaction, it is worthwhile to take one step back and seriously think of what customer satisfaction really is. Even if this topic has been deeply researched, there is no consensus in the definition of customer satisfaction [4]. Giese and Cote [5] define satisfaction as "response (emotional or affective) pertaining to a particular focus (product, consumption experience, etc.) determined at a particular time (immediately upon purchase, after consumption, based on accumulated experience)." Some research [6] defines it as "a cumulative evaluation of a customer's purchase and consumption experience to-date." There is also definition that "the important service attributes and measure customer's perception of those attributes and overall customer satisfaction [7]." As we can see, satisfaction is so difficult to be explicitly defined. All of these definitions are entangled with capturing some traits of the state of satisfaction or what satisfaction produces. Besides, all of these definitions can hardly be used in corporate practice. As long as there is no agreement being made on the definition of customer satisfaction, debates over which attributes are the best reflections of customer satisfaction would not end. Thus, it seems more practical to focus on measuring the behavioral reflections of satisfaction rather than defining sat isfaction. How do you show loyalty to a brand/product/service? Or what will you do if you are satisfied with a brand/product/service? It draws us back to the concern that to what extent it is likely to reflect customer satisfaction either by giving referral, buying more, not using competitors' products, giving visually support, or other ways.

2   Past Research on Customer Satisfaction Measure

2.1   Net Promoter Score

A variety of IS customer satisfaction research has been discussing the construct of satisfaction, or metrics of satisfaction [8]. Even if there is no such a perfect measurement yet, the net promotor score (NPS) is one of the simplest as well as the most widely adopted customer satisfaction and loyalty measurement. NPS asks customer's willingness to recommend a product or service to other people, evaluated on a scale from 0 to 10. Based on the score given, it divides all customers into three groups, naming detractors, passives, and promoters accordingly. The net promoter score is calculated by subtracting detractors from promoters. The net promoter score is used as the estimate for customer loyalty and business growth.

Compared with other traditional customer satisfaction measures, NPS asks fewer questions and is very easy to calculate. It reduces the barrier for customer satisfaction data collection greatly. Customer feels less bothered by one simple question than a set of questions. Many organizations conduct their NPS study on a monthly or weekly pace. Some even monitor their NPS performance in a real-time matter. NPS is very much explicit and self-explained. It diagnoses the health of business from the customer side, and notifies executives for adjustment or changes. Fred Reichheld [9] called NPS the ultimate question for the sustainable growth of business. With the persistent endeavor of Reichheld and his follower, nowadays, NPS has been adopted by many leading B2C companies and organizations of a variety of industries and business. An important outcome of this NPS phenomenon is that individual company or organization is able to compare their performance with competitors. More than that, NPS benchmarking forms a kind of standard in a sense that who satisfy customers better regardless of industries and business. That creates an atmosphere of customer first rather than profit first. It also allows dialogues between corporates from varied business in the scope of customer centered economy.

From the nation level, NPS has also made great contribution in the process of experience economy. In China, for instance, the government recently founded a special organization to build nation-wide customer NPS (C-NPS) management system [10]. Their research covers major domestic and foreign brands from FMCG, durable consumer goods, and service industries. The result is released publicly, aiming to promote customer satisfaction in regular corporate performance evaluation as well as to facilitate the so called customer centered culture in Chinese economy.

2.2   Criticism to NPS – from Intention to Implementation

In spite of its world-wide popularity, discussions and notions over NPS is not overwhelmingly positive. NPS has been challenged for its doubtful in predicting customer loyalty behaviors [11] and in helping make management decisions [12]. The underneath rationale of NPS lies in that referral intention is believed to be the very direct reflection of loyalty. Furthermore, NPS put emphasis on customer mind share. Customer mind share is reflected via the proportion changes of customer groups with different levels of referral intention. It claims that improving NPS can help companies to win bigger market share.

Along with more practice in NPS, it is challenged that the predictive validity of NPS for loyalty behavior. Some research compared NPS with traditional ACSI (American Customer Satisfaction Index) model in predicting company growth, and found no better performance with NPS [13]. Higher NPS score does not necessarily promise more positive comments for your service, or more purchase for your product, or even not more actual recommendatory behaviors for your website. NPS itself is unable to fix the gap between intention and actual behavior. Besides, using NPS alone is difficult to provide actionable plan for company executives or operation staffs. The user experience research sector in e-commerce companies are often put in a situation to explain to their product and merchandizing fellows about how the score is linked to website GMV (Gross Merchandise Volume) and what they can get from the score. For business with well-established profit model and steady sales growth, their NPS score may not have major changes over time given that the business is in a relatively stable stage [11]. At the same time, for newly developed e-commerce business, NPS score alone is not reliable enough to reflect customer satisfaction. Since the score can be very sensitive to major website events and has big variation across different customer groups depending on their familiarity to the website.

2.3 Continuous Purchase Intention and Satisfaction

In the realm of customer satisfaction research, continuous purchase intention (CPI), also called repeat purchase intention, is another attribute that has been thoroughly researched. Continuous purchase intention refers to the subjective probability that a customer will continue to purchase a product from the same online seller [14]. Compared with referral intention, CPI may have higher predictive influence on the share of wallet of business. Some studies use CPI as an equivalent metric for satisfaction. However, how CPI correlates with customer satisfaction and loyalty is not so obvious and direct as NPS. Customers with higher satisfaction level are very likely to shop again; whereas, customers' continuous shopping may be due to various reasons rather than being satisfied or loyal. Although some empirical studies find indirect positive correlation existing between CPI and loyalty [15, 16] argue that CPI may not represent loyalty effectively. They extend loyalty into a relationship construct based on the different characters and various degrees of relationship strength, and claim that CPI correlates differently with different types of loyalty relationship.

More research discusses determinants or the construct of CPI [17], exploring ways to improve repeat purchase. Prior research has indicated a set of determinants of CPI, including but not limited to perceived usefulness, trust, satisfaction, switching cost, and perceived value. Research reveals that perceived value includes both utilitarian value and hedonic value. It is the main driver for customer to repeatedly purchase from the same store [18, 19]. Utilitarian value is proposed as a construct formed by product offerings, product information, monetary savings, and convenience. Hedonic value is proposed as a construct of six hedonic benefits, which are adventure, gratification, role, best deal, social, and idea. Other researches find that customers' online shopping habit moderates the influence of those determinants' influence on CPI [17]. For instance, the more experience a customer have with shopping in one particular store, the more likely she or he will come back and shop again. Despite of the presence of large amount of CPI research, applicable implications are rarely discussed.

2.4 Other Research Model on Measuring Customer Satisfaction

Given the shortages of NPS, many endeavors have been made in exploring a more precise measurement for customer satisfaction and loyalty and how the measure can promote business growth. In the aim of that, measures with more explicit predictive correlation with actual sales growth need to be introduced. A customer can be likely to recommend to other people without buying more himself. Also, a customer satisfaction measure system will work better than a single satisfaction score.

Interestingly, we notice that other research explored similar idea. In a study conducted by [20], researchers asked consumers "How do you show loyalty to the firms you do business with." The top two answers were "spreading the word and telling others" and "buying more", with a selection of 78 % and 69 % respectively. Further than that, Aite Group [12] started measuring referral performance score. In their metric, customers were divided on two dichotomous dimensions, referral (refer and don't refer) and business growth (customers who increased consumption of the business and customers who do not increase consumption). The score was calculated by multiplying the percentage of customers that refer by the percentage of customers that grow their relationship. This is a worthy trying of combining both loyalty intention and loyalty behavior in one measure. The different customer segments sliced by referral intention and business growth provide valuable trace. It shows clearly how your customer groups with different referral and consumption pattern compose. It also calls attention to the inconsistency between behavior and intention, and what can be done to transform inconsistent customers to a better relationship stage with your business. However, depending on business features, customer segments sliced by business growth can be misleading and may not be appropriate for some business. Business relationship growth involves many variables, such as amount of spending, frequency of consumption, customer quality, length of doing business, and so no. Of some many variables, it brings out another problem that which is the proper one to pick out as customer's behavioral loyalty contribution. Moreover, the metric tells only where you are, however, it is still a myth that where to go.

In the China Customer Satisfaction Index Model (C-CSI) [21], three metrics are considered, including total satisfaction (TS), factor satisfaction (FS), and continuous purchase intention (CPI). TS and CPI are both measured on a 5-point Likert scale, and calculate the percentage of the top 2 answers, very satisfied and satisfied, and willing to buy very much and willing to buy, respectively. FS considers both the satisfaction and importance of a set of sub-attributes of products, service, or images. Each satisfaction attribute is weighted accordingly. C-CSI score is the sum of the three metrics, with each given a specific weight. The formula is

$$C - CSI = TS * 0.4 + FS * 0.4 + CPI * 0.2$$

As we can see, rather than composed by a single score, C-CSI adopts repeat purchase and satisfaction attributes into its measure system. Corporate performance can also be measured and compared on specific influence factors. Even though C-CSI still measures from a purely cognitive level, it extends satisfaction and loyalty to repeat purchase intention, which is helpful for companies to know how their market is going to change.

3   From Customer Satisfaction to Customer Experience

3.1   Taobao International and Tmall Global

When building customer centered experience testing system in an e-commerce setting, not only satisfaction and loyalty, but also practical implications for business growth should be considered. As discussed earlier, the practical value of customer satisfaction measurement is determined by the stage of business and market maturity. If this business factor is taken into account as early as possible, fewer barriers would be expected in either communicating results or facilitating further actions.

In our case, the business we service for is Taobao International and Tmall Global. Taobao International is a platform to connect Chinese domestic sellers and oversea individual buyers. On the contrary, Tmall Global is aimed to help Chinese domestic individual buyers to purchase oversea products easier. No matter either an import or an export direction, the two international B2C websites are both quite young, and are in a stage of introducing the marketplaces to more customers.

3.2 User Experience Pulse Tracking

Reviewing different endeavors in exploring a better customer satisfaction, although some look for a revolutionary replacement for NPS, evolutionary approaches are more commonly used. To continuously and systematically track customer satisfaction and loyalty for our websites, Taobao International and Tmall Global, we also take a more evolutionary approach. Since both websites are in early stage of business growth, it becomes the first and primary priority to building reputation and retain customers. This big issue, when translating into customer satisfaction tracking, lays priority on how do they like our websites, and how much likely they will buy again. Furthermore, while working with merchandizing and product fellows side by side, we have really made a lot of efforts on transforming the original customer feelings and thinking into interpretations that are meaningful to different stakeholders. For a useful tracking system, satisfaction metric alone is not expected to answer all "Why?" questions behind. It is vital to inform different stakeholders the good as well as the not good enough experience customers' have with our websites. Considered all the factors above, our measure system is extended from customer satisfaction tracking to customer experience tracking. Three key metrics are used, which are NPS, CPI, and PSAT (product satisfaction), naming together User Experience Pulse Tracking (UEPT) (Fig. 1).

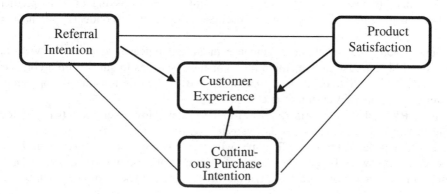

Fig. 1. User experience pulse tracking model

3.2.1 NPS and Why?

NPS is the first and foremost metric in UEPT. First, referral intention has high correlation with loyalty and loyalty behavior according to prior research. Second, NPS is one of the most often used satisfaction and loyalty measure internationally. Many research entities and enterprises share data with the public. It allows comparison with similar products horizontally. Third, besides knowing the scores, we also want to know reasons behind. It is worthwhile to know what make them to recommend or not to recommend for explanatory and practical purposes. Based on traditional NPS practices and our website features, we generate 21 referral determinable factors. The 21 items list out the key user-faced touch point throughout a complete purchase experience, including product, price, promotion, payment, logistics, customer service, and website design. For customers who give a score of 7 or above, who are passives or promoters according to NPS system, we ask them to select reasons from the 21 items for making a referral to others. For customers who give a score of 6 or below, who are the detractors, we ask them to select the items that making them not recommending our website as well.

3.2.2 Continuous Purchase Intention

Given the practical importance in business growth, CPI is the second metric added into UEPT. A study [14] shows that an average customer must shop four times at least in a same online shop before the shop can make profit from the customer. High continuous purchase can bring increased gross profit rate for e-commerce websites, therefore, it leads to better ROI performance and higher profit [22]. Now some people may wonder why not asking customers' repurchase behavior directly. One risk for measuring behavior directly is that repurchase behavior is often uncontrollable. Purchase behavior is often triggered by factors irrelevant with websites, many other random factors are involved at the same time. Every purchase is independent from the other, it is risky to predict one purchase by using the prior one. Whereas intention is relatively stable and is generally acknowledged to play a significant role in the prediction of future behavior. Besides, it is a memory burden to ask customers to recall how many times they have purchased. Plus that the reliability of recalling is doubtful. Self-reported data shall have higher reliability that collecting customers' intention versus asking them to predict behavior in the future. It will be more practical to research respondents' purchasing data if necessary.

Furthermore, high continuous purchase intention indicates more active website traffics and higher customer retention rate. For new websites to survive on a competitive battlefield, CPI tracking is a vital reference in regards to strategic operation planning for improving customer retention.

In UEPT, CPI asks customers on a 0 to 10 scale: "How likely is it that you are going to continue to purchase on our website?" Customers who give a score of 7 or above are considered the high CPI type, whereas customers score lower than 7 are considered the low CPI type. The question is open to all respondents, however, only those who have made one order at least on the website are taken into calculation.

3.2.3   Product Satisfaction

Product satisfaction (PSAT) is another index that have grown in popularity over the last couple years. There has been debates that whether PSAT or NPS is more important than the other. In fact, drivers of PSAT or NPS are not identical [23]. PSAT depends on your customers' expectations on products and it emphases on the state of content of the user; whereas NPS asks customers if they believe your product is worth recommending to others. It indicates how customers rank your product compared with other competitors. There is known a strong correlation between the two metrics. Both are business-outcome metrics that are equally important to measure. In UEPT, PSAT asks respondents "How satisfied are you with our website based on your experience with it?" It is measured on a 5-point Likert scale, from very dissatisfied to very satisfied.

3.3   An Integrated System

In UEPT, the three scores are present as a complete customer experience tracking system, each index is reported independently. Some other satisfaction models apply generated metric by using statistical methods, such as ACSI and C-CSI. However, metrics produced by statistical modeling on the average are complex to explain. For inner stakeholders who do not have much patience with statistics, it adds extra burden on using the metrics. The three metrics in UEPT have all been applied maturely with plenty of successful cases, and are familiar to our stakeholders as well. Hence, it is much more effective and efficient to report the three metrics rather than creating a new one.

What is more, the three metrics together create rich and flexible customer dimensions. For example, when segmenting customer by using CPI and NPS together, it becomes possible to know that how much customers truly love us, whether it is verbal support only or it potentially increases sales. The extended customer segments also bring richer and more valuable information than the single dimensional segments of detractors/passives/promoters. It is valuable for marketing and merchandizing fellows to know the proportion of each of the segments and how the proportions change over time, and then seek solutions. For example, customers who do not recommend the website but are very likely to purchase again themselves may stay merely because they can hardly find alternatives. Customer satisfaction needs to be present to convert the mere repeat purchasers to committed purchasers [4].

In addition, it has also been found that generated metrics have reduced acuteness to website fluctuations since the numbers have been weighted. It is much easier to use NPS, PSAT with which industry benchmarking has been well established with public recognition, allowing quick comparison with other players. In general, NPS, CPI, and PSAT are strongly correlated, each of them contributes to satisfaction and loyalty. Moreover, using further referral factor questions, UEPT is able to help to identify the root causes for the up and down with customers' attitude changes and improve (Fig. 2).

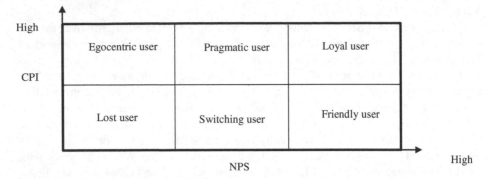

Fig. 2. Customer segments model

4   Discussions

After reviewing various prior research on customer satisfaction and loyalty, there has not been any metric or model reached consensus. We adapted an evolutionary approach to develop the UEPT model. An innovative way was proposed to segment customers by using CPI and NPS, which gave us rich insight into customer attitude and root causes.

We also created a live system to continuously improve the questions used in referral factors in order to provide more meaningful information to business. The current 21 referral factors were reviewed frequently for refinement. We compared the selection of each referral factor for recommending or not recommending with their opening question feedbacks regarding to their complaints and what they believe we can make improvements to better serve them. We found factors and conditions that had been left out. For instance, if a new factor emerged as a frequently mentioned factor in their referral decision, which is not in the UEPT, we would add it to the questions.

Also, we think the referral factors need to be refined accordingly for different websites. The UEPT for Taobao International and Tmall Global are using the same referral factors for the purpose of keeping measurement consistent. The disadvantage is that the factors are less website specific and are less detail oriented. Besides, Taobao International and Tmall Global are facing different user groups and have different functions and services. It will be helpful to apply website customized referral factors. In general, how customer satisfaction and loyalty research can promote business growth requires persistent attempts.

For future research, we have not closely studied the relationship between NPS and PSAT. Occasionally, NPS and PSAT would change in opposed directions. There were no sufficient data to explain why customer are more willing to recommend us while they are less satisfied, or the other way around. Further research are needed to explore this area.

References

1. eMarketer.   http://www.emarketer.com/Article/Worldwide-Smartphone-Usage-Grow-25-2014/1010920

2. Wind, J., Rangaswamy, A.: Customerization: the next revolution in mass customization. J. Interact. Mark. **15**(1), 13–32 (2001)
3. Parasuraman, A., Grewal, D.: The impact of technology on the quality-value-loyalty chain: a research agenda. J. Acad. Mark. Sci. **28**, 168–174 (2000)
4. Yeoh, E., Chan, K.L.: Malaysian low cost airline: key influencing factors on customers' repeat purchase intention. World Appl. Sci. J. **12**, 35–43 (2011). (Special Issue of Tourism & Hospitality)
5. Giese, J.L., Cote, J.A.: Defining customer satisfaction. Acad. Mark. Sci. Rev. **1**, 1–24 (2002)
6. Auh, S., Johnson, M.D.: Compatibility effects in evaluation of satisfaction and loyalty. J. Econ. Psychol. **26**, 35–37 (2005)
7. Zeithaml, V.A., Bitner, M.J.: Services Marketing. Integrating Customer Focus across the Firm. Irwin McGraw-Hill, New York (2000)
8. Cheung, C.M.K., Lee, M.K.O.: Research Framework for Consumer Satisfaction with Internet Shopping, City University of Hong Kong, China. Sprouts: Working Papers on Information Systems, vol. 5, no. 26, (2005). http://sprouts.aisnet.org/5-26
9. Reichheld, H., Markey, R.: The Ultimate Question 20 How Net Promoter Companies Thrive in a Customer-Driven World. Harvard Business Review Press, Citic Press, Beijing (2013). Translated by Yang, Y
10. Chinabrand. http://www.chn-brand.org/c-nps/cnpsInfo.aspx
11. Huang, G., Wang, H.L.: Improving the predictive validity of NPS in customer satisfaction surveys. Paper presented at the meeting of Human Computer Interaction International, Crete, Greece (2014)
12. Shevlin, R.: It's time to kill the net promoter score, The Financial Brand. http://thefinancial brand.com/47237/its-time-to-kill-the-net-promoter-score/
13. Verint, Net promoter score (NPS) criticisms and best practices. http://blog.verint.com/net-promoter-score-nps-criticisms-and-best-practices
14. Chiu, C., Wang, E., Fang, Y.H., Huang, H.Y.: Understanding customers' repeat purchase intentions in B2C e-commerce: the roles of utilitarian value, hedonic value, and perceived risk. Inf. Syst. J. **24**, 85–114 (2014)
15. Anderson, E.W., Sullivan, M.W.: Customer satisfaction and retention across firms, presentation at the TIMS College of Marketing Special Interest Conference on Service Marketing, Nashville, TN (1990)
16. Wakenshaw S., Woodruffe-Burton, H.: Can 'Share of Wallet' and 'repeat purchase intention' measure store loyalty: an empirical investigation. https://www.academia.edu/10259286/Can_share_of_wallet_and_repeat_purchase_intention_measure_store_loyalty_an_empirical_investigation
17. Chiu, C., Hsu, M.H., Lai, H.C., Chang, C.M.: Exploring online repeat purchase intentions: The role of habit. http://www.pacis-net.org/file/2010/S06-01.pdf
18. Gutman, J.: Means-end chains as goal hierarchies. Psychol. Mark. **14**, 545–560 (1997)
19. Kim, H.W., Gupta, S.: A comparison of purchase decision calculus between potential and repeat customers of an online store. Decis. Support Syst. **47**, 477–487 (2009)
20. Zendesk. https://www.zendesk.com/resources/building-customer-loyalty
21. Chinabrand. http://www.chn-brand.org/IndexProducts/main_frame.asp?mainmode=1&sub menu=2
22. iResearch. http://www.infomorning.com/szb/html/2012-09/26/content_4757.htm?div=-1
23. Madhurima B.D.: Which is more important? Net Promoter Score or Customer Satisfaction Score. Metrics and Skills. http://www.pakragames.com/plugged-in/entry/which-is-more-important-net-promoter-r-score-nps-or-customer-satisfaction-score-csat-training.html

E-Commerce Purchase Intention in Emerging Markets: The Influence of Gender and Culture

Dimitrios Rigas[(⊠)] and Nazish Riaz

University of West London, London W5 5RF, UK
{dimitrios.rigas,nazish.riaz}@uwl.ac.uk

Abstract. This paper explores the external factors that influence the decision making process of young Asian females when they shop online for fashion clothing. The empirical investigation was carried out with a positivistic approach and a sample size of 142 young females in Pakistan. As females get more financially independent in developing Asian nations it leads to a question whether their buying decisions are still dominated by external factors? It was found that young educated adult Pakistani females make on-line purchase decisions under a significant influence of a highly collective and masculine environment. These results could be extrapolated to other similar cultures and emerging e-retailing areas.

Keywords: Socio-technical issues · E-commerce user interfaces · Culture · Purchase behavior · Consumer behavior · Emerging markets · Decision-making process · Theory of reasoned action

1 Introduction

It is widely common in the developed world that women make independent e-retailing decisions. However, for some developing countries (e.g. Pakistan) the female buying behavior appears to be affected by cultural variables (e.g. masculinity). According to Bearden et al. [1], the most important determinant of an individual's behavior is the influence of another individual.

This study has taken an opportunistic Pakistani female user sample. This retail market was approximated at 42 billion USD reporting an annual sales growth of approximately 105 million USD (Punjab Board of Investment and Trade 2013). This indicates an increase in economic growth and spending power of consumers. One of the most important contributing factors towards this new consumption pattern is the young generation, which account for 73 % of the total population (under 35 years of age) of which 33,632,395 are females [2].

Previous studies examined the influence of cultural variables to buying behavior and purchase decision-making of consumers. These include family structure and size, religion, and collectivism. Bearden et al. [1] suggest that the most important determinant of an individual's consuming behavior is the influence of others. Cultural and idiosyncratic values often influence e-commerce user behavior [3–5]. This type of

© Springer International Publishing Switzerland 2015
P.L.P. Rau (Ed.): CCD 2015, Part II, LNCS 9181, pp. 90–100, 2015.
DOI: 10.1007/978-3-319-20934-0_9

influence distils into a shared set of on-line consumer decision-making values [6] that pass on from generation to generation [7, 8]. Bagozzi et al. [9] define it as a combination of social and psychological processes that people endure through the acquisition, use and disposal of products, practices or services. These processes also gender dependent [10] with different needs and behavior of consumption [11]. Culture is another influencing parameter [12]. It involves conscious and unconscious values, attitudes, ideas and symbols that help to shape up on-line consumer behavior.

The understanding of these influencing factors to consumer behavior in emerging markets is particularly important for the development of e-commerce interfaces. This paper aims to understand these issues better.

2   Culture and e-Commerce

In emerging e-commerce markets, such as the one in Pakistan that this study has focused, male dominance influences women decisions. As there is lack of education and less awareness amongst women in the urban and rural areas, the success of e-commerce is not as in the Western countries. However, the e-commerce platforms and e-commerce interfaces are on the rise and slowly businesses have started to have their presence on the web. This has been a result of the multimodal interfaces and avatars, which as described by Rigas and Alty [19] help to communicate with the target audience. Moreover, Rigas [20] supported the idea of auditory and ear-cons in the user interfaces for effective communication. These additions could play a vital role in an emerging e-commerce market such as the one in Pakistan.

2.1   Hofstede Cultural Typology

Hofstede Cultural Typology, as shown in Fig. 1, shows five points through which the culture of a country can be analyzed. The higher the number the more that aspect is persistent in the culture. Power distance indicates the degree to which the less powerful and dominant members of the society accept the power to be distributed unequally. High power distance indicates that all the individuals are not dealt with equality. The level of inequality is usually sanctioned equally by the leaders and the followers. Individualism reflects the extent to which the individuals of a particular society are bonded into groups.

In an individualistic culture, the members of a society are mainly concerned only about their own interests and do not take into consideration the interests of other members of the society. Whereas, a society having a collectivist culture is more interested in the interest of its group into which they are strongly bonded. Personal interest, likes and dislikes are usually overlooked and ignored for the sake of common interest of the group in such a society.

Pakistan displays a collectivist culture. A study on China found that collectivist values influence the purchasing decision most [22]. It is believed that due to being a highly collective society, the basic norms and values shared amongst the society and the suggestions and likes or dislikes of close family members are of great value and

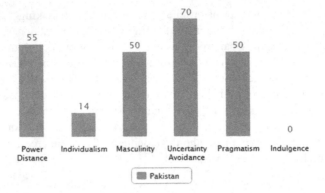

Fig. 1. Hofstede's cultural dimension [21]

influence when a Pakistani individual would make a purchase decision. Pakistan being a masculine society not only interrelates its values with the role of men but is also to a great extent influenced by the dominance of men and their super ordinate position over females. This context makes the male dominance and the power of men a predominant factor, which is likely to affect the purchase decision of Pakistani women.

2.2   ABC Model of Attitude

Pakistani, which has a very collectivist culture, people tend to form attitudes that full fill their social identity functions, and there is not a constant relationship between attitude and future behavior [13, 14]. There can be a possibility of having a converse relationship, where the behavior would come first determining the attitude. In a collectivist culture, the shared experiences within a group of a particular brand or product would be more influential as compared to an individualistic culture [15]. Hence, it is assumed that within a Pakistani society, women have a standard learning hierarchy approach, as illustrated in the diagram above, when making purchase decision and they carry out an extensive problem solving process before making a purchase.

Considering the notion of culture suggested by Hofstede [21] as *"collective programming of the mind"* it is then important to understand culture by further studying attitudes, beliefs and values which are shared amongst certain group of people. Attitude is a cultured and learned tendency to react or respond in a consistent and steady manner towards a given article or object.

3   User Study: Results, Discussion and Analysis

A positivist approach was taken in this study. A structured questionnaire was designed to investigate the different stages of the decision-making purchasing process and input variables to this process of young adult females. The sample was opportunistic and taken in Pakistan. It consisted of 142 female respondents aged between 18 and 35 years old. This age profile of respondents consisted of 26–30 years old (36.1 %), 21–25

(35.4 %) and 18–20 (4.9 %) as shown in Fig. 2. Figure 2 shows the educational profile of the sample. It consisted of 65 respondents (45.5 %) with a postgraduate qualification and 40 (28 %) with an undergraduate education. The results are discussed in relation to the purchase decision-making process, attitudes and the theory of reasoned action. Results indicated that from the age of 26 onwards, their spouses will influence their purchasing decision-making process of potential e-commerce female users. Females aged between 21 and 25 are more likely to be influenced by males members of their family (e.g. fathers or brothers).

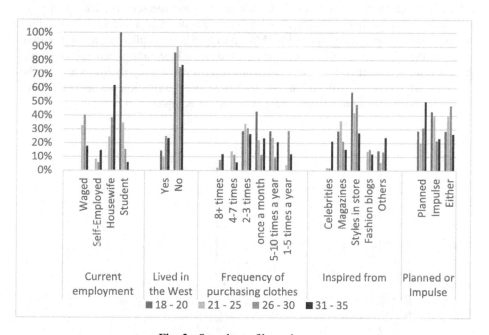

Fig. 2. Sample profile against age

A total of 144 respondents took part in the survey consisting of females only between the ages of 18–35. 142 respondents gave valid responses (98.6 %) and two gave invalid responses (1.4 %). The first largest group (36.1 % of respondents) who filled in the questionnaire were aged 26–30. The second largest group (35.4 % of respondents) were aged 21–25. The smallest group (4.9 %) was aged 18–20. The majority of females (aged 21–25) were single and considered themselves independent to make their own decisions regarding purchasing fashion clothing on on-line and offline. However, the analysis suggests that these females are actually most dependent and influenced by males. This can be related to the fact that single women usually live with their family and hence there are more men who can influence their decisions such as their father, brothers or uncles or even males from the extended family.

3.1   Sample Profile Against Marital Status

A cross tabulation between age group and marital status, as shown in Fig. 3, indicates that the highest percentage of married females (21.0 %) were between the ages of 31–35; 19.6 % between ages 26–30; and the highest percentage of single females (21.7 %) between ages 21–25. Results suggest that from the age of 26 onwards, it is more likely that Pakistani females are married and hence may be more likely to be influenced by males, specifically their husbands in their decision making process. However at the age of 21–25 they are either staying at home and influenced by other males of the family such as father or brothers or are relatively independent compared to married females. In a masculine society females tend to spend more time at home and in domestic activities and also tend to face gender inequality. Married females in a collective and masculine society of Pakistan are believed to be dominated by their husbands, where men not only take control over most of the house matters but also purchasing their clothes. In the buying decision process, women not only look for more information but also take more options into consideration, making the process more complex.

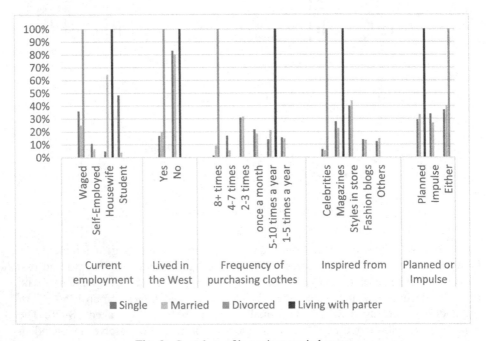

Fig. 3. Sample profile against marital status

Results also suggest that married females were significantly influenced by their husbands (only) when making decisions for purchasing fashion clothing. The fact that females cannot purchase against the will of their father or husband, who are considered the 'head of the house' in Pakistani society, may influence this. Consequently, Pakistani females try to consume products, which are accepted by their husbands, fathers, or other family members.

3.2 Decision Making Factors Against Age Group

In a collective society, most young adult women do not live on their own, but there are a number of few females who live outside of their families. Some live because of their jobs and some live away from their families because of their studies. To have a better understanding of the influences which young women have on them whilst making a purchase decision the age group to which they belong and with whom they live with has been crosstublated in Fig. 4. From the same Fig. 4. it can be seen that 61.0 % live with their family. 24.8 % disagree that they make independent decisions in the absence of influence of males. Only 5.7 % of those staying at home agreed that they make independent decisions in the absence of male influence. 14.9 % of respondents living with their spouses disagreed that they make independent decisions and only 2.1 % agreed that their decisions are independent. Whereas it can be seen that only 1 respondent, living alone, claimed that she makes independent decisions and surprisingly 2.1 % females living alone, the samples shows that they were influenced by males when making their purchase decisions. It was expected that young women living with their family or husband are likely to be influenced by men, but these results have strongly revealed the influence that men have even to those females living alone. This indicates the strong influence and that, women tend not to overlook or avoid the influence of men when purchasing.

Results show that 29.7 % of young women living with their families agreed that they consider other people's opinions when they making purchasing decisions. However, 15.9 % disagree that they consider other's opinions. This can be due to many factors. Within a family, other's opinions matter. For example, if an uncle lives in the same house the tradition in a collectivist society is to take their opinion and ideas. For clothing, the aunt would be involved in giving her opinions for purchasing. If that clothing is bought against her approval it may lead to conflict, therefore allot of sensitivity is involved. However in e-commerce, women do not seek much permission and approval, because purchases on the internet are favored by friends or reviews that recommend others to purchase.

Out of all respondents, 54 (which is the largest group) agree that females who are financially dependent on males, significantly consider males views at the final stage of deciding to purchase. Only 26 respondents disagree to this statement, which suggests that a large number of young Pakistani women believe that females financially dependent on males are more likely to consider their views. This belief can be due to either personal experience or observation, as a large number or respondents live with their family, and are either students or married; i.e. financially dependent on males.

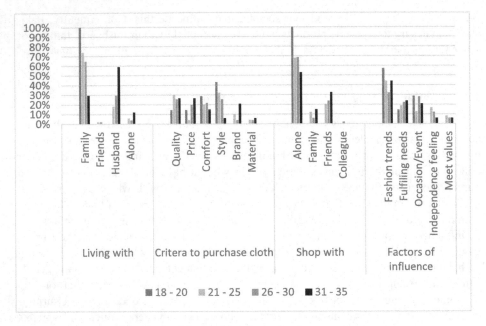

Fig. 4. Decision making factors against age group

3.3 Decision Making Influencing Factors According to Marital Status

A large proportion of the sample (41 respondents) claimed that family suggestions were the most influential to making new purchases (29.1 %). 28 respondents (19.9 %) claimed that were influenced by friends, 27 respondents (19.8 %) were influenced by celebrity styles and 26 respondents (18.4 %) were influenced by spouses. However, 12.8 % declared other factors.

Figure 5 shows that 41 respondents (29.5 %) agreed that males from an extended family have an influential role towards the purchase clothing of young women. Whereas 40 respondents disagreed to the above given statement. Furthermore, 11 respondents strongly disagreed, hence if calculated larger number of respondents disagree that males from extended family play an influential role towards the purchase of fashion clothing.

The second most important factor for deciding to purchase is 'a spouse's suggestion', as given by 40 respondents (28.8 %). 'A friend's suggestion' was the next most important factor given by 32 (25.80) respondents followed by a 'celebrities style' with 27 (21.77 %) respondents and 'a family suggestion' with 25 (20.16 %) respondents. This suggests that 'family, friend or spouse suggestion', are the main factors that encourage young adult Pakistani women to purchase something new. This study proposes that male dominance plays the most critical part and role in influencing the decision process and purchases of young Pakistani women. Although, it is important to understand and distinguish between the influence of closely related males and males from the extended family. Results also suggest that they were not considerably influenced by males in their extended family (e.g. uncles, cousins). This may be associated with a growing desire to have a more individualistic lifestyle. Males who are directly related to these young women (e.g. fathers, brothers and spouses) had the greatest influence on them for purchasing decisions.

Fig. 5. Decision making factors against marital status

3.4 Education and Buying Behavior

It is believed that women's rational decision making is also influenced by emotion. Women think more contextually and holistically. To observe this and as well to relate that either women only take opinions of others whilst they are living with influential people or they undergo this process at all times, despite whomever they live with the relevant cross tabulation is shown in Fig. 6. These results suggest that despite living circumstances (e.g. financial independence), Pakistani female consumers are influenced by their family, society, and colleagues; particularly males. They undergo an extensive thinking process, where they place their beliefs first, and these beliefs are the perceptions of the expected reaction from the society of males of undergoing a certain action. In fact, 47.2 % of the total respondents did not purchase the clothes they preferred, suggesting that influencers (as mentioned above) enforce restrictions and set criteria, thereby limiting Pakistani females ability of carrying out independent purchase decisions.

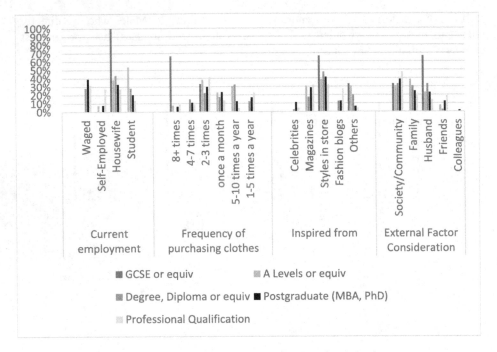

Fig. 6. Highest level of education and buying behavior

4 Conclusion

Pakistani females (of any marital status) are influenced by males in their e-retailing decisions. They not only change their e-retailing decision at the last stage of the decision-making process but, also, in many cases, they allow males to make their fashion clothing purchase decision. The data suggests that when it comes to on-line shopping and e-commerce, young educated adult Pakistani females make on-line purchase decisions under a significant influence of a highly collective and masculine environment. The case study and results also demonstrate this to be true for the Pakistani society when shopping in-stores as well, but by extrapolating these findings, this is very likely to be true in several similar emerging markets in the same geographic region. Although, the empirical data gathering was in relation to fashion clothing, it is believed that the same results will also apply to other e-retailing areas.

The external influencing factors were *society, family, spouse* and *colleagues* for on-line decision-making in e-commerce platforms. The 'traditional family structures' and 'collective society' may change the final purchase decision of young adult women in emerging markets. Furthermore, from the perspective of decision-making process model [16], theory of reasoned action [17, 18] and attitude model, they appear to adopt a thinking process under which their purchasing choices are shaped by the reaction of their male counterparts when purchasing a product on-line. It has been observed as a whole, that the majority of the females, either single or married, are influenced by males to such an extent that not only can they change their decision at the last stage due to their influence, but also allow them to make their decisions.

For the development of e-commerce interfaces, this data suggests that the interaction and marketing presentation must be suitable and appeal not only to the purchaser (i.e. adult female) but also to the males in their immediate environment. Given the strong influence of males, the associated reviews of a product must also depict the gender of the reviewer given that a review from a male even for a female product is expected to have stronger influence than the same review originated by a female. This emerging paradigm of e-commerce transaction in developing markets is somewhat different to the traditional e-commerce interface approach that is traditionally used in developed markets.

References

1. Bearden, W.O., Netemeyer, R., Teel, J.: Measurement of consumer susceptibility to interpersonal influence. J. Consum. Res. **15**, 473–481 (1989)
2. Pakistan Infrastructure Report - 2014, Business Monitor International, London (2014)
3. Arnould, E.J., Thompson, C.J.: Consumer culture theory (CCT): twenty years of research. J. Consum. Res. **31**(4), 868–882 (2005)
4. Brey, P.: Evaluating the social and cultural implications of the Internet. Comput. Soc. **36**(3), 41–48 (2006)
4. Ilyas, S.: An integrative framework for consumer behavior: evidence from Pakistan. Int. J. Bus. Manage. **6**(4), 120 (2011)
5. Luna, D., Gupta, F.S.: An integrative framework for cross-cultural consumer behavior. Int. Mark. Rev. **18**(1), 45–69 (2001)
7. Traindis, H.C., Chan, D.K.-S., Bhawuk, D.P.S., Iwao, S., Sinha, J.B.P.: Multimethod probes of allocentrism and idiocentrism. Int. J. Psychol. **54**, 323–338 (1995)
8. Triandis, H.C.: Culture and Social Behavior. McGraw-Hill, New York (1994)
9. Bagozzi, R., et al.: The Social Psychology of Consumer Behaviour. Open University Press, Buckingham (2002)
10. McCrae, R.R., Costa, P.T.: The stability of personality: observation and evaluations. Curr. Dir. Psychol. Sci. **3**, 173–175 (1994)
11. Żelazna, K., Kowalczuk, I., Mikuta, B.: Ekonomika konsumpcji, elementy teorii. Szkoła Główna Gospodarstwa Wiejskiego, Warszawa (2002)
12. Keegan, W.J., Green, M.C.: Global Marketing. Pearson, Boston (2015)
13. Streeter, L.G.: Brush up on ABCs of model behaviour, Final Edition, Infomart, a division of Postmedia Network Inc., Edmonton, Alta (2007)
14. de Mooij, M., Hofstede, G.: Cross-cultural consumer behavior: a review of research findings. J. Int. Consum. Mark. **23**, 181–182 (2011)
15. Chang, P., Chieng, M.: Building consumer-brand relationship: a cross-cultural experience view. Psychol. Mark. **23**(11), 927–959 (2006)
16. Engel, J.F., Kollat, D.T., Blackwell, R.D.: Consumer Behavior. Holt, Rinehart & Winston, New York (1968)
17. Fishbein, M., Ajzen, I.: Belief, Attitude, Intention and Behaviour: An Introduction to Theory and Research. Addison-Wesley, Reading (1975)
18. Fishbein, M., Stasson, M.: The role of desires, self-predictions, and perceived control in the prediction of training session attendance. J. Appl. Soc. Psychol. **20**, 173–198 (1990)

19. Rigas, D.I., Alty, J.L.: Using sound to communicate program execution. In: Proceedings of the 24th EUROMICRO Conference, vol. 2, pp. 625–632 (1998)
20. Rigas, D.I.: Guidelines for Auditory Interface Design: An Empirical Investigation. Ph.D. thesis, Loughborough University of Technology (1996)
21. Hofstede, G.: Cultures and Organizations: Software of the Mind. McGraw-Hill, London (1997)
22. Luo, Y.: Analysis of culture and buyer behavior in Chinese market. J. Asian Cult. Hist. 1(1), 25–31 (2009)

Cultural Capital at Work in Facebook Users' Selection of Different Languages

Jieyu Wang[1](✉) and Satarupa Joardar[2]

[1] Department of Information Systems, University of Maryland,
Baltimore County, Baltimore, MD, USA
wajieyu1@umbc.edu
[2] Department of Language Literacy and Culture,
University of Maryland, Baltimore County, Baltimore, MD, USA
joardar1@umbc.edu

Abstract. As the number of international users on Facebook has increased, users with multi-lingual backgrounds showed their diversity in language selections. Some research has studied how Facebook affects users' social capital. This study examines users' language selection behaviors and analyzes their selections by applying the concept of cultural capital. It aims to provide information to designers to develop cross-cultural applications or web pages on Facebook, for example, advanced translation tools or different language versions of web pages with cultural elements. The cross-cultural design might attract more international users and improve the website's usability. Through observing 83 active Facebook users' status updates and interviews with 10 users with multi-lingual backgrounds, we find that audience, locality and context are three important factors that affect users' language selections. It showed that users' language proficiency plays a role when users choose the language in their posts and comments. The characteristics of different languages also affect users' language selections when they update their status and interact with other users on Facebook. Furthermore, some users prefer to use their native languages or heritage languages other than English on Facebook because they want to show their cultural capital and keep their cultural heritage alive.

Keywords: CSCW · Cross-cultural design · Cultural capital · Multi-lingual · Locality · Context · Audience · Language proficiency

1 Introduction

With the fast development of social computing, Facebook is one of the most popular social networking websites. It is an English language based website. However, as the number of web users who are speakers of other languages increases, the role of language on Facebook is becoming important. By the end of 2014, Facebook had more than 208 million users in North America while there were over a billion users all over the world [3]. A significant proportion of Facebook users are not native English speakers. In order to meet the language requirements from a vast variety of users, Facebook has introduced a translation tool. However, the translation tool is limited to specific languages and different Facebook settings. For example, Hindi comments on

© Springer International Publishing Switzerland 2015
P.L.P. Rau (Ed.): CCD 2015, Part II, LNCS 9181, pp. 101–109, 2015.
DOI: 10.1007/978-3-319-20934-0_10

wall posts cannot be translated into English yet. This translation function is only offered on Facebook pages instead of profiles. The translation tool can reduce language barriers and help users in certain situations. Yet it cannot remove the barriers. Users with multi-lingual backgrounds are still using different languages due to their selections.

The goal of this paper is to examine Facebook users' language selection behaviors, especially the reasons that contribute to their selections. We observe and analyze when and how Facebook users use different languages while communicating with others. We try to figure out important factors which impact users' language selections on Facebook. We hope these factors might bring some implications to designers in their future cross-cultural design.

2 Related Work

Languages on Facebook are important factors that influence users' behaviors or communications, especially with those who have multi-lingual backgrounds. Few research has studied users' language selections on Facebook and the reasons that behind their selections. Tang et al. [5] collected 30 participants' Facebook status updates data and did quantitative analysis to find that language barriers influenced users into different circles and private control.

A number of studies have analyzed the relationship between the social capital and Facebook. Burke et al. [2] carried out longitudinal surveys to observe 415 Facebook users' log activities in order to explore how users' social capital was influenced by Facebook. They found that some users' social capital had been increased by receiving messages. Meanwhile, users who passively viewed news on Facebook also increased their social capital.

Yoder and Stutzman [7] aimed to find out where on Facebook could users produce social capital and transmit it to others. They designed a web questionnaire and sent to the 6000 students at the university. They got 574 responses with a reasonable response rate. By employing structural equation and regression models, they found that social capital could be produced by intensive wall posts. These posts were public and one to one/many communications.

Social capital is an "the actual or potential resources which are linked to a durable network of more or less institutionalized relationships of mutual acquaintance or recognition" [1]. It was first articulated by Bourdieu in the field of social sciences. Bourdieu also introduced another type of capital, "cultural capital". Cultural capital can include a broad range of goods such as art, education and forms of language [1]. Few research has been done to examine the effect of cultural capital on Facebook users' activities. In this paper we explore how users with multi-lingual backgrounds used languages as their cultural capital on Facebook and how this capital affected their communication with other Facebook users.

Locality and audience also influence users' language selections when they interact with each other. Lutters and Ackerman [4] did a field study on a Disney BBS, "The Castle". They found that the geographic locality was one of the important reasons that made the BBS thrive. On Facebook non-native English users outside their native countries and in their native countries have different language selection tendencies which are influenced by their current locality. Users outside their native countries tend to use English as their formal selection on Facebook while users in their native countries tend to use their native languages in all situations.

Not only locality but also the audience affects users' language selections. Users of Facebook have an audience of weak ties and strong ties. Weak ties are non-intimate and not regularly maintained connections. For example, co-workers on Facebook have weak ties. Strong ties show a relationship of intimacy and kinship, for example, ties between close friends and families [6]. Users who have multi-lingual backgrounds on Facebook tend to share more self-disclosure messages in their native languages to the audience who has strong ties with them, for example, their family members and their old friends in their country. The geographic locality also plays a role in this situation. In sum, multilingual users with different locality and audience share their information and cultures on Facebook. They create dynamic cultures on it.

In this paper we aim to find out how languages impact users' interaction. By analyzing when and why users select English or other languages, we aim to explore what is the function of languages in certain situations. The paper tries to offer detailed analysis on users' language selections for the design of advanced translation tools or the cross-cultural design of different language web pages on Facebook.

3   Methods

This study carried out participatory observation and supported the data with semi-structured interviews. The first author participated and observed the status update of users on Facebook. The observed users were 83 Facebook users who regularly log in Facebook and update their status. Most of them are or were graduate students at a university in the east coast. Among these participants 77 of them are non-American users with multilingual backgrounds within or outside the United States. Their native countries are Argentina, China, Columbia, French, Germany, India, Pakistan, Japan, Malaysia, and South Korea. There are in total 78 users who have multilingual backgrounds. The first author participated in their posts and comments, which helped her to get a deep understanding of the users' behaviors in the field. She also observed the users' wall posts and comments for over three months. She collected 12 typical intercultural communications among the users.

In order to reduce bias and increase result credibility, we conducted semi-structured interviews with open-ended questions to get results from users on their specific language selections in their wall posts and comments on Facebook. We totally interviewed 10 Facebook users. Five of them whose native countries are China, Columbia, India, Malaysia, and South Korea were interviewed face-to-face. One German user was interviewed through an online video call. Four users in India, Pakistan and the United States were interviewed through emails. We made audio records for the interviews.

Once the data were collected, the transcripts of the interviews were made immediately. The interviews were in the following areas of interest:

- The users' multilingual backgrounds and their language proficiency
- The languages they used on Facebook
- The situations and reasons that they used English on Facebook
- The situations and reasons that they used their native languages or languages other than English on Facebook

In order to analyze the qualitative data from the observation and interviews we created an NVivo project to import the transcripts of the interviews and the 12 scenes from the observation. NVivo is a software application for qualitative research analysis. It can interpret qualitative data and unstructured data. We did open-coding of the observation and interview data to generate themes independently. We discussed our themes and reached agreements on the final generated themes. For the interview data we used the first letter of each participant's country combining with numbers to represent the participant. For example, Interviewee I2 stands for the second Indian interviewee.

4   Results

From observation we found that audience, context and locality were important factors that impacted user' language selections. Non-native English speakers used English as a formal and communicative language to all users. They used their native languages to limit the audience to family members and certain friends. Locality also affected their language selections. Non-native English users in their native countries tended to prefer the native languages rather than English. Users in native English speaking countries tend to use English more often than using their native languages other than English. Users' language selections also depended on different contexts. When the posts or comments were in English, users were likely to respond in English. On the contrary, when the posts and comments were in languages other than English, they were likely to join the context and use certain languages other than English. For native English speakers, they posted in other languages when they could not express themselves well in English.

The data from the interviews supported the observation data. It showed further and detailed information in the reasons for the interviewees' language selections. We found that English proficiency impacted users' language selections. Non-native English users who had high English language proficiency preferred to use English on Facebook in a native English speaking country. Users who had high language proficiency both in English and their native language often used code-switching from their native language to English in their posts and comments. One native Bengali speaker from India mentioned that being comfortable in both English and Bengali. She used English for "slightly formal communications" while her native tongue Bengali was "the medium for more spontaneous conversation."

Different characteristics of languages also affected users' language selections. For example, the Malaysian interviewee pointed out that she preferred to write in English when she posted her status on Facebook.

> Personally I usually post in English because of my personal preference and besides I think it sounds too fancy, extravagant in my native language." (Interviewee M)

Certain users who had multi-linguistic and cultural backgrounds with higher education were likely to be considered to obtain more cultural capital. They used their native languages or heritage languages when possible on Facebook to show their identity and protect their cultural heritage. For example, the German interviewee stated that she used German to interact with German users.

> I think, I really stick to German there whenever possible... The usage of German in the US and on Facebook among other German speakers is also a sign of identity to send a signal, that I speak English, but that my native language and my culture is German. (Interviewee G)

5 Discussion

The results indicated that people in different localities followed a similar pattern to use related languages. For example, users in the U.S. were likely to use English as the dominant language on Facebook. Users in Latin America used Spanish as their primary language. Users in Germany and Japan used German and Japanese as their preferred languages. Non-native English users in different localities displayed different patterns in their language selections. They chose English as their preferred language when they stayed in English speaking countries.

> (I use) English, cause I am currently living in USA, so my current activity is here, and the common language with the people here is English. (Interviewee K)

The German interviewee who lived in Germany pointed out when she was in the U.S., she set up her Facebook account in English. But now she has difficulties accessing German terms.

> My language setting on Facebook is English. I lived in the US when I set up my FB account and "lived" with the English language. At that point I set the language to English on all Computer Applications. For that reason I am often missing the German terms for these applications. (Interviewee G)

The observation data showed that the users' language selections changed in different context. When a post was initiated in English, the following comments were likely to be in English. When a post was initiated in another language, the following comments tended to be in that language used by their friends from the same country. Or it could be in English used by their friends around the world. The interview data also supported this finding. The Spanish, Malaysian and American interviewees expressed that they paid attention to the context who commenting on posts.

> I use the same language in which the comment was posted. Because I think is polite to follow the comments in the same language. (Interviewee K)

Also it depends on how other people's commenting, if a person converse with me in English, I will reply it using English and vice versa. (Interviewee M)
If the original posting was in French, I respond in French, for the most part, unless I feel like writing in English or I see that most of the comments are in English. (Interviewee A)

Users' language selections were not only influenced by linguistic context, but also the cultural context. One Indian interviewee gave an example that in one of her posts she introduced the international Labor Day to her American friends. Coincidentally, the German interviewee also mentioned the reason why she chose German to post about the International Women's Day.

It depends on the context. Today is May Day, the international labor day, which is an official holiday in my native country, India. I posted the status updates, discussing the origins of this holiday and how it first started in Chicago. But ironically it is not the holiday in USA. So this status was in English because I was trying to reach my American friends. (Interviewee I1)
Interestingly I mentioned the International Women's Day in German. Thinking of it, I think that during my stay in the US, I never heard so much about it, so maybe subconsciously I decided, that this message would mean more to my German-speaking friends than my English-speaking friends and that it is somehow less applicable to the people I know from the United States, although it of course is international. (Interviewee G)

Audience was an important factor that affected users' language selections on Facebook. From the observation, the first author found that audience who had strong ties with the users was the special group. This group often included the users' family members, relatives such as cousins, and friends that grew up together. They shared the same cultural background and similar life experiences. When the users communicated with this group, they usually used their native languages. This cultural capital helped them to show their intimacy relationship. In the interviews, the Indian, Korean and Malaysian interviewee mentioned that they communicated with their families and friends in their native languages.

If my dad, I will use Bengali (native language) even though he speaks English because our relationship is closer than any other people. (Interviewee I1)
For my family in Korea, I use Korean. Otherwise, I usually us English. (Interviewee K)
If I initiate a post, usually it's always in English. But most of the time, my relatives and my friends back home prefer to converse with me in Malay, so I reply them back in Malay. (Interviewee M)

The users usually used English to audience with weak ties, for example, general friends. They also used English to broadcast their messages to a wider audience. The interviewees from Columbia, Germany, Indian, Pakistan, and Korean all stated that they use English to interact with friends worldwide.

I have friends from different countries with other languages, so the easy way to communicate with them is using English. (Interviewee S)
I use English, when the intended audience of the message is international. I probably use English 60–70 % of the time since most of my Facebook friends don't speak German. Also, I started using Facebook when I lived in the US, so I still connect Facebook to English. (Interviewee G)
I most often use English to communicate with all my contacts. I have contacts from different parts of the world. In order to reach all of them, I usually use English. (Interviewee I)
Most of times, Cause my most Facebook friends are from all over the country. English is the common language for communication. (Interviewee K)

I tend to use more of English to make the discussion more inclusive of those friends of mine who understand English only. (Interviewee P)

The users sometimes used their native languages as language barriers to limit their audience. For example, the Indian interviewee used her native language, Bengali, to keep her message private. The Korean interviewee did not want to show her emotions to all her friends. She chose her native languages to limit her audience. Another Indian interviewee uses her native language, Bengali, for inside-jokes and one-on-one conversation, which is yet another example of limiting an audience on Facebook.

I use my native language to have a private conversation with someone. There is an translation function, it will not work if I write Bangali in English scripts. So it is pretty private to people who speak the language. People can read it but it will not make sense to them. (Interviewee I1)
Sometimes I want to post my status (emotional) – mostly negative then I use Korean so that other people can't understand. (Interviewee K)
Bengali inside-jokes, quotes from Bengali movies/books, or Bengali idioms intended solely for my Bengali Facebook friends. One-on-one conversations with Bengali friends, almost always feel more appropriate in Bengali. (Interviewee I2)

The users' language proficiency had an impact on their language selections on Facebook. For users who had higher language proficiency in certain languages, they could choose freely what they wanted to use to express their opinions. For example, the Korean and Indian interviewees' English language proficiency was as good as their native languages. Also because they have been stayed in the U.S. till now, they preferred to use English when post their status.

English. I am used to use English. I have created my Facebook here in America, which is English version. I couldn't find any difference between two languages. (Interviewee K)
English is like my native language. It is really based on the context and the person that I'm communicating with. (Interview I1)

The users with high language proficiency sometimes used code-switching when they posted or commented on Facebook. For instance, the Indian interviewee used three languages (Indian, Bengali, and English) as her native languages. She mentioned that all her Indian friends and she used code-switching. It was natural for them to do it.

The respondent from Pakistan was proficient in languages other than English, like Urdu, Punjabi, Sindhi, or Wolof, a language spoken in Senegal and a few other African nations, which this respondent was learning. She mentioned that she was comfortable using different languages with Facebook friends who were bi- or multi-lingual.

Interacting with folks who are bi/multilingual in the same languages that I'm familiar with, I do at times take the liberty of using languages other than English, like Urdu, Punjabi, Sindhi, or Wolof, so I use these languages at times when communicating with friends (Interviewee P)

The Malay interviewee pointed out that she needed to be careful about using English when communicating with her friends in her home country. She needed to pay attention to the context because not all her friends had a high level of English proficiency. If she always used English to interact with her friends in her country, they would consider that she was showing off.

I think I have to be cautious and alert people preferences in conversing with me, cause speaking too much English may cause perception that I'm showing off. (Interviewee M)

As we mentioned in the result, the characteristics of different languages also affected users' language selections. The Malay interviewee usually used English when she updated her status. She explained that English is formal, while Malay is too flowery to her. In a similar vein, the Pakistani respondent mentioned the broad reach of the English language, and its inclusiveness and success in reaching a large group of people were reasons why she used English on Facebook:

> Also, if I'm having a discussion about some social issues, politics etc., I tend to use more of English to make the discussion more inclusive of those friends of mine who understand English only (Interviewee P).

The users with more cultural capital intentionally used their native languages or heritage languages on Facebook to keep their cultural heritage. The German interviewee pointed out that she did not like the English-only movements in the U.S. when she stayed in the U.S.

> While living in the US, I always spoke German to Germans unless non-German speakers were involved in the conversation and I never liked it when Native speakers of other languages than English used English to talk among each other. My dislike for this has to do with the cultural imperialist tendencies of the US. The usage of German in the US and on FB among other German speakers is also a sign of identity to send a signal, that I speak English, but that my native language and my culture is German (Interviewee G).

The first author also observed that Chinese users had the tendency to use Chinese with their Chinese friends on Facebook even though they lived in the United States. The Chinese user expressed that this contributed to his identity and cultural habits. Meanwhile, the American interviewee who married a native French speaker spoke in French to her baby girls. She also posted in French on Facebook. She mentioned that when she found that it was difficult for her to express her ideas in English, she would use French.

> I choose to use French when what I have to say doesn't translate well into English. For example, my last post in French, had to do with a conversation I had with Hawa. She had said something really funny, but in French. It just doesn't translate well into English, so I posted in French. (Interviewee A)

6 Conclusion and Future Work

Facebook is one of the most popular social networking sites in the world. With its increased international users, the language-based communication has huge space for advanced translation and cross-cultural design. This study explored when and why users with multi-lingual backgrounds used different languages on Facebook. Audience, locality and context were three important factors that impacted users' language selections. Users' language proficiency, the characteristics of languages, and users' cultural capital also affected their selections on language usage on Facebook.

In this study we used participant observation and interviews to collect the data. Participant observation helped us to get basic guidelines of users' language selections. The interviews allowed us to get an in-depth look at the users' language selections. We interviewed 10 users in this study. Future studies can focus on interviewing more users with even more varied linguistic backgrounds. An ethnographic study could be carried out in order to collect more valuable information from users' language selection behaviors.

Acknowledgement. We would like to thank our international friends for their strong support, nice cooperation, and prompt responses.

References

1. Bourdieu, P.: The forms of capital. In: Richardson, J. (ed.) Handbook of Theory and Research for the Sociology of Education, pp. 241 258. Greenwood Press, New York (1985)
2. Burke, M., Kraut, R., Marlow, C.: Social capital on facebook: differentiating uses and users. In: SIGCHI Conference on Human Factors in Computing Systems (CHI 2011), pp. 571–580. ACM, New York (2011)
3. Internet World Stats. http://www.internetworldstats.com/facebook.htm
4. Lutters, W., Ackerman, M.: Joining the backstage: locality and centrality in an online community. Inf. Technol. People. **16**(2), 157–182 (2003). MCB UP Limited
5. Tang, D., Chou, T., Drucker, N., Robertson, A., Smith, W., Hancock, J.: A tale of two languages: strategic self-disclosure via language selection on facebook. In: ACM 2011 Conference on Computer Supported Cooperative Work (CSCW 2011), pp. 387–390. ACM, New York (2011)
6. Wellman, B., Gulia, M.: Net surfers don't ride alone: virtual community as community. In: Kollock, P., Smith, M. (eds.) Communities in Cyberspace. University of California Press, Berkeley (1997)
7. Yoder, C., Stutzman, F.: Identifying social capital in the facebook interface. In: SIGCHI Conference on Human Factors in Computing Systems (CHI 2011), pp. 585–588. ACM, New York (2011)

Culture for Transport and Travel

Applying Soundscape to Creating an Interactive and Cultural Centered Experience

Hsiu Ching Laura Hsieh[✉] and Chiao Yu Hwang

Department of Creative Design,
National Yunlin University of Science and Technology, Douliu, Taiwan
laurarun@gmail.com

Abstract. Soundscape, the composition of Sound and Landscape proposed by Schafer [2] in 1970s, refers to the environmental landscape composed of sound. Extended from acoustic studies, soundscape study stresses more on the bonding relationship between sound and social culture. This research aims to apply sound as the key element to design travel web and mobile applications could have travel offer cultural experience and emotional awareness and further construct a new design. Focusing on local sound, local soundscape is investigated in this study. Assisted with literature review, field research, and in-depth interview to analyze local characteristics and soundscape, the design elements are integrated in the travel web design, the soundscape with rich historical, geographic, ecological, and cultural information is confirmed, and the soundscape web design framework is proposed. The framework does not simply plan travel map and local travel web, but could provide designers with the abstract method for soundscape elements for being applied to digital media, mobile application design, and experience design. Finally, several suggestions and considerations are concluded.

Keywords: Soundscape · Travel web · Mobile travel application

1 Introduction

Making a comprehensive survey of current travel web and mobile applications, most of them focus on visual perception, but few apply five senses as the experience media. As a matter of fact, visual perception indeed presents 80 % of human senses that visual perception leads people's cultural experience and perception. However, it is wondered whether using sound for people experiencing culture could enhance the memory and understanding of culture. It becomes the investigation in this study whether applying sound as the key element to design travel web and mobile applications could have travel offer cultural experience and emotional awareness and further construct a new design.

2 Literature Review

2.1 Cultural Value of Soundscape

Soundscape, the composition of Sound and Landscape proposed by Schafer [2] in 1970s, refers to the environmental landscape composed of sound. Extended from

© Springer International Publishing Switzerland 2015
P.L.P. Rau (Ed.): CCD 2015, Part II, LNCS 9181, pp. 113–120, 2015.
DOI: 10.1007/978-3-319-20934-0_11

acoustic studies, soundscape study stresses more on the bonding relationship between sound and social culture. From various aspects, such as musicology, sound and image studies, ecology, and sociology, soundscape study presents distinct reference and applications. From the aspect of musicology, Schafer [2] proposed the idea of soundscape triangle by considering soundscape as The Music of the Environment and regarding soundmark, signal, and keynote as the analysis reference. Nevertheless, it could hardly prove the cultural value of soundscape simply from the aspect of musicology. Wang [6] therefore followed the idea of soundscape triangle proposed by Schafer [3], combined the ecological triangle structure developed by Tilly [5] from the aspect of sociology, and integrated soundmark, signal, and keynote into the social context of human, space, and activity to develop the city soundscape study structure. Furthermore, local soundscape value was classified according to historical sound, cultural sound, social sound, and natural sound with Soundmark so as to design urban soundscape with cultural value. Soundscape presents the cultural value for local marketing and local asset.

Schafer [2] indicated in Five Village Soundscape that, in addition to artificial sound and natural sound, soundscape further covered "historical memories". Soundscape is defined by Ministry of the Environment, Japan, as "sound environmental goods" and "sound cultural goods", which are a part of "cultural heritage". Apparently, the cultural value of soundscape is not simply the cultural heritage, but could rich the urban "sound expression" when regarding a city as an "organism", in which the "exchange circle" composed of soundscape contains the positive exchange among people, space, activities, and sound in the city [5].

2.2 Shuilin is Defined in this Study as the Area for Soundscape Collection

Shuilin is a plain located in the northwest of Chianan Plain, where more than a half of villagers are farmers and "Shuilin yam" is the representative produce. Such an agricultural structure allows Shuilin conserving the early agricultural society, culture, and landscape with thick friendliness. As one of the earliest developed cultivation areas, Shuilin conserves the religious and historical characteristics as well as western rural characteristics and presents cultural landscapes with settlement characteristics. Especially, regional kin temples still conserve the special ceremonies; various temples and ancient buildings become the primary cultural heritage in Shuilin.

2.3 Related Works

Sinha et al. [4] developed the application to monitor noise in a city. The soundscape application involves capturing of audio data using user's mobile phone, extracting the attributes and posting the same to the backend, running analytics on the same and then displaying it using a legend-based heat-map on a dashboard. Zhang and Huang [9] stateed that today's effervescent cities produce lots of new sounds while accelerating the terminating of traditional ones. They proposed to evoke the lost memories of neglected sounds by forming an interactive, emotional centered experience. They developed the application "More Than Sound", an on-line social soundscape with three major components: a mobile application, a web and a public sound installation, outlining social scenes and life stories, it stimulates the visitors to form a deeper comprehending of their living environment through cities' splendid sound silhouette. Finney and Janer [1] apply unstructured databases for soundscape creation, and depict an autonomous soundscape system for virtual reality environments that use the Freesound database to augment scenes from Google Street View with sounds. Words that portray objects in the scene, referring to sound sources, are used to search the database for recordings, which are then operated into a total soundscape for that scene. Resulting soundscapes were found to illustrate the scene effectively for subjects when assessed.

3 Methods

Step 1:   Taking Shuilin for the investigation, the soundscape structure proposed by Wang [7] is applied to the field research on human, space, and activity with observational method for soundscape collection.

Step 2:   The soundscape characteristics are further picked out and supplemented through literature review and in-depth interview with local citizens. Besides, local soundscape value is classified into historical sound, cultural sound, social sound, and natural sound, based on phonetic indicators, for analyses.

Step 3:   The idea of "time" is included to make the travel concept map of Shuilin sound scape, which is cross-organized from present sound, lost sound, and new sound with Step 2.

Step 4:   The idea of "time" is included to make the travel web and application concept map of Shuilin soundscape, whose feasible direction is cross-organized from present sound, lost sound, and new sound with Step 2.

3.1   Analysis of Shuilin Soundscape

The general investigation areas are selected according to *164 Happy Trips* in Shuilin, published by Yunlin Country Government [8]. Observational method is utilized for the field work to collect the soundscape in the routes and further investigate what local citizens regard as characteristic local sound with in-depth interview. After observing the places and collecting the sound through observational method, in-depth interview with local citizens is proceeded for the complete and objective sound collection so as to supplement and filter the characteristic soundscape in Shuilin. Soundscape presents "historical memories" [3]. Current and past local cultural heritage could be understood from soundscape. By the lapse of time, soundscape would change, disappear, or emerge the new one. Promoting local tourism aims to have travelers deeply understand local culture and evolution.

Based on the characteristics of phonetic indicators in Shuilin, historical sound, cultural sound, social sound, and natural sound as the vertical axis and present sound, lost sound, and new sound as the horizontal axis (proposed in this study) are classified in the Table 1, expecting to highlight the time evolution and distribution characteristics of Shuilin soundscape.

From Table 1, Shuilin soundscape appears thick rural characteristics in Taiwan in terms of social sound and natural sound, including sound of people and distinct sound of vendors in markets, sound of agricultural machines, biological sound in natural farms, and sound of strong wind in the west. The dense life in early western rural societies in Taiwan is conserved, as it is precious in modern urban societies. The original natural ecology, such as golden bats, is restored the sound of bats with machines by A local cultural museum. It is considered as an alternative soundscape experience.

In regard to historical sound, Shuilin, as one of the earliest cultivation areas, presents distinct culture generated by cultivation. The major characteristic is the kin

Table 1. Analysis of Shuilin soundscape

Features of phonetic indicators	Present sound	Lost sound	New sound
Historical sound	• Sound of machine in He Hsing Rice Miller (it is still working nowadays) • Shun Tien Temple, • Siang Yu Temple, • Tung Tien Temple, • Chi Hsing Temple (religious carnival sound of firecrackers and sound of people in festivals)	• Chi Historical Place (sound of activity in space) • Ancient sugar railways (railways and sound of train whistle) • Chi Chiao Well in Chung Chuang (sound of water-drawing)	
Cultural sound	• Sound of making scaffold ing stage for glove puppetry • Sound of performance		• Sound of making musical instrument in the ukulele factory • Sound of playing
Social sound	• Sound of people and dis tinct sound of vendors in Shuilin markets • Chatting sound in Niao Song Restaurant • Sound of sugarcane scraping • Sound of selling in Liang Hsin Chinese herb tea • Sound of polishing in Tai Yuan bamboo art • Mechanical sound in Shuitien tiller • Cooking sound in the kitchen of Niao Song Restaurant		

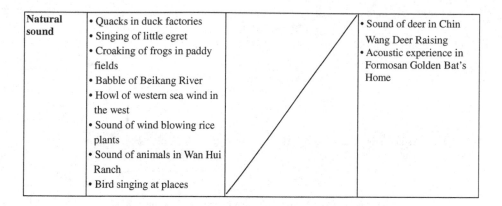

| Natural sound | • Quacks in duck factories
• Singing of little egret
• Croaking of frogs in paddy fields
• Babble of Beikang River
• Howl of western sea wind in the west
• Sound of wind blowing rice plants
• Sound of animals in Wan Hui Ranch
• Bird singing at places | | • Sound of deer in Chin Wang Deer Raising
• Acoustic experience in Formosan Golden Bat's Home |

temples in the cultivation areas. Such temples present special historical sound, especially the worship, which still conserves the historical custom characteristics. Nonetheless, the historical sound in some places is disappearing, among which sound of train whistle on sugar railways, sound of space in Chi Historical Place, and sound of water-drawing of Chi Hsing Well are lost. Sound of firecrackers and music in temples during festivals and sound of machines in He Hsing Rice Miller are conserved currently; Fanshu Matsu in Shun Tien Temple and He Hsing Miller are particularly apparent. The place is full of temple soundscape with cultivation history and the operation sound of miller for more than a century. Regarding cultural sound, cultural sound in Shuilin does not appear siginficant local characteristics. However, ukulele has become a new culture mark in Shuilin. With the integration and exchange between a local cultural museum (Kuan Chi Guitar Factory) and locals, the soundscape of ukulele is gradually combined with Shuilin and become a new representative of cultural sound.

3.2 Design Concept of Shuilin Soundscape Tourism

From above analyses, the soundscape elements are organized, in which several places are suitable for local tourism. The designed Shuilin soundscape travel web prototype presents international characteristics that it is designed bilingually, Chinese and English. First, Chinese and English could be selected in Introduction page to switch to the Home page of "Sonic Travelling in Shuilin", which is introduced on the left of Home page, while the Shuilin map is shown on the right. Scenic spots shown with different colors could be clicked in order to listen to the environmental sound and show the visual images of scenic spots. The design process concept framework is shown and analyzed as below (Fig. 1).

Route 1 offers historical learning, experience, and imagination. The historical sound of Shuilin is divided into the conserved sound and the lost sound. Most of the conserved sound are related to festival activities in temples, which are restricted the time and could not connect with the soundscape spots. For this reason, the sound of machines in He Hsing Miller, which is next to Shun Tien Temple, is suggested as the center of the route. It could be connected to temples with sound and lost historical

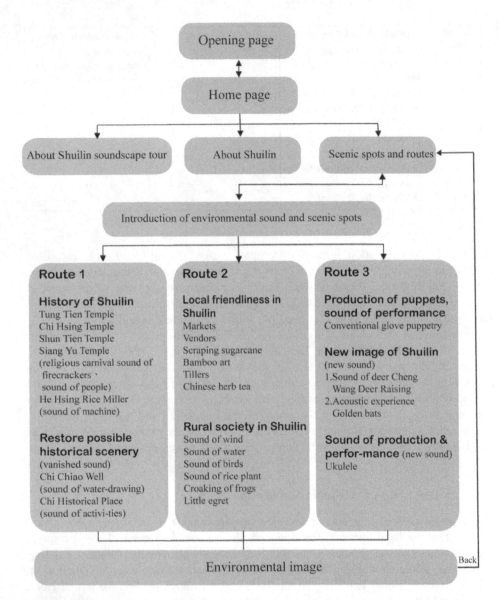

Fig. 1. Design process framework for Shuilin soundscape travel prototype

soundscape spots. With the title of "Passing through the century, the past imagination of Shuilin", the travelers could know the Shuilin history, listen to the existing historical soundscape, reconstruct the lost historical soundscape in Shuilin, such as ancient sugar trains, and enhance the in-depth experience of town travel by the introduction of cultivation, temple, and industrial history.

Route 2 offers the geography, social learning, and experience in western Taiwan. The social sound and natural sound of Shuilin reflect the rural social structure and the geographic characteristics in western Taiwan. Such soundscape therefore is integrated with local geography and social information to plan the learning and experience route for students. Not only could the geographic characteristics in western Taiwan be known, but the soundscape with friendliness and life in disappearing rural societies could be contacted.

Route 3 provides diverse developing sonic experience in Shuilin. Local characteristics are actively developed in Shuilin. The introduction and transformation of new and old industries have the soundscape appear more diversity. Combining such new characteristic soundscape with the history travel could correspond to the past and future of Shuilin and realize the ecological and social characteristics in Shuilin with the geographic society so as to present the active dimension of Shuilin.

4 Conclusion and Suggestion

Focusing on local sound, local soundscape is investigated in this study. Assisted with literature review, field research, and in-depth interview to analyze local characteristics and soundscape, the design elements are integrated in the travel web design, the soundscape with rich historical, geographic, ecological, and cultural information is confirmed, and the soundscape web design structure is proposed. The analysis framework is based on sociology to discuss the cultural value generated by including soundscape in the travel web design and development as well as allow the users knowing culture and acquiring pleasant emotion and use experiences. The framework does not simply plan travel map and local travel web, but could provide designers with the abstract method for soundscape elements for being applied to digital media, mobile application design, and experience design.

Finally, several suggestions and considerations are proposed for successive research.

1. Application of "Sonic Travelling in Shuilin" prototype. The prototype allows the successive research developing more diversely. For example, the design of multi-media interactive system could be placed in the exhibition for interacting with the participants; and, the design of websites would allow the users uploading new sound with the mobile travel application.
2. Verification of "Sonic Travelling in Shuilin" prototype. To ensure the success of the soundscape prototype, local elders and travelers could be continued in-depth interviews and usability test. With such verification, favorable improvement for the soundscape design prototype could be proposed.
3. "Lost historical sound" is an interesting idea. A new in-depth human-machine interactive travel model could be developed by combining visual perception or text data with travel for deeper imagination.
4. The classification and application of soundscape in this study could be the reference of relevant interactive design in the future.

References

1. Finney, N., Janer, J.: Soundscape generation for virtual environments using community-provided audio databases. In: W3C Workshop, Augmented Reality on the Web, Barcelona, Spain (2010)
2. Schafer, R.M.: The Turning of the World: Toward a Theory of Soundscape Design. University of Pennsylvania Press, Toronto (1978)
3. Schafer, R.M.: Five Village Soundscape, No. 4. Music of the Environment Series. ARC Publications, Vancouver (1977)
4. Sinha, P., Ghose, A., Bhaumik, C.: City soundscap. In: The Proceedings of the 13th Annual International Conference on Digital Government Research, pp. 298–299 (2012)
5. Tilly, C.: An Urban World. Little Borwn & Company, Boston (1974)
6. Wang, C.S.: Soundscape's expression in the two-city case: imagination of environmental sociology. J. Build. Plann. **10**, 89–98 (2001). National Taiwan University
7. Wang, C.S.: Cross-cultural comparative study on 100 soundscape in Taiwan and major urban rapid transit soundscape in Asia. Project report for Ministry of Science and Technology, executed by National Tsing Hua University's Center for General Education (2008)
8. Yunlin Country Government: 164 Happy Trips in Shuilin. Shuilin Township Office, Yunlin County (2013)
9. Zhang, L., Huang, J.: Original-ecology sounds of cities' impression. In: Rau, P.L.P. (ed.) HCII 2013 and CCD 2013, Part II. LNCS, vol. 8024, pp. 356–363. Springer, Heidelberg (2013)

Design of Vehicle-to-Vehicle Communication System for Chinese and German Drivers

Xiang Ji, Lukas Haferkamp, Chieh Cheng,
Muanphet Charunratanavisan, Andreas Neuhaus, Na Sun,
and Pei-Luen Patrick Rau[✉]

Department of Industrial Engineering, Tsinghua University,
Beijing 100084, China
rpl@mail.tsinghua.edu.cn

Abstract. Vehicle-to-Vehicle communication system is a designed to deal with the growing car accidents during the recent years. It allows drivers to communicate with each other visually and aurally. This study investigates the relationships between the communication styles of Vehicle-to-Vehicle system and drivers' driving behaviors in Chinese and German cultures. Results showed that all three styles (text, voice and emoticon) have significant effect on Chinese drivers, but only emoticon has effect on German drivers. And Chinese drivers like voice most while German drivers like emoticon most. Cultural differences, privacy issues and driving experience are discussed to explain the results.

Keywords: Communication styles · Emotion · Attitude · Cultural difference

1 Introduction

Roads become congested and accidents have steadily risen during the recent years. Research has shown that driving risks arise from the drivers themselves, the surroundings and technical issues regarding their vehicles. Offensive driving behavior from other drivers may induce negative driving emotion, influence driving behaviors and decrease driving performance. Therefore the communication between drivers has drawn a lot of attention.

New technologies constantly arise to cope with those problems. One example is Vehicle-to-Vehicle communication system (also abbreviated as V2V system), which allows drivers to know the exact position and speed of surrounding vehicles and aims to assist drivers by transmitting information between vehicles.

There are different communication styles between drivers. Studies show that different styles may cause different effects on receivers' emotion and attitude, and influence drivers' driving behaviors. Therefore, this paper aims to investigate the relationship between the communication styles of V2V system and driving behaviors in different cultures.

© Springer International Publishing Switzerland 2015
P.L.P. Rau (Ed.): CCD 2015, Part II, LNCS 9181, pp. 121–128, 2015.
DOI: 10.1007/978-3-319-20934-0_12

2   Literature Review

2.1   Driving Behavior Model

Most of driving behavior models are deduced from TPB model [1], which has long been used to explain the reason of some aggressive driving behavior like over-speeding and drunk driving [2, 3]. This model shows that attitude contributes to certain behavior. This is also proved in a study that a high-risk perception lead to a high risk-driving attitude, which is closely related to higher tendency of risky driving [4]. Therefore attitude is a significant predictor for potential driving behavior.

Some studies scientifically proven there is a connection between emotions and driving skills or performance. Anger leads to decreased subjective safety level and degraded driving performance; while happiness leads to degraded driving skills [5]. And driving anger is a very important emotion for drivers, since it leads to stronger acceleration and higher speed [6], and reduces risk perception [7]. Furthermore, one study showed there is no significant difference between traffic-related and traffic-unrelated emotions [4].

In conclusion, driving attitude and emotion can be changed by short sudden stimulus and can be regarded as two main predictors for driving behavior.

2.2   Effects of Communication Styles

There are three common communication styles. The first one is visual stimulus including text, images and video. It is a traditional communication style used in vehicle systems to transmit messages, like the navigation system, the instrument panel, and the in-vehicle control systems. Many psychological studies have proved that text and image can induce the receiver's emotions. Studies regarding vehicles also proved this. It is indicated the process of text in and output may cause the drivers' distraction [8], and negative distractions reduced lateral control and slowed driving speed [9]. Besides, some studies also focus on the relation of images and visual stimulation to driving performance. A direct effect was measured by Tricka et al. [10]. Their study discovered a decrease in driving performance for negative and an increase of driving performance for positive images. So visual stimulus is a useful way to influence driving behaviors. And visual stimulus can be separated into different levels, since images transmit richer information than text.

Another communication style is audial stimulus, including sound, voice and telephone. For example, the new navigation system, taxi broadcasting station, and some cars can play music automatically to correspond to the drivers' emotion. Studies showed that happy music had the strongest effect on the driver that their mean speed decreased and their lateral control deteriorated; while sad music makes them drive slower and keep their vehicle in its lane [11]. But another study in Spain showed a contrast result that a (not emotional) beep reduced the frequency of accidents in the upcoming risky situation, while the emotional cues did not [12]. This means that not all emotional stimulus have an effect on driving behaviors.

The third communication style is haptic stimulus, including vibration, temperature, and so on. For example, some new cars can adapt the in-car temperature according to drivers' emotion to help drivers calm. Some cars used shaking chairs to awaken drivers so that it can prevent drivers from sleeping on the road. But few studies have shown the connection between haptic stimulus and driving behavior.

In conclusion, there are different communication styles: visual stimulus, audial stimulus and haptic stimulus. And studies have shown connections between driving behaviors and visual or audial stimulus.

2.3   Cultural Difference in Driving Behavior

Cultures can be generally divided into high-context cultures and low-context cultures. Studies have shown that human decisions and behaviors can be influenced by different cultures [13]. This conclusion can be also used in the vehicle domain. Studies showed significant cultural differences in driver self-assessment among U.S., Spanish, and West German drivers, for example, U.S. drivers assessed themselves as safer than West German and Spanish subjects [14]. A similar study was conducted again in China. The results indicated that Chinese drivers and German drivers have a different perception of driving anger that Chinese drivers showed lower angry level than German drivers. Besides, Chinese drivers will get higher angry level as their age grows, while German drivers are in the contrast [15].

Therefore, culture is a significant variable contributing to driving behavior. But these results are concluded by questionnaire using different scenarios. In our study we will only take one scenario (offensive driving) into consideration to compare the difference between Chinese and German drivers.

3   Research Framework and Methodology

3.1   Research Framework

Studies have proven a connection between of driving behavior and V2V system, but few studies emphasized the differences between different communication styles through the emotion and attitude. Besides, although some studies have been focusing on the cultural difference in driving behavior, none could emphasize the interaction effect between the cultures and communication styles. Therefore, this study assumes an effect of V2V system and explores the effect of different communication styles on the drivers' emotion and attitude in different cultures. This study will be conducted in order to answer the following research question:

What effects do the different communication styles have on driving behaviors through emotion and attitude in Chinese and German cultures?

The independent variables are communication styles with 4 levels (text, voice, emoticon and no communication) and cultures with 2 levels (German and Chinese).

3.2   Task and Participants

Participants were required to watch scenarios with 4 different levels of communication styles shown in slides with pictures and text descriptions in a Latin-Square sequence design. All scenarios were given time pressure, and the other driver's behavior was designed as aggressive and against law to enhance the emotion inducted by the scenarios.

Twenty-four participants were invited to take part in the experiment: 12 Chinese and 12 German participants. Only experienced male drivers (with more than 2 years driving experience) were accepted, since novel drivers and female drivers will have more emotions (for example, fear and anxiety) than experienced male drivers. All participants are all graduate students in Department of Mechanical Engineering, Tsinghua University. The information of participants is shown in Table 1.

Table 1. Information of participants

Items	Chinese	German
Age (years old)	Mean 24.17, SD 1.19	Mean 24.25, SD 0.97
Driving Experience (years)	Mean 2.71, SD 1.83	Mean 5.92, SD 2.02

Participants filled in a questionnaire about their personal information and driving experience before the experiment. And during the experiment after watching each scenario, they were required to answer a questionnaire about their emotions and attitudes. After all scenarios, they would receive a short interview about their feelings and preference about different communication styles.

4   Results and Analysis

The two parameters measured in this experiment are emotion and attitude of the driver after receiving different styles of V2V system. Data about emotions and attitudes of the drivers are collected by questionnaire and analyzed by repeated measure ANOVA.

Table 2. Comparison of emotion level towards different styles

Styles	Cultures	Negative emotion	Positive emotion
No communication	Chinese	Mean 5.57, SD 0.89	Mean 2.08, SD 0.84
	German	Mean 4.38, SD 2.24	Mean 1.75, SD 0.79
Text	Chinese	Mean 4.17, SD 1.49	Mean 2.92, SD 1.10
	German	Mean 3.80, SD 0.97	Mean 2.22, SD 1.12
Voice	Chinese	Mean 3.60, SD 1.17	Mean 3.50, SD 1.31
	German	Mean 3.77, SD 1.19	Mean 2.06, SD 0.85
Emoticon	Chinese	Mean 4.45, SD 1.26	Mean 2.56, SD 1.38
	German	Mean 4.03, SD 1.31	Mean 2.47, SD 1.20

4.1 Emotion

Table 2 shows the comparison of the emotion level towards different styles between Chinese and German participants.

Negative Emotion. There is marginal significant interaction effect between communication styles and cultures. When offended by other drivers without communication, Chinese drivers would feel angrier than German drivers ($F = 7.21$, $p = 0.014$). But there is no significant difference between Chinese and German drivers in other conditions.

For Chinese drivers, they ranked higher angry level in the scenario without communication than text ($p = 0.000$), voice ($p = 0.000$) and emoticon ($p = 0.006$), meaning that all three styles have a significant effect on decreasing Chinese drivers' negative emotion.

For German drivers, results showed that the effect of communication styles on German drivers' negative emotion is not significant ($F = 1.43$, $p = 0.243$).

Positive Emotion. There is significant interaction effect between communication styles and cultures. ($DF = 20.00$, $p = 0.006$). When receiving a voice communication after being offended by other drivers, Chinese drivers would feel more happy and relaxed than German drivers ($F = 10.21$, $p = 0.004$). But there is no significant difference between Chinese and German drivers in other conditions.

For Chinese drivers, they ranked significantly lower positive emotion level in the scenario without communication than text ($p = 0.000$) and voice ($p = 0.000$), meaning that text and voice have a significant effect on increasing Chinese drivers' positive emotion.

For German drivers, results showed that that the effect of communication styles on German drivers' positive emotion is not significant ($F = 2.22$, $p = 0.094$).

4.2 Attitude

Table 3 shows the comparison of the attitude level towards different styles between Chinese and German participants.

Table 3. Comparison of attitude level towards different styles

Styles	Cultures	Negative attitude	Positive attitude
No communication	Chinese	Mean 5.96, SD 0.96	Mean 2.38, SD 1.11
	German	Mean 5.83, SD 1.60	Mean 2.42, SD 1.28
Text	Chinese	Mean 4.38, SD 0.93	Mean 4.29, SD 1.27
	German	Mean 5.38, SD 1.35	Mean 3.13, SD 1.32
Voice	Chinese	Mean 4.42, SD 1.16	Mean 4.63, SD 1.33
	German	Mean 5.46, SD 1.30	Mean 3.25, SD 1.08
Emoticon	Chinese	Mean 5.25, SD 0.92	Mean 3.50, SD 1.17
	German	Mean 5.21, SD 1.50	Mean 3.54, SD 1.41

Negative Attitude. There is significant interaction effect between communication styles and cultures. (DF = 20.00, p = 0.008). When receiving a text communication after being offended by other drivers, Chinese drivers would feel think the other driver less offensive and impolite than German drivers (F = 4.46, p = 0.046). But there is no significant difference between Chinese and German drivers in other conditions.

For Chinese drivers, they ranked significantly higher negative attitude level in the scenario without communication than text (p = 0.000) and voice (p = 0.001), meaning that text and voice can decrease Chinese drivers' negative attitude.

For German drivers, results showed that the effect of communication styles on German drivers' negative attitude is not significant (F = 1.80, p = 0.156).

Positive Attitude. There is significant interaction effect between communication styles and cultures. (F = 4.069, p = 0.010). When offended by other drivers, Chinese drivers are more willing to understand and forgive the other driver than German drivers with a text (F = 4.88, p = 0.038) or voice communication (F = 7.72, p = 0.011). But there is no significant difference between Chinese and German drivers in other conditions.

For Chinese drivers, they ranked significantly lower positive attitude level in the scenario without communication than text (p = 0.000), voice (p = 0.001) and emoticon (p = 0.003), meaning that all three styles have a significant effect on increasing Chinese drivers' positive attitude.

For German drivers, they ranked significantly lower positive attitude level in the scenario without communication than emoticon (p = 0.003), meaning that the emoticon can increase German drivers' positive attitude.

5 Discussion

From the result part, we can conclude that all three styles (especially text and voice) can influence Chinese drivers' driving behavior while only emoticon can influence German drivers' driving behavior. Besides, interviews after the experiment showed that Chinese drivers like voice most and German drivers like emoticon most.

One reason is that Chinese are always described as high-context culture and think in holistic way [16]. Therefore they would focus more on the relationship between objects and emphasize the existence of change. They try to collect as much information as possible to get a better control of the surrounding and understand the context. This is consistent with their reaction for V2V system. In our experiment, Chinese participants believed that they could obtain more information to control driving situation through V2V system. And voice can transmit more information than text using tone and rhythm, which help Chinese drivers understand the motivation of the sender. As a result, Chinese drivers think the V2V system helpful and they like the voice best. On the other hand, German are always described as low content culture. They think in analytic way. In our experiment, German drivers like emoticon most because emoticon could be regarded as more direct and clear compared to voice and text. Besides, some German participants mentioned that they could control the car and their behavior by themselves so the V2V system was unnecessary and useless.

Moreover, privacy issue was also considered in this study. Some German participants mentioned that communications from the other driver violated their privacy. It was not comfortable to receive others' information in their own driving space; while other research indicated that Chinese are usually not as sensitive as western culture in privacy issue. This lead to a low acceptance of V2V system by German drivers.

Also, bias of emotion caused by different interpretation of emoticon was another reason. Both German and Chinese participants mentioned that if emoticon only showed sad face without context could be explained in either sorry or ridicule. Emoticon design issue can be discussed more in the future.

And the difference between two groups could also influenced by driving experience. In this study, German participants had more driving experience and were more skilled than Chinese participants. There were no Chinese participant had long-distance driving experience, but eight participants from Germany did. It is rational that skilled drivers do not need help while driving so that they may have lower aspiration to receive additional information and use V2V system than novel drivers.

6 Conclusions

This study made an investigation of the effect of communication styles on driving behavior in different cultures. Repeated measure ANOVA analysis was conducted to understand different effects on driving behaviors of cultures and communication styles measured by emotion and attitude. Results showed that all three styles (text, voice and emoticon) have a significant effect on Chinese drivers, but rarely have effect on German drivers. According to the interviews, we find Chinese drivers like voice most and German drivers like emoticon most. This can be explained by high/low context culture and holistic/analytic thinking. Besides, the acceptance of V2V system and privacy issues are also discussed in our study.

There are still some limitations in our study, so future research can be done with empirical studies to validate the findings in the survey or with field observation to acquire real data to study the effect of communications on driver behaviors.

Acknowledgements. This study was funded by a Natural Science Foundation China grant 71188001 and State Key Lab Automobile Safety and Energy.

References

1. Ajzen, I.: The theory of planned behavior. Organ. Behav. Hum. Decis. Process. **50**(2), 179–211 (1991)
2. Warner, H.W.: Drivers' decision to speed: a study inspired by the theory of planned behavior. Transp. Res. Part F: Traffic Psychol. Behav. **9**(6), 427–433 (2006)
3. Chan, D.C., Wu, A.M., Hung, E.P.: Invulnerability and the intention to drink and drive: an application of the theory of planned behavior. Accid. Anal. Prev. **42**(6), 1549–1555 (2010)
4. Hu, T.-Y., Xie, X., Li, J. : Negative or positive? The effect of emotion and mood on risky driving. (E. Ltd., Hrsg.). Transp. Res. Part F **16**, S.29–S.40 (2012)

5. Jeon, M., Walker, B.N., Yim, J.B.: Effects of specific emotions on subjective judgment, driving performance, and perceived workload. Transp. Res. Part F: Traffic psychol. Behav. **24**, 197–209 (2014)
6. Ernst Roidl, B.F., Frehse, B., Höger, R.: Emotional states of drivers and the impact on speed, acceleration and traffic violations—a simulator study. (E. Ltd., Hrsg.). Accid. Anal. Prev. **70**, 282–292 (2014)
7. Lu, J., Xie, X., Zhang, R.: Focusing on appraisals: how and why anger and fear influence driving risk perception. J. Saf. Res. **45**, 65–73 (2013)
8. Peng, Y., Boyle, L.N., Lee, J.D.: Reading, typing, and driving: how interactions with in-vehicle systems degrade driving performance. Transp. Res. Part F: Traffic Psychol. Behav. **27**, 182–191 (2014)
9. Chan, M., Singhal, A.: Emotion matters: implications for distracted driving. Saf. Sci. **72**, 302–309 (2014)
10. Tricka, L.M., Brandigampola, S., Enns, J.T.: How fleeting emotions affect hazard perception and steering while driving: the impact of image arousal and valence. (E. Ltd., Hrsg.). Accid. Anal. Prev. **45**, 222–229 (2011)
11. Pêcher, C., Lemercier, C., Cellier, J.-M.: Emotions drive attention: effects on driver's behaviour. Saf. Sci. **47**, 1254–1259 (2009)
12. Stasi, L.D., Contreras, D., Cañas, J., Cándido, A., Maldonado, A., Catena, A.: The consequences of unexpected emotional sounds on driving behaviour. Saf. Sci. **48**, 1463–1468 (2010)
13. Yi, J.S., Park, S.: Cross-cultural differences in decision-making styles: a study of college students in five countries. Soc. Behav. Pers.: Int. J. **31**(1), 35–47 (2003)
14. Sivak, M., Soler, J., Tränkle, U.: Cross-cultural differences in driver self-assessment. Accid. Anal. Prev. **21**(4), 371–375 (1989)
15. Liu, R.-z., Zhou, R.-l., Oeh, M.: Driving angry behavior of drivers in Mainland China and Germany. Chinese J. Ergon. **19**(1), 10–15 (2013)
16. Nesbit, S.M., Conger, J.C.: Evaluation of cognitive responses to anger-provoking driving situations using the articulated thoughts during simulated situations procedure. Transp. Res. Part F **14**, 54–65 (2011)

Investigation of a Driver-to-Driver Communication Method Through Rear Window Display for Chinese

Na Liu[1(✉)], Ruifeng Yu[1], Deyu Wang[1], and Yunhong Zhang[2]

[1] Department of Industrial Engineering, Tsinghua University, Beijing, China
{n-liu14, wangdy11}@mails.tsinghua.edu.cn,
yurf@mail.tsinghua.edu.cn
[2] China National Institute of Standardization, Beijing, China
zhangyh@cnis.gov.cn

Abstract. There exists major information asymmetry of traditional driver-to-driver communication method that may result in misunderstandings among drivers. In this study, a driver-to-driver communication method through rear window display was designed and evaluated. Drivers can express their feelings when they drive or explain their intentions before performing specific actions. Their feelings or intentions were presented by text signs or emoticon signs on the rear window. The study investigated the effect of driver-to-driver communication on people's perception and preference for two information presentation types. The experiment used three typical driving scenarios, i.e. normal driving, cutting in line and overtaking. The results indicated that information communication had a significant effect on people's perception. Their preference for the information presentation types depended on driving scenarios. Suggestions about the design of information display through rear window were provided to increase the communication effectiveness among drivers and thus improve driving safety.

Keywords: Information display · Emoticon · Text · Driver-to-driver communication

1 Introduction

Daily vehicle driving is a common activity in modern society. The number of private vehicles was about 88.39 million and the number of drivers was about 0.25 billion in China until 2012 [1]. More frequent driving increased the opportunities for driver interaction.

In road transportation, communication can be seen as the interaction between the drivers, the vehicles and the environment (road, signage, signals and other road users) [2]. As car drivers are sitting behind the wheel, the traditional driver-to-driver communication is realized through a limited set of channels, including signals, lights, horn, and behavior. It can be direct using hand and electronic signals, or indirect, like the

P.L.P. Rau (Ed.): CCD 2015, Part II, LNCS 9181, pp. 129–139, 2015.
DOI: 10.1007/978-3-319-20934-0_13

sound of squealing of tires, change in vehicle trajectory etc. Both direct and indirect communication methods use visual and auditory channels, with visual providing the majority of information [3]. Interactions through these channels are not as effective as common communication ways in daily life, such as speech, facial expression, gestures, etc. It is difficult for drivers to clearly understand what the intentions of the other drivers are [4]. If a driver is not aware of other road users' real intentions, it can lead to misunderstandings, which can potentially cause stress and extreme emotional responses [4]. Research related to driver-to-driver communication device suggests that the driver-to-driver communication plays a very important role in ensuring safety in road transportation [2]. It was found that drivers would be willing to use a hypothetical device to send messages to other drivers [5].

During the tasks of driving, drivers perceive other traffic participants and the environment mainly through visual channels. Visual display mounted on vehicles is a compatible way of information presentation while driving. Observers would instantly understand the source of the information. A series of patents related to digital message display for vehicles have been claimed. The digital message display for vehicles is a device to be mounted on the rear window of an automobile, capable of displaying a number of pre-defined messages [6]. U.S. Pat. No. 5500638, issued on Mar. 19, 1996 to I. George, disclosed a vehicular goodwill message system that was intended to issue a message on command from the operator of a vehicle. The system allows for the display of four pre-defined messages including courtesies such as "SORRY" or "THANK YOU!", and distress messages such as "PLEASE HELP" or "PLEASE CALL 911", which may be signaled to a trailing driver. U.S. Pat. No. 5,905,434, issued on May 18, 1999 to P. Steffan, showed a vehicle communication device that was another example of a message display that allows the driver of a vehicle to select from a number of preset and pre-programmed messages to be presented on a display device mounted on the exterior of the vehicle. We are concerning about whether presenting information through rear window display is a proper way for driver-to-driver communication.

Information presented by displays can be categorized as dynamic and static. Dynamic information continually changes, such as traffic lights, and temperature gauges. Static information remains fixed over time, such as printed alphanumeric data, graphs and labels [7]. Typical display types include verbal signs, symbolic signs and so forth [7]. Previous studies compared the effectiveness of some information presentation types [8–10]. The utilization of various information presentation types depends on specific scenarios. It needs to investigate people's preference for information presentation types for driver-to-driver communication through rear window display.

The purposes of the study are to investigate the effect of driver-to-driver communication on people's perception and to evaluate people's preference for two kinds of information presentation types, text and emoticon, for rear window display on three driving scenarios. The study is expected to provide design suggestions for the information presentation types on the rear window when drivers communicate with other drivers.

2   Method

2.1   Participants

Twenty participants (10 male and 10 female, mean age = 32.2, standard deviation of age = 4.5) were recruited to participate in the experiment. They were licensed drivers and had driving experiences for more than three years. All participants had normal or corrected normal visual acuities and healthy physical conditions.

2.2   Design and Variables

The study identified three scenarios, i.e. normal driving, cutting in line and overtaking. In cutting in line and overtaking scenarios, driver-to-driver communication was vital for eliminating misunderstandings. The driver of the front car performed a seemingly aggressive driving maneuver which might cause anger on the driver of the following car. However, the driver of the front car did not intend to cause any harm to others. In such cases, it was expected that an additional channel of communication was provided so that the driver of the front car could effectively inform the driver of the following car about the intentions of his or her behavior. The scenarios were reviewed by experienced drivers so that they were representative. In all scenarios, there were two vehicles, denoted by vehicle A (observer vehicle) and vehicle B, each having a driver, driver A and driver B, respectively.

In normal driving scenario, driver A approached driver B from behind and seeing the rear window display which indicated the feeling of driver B. The first independent variable was information content, and it had two levels, positive information and negative information. The second variable was information presentation types, and it also had two levels, emoticon and text. The dependent variables were participants' perception of these four settings (2 information content × 2 information presentation types) and their preference for presentation types.

In cutting in line scenario, driver A was waiting in line to go through an intersection. Driver B overtook from an adjacent lane and cut in the line in front of driver A. Driver B would like to let driver A know his situation and to express his gratitude. In this scenario, information communication existed or not. When there was information displayed, it either presented by text or by emoticon. The information presented the driver's motivation and explanation of his behavior. The dependent variables were participants' perception and preference.

In overtaking scenario, driver A ran normally on urban expressway. Driver B changed the lane and went in front of vehicle A with very close distance. Driver B wanted to express his apology to driver A. In this scenario, the information communication existed or not. It only used text displaying driver A's explanation. Participants were required to give their perception and cognition after seeing the information presentation.

During the experiment, participants were set as drivers in vehicle A who saw the driving behavior of vehicle B and received the information displayed on the rear window in vehicle B. Participants reported their perception to the behavior and preference for the display by filling in a questionnaire. The test settings in each scenario were as follows,

- In normal driving, the information content was the feelings of drivers in the front. When the feeling was positive, text "I am happy (presented in Chinese)" or emoticon " ☺" was shown. When the feeling was negative, text "I am upset (presented in Chinese)" or emoticon " ☹" was shown (Fig. 1).
- In cutting in line scenario, information was either displayed or not. When communication existed, the information was either text "Sorry, in a hurry (presented in Chinese)" or emoticon " ☺" (Fig. 2).
- In overtaking, information was either displayed or not. When communication existed, the display used text type, "Sorry, in a hurry (presented in Chinese)" (Fig. 3).

Fig. 1. Information display in normal driving scenario. Happy emoticon; Upset emoticon; "I'm happy" (presented in Chinese); d. "I'm upset" (presented in Chinese).

Fig. 2. Information display in cutting in line scenario. Happy emoticon; "Sorry, in a hurry (presented in Chinese).

Fig. 3. Information display in overtaking scenario. "Sorry, in a hurry" (presented in Chinese)

2.3   Measurements

Participants reported their perception and evaluations by filling in a questionnaire. All the questions in the questionnaire were measured by a five-point Likert scale from strongly disagreement to strongly agreement (1 = "strongly disagreement" and 5 = "strongly agreement"). The questionnaire composed of two parts, the perception part, measuring participants' feelings of the information communication, and the evaluation part, measuring participants' preference for the information presentation types.

In normal driving scenario, participants' perception of the information communication was measured in five dimensions: the extent of being eased or worried on following the vehicle, being pleased or upset with the display, being annoyed by the display, and the extent to which it is interesting to me and it is silly to me. The ergonomics features of the display, concerning clearness, distraction degree, and willingness to use were measured as well. When the content was positive, participants were asked to give their ratings on the item "at ease and pleased by the information communication". When the content was negative, participants needed to rate the worrying and upsetting level.

Participants' perception about the behavior of cutting in line and overtaking was measured in three main dimensions: the extent of being annoyed by the cutting in line behavior or overtaking behavior; the extent in which I think the driver was malicious and I think the driver may have a reason. Participants' willingness to use the information communication display was measured as well.

2.4   Apparatus

The experiment was conducted in a full-cabin Daewoo Nubira driving simulator. It was installed in the laboratory in the Institute of Human Factors and Ergonomics in Tsinghua University. The experiment scenarios were presented to the participants through video clips and projected to a curved screen in front of the car cabin. The car cabin simulated the real in-vehicle driving environment. Participants were seated in the car cabin and watched the scenarios on the screen.

The videos were recorded beforehand on the real road. A digital camera mounted on an observer vehicle (vehicle A) recorded the scenes where another vehicle (vehicle B) performed the actions and displayed information on the rear window just as the design of the experiment scenarios. A tablet (iPad, "9.7", with a pixel resolution of 2048 × 1536) fixed on the back of the headrest of rear right seat on the vehicle B was used as the display media. In the lab experiment, participants received the information through videos and their vision angle was the same as the observer vehicle.

2.5   Procedures

After arriving at the laboratory, participants signed the informed consent and completed a general survey about their demographic information. The participants were asked to sit into the simulator to get ready for the test. Then the participants were asked to watch a five-minute video clip of general driving to get familiar with the system and get immersed in the virtual driving environment. After that, the videos of three experiment scenarios were played for the participants. In each video clip, about two minutes in the beginning was for warm-up. The video lasted 15 min in each scenario. When information communication existed, information was displayed three times in each presentation setting. After seeing each video clip, they filled in the questionnaire to give their perception of the information communication method and their preference for the information presentation types. Each participant spent about one hour finishing the experiment.

3 Results

3.1 Normal Driving

160 ordinal scale data (20 participants × 8 questions) was collected. The one-sample Wilcoxon sign rank test was used to measure the effect of positive and negative information display on drivers' perception. Results indicated that positive emoticon information display had significant effect on participants' feelings (Table 1). Participants tended to feel pleased, eased, less annoyed with the information display and thought that the communication was interesting and not silly (p's $< .05$). After seeing the positive text display on the rear window, participants felt eased following the vehicle, felt pleased, less annoyed with the information communication and thought it interesting significantly (p's $< .01$) (Table 2). The negative information display (both text and emoticon) had significant effect on drivers' feelings (Tables 3 and 4). When the participants saw the negative display mounted on the front car, they felt worried about the information content (p's $< .05$).

Nonparametric Mann-Whitney test was conducted to compare the effect of the two types of information presentation on participants' preference from three aspects, clearness, distraction degree and intention to use the device. The results showed that participants preferred the emoticon display because it showed information more clearly than text display ($p < .05$) (Table 5).

Table 1. Results of positive emoticon display in normal driving scenario

Item	Estimation of a median	Wilcoxon statistics	p value
At ease on following the vehicle	4.00	100.5	0.023
Pleased with the display	4.00	136.0	<.001
Annoyed by the display	1.50	<0.1	<.001
It is interesting to me	4.00	122.0	0.033
It is silly	2.50	13.0	0.025

Table 2. Results of positive text display in normal driving scenario

Item	Estimation of a median	Wilcoxon statistics	p value
At ease on following it	4.00	121.0	0.007
Pleased with the display	4.00	99.0	0.004
Annoyed by the display	2.00	4.0	0.004
It is interesting to me	3.50	98.5	0.004
It is silly	2.50	35.0	0.164

Table 3. Results of negative emoticon display in normal driving scenario

Item	Estimation of a median	Wilcoxon statistics	p value
Worried on following it	4.00	91.0	0.002
Upset with the display	3.50	57.0	0.170
Annoyed by the display	3.00	50.0	0.410
It is interesting to me	2.50	25.0	0.090
It is silly	3.00	29.0	0.756

Table 4. Results of negative text display in normal driving scenario

Item	Estimation of a median	Wilcoxon statistics	p value
Worried on following it	4.00	120.0	0.001
Upset with the display	3.00	30.0	0.407
Annoyed by the display	3.50	74.0	0.187
It is interesting to me	3.00	57.0	0.887
It is silly	3.00	44.5	0.972

Table 5. Comparison of two display methods

Item	Estimation of a median difference	p value
I could see it clearly	1.00	0.017
It is distractive for me	−0.50	0.285
I am willing to use this device	0.50	0.579

3.2 Cutting in Line

Participants' perception about the behavior of cutting in line was measured by three items, "I felt annoyed by this behavior", "The driver may have a reason" and "The driver is malicious". 120 ordinal scale data (20 participants × 6 questions) was collected. Nonparametric Mann-Whitney test was used to measure the effect of information communication on participants' perception (Table 6). The results showed that text display made participants significantly believe that the drivers cutting in line had some reasons for doing that ($p < .05$) and they were not malicious ($p < .05$), and participant felt less annoyed after seeing the text display than without information communication significantly ($p < .01$). On the other hand, the emoticon display did not show significant influence on participants' feelings (p's $> .05$) (Table 7).

Three items with respect to clearness, distraction degree and willingness to use were utilized to measure participants' preference for two display types. Nonparametric Mann-Whitney test results showed that participants were more willing to use text display than emoticon display significantly ($p < .01$). It did not show significant difference on clearness, distraction degree between two information presentation types (p's $> .05$).

Table 6. With text display and without information display comparison

Item	Estimation of a median difference	p value
Annoyed by cutting in line behavior	1.00	<.001
The driver may have a reason	−1.00	0.031
The driver is malicious	1.00	0.034

Table 7. With emoticon display and without information display comparison

Item	Estimation of a median difference	p value
Annoyed by cutting in line behavior	0.00	0.152
The driver may have a reason	0.00	0.190
The driver is malicious	0.00	0.190

3.3   Overtaking

80 ordinal scale data (20 participants × 4 questions) was collected. Nonparametric Mann-Whitney test was used to compare the ratings of the two settings, i.e. with information displayed by text and without information displayed (Table 8). Although people still thought that the behavior was dangerous (no significant difference between the two groups, $p > .05$), and they felt less annoyed ($p < .05$) and were more inclined to think the driver had reasons for this behavior ($p < .01$). Nearly half of the participants reported the text in the display could not be seen clearly and distracted their attention. Despite this legibility problem, more than half of them had the intention to use this display.

Table 8. Comparison of text display and without information display

Item	Estimation of a median difference	p value
It is dangerous	0.00	0.989
Annoyed by this behavior	1.00	0.022
The driver may have a reason	−1.00	0.002
The driver is malicious	1.00	0.120

4 Discussion

A typical scenario that may induce anger on drivers is traffic jam accompanied by unlawful or immoral driving behaviors. As the driver drives through an intersection, driver A lined up along with the traffic. Driver B overtook through an adjacent lane and drove up in front of driver A. Such a cutting-in-line behavior may easily arouse the anger on driver A. In the given context, misunderstandings between drivers would induce or exacerbate road rage. It has been proven that road rage is a causal factor to traffic accidents [11]. Aggressive driving is a common cause for road rage in drivers [12]. As a driver is impatient or in emergency, he may perform driving actions that cause physical or mental harm to others. In some cases, drivers only wish to bring some benefits to themselves, without any intention to produce any harm to others. Such actions are still perceived as aggressive by other drivers and arouse discomfort and anger on them. In this situation, it is necessary to provide an additional channel to enhance driver-to-driver communication and therefore to promote driving safety and efficiency. It was found that participants' perception was influenced significantly by the information display on the rear window of other drivers. People's stress relived after seeing the information display. The information communication through rear window between drivers would reduce extreme stress and improve traffic safety to some extent.

The study tested participants' preference for two typical information presentation types, verbal signs (text) and symbolic signs (emoticon). It was found that people's preference depended on driving scenarios. In normal driving scenario, driver A saw the status information of drivers in the front vehicle and did not need to fully comprehend the meanings of the information. Symbolic signs would deliver the information effectively and efficiently. Previous studies have indicated that signs with symbolic messages can be understood more quickly than those with verbal messages. Visually degrading the signs resulted in a greater decrement in performance for verbal than for symbolic signs [13]. Text, icon and modified icon have been compared in higher-velocity condition. It was found that the two iconic versions were superior to the text version [14]. Icon signs were visible at much greater distances than were text signs for people of different age [15]. In this study, participants preferred to use emoticon in normal driving scenario because they considered that emoticon showed information more clearly than text.

The main purpose of the information communication in cutting in line and over-taking scenarios was to explain to the driver of the following car about the behavior performed by the front car. In this situation, the information and messages should be clear to see and quick to comprehend. In addition, the information should help explain the intentions of performing such behavior. Symbolic signs were assumed to be improper as it could not present the reasons for taking such actions. In the experiment, we presented "Sorry, in a hurry (presented in Chinese)" on the experiment display. The results indicated that emoticon signs were not proper. Participants were more willing to use text type than emoticon type in cutting in line scenario.

Visual workload affects driving performance in various ways [16]. It may reduce the speed and increase lane keeping variation. When visual attention is diverted from the road, the driver cannot give any tracking response, which results in periods with fixed steering wheel angle. In normal driving scenario, as both vehicles are travelling at high speed, visual workload of the driver behind is relatively high. It is required that the information in the scenario is simple and highly readable. Emoticon presentation type is recommended in this situation. In cutting in line scenario, as the both vehicles are nearly stationary, the visual workload of the driver behind is relatively low, more detailed information can be displayed. Thus, text presentation type is a proper design in this situation.

5   Conclusion

The study investigated the effect of driver-to-driver information communication on people's perception. It compared the two information presentation types, text type and emoticon type, to figure out which was better in information communication on rear window display. A driver-to-driver communication interface was designed and an experiment was conducted to fulfill the study goals. The experiment used three typical driving scenarios, normal driving, cutting in line and overtaking. The results indicated the information display through rear window had significant effect on people's perception. It was necessary to provide additional channel for information communication among drivers. People were willing to receive information of other drivers through rear window and their stress relieved when information communication existed. The design of information presentation should take driving scenarios into consideration. In normal driving, emoticon type was better than text type because emoticon was easy and quick to comprehend. In cutting in line scenario, text type could deliver more detailed information and explain drivers' intentions, which was better than emoticon type. Information communication through rear window could increase the communication effectiveness among drivers and thus improve driving safety.

Acknowledgement. The authors would like to acknowledge the support from the Natural Science Foundation of China (71071085), Natural Science Foundation of China (71471098), National Key Technology R&D Program of the Ministry of Science and Technology (2014BAK01B03) and China National Institute of Standardization through the "special funds for the basic R&D undertakings by welfare research institutions" (552013Y-3078).

References

1. National Bureau of Statistics of China. http://www.stats.gov.cn/tjsj/ndsj/2013/indexeh.htm
2. Pillai, S.S., Ray, G.G.: Ergonomics intervention in automobile driver communication in a developing country. In: The 2014 European Conference on Cognitive Ergonomics, p. 8. ACM (2014)
3. Macadam, C.C.: Understanding and modeling the human driver. Veh. Syst. Dyn. **40**, 101–134 (2003)
4. Renner, L., Johansson, B.: Driver coordination in complex traffic environments. In: The 13th Eurpoean Conference on Cognitive Ergonomics: Trust and Control in Complex Socio-Technical Systems, pp. 35–40. ACM (2006)

5. Lamas, R., Burnett, G., Cobb, S., Harvey, C.: Driver link-up: exploring user requirements for a driver-to-driver communication device. In: The 6th International Conference on Automotive User Interfaces and Interactive Vehicular Applications, pp. 1–5. ACM (2014)
6. Somuah, E.: Digital message display for vehicles: Google patents (2004)
7. Sanders, M.S., McCormick, E.J.: Human Factors in Engineering and Design. McGraw-Hill, New York (1987)
8. Benbasat, I., Dexter, A.S.: An investigation of the effectiveness of color and graphical information presentation under varying time constraints. MIS Q. **10**, 59–83 (1986)
9. Speier, C., Vessey, I., Valacich, J.S.: The effects of interruptions, task complexity, and information presentation on computer-supported decision-making performance. Decis. Sci. **34**, 771–797 (2003)
10. Tractinsky, N., Meyer, J.: Chartjunk or goldgraph? Effects of presentation objectives and content desirability on information presentation. MIS Q. **23**, 397–420 (1999)
11. Galovski, T.E., Malta, L.S., Blanchard, E.B.: Road Rage: Assessment and Treatment of the Angry, Aggressive Driver. American Psychological Association, Washington, DC (2006)
12. Dukes, R.L., Clayton, S.L., Jenkins, L.T., Miller, T.L., Rodgers, S.E.: Effects of aggressive driving and driver characteristics on road rage. Soc. Sci. J. **38**, 323–331 (2001)
13. Ells, J.G., Dewar, R.E.: Rapid comprehension of verbal and symbolic traffic sign messages. Hum. Factors J. Hum. Factors Ergon. Soc. **21**, 161–168 (1979)
14. Long, G.M., Kearns, D.F.: Visibility of text and icon highway signs under dynamic viewing conditions. Hum. Factors J. Hum. Factors Ergon. Soc. **38**, 690–701 (1996)
15. Kline, T.J.B., Ghali, L.M., Kline, D.W., Brown, S.: Visibility distance of highway signs among young, middle-aged, and older observers: icons are better than text. Hum. Factors J. Hum. Factors Ergon. Soc. **32**, 609–619 (1990)
16. Lansdown, T.C.: Causes, measures and effects of driver visual workload. In: Hancock, P.A., Desmond, P.A. (eds.) Stress, Workload and Fatigue, pp. 351–369. Erlbaum, Mahwah (2001)

On the Qualitative Research Approach and Application of the "VTIO" Model Based on Cultural Differences

A Case Study of Changan Ford Mazda Automobile Co., Ltd

Lei Liu[1](✉) and Lin Ma[2]

[1] School of Economics and Management, Tsinghua University,
Beijing, People's Republic of China
liul3.ll@sem.tsinghua.edu.cn
[2] Beihang University, Beijing, People's Republic of China
malin2014@buaa.edu.cn

Abstract. In the context of globalization, cultural differences resulted from diverse cultural backgrounds have formed a main influential factor in the development of joint ventures. Using a qualitative research approach, this paper first establishes the "VTIO" model, which serves as a model for analyzing cultural differences. Production mode is set to the center of the "VTIO" model. The core of culture is concluded as "sentiment, ethics and law". V (value), T (thinking mode), I (interpersonal relationship) and O (organizational behavior) are considered as representations of culture. Based on the "VTIO" model, the paper comprehensively studies the typical examples of cultural differences among China, the US and Japan from the abovementioned four aspects of cultural representations. Furthermore, a case study of Changan Ford Mazda Automobile Co., Ltd is presented in this paper with an analysis of the representations of its corporate culture. Finally, this paper proposes some relevant coping strategies regarding cross-cultural management, providing some suggestions for cross-cultural management in Sino-foreign equity joint ventures.

Keywords: Qualitative research · Cultural differences · VTIO · Case study

1 Introduction

In recent years, accompanied by the rapid development of Chinese economy, the business form of joint ventures has existed for quite a long period of time. However, the success rate of joint ventures so far is still low. According to the results of international investigations and researches, 30 %−40 % of international joint ventures are not successful. According to previous studies, 15 % of Sino-foreign equity joint ventures in China (including transnational companies) terminated before the end of its expected life expectancy. 70 % of corporate cooperations are not harmonious (Tian, 2012). Studies on cross-cultural management have long been a hot topic in the academic field.

© Springer International Publishing Switzerland 2015
P.L.P. Rau (Ed.): CCD 2015, Part II, LNCS 9181, pp. 140–149, 2015.
DOI: 10.1007/978-3-319-20934-0_14

Some related theories proposed by foreign scholars are cultural dimensions by Hofstede (1984), six value orientations by Kluckhohn & Strodtbeck (1961) stages of conflicts by Pondy (1967) Thomas (1992) and Robbins (1994), and the "inverted U" relationship between conflict and organizational effectiveness by Brown (1983). These theories cover the extraction of index factors, the analysis of different stages of cultural harmony and conflicts, and the analysis of conflict levels and organizational effectiveness, providing significant theoretical references to cross-cultural studies. However, the influence of cultural factors is closely linked to specific environments. Especially in recent years, cross-cultural studies focus more on combining theories with a certain aspect of practice, such as the application of cross-cultural theories in marketing (Luo et al., 2014;Mower et al., 2013), share of knowledge between organizations (Hau et al., 2013;Qiu et al., 2013;Wei et al., 2010). So it is not proper just to simply transplant the index factors of cross-cultural theories into practices. There is still a lot to be studied in combining theories with practices (Craig & Douglas, 2011).

The development of cross-cultural management in China started relatively late. Yu and Jia (1997) proposed the CMC model which is a management model coping with the internal cross-cultural conflicts of joint ventures. Zhang and Wang (2002) analyzed and studied the cross-cultural conflicts caused by the managers with overseas assignments. Qiu (2003) put forward the influence of cross-cultural conflicts on joint venture management, the specific representations, causes and resolutions. Chen et al.(2005) concluded some influential factors on cross-cultural management in Sino-foreign joint ventures supported by some practical cases of Sino-foreign cross-cultural management. Wang and Wang (2010) discussed cultural management from the two dimensions of the static operation mode-cultivation of corporate culture and the dynamic operation mode-accumulation of corporate culture. Additionally, Lv (2007), Xie et al.(2012) studied the topic from the perspective of cross-cultural communication.

Although the studies in the field of cross-cultural management have existed for a while, the research results abroad are mainly based on the western cultural contexts, which are profoundly different from the Chinese culture and Asian culture and therefore cannot be applied to the Chinese context directly (Wei et al., 2010). Domestic studies focus more on the coalition and merging of different cultures and haven't touched upon the strategies of cross-cultural management from the perspective of the essence of cultural differences.

This paper seeks to study the differences of cultural features among China, the US and Japan from a comprehensive and thorough perspective. It also looks into the case of Changan Ford Mazda Automobile Co., Ltd. (CFMA), which is a typical case of influenced by a myriad of cultures of the three countries. The paper analyzes the corporate culture of CFMA from three dimensions, which are the production mode extended from the corporate culture, organization and effectiveness. From the cultural dimension, there are many cultural elements from the US and Japan in the cross-cultural companies in China. Therefore it is of critical strategic significance to distinguish the differences and avoid conflicts. From the dimensions of organization and effectiveness, there are more and more organizations involving Chinese, American and Japanese cultural elements. The cross-cultural management strategies, which are applicable for enterprises, also suit other organizations. From the perspective of the enterprise, this paper is of great referential values for the joint ventures, such as CFMA, to learn how to prevent management conflicts and integrate the diverse cultural resources.

2 Methods

This paper adopts the qualitative research method. By searching for the keywords of "cross-cultural", "cultural difference", "Chinese culture", "American culture" and "Japanese culture" using the search engines of Google (in Chinese, Japanese and English) and Baidu, the study collected 8,019 results which were later categorized into three types: articles, blog posts and BBS comments. After classification, the blog posts were divided into eight main categories including values, organizational behavior, attitudes towards gender and nationality, thinking mode, rationality and sensibility, behavior mode, interpersonal relationship, labor and payment policies. Each category can be further subdivided into secondary subcategories which amount to 34 in total. Therefore, the search and analysis of second-hand information generated 8 primary categories and 34 secondary subcategories.

The paper also uses the Delphi method to further study and discuss the in-formation extracted from the second-hand materials. The colleagues who were invited to attend the Delphi method came from different academic backgrounds including one from demography, two from sociology, 2 from economics, 4 from business management, 1 from system science, 1 from management engineering and 2 from education. Some of the colleagues had the working experiences in governmental departments, state-owned enterprises and transnational companies. The study consists of three rounds of con-sultation on the 8 primary categories and 34 secondary subcategories. And the partic-ipants are allowed to add new contents. After every round of consultation, the replies are gathered and sorted and the most acknowledged categories rated by the participants are extracted. The extracted elements are classified and will be further discussed in the next round of consultation, especially those newly proposed ones. By using this method, the two primary categories, which were attitudes towards gen-der/nationality and labor/payment policies including 5 secondary subcategories attached, were excluded after the first round of consultation. After the second round, rationality/sensibility and behavior mode were deleted. The subcategories attached to them were either deleted or merged into other categories. After the third round of consultation, four primary cate-gories were kept including values, thinking mode, organizational behavior and inter-personal relationship, with the 25 secondary subcategories attached to them.

3 Analysis and Discussion

3.1 The "VTIO" Model

Based on previous studies and achievements, this paper further studies the phenomenon of cultural differences and concludes the "VTIO" model. The basic principles are as follows. Cultural differences are reflected mainly in value, thinking mode, interpersonal relationship and organizational behavior. The decisively influential factors of cultural differences are "sentiment, ethics and law". Further explained on the physical and psychological levels, the influential factor of "sentiment, ethics and law" is the production mode, which will finally influence the organizational effectiveness (productivity).

According to Karl Marx' theory of political economy, the economic basis decides the superstructure. "To study the connections between spiritual production and material production, one must investigate certain type of material production from a historical point of view. If material production is not judged in its specific historical form, then it is impossible to understand the feature of the correspondent spiritual production and their mutual effects". Therefore the production mode determines "sentiment, ethics and law", which in turn influence the production mode to some extent.

"Sentiment, ethics and law" are the core and essence of culture. All kinds of management involve the management of "sentiment, ethics and law", ranging from managing the countries, societies, to enterprises and organizations. Here, the concept of "sentiment, ethics and law" is in the broad sense. Sentiment means relationship, which covers the extensive relationships including kinship, friendship, the relationships with colleagues, compatriots and the relationship between the old and the young. Ethics here means the "universal ethics", what "everybody feels the same about" as in a Chinese idiom. Ethics here are also associated with "manners", which are the rules people follow in everyday life. Law, in the broad sense, covers national laws, regulations and the rules and policies within an organization. Even social customs can be seen as one form of law. Therefore, sentiment is a soft culture, which is flexible to be manipulated by individuals to different extents. Law is a hard culture, serving as a strict and fixed measurement. Once published, the law becomes the "golden rule" which people are required to follow. Any behaviors violating the law will be punished accordingly. While ethics serve as a mediator between sentiment and law, balancing the soft culture and the hard culture. The core of culture is the integration of "sentiment, ethics and law". Because of different preferences for "sentiment, ethics and law" in diverse cultures, the cultural differences among different countries arise. Accordingly, the external representations of culture are the four aspects of values, thinking mode, interpersonal relationship and organizational behavior. The differences in these four aspects formed diverse cultural phenomena in different countries. Therefore, production mode, as the economic basis, decides the preferences for "sentiment, ethics and law". "Sentiment, ethics and law" influence and decide values, thinking mode, interpersonal relationship and organizational behavior. Meanwhile, values, thinking mode, interpersonal relationship and organizational behavior have mutual impact on each other following the sequence of the order.

Looking at the cultural differences of China, the US and Japan in coping with "sentiment, ethics and law", it can be concluded as follows. Chinese culture is typically represented by Confucian culture while also influenced by Taoism in terms of social system. Confucianism and Taoism advocate different principles. Confucian theories pursue the "Doctrine of the Mean (centeredness)" while the Taoists follow the theory of "non-action". Simply put, Confucianism resorts to the rituals in cultural traditions while Taoism resorts to the principle of the earth. So Confucianism is a positive theoretical system (so-called "Yang)" and Taoism is negative (so-called "Yin"). The yin-yang combination of Confucianism and Taoism constructed the distinctive feature of Chinese culture, which emphasizes groups, morality and practical uses. American culture is a low-context culture, which originates from the ancient Greek culture and the Jewish Christianism. It is a social culture of commercialism and citizenship based on common people as its main body. Therefore the core of American culture is individualism and rationalism, focusing on individuals, science, critical thinking and law. American culture determines the mode of American enterprises to be internationally structured, which is also known as the bipolar mode. Japanese culture is high-context, which is profoundly influenced by Chinese culture and is also based on the ethics of Confucianism. Therefore the Japanese culture highlights teams, ethics and laws, making it an internationally constructed mode with the centralized power in Tokyo.

Judging from the representations, on the level of the value, traditional Chinese culture values spiritual beings more than materials. Although there is no deeply rooted religious tradition, Chinese people adhere to traditional moral values. While American culture values materials more than spirits, with very strong religious beliefs. Japanese culture values materials as much as spirits, but values more about the collective interest.

In terms of thinking mode, China is a society of totally "imagery thinking". The individual image outweighs rational analysis. The thinking mode is non-quantitative and non-systematic, focusing on team spirits while maintaining a certain level of individual awareness. The US is a society of "quantitative thinking", which highlights critical thinking and benefit-risk analysis with strong systematic and rational thinking ability and individualism. Japanese culture is "half-imagery", which values both personal impression and the benefit-risk analysis. It values the group, rational thinking and has a strong sense of teamwork.

Regarding interpersonal relationship, there is a traditional Chinese idiom "unnecessary and over-elaborate formalities", which reflects the importance of interpersonal relationship in the social life of Chinese people. The closest circle of interpersonal relationship for Chinese people includes relatives, compatriots, classmates, neighbors and colleagues. And these relationships are obligatory, which means that there is very limited space for individuals to choose their relationships. While in the US, relationships are not compulsory but free to choose. Their most intimate circles include relatives, friends, classmates and colleagues. Japan is likewise a country that values relationships. Their closest circle of interpersonal relationship is quite similar to the Chinese one, including relatives, compatriots, classmates and colleagues, obligatory and nearly impossible to select.

On the level of organizational behavior, Chinese people have the value of organizational dependency, which is the so-called "Iron Rice Bowl". Meanwhile, they also have individual dependency which is reflected in the arrangement system based on seniority. The leaders have the right to nominate employees for promotions. Many positions are specifically set for some individuals. The one in power has the decisive authority. In terms of competition, Chinese people follow the "Doctrine of the Mean", which results in a balanced situation without active competitions. In American culture, free competition is advocated. The employees are promoted for their talents. The decision power is diluted. In Japan, there is a very strong value of group dependency and awareness. The decisions are made by multiple leaders. Competition exists externally among different groups rather than within one group.

3.2   The Features of the Cultural Difference Among China, the US and Japan

According to the "VTIO" model, "sentiment, ethics and law" influence and determine the profound differences between different cultures, which are further reflected in values, thinking mode, interpersonal relationship and organizational behavior. The paper further studies the distinctive features of cultural differences among China, the US and Japan, as is shown in Table 1.

3.3   A Case Study of the "VTIO" Model-the Corporate Culture of Changan Ford Mazda Automobile Co., Ltd

Changan Ford Mazda Automobile Co., Ltd (hereinafter "CFMA") is a large-scale Sino-foreign joint venture established by Changan Group, a famous automobile enterprise in China, Ford Auto, a world leading automobile company and Mazda automobile company. As a joint venture founded by three parties involving China/US/Japan, the culture of CFMA is a melting pot of typical Chinese, American and Japanese cultures.

Based on the results abovementioned regarding the cultural differences of China, the US and Japan by applying the "VTIO" model, this paper further studies the corporate culture of CFMA.

1. Different values are reflected in everyday tasks. American managers in CFMA always make clear clarifications of the job contents, specific tasks and distribution of tasks. They would divide their own tasks clearly from others' tasks. But this doesn't mean that they are not ready to help each other. The American managers are willing to help. However, if you do not ask them for help, they wouldn't offer their help straightforward. This type of difference in values often leads to the misunderstanding of Chinese employees thinking that the foreign managers are indifferent and self-centered. While the foreign man-agers would in turn think the Chinese employees are inactive and less responsible. In Japanese culture, teamwork is also valued. Chinese teamwork is often based on kinship, while the Japanese teamwork is not. Japanese people value the honor of the team and are willing to do extra work for the team. While the Chinese people only value the team with the authorities and have a fragile relationship with the enterprise itself. The level of payment decides how much labor they would devote.
2. The typical representation of diverse thinking mode is evident in the issue of whether publishing the notice for the punishment of employees. Chinese managers prefer to publicize both compliment and punishment, while American managers value positive reinforcement by publicizing compliment only. They consider the revelation of punishment as a violation of privacy, which will harm the individual's self-esteem. For Chinese managers, small mistakes can be kept confidential, however, big and severe mistakes must be publicized. The punished individual will be informed in advance before the notice being put out. It is considered to be a useful warning and beneficial for the development of the individual. In Chinese enterprises, this is a very normal way of punishment. Such cultural conflict regarding

Table 1. Cultural differences of China/US/Japan

Category		Chinese culture	American culture	Japanese culture
Value	Philosophy: materialism/spiritualism	Emphasizing spiritualism: a. justice outweigh profit b. balance between justice and profits c. profit outweighs justice	Emphasizing materialism: money is everything	Balance between materialism and spiritualism
	Religious influence	Weak	Strong	Weak
	Adventurous spirit	Lack	Strong	Weak
Thinking mode	Feature	Imagery	Quantitative	Quantitative + Imagery
	Starting point	Personal impression	Benefit-risk	Benefit-risk + Personal impression
	Pattern	General and non-rational	Systematic and rational	General and rational
	Method	Non-quantitative and non-procedural	Quantitative and procedural	Procedural
	Awareness	Team + individual Team > individual	Strong individualism	Strom team spirit
	Punctuality	Weak	Strong	Strong
Interpersonal relationship	Principle	Optimum	Innovation	Optimum + Innovation
	Closest circle	Relatives, compatriots, classmates, colleagues and neighbors	Relatives, friends, classmates and colleagues	Relatives, onpatriots, colleagues classmates, and neighbors
	Nature	Obligatory, no freedom of choice	Free to choose, optional	Obligatory, less freedom of choice
Organizational behavior	Tenet	Organizational and Individual dependency	Competition, the most capable wins	Group dependency
	Structure	Power, Seniority	Equality, independence and freedom	Annual achievements + practice
	Promotion	Leader nomination	Free competition	Natural rotation
	Position setting	Position set for people	Position chooses the one who fits	Position set for a duty
	Decision	Vertical + top-down	Horizontal + vertical	Vertical + horizontal
	Competition	Doctrine of the Mean + competition to be motivated	Free competition	Internal harmony, external competition
	Management	Kinship	Contract	Corporation

whether publishing the punishment is a vivid example of the difference in values towards "individualism". Chinese culture under the influence of Confucianism sees "minimizing oneself" as the noblest state of mind, advocating obedience and self-control. American culture emphasizes the central status of "oneself" in its value system, promoting self-dependency, responsibility and self-esteem. Therefore, the American managers would consider publicizing punishments as an action harmful for the "self-esteem" of the employees, while the Chinese managers wouldn't agree.

3. In terms of interpersonal relationship, Chinese and Japanese employees rarely question their bosses face-to-face, while American employees would ex-press different opinions directly, including the questioning and doubts towards the corporate policies. Chinese employees at CFMA usually prefer to gossip be-hind people's back, rather than express their opinions directly when there is dis-agreement. But the American employees would often express their feelings more straightforward.

4. Regarding organizational behavior, the collectivism and the tendency to avoid high risks in Chinese culture urge Chinese managers at CFMA to consult other employees' ideas before making important decisions. They will attempt to maintain harmony and reduce potential factors which may induce conflicts. But in American culture, there is a typical tendency of individualism and low risk avoidance. The authority group within the enterprise, which bears similar responsibilities and honors with the Japanese groups, often makes decisions. American people tend to make decisions by individuals, who will shoulder the final responsibilities of the decisions. As is the case in CFMA, the decision-making processes on the Chinese and Japanese sides are often cautious but slow. The American managers often solve the problems right away with a very quick speed of decision and work tempo. This may result from the different structures of "responsibility, right and interest" in three cultures. Under the influence of collectivism, the "responsibility, right and interest" structures for Chinese and Japanese managers are imbalanced, which means that more responsibilities are shouldered while there are not enough material profits or authority empowerment for that. But for American managers, the "responsibility, right and interest" structure is basically equivalent and balanced.

4   Conclusions and Suggestions

Based on extensive researches, this paper creates the "VTIO" model, which is used for analyzing and studying cultural differences. The model is centered on the production mode, setting "sentiment, ethics and law" as the core of culture with four forms of representations of value, thinking mode, interpersonal relationship and organizational behavior. Therefore the analysis of cultural difference is derived from the production mode and is based on "sentiment, ethics and law", the core of culture.

This study shows that the "Doctrine of the Mean" is the center of Chinese culture. American culture values individualism the most. Teamwork is placed at the most prominent place in Japanese culture. Therefore the China/US/Japan joint ventures can examine and distinguish the conflicts or ineffective management in their enterprises accordingly which may be caused by cultural differences so as to avoid cultural conflicts and facilitate the integration of different cultures. Based on this finding, it is necessary to combine the valuable essence of traditional Chinese culture with the advanced management philosophy and ideas in the western world, which can keep the advantages of western management and make it suitable for the status quo of China as well. This will definitely be the ideal method to promote cross-cultural integration in China/US/Japan joint ventures. Accordingly, this paper proposes the following solutions.

1. Extract and integrate the advantages of different cultures, creating a universal cultural system suitable for the development of enterprises.

The core of corporate cultural construction is recognition and sharing. If a culture is not recognized by its recipients, then it is valueless. And the key of recognition is participation and sharing. Therefore companies should ab-sorb/construct new cultural systems suitable for joint ventures under the premises of recognition and participation.

2. Strengthen cultural understanding, improving the training of new cultural systems

American and Japanese sides, it is highly recommended for different parties in joint ventures to understand each other's culture, which can be effectively be realized by new cultural training. The training may include: a. an introduction to the essence of Chinese culture and the corporate culture of the original company; b. trainings on cultural communication skills; c. trainings on the coping strategies of cultural conflicts.

3. Upgrade the management level, building a cross-cultural team

In the context of globalization, it is critical to use modern cooperation spirit and open-minded and integrated attitudes to shape and modernize the traditional concept of collectivism. Therefore in the cross-cultural integration process of joint ventures, the companies should emphasize modern and trans-original cultural management philosophy and management ideas. It is important to deeply understand the cultural differences of different countries using both imagery thinking and quantitative thinking, to create a cross-cultural leadership with great strengths and the effective demonstration effect of individuals.

References

Brown, L.D.: Managing Conflict at Organizational Interfaces. Ad-dison-Wesley, Reading, MA (1983)

Chen, X., Li, B., Shen, J.: The cross-culture management model of shanghai automobile industry based on common interest. Soft Sci. **4**, 56–58 (2005). (in Chinese)

Craig, C.S., Douglas, S.P.: Assessing cross-cultural marketing theory and research: a commentary essay. J. Bus. Res. **6**, 625–627 (2011)

Hau, Y.S., Kim, B., Lee, H., Kim, Y.: The effects of individual motivations and social capital on employees' tacit and explicit knowledge sharing intentions. Int. J. Inf. Manag. **2**, 356–366 (2013)

Hofstede, G.: Culture's Consequences: International Differences in Work-Related Values, vol. 5. Sage Publications, Beverly Hills, CA (1984)

Kluckhohn, F.R., Strodtbeck, F.L.: Variations in Value Orientations. Greenwood Press, Oxford (1961)

Luo, C., Wu, J., Shi, Y., Xu, Y.: The effects of individualism-collectivism cultural orientation on ewom information. Int. J. Inf. Manag. **4**, 446–456 (2014)

Lv, H.: Empirical research of internal intercultural communication cues facets in company. Soft Sci. **5**, 127–130 (2007). (in Chinese)

Mower, J.M., Pedersen, E.L., Jai, T.: Concept analysis of "cross-cultural marketing": an exploration. J. Glob. Fash. Mark. **1**, 4–19 (2013)

Pondy, L.R.: Organizational conflict: concepts and models. Admin. Sci. Q. **2**, 296–320 (1967)

Qiu, L., Lin, H., Leung, A.K.: Cultural differences and switching of in-group sharing behavior between an american (facebook) and a chinese (renren) social net-working site. J. Cross Cul. Psychol. **1**, 106–121 (2013)

Qiu, Y.: Harmony in diversity- an analysis of the cultural differences in si-no-foreign joint ventures. Corp. Stud. **4**, 22–25 (2003)

Robbins, S.P., Waters-Marsh, T., Cacioppe, R., Millett, B.: Organisational Be-haviour: Concepts, Controversies and Applications: Australia and New Zealand. Prentice Hall, Englewood Cliffs, NJ (1994)

Thomas, K.W.: Conflict and conflict management: reflections and update. J. Organ. Behav. **3**, 265–274 (1992)

Tian, H.: A Study On Cross-Cultural Conflicts and Effectiveness of Sino-Foreign Joint Ventures. Economic Science Press, Beijing (2012). (in Chinese)

Wang, W., Wang, B.: Two dimensions of operational management model of modern corporate culture. Manag. World **8**, 184–185 (2010). (in Chinese)

Wei, J., Liu, L., Francesco, C.A.: A cognitive model of intra-organizational knowledge-sharing motivations in the view of cross-culture. Int. J. Inf. Manag. **3**, 220–230 (2010)

Xie, D., Fan, L., Yi, J.: Experiment research on index system of employees communication techniques in transnational corporation-based on sense-making theory. Soft Sci. **5**, 116–119 (2012). (in Chinese)

Yu, W., Jia, Y.: The new cmc model and its application. Appl. Psychol. **1**, 3–10 (1997). (in Chinese)

Zhang, X., Wang, Y.: International Management: Managing in the Era of Globalization. China Renmin University Press, Beijing (2002). (in Chinese)

Driving Safety Considered User Interface of a Smartphone: An Experimental Comparison

Sanaz Motamedi[1(✉)], Mahdi Hasheminejad[2], and Pilsung Choe[3]

[1] Mechanical, Industrial and System Engineering Department,
University of Rhode Island, Kingston, USA
sanaz_motamedi@my.uri.edu
[2] Engineering and Technology Department, Tarbiat Modares University,
Tehran, Iran
mehdi@hasheminezhad.com
[3] Departments of Mechanical and Industrial Engineering, Qatar University,
Doha, Qatar
pchoe@qu.edu.qa

Abstract. With the rapid advancement of mobile technology, information searches by drivers using smartphones have increased despite the potential risk of accidents. The small screen size of smartphones greatly distracts driving performance. Apart from traffic regulations that prohibit smartphone usage while driving, a better user interface design of smartphones for drivers is also a critical issue in regard to increasing driving safety and user satisfaction.

In this study, a human factors experiment was conducted to evaluate driving performance while searching for information (browsing news) in a fixed-base driving simulator. The simulator simulated an urban driving environment with heavy traffic condition. A total of 12 subjects aged 25–35 years old participated in the experiment. A between-subject design compared three methods of user interfaces: Pop-up, Full-screen, and Auto-zooming. Effectiveness, efficiency, and satisfaction were measured as the usability principles. Results show that the more complex the visual tasks, the more unsafe distractions will occur while driving.

Keywords: Localization · Driving safety · Website layout adaptation · Smartphone interface · News reading on smartphone

1 Introduction

Checking news is a popular action for most people every day. In recent years the trend of using a smartphone while driving, and browsing the news as secondary task, is increasing. Any visual secondary task, i.e. browsing news, while driving is often done in spite of the potential risk of car accident. According to statistics from the National

© Springer International Publishing Switzerland 2015
P.L.P. Rau (Ed.): CCD 2015, Part II, LNCS 9181, pp. 150–160, 2015.
DOI: 10.1007/978-3-319-20934-0_15

Safety Council, 26 % of crashes (1.5 million) involved Smartphone usage distraction in 2012.[1] Yu et al. revealed that driving is one of the top activities during which people used their smartphone as a secondary task, in addition to walking and waiting. It is worth noting that, in 64 % of these situations, the users were browsing the news [1]. These statistics show the practical need for a particular consideration of user interface (UI) design for browsing the news on a smartphone while driving.

Research showed that only 24 % of mobile news consumers reported that they use applications (apps) to check news [2]. Despite the publication of a variety of apps, many users still abstain from relying on them, and check news through following significant reasons:

- Apps switch news websites' layout, which can impede users' browsing while driving
- Apps may compound or exclude parts of their respective original websites; missing parts (e.g. pictures, old news) can be found by viewing original news websites
- Smartphones' lack of memory influences speed and installations

In addition to mobile apps, mobile web browser is another option for browsing the news. A survey was conducted to identify mobile users' experiences using mobile web browsers. According to the result, 82 % of participants disliked this way of browsing due to, for example, bad content layout and slow interface [2]. Therefore, the mobile web browser needs a lot of improvement. This paper seeks to consider all of these challenges to obtain optimal UI news websites for use while driving.

In line with UI design importance, the interface style, which is dependent on language, should be carefully studied. A written language can influence browsing performance while driving because information perception and processing highly depend on the style of the written language in the information system [3]. In terms of writing, Persian, Arabic, Urdu, Pashto, and Dari languages share the same letters and altogether these speakers constitute 10 % of the world's population [4]. The language of news considered in this study is Persian because the Persian language has different alphabets and style.

The objective of this article is to propose better website adaptation on smartphones for browsing news written in Persian while driving.

2 Literature Review

2.1 Page Adaptation for Smartphone

Different ways to adapt websites on smartphone screens are direct, manual, and automatic [5]. Direct adaptation is not a suitable method due to some small device limitations such as a small screen. Manual methods are expensive to develop for each particular website. For these reasons, this research utilizes automatic methods. Motamedi, et al. categorized the automatic adaptation in four sub methods [6].

---

[1] http://www.nsc.org/DistractedDrivingDocuments/CPK/Attributable-Risk-Summary.pdf.

Format Conversion. In this method, a website is splitted in different parts that connect with links to have better UI on small size screens [7]. But the weak point of this method is deep structure, which creates confusion for users who are familiar with a website's original view [8].

Overview. At the outset, this method provides the original view of websites at the beginning. In this way, users are allowed to use their skills and memories to navigate the website even on their smartphones. B. Mackay et al. proposed the "Gateway" method in which users click or rollover the individual sections [7]. Then the selected section is expanded over the original view of the website [6].

Summarization. As you can guess from the name of this method, all contexts are summarized based on key words. Although this method can summarize the whole website on the small screen size of smartphone, it has two disadvantages: tables and pictures are eliminated from websites after summarization, and key words are developed manually for each website paragraph, which takes a lot of time and effort [9].

Linearity. In this method, website layouts are changed to a long linear list which adapts to the small screen size of a smartphone. This long linear list, a menu, is generated with all the extracted links and content appearing as menu items. By doing this, websites effectively separate navigation and action, making navigation simply a matter of selecting a link to follow from a list [10]. However, this method changes the original layout of the website, which can create confusion for users.

Among these categories, the *overview* method is less expensive and has a better user interface due to its allowing users to have the same layout of an original website seen on a desktop computer [7]. In this study, three *overview* methods were compared while driving.

2.2 Persian Language Complexity in Terms of UI Design

Persian language letters are different from English or Latin in many ways, for instance: starting from right to left for writing, connecting letters within a word (even in printed writing, see Fig. 1), twenty-eight letters having separate parts (as circled in Fig. 1), and requiring a larger optimum font size in terms of readability [11]. The Persian language, which shares letters with similar languages such as Arabic, Urdu, Pashto, and Dari, has thirty-two letters which have different shapes based on their position in words and sentences. Including all shapes and sizes, the Persian language has 115 effective letters [12]. All of these differences make Persian a complicated language in terms of UI design [13]. These differences influence the perceptions and performance of Persian users searching websites [6].

Fig. 1. Comparing the complexity of english and persian languages

3 Methodology

3.1 Design

The experiment was a 3 × 1 variables design (browsing methods: Pop-up, Full-screen, and Auto zooming) for analyses of efficiency, effectiveness, and satisfaction.

Browsing Methods. This paper utilized the same browsing methods introduced by Mohamed et al. [6]. As the study concluded, the overview method is a better method for smartphones due to using the same layout as the website's original appearance [6]. The innovation of this study is the use of three different *overview* methods which are compared while driving, as a secondary task instead of a first task.

Many screen adaptations for smartphones such as apps and mobile browsers exclude or compound some part of news websites. However, these browsing methods avoid do so and try not change layout of news websites by considering the lack of space. Moreover, by cutting zooming action during checking news, these methods improve UI. In detail, we used JavaScript functions to detect all clicks and capture the background based on a predefined method. Figure 2 illustrates the screen shot of the first look at the website, which is same in all three methods used in this study, and the original website. After clicking on the screen each method acted differently (see Fig. 3).

Fig. 2. The first screen shot of all three methods

First method: Pop-up. In this method, the selected and clicked news would Pop-up in a bigger font size on the website; this is expanded and superimposed on top of the overview [6]. Figure 3(a) shows the example of a Pop-up method after one click on the desired news.

Second method: Full-screen. In this method, after having an overview of the news website, a user can read the whole selected news in full-screen mode only using one click [6, 7]. You can see the screen shot of this method after one click in Fig. 3(b).

Third method: Auto-zooming. In this method, after having the overview, a user is able to automatically zoom in and out of any of the selected news on the website; however, this is not a concern of our study. In order to read the whole news content, a user needs to double click [6]. In this case, the user can read in full screen mode, which is similar to Full-screen method. This method is depicted in Fig. 3(c).

A) Pop-up method   B) Full-screen method   C) Auto-zooming method

Fig. 3. Screen shot of all three methods after one click

3.2   Participants

This study compared these methods to obtain the best news website adaptation for smartphones via an experiment performed by 12 people ranging from 25–35 years old. All participants were randomly selected from the local Persian population. The participants had annual driving experience of at least 15,000 miles. These drivers have held a valid license for at least two years and count as active drivers (i.e., they have driven at least 30,000 miles in their lifetimes). Persian is the mother tongue of all participants. Inexperienced and elderly drivers are excluded in this study due to low driving performance. The participants reported normal or corrected-to-normal vision.

3.3   Apparatus

A virtual-reality driving simulator was employed in the experiment, specifically the TranSim VS IV driving simulator produced by the L3 Corporation. The simulator provides high-fidelity, real-world driving environments that can be customized for various applications. It is a fixed-base simulator consisting of a regular driving module and three channel plasma monitors in an immersive driving environment that combines the look and feel of a real vehicle. Participants interact with the simulator using a sedan steering wheel and pedals that provide real-time feedback. As Wang et al. [14] pointed out, driving simulations can be safe and effective environments to evaluate drivers' electronic device interfaces.

A separate computer was used to run and control the simulator through the Operator Console (OPCON) software. Another software, "Scenario Builder", was used to create desired test conditions for various scenarios. These driving scenarios were designed to be predictive of driving performance in naturalistic settings and standardized road tests. Simulated "real-world" driving events were included that placed relatively greater or lesser demands on the effective utilization of: (1) executive control processes, (2) visual search mechanisms, and (3) selective attention mechanisms underlying the appropriate processing of both relevant and irrelevant orienting cues (Fig. 4).

Furthermore, in this study drivers were equipped with a smartphone. Due to smartphones' different sizes, this study used one common small device, the Google Nexus 5 Android Phone. The size of this Smartphone is 5.4" × 2.7" × 0.3", and the main display's resolution is 1920 × 1080 pixels. This smartphone was equipped with a framework that can adapt a Persian news website with these methods. In order to avoid Internet speed effects this experiment conducted offline.

Fig. 4. Driving simulator

3.4 Procedure

Firstly, an orientation video was played to explicitly explain the experiment to the participants. Then, participants were asked to perform a ten minutes warm-up run, followed by the experiment. In total, a participant went through three scenarios in a random manner. At the beginning of each scenario, the participant was informed that what kind of browsing methods (Pop-up, Full-screen, and Auto-zooming) should be used.

In each scenario, a participant drove about one mile on a city roadway, which took approximately two to three minutes. The participant was asked to keep their speed in the 25–35 mile per hour range. In order to simulate the city environment, five challenging events occurred in each scenario. For example, challenging events included events where other drivers or pedestrians emerged suddenly, thus provoking collisions if not avoided. By demanding active action from the driver, we were able to obtain an assessment about the driver's performance and response. In order to avoid the learning curve effect, three similar scenarios were designed. These scenarios share similar road environments, urban roadways, and routes. However, they differ in terms of objects — the people and cars used in the scenarios.

Lengths of selected news, randomly assigned to each method, were almost the same (M = 87.16, SD = 1.16). It is worth noting that since the news locations were randomly changed when participants browsed the websites, they were not able to use their memory to guess the location of the news.

After a warm-up run in which participants familiarized themselves with the scenarios and browsing methods, the experiment began. Participants were asked to complete two tasks. In the first task, participants, while driving in the scenarios, browsed the news, which meant that they needed to find, read aloud (heard by the researchers), and understand the browsed news using the methods. Time of task is one of our responses and was measured through captured video using a timer on the screen of the smartphones. This data objectively measured the efficiency of the methods. Moreover, participant driving performance was recorded and monitored by two researchers in order to evaluate the participant performance in scenarios based on a grading system, which will be explained in following section. The overall score of driving performances is the response for measuring effectiveness of each method.

In the second task, participants were asked to complete a questionnaire. In the first part of the questionnaire, participants answered multiple questions about the news they read during the scenarios. If they were not able to identify the correct option, their data was excluded. In the other part of the questionnaire, participants rated (from 1 = not satisfied to 5 = very satisfied) the ease-to-use (satisfaction level) of each method for checking the news.

3.5 Variables

There are a wide variety of usability measurements. Usability is counted as a primary factor in UI and the consequent success of any kind of adaptations. Users' satisfaction, time efficiency, and effectiveness are the elements of usability based on ISO 9241. Therefore, this study evaluated usability of these methods by measuring time completion of the tasks, driving performance, and subjects' opinion about ease-to use of methods.

The independent variables were the browsing methods while the dependent variables measured were effectiveness, efficiency, and satisfaction (ease-to use) level of methods.

As mentioned above, effectiveness of methods measured by driving performance was assessed by a grading system. This system calculated the overall score (from 100) of participants' driving performance while browsing the news. Ten categories with different weights are included in this grading system (Table 1) [15].

Table 1. Categories and weights

Category	Over Speed Limit	Following Distance	Lane Position	Collision
Weight	2	2	6	8
Category	Over Speed Limit	Speed Maintenance	Violating Sign/Light	Visual Focus
Weight	1	1	4	2

The other dependent variable is efficiency of methods, which was measured with task completion times. The time was recorded precisely via capturing a screenshot from a smartphone's screen during the experiment. Moreover, experienced subjects were asked to rate the browsing methods according to satisfaction (ease-to-use).

One-way analysis of variance (ANOVA) with the significant level of 0.05 was utilized for within-subject analysis. Three methods, as independent variables, analyzed three dependent variables: efficiency, effectiveness, and satisfaction.

4 Results

Two of the 12 drivers who participated in this experiment are excluded from the experiment results. These two drivers could not correctly answer the first part of questionnaire, which was about the news that they read during the experiment. Next, the normality assumption of user performance data obtained from the captured video and driving simulation were checked. All data passed the normality test (with $\alpha = 0.05$), which ensured the validity of the comparison analyses. Then, the results were analyzed using one-way ANOVA (with 95 % confidence level) procedure (see Table 2).

Table 2. Summary of ANOVA results

Source of Variation	SS	Df	MS	F	P-value
Effectiveness	120.9	2	60.4	0.70	0.504
Efficiency	681.3	2	340.7	5.05	0.014
Satisfaction	16.47	2	8.23	6.84	0.004

According to the results, there was no significant method in terms of effectiveness (F-value = 0.70, p-value = 0.504). As noted above, the driving performance was considered as a response for effectiveness. With 95 % confidence, the mean of the driving performance for all three methods was between 73.00 and 79.86. Figure 5 illustrates the 95 % confidence interval of each method particularly for mean and median.

In terms of efficiency, methods had significant impact (F-value = 5.05, p-value = 0.014). Figure 6-a illustrates the main effect of this significant factor. In this figure, it is clear that subjects needed less time to complete the browsing task with method 3 (Auto-zooming).

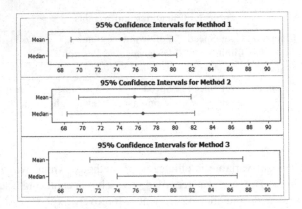

Fig. 5. Confidence interval for methods

Based on subjects' points of view, methods significantly affected their satisfaction (F-value = 6.84, p-value = 0.004). According to the main effect plot (see Fig. 6-b), the best method in terms of subjects' satisfaction was method 2 (Full-screen) and with roughly 0.2 difference with method 3 (Auto –zooming), the second best method.

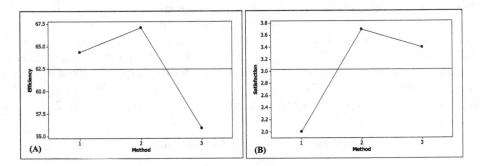

Fig. 6. Main effect plot: (A) efficiency (B) satisfaction

5   Discussion

In contrast to previous research [7, 9] that compared direct and/or linear website adaptation for smartphones, this research considered three methods from the *overview* category. In addition, this comparison was conducted in a driving simulator to measure the effectiveness, efficiency, and satisfaction of these methods as a secondary task while driving. The other innovation of this study was utilizing Persian as the news language due to its different shape and letter complexity.

Results revealed method 3 was the most efficient method. Method 3 provided the Full-screen of the news after two clicks on the smartphone's screen. In this way, a user did not need to zoom in on the content because the letters became bigger and more readable [6]. Furthermore, method 3 is extremely similar to the way users on desktop computers browse the news (double clicking to open the news). Thus, in method 3, users spend less time (more efficient) browsing (= finding + reading) news.

Regarding subjects' rating, method 2 was the most satisfying method among the three methods. As previously mentioned, this method provided the full-screen of the news, which provided more room and improved letters' readability after only one click. As result, subjects were satisfied with method 2 for browsing tasks. However, considering the actual time that they spent completing the tasks (browsing news), users invested significantly more time (lowest efficiency) on this method. This is because of the limited capacity of the human brain, which cannot properly process the secondary task. Drivers clicked two times instead of once as they became acclimated to the task. In other words, the reason for the low efficiency of this method was not being familiar enough with needing only one click to open the desired news while driving (as secondary task), whereas users had better efficiency as primer task [6].

Effectiveness was not significant factor based on the analysis. However the confidence interval still revealed interesting information about this factor. Method 1 had the lowest mean for driving performance compared to the other methods. As a result, method 1 could be the most distracting method for drivers. This distraction could be the result of the smaller window method 1 provided after one click.

Comparing driving performance while browsing news with driving performance while hands-on texting [15], this finding can lead to the conclusion that browsing news distracts drivers more than texting. Longer context and smaller font could cause this increased distraction.

6 Conclusion

This study identified the usability of three website adaptation methods — Pop-up, Full-screen and Auto-zooming — for browsing news while driving in a city environment. Through the driving simulator, driver performances were examined under the effect of browsing news. Moreover, the efficiency of these methods was measured by recording completion times of the browsing task. Users' satisfaction was assessed subjectively immediately after the driving test. As a result, Auto-zooming and Full-screen methods were found to be the most efficient and satisfying methods, respectively, for browsing the news while driving. In addition, the Pop-up method was found to be the most distracting browsing method for drivers. The results gained from the study support the notion that the more complex the visual tasks, the more unsafe distractions are while driving.

Although this research employed a high fidelity simulator with a high level of experimental control, in real-life driving settings, such as naturalistic studies, an expanded number of participants are needed in order to ensure the validity of the findings. In future studies, other factors such as weather condition, traffic density, visual conditions (day/night), and different languages should be considered.

References

1. Yu, C., Miller, R.C.: Enhancing mobile browsing and reading. In: CHI 2011 Extended Abstracts on Human Factors in Computing Systems, pp. 1783–1788. ACM (2011)
2. Purcell, K., Rainie, L., Rosenstiel, T., Mitchell, A.: How mobile devices are changing community information environments (2011). http://www.stateofthemedia.org/2011/Mobile-survey
3. Wickens, C.D., Lee, J.D., Liu, Y., Becker, S.E.: An Introduction to Human Factors Engineering, 2nd edn. Pearson Education Inc., New Jersey (2004)
4. Roy, K., Alaei, A., Pal, U.: Word-wise handwritten Persian and Roman script identification. In: Frontiers in Handwriting Recognition (ICFHR), pp. 628–633. IEEE (2010)
5. Mohomed, I., Chin, A., Cai, J.C., de Lara, E.: Community-driven adaptation: automatic content adaptation in pervasive environments. In: WMCSA 2004 Sixth Workshop on Mobile Computing Systems and Applications, pp. 124–133. IEEE (2004)
6. Motamedi, S., Hasheminezhad, M., Choe, P.: Improving the user interface for reading news articles through smartphones in persian language. In: Rau, P. (ed.) HCII 2013 and CCD 2013, Part I. LNCS, vol. 8023, pp. 440–449. Springer, Heidelberg (2013)
7. MacKay, B., Watters, C.R., Duffy, J.: Web page transformation when switching devices. In: Brewster, S., Dunlop, M.D. (eds.) Mobile HCI 2004. LNCS, vol. 3160, pp. 228–239. Springer, Heidelberg (2004)
8. Cai, J.: Page layout adaptation for small form factor devices. In: Department of Computer Science, Toronto, pp.1–12 (2006)
9. Virpi, R., Popescu, A., Koivisto, A., Vartiainen, E.: Minimap: a web page visualization method for mobile phones. In: Proceedings of the SIGCHI Conference on Human Factors in Computing Systems, pp. 35–44. ACM (2006)
10. Schilit, B.N., Trevor, J., Hilbert, D.M., Koh, T.K.: Web interaction using very small internet devices. Computer 35(10), 37–45 (2002)
11. Abubaker, A.A., Lu, J.: The optimum font size and type for students aged 9–12 reading Arabic characters on screen: a case study. J. Phys: Conf. Ser. 364(1), 012115 (2012). IOP Publishing
12. Alaei, A., Pal, U., Nagabhushan, P.: A comparative study of persian/arabic handwritten character recognition. In: ICFHR, pp. 123–128 (2012)
13. Kanoun, S., Ennaji, A., LeCourtier, Y., Alimi, A.M.: Script and nature differentiation for Arabic and Latin text images. In: The Proceedings Eighth International Workshop on Frontiers in Handwriting Recognition, pp. 309–313. IEEE (2002)
14. Wang, Y., Mehler, B., Reimer, B., Lammers, V., D'Ambrosio, L.A., Coughlin, J.F.: The validity of driving simulation for assessing differences between in-vehicle informational interfaces: a comparison with field testing. Ergonomics 53(3), 404–420 (2010)
15. Motamedi, S., Wang, H.J.: Is hands-free texting a better alternative of text driving? In: 56th Annual Transportation Research Forum Program, pp. 48–49 (2015)

Exploring Smart-Car Space in Urban India

Sarita Seshagiri$^{(\boxtimes)}$ and Aditya Ponnada

Samsung R&D Institute, Bangalore, India
{sarita.s,a.ponnada}@samsung.com

Abstract. Driving is a quotidian activity that people across cultures have long engaged in. Given the pervasive need for information on the go, the smart-car era is well nigh. To develop solutions in this direction, an understanding of users' needs with respect to their cars is necessary. In this paper, we present our exploratory study of user's driving behavior in urban India. We found that the basic need for a smart-car begins even before entering a car and is not confined to driving alone. Activities before and during driving cyclically impact each other. Moreover, we found that driving is not limited to users alone, but also involves critical participation from users' social circles. From these findings, we discuss design implications that can impact pre-driving and while-driving modes and can thereby inform future research in smart-cars for urban India.

Keywords: Ubiquitous computing · Smart-cars · Qualitative research

1 Introduction

Automobiles since their invention have catered to our basic need for transport. However, driving also entails a constant need for information, communication and entertainment. Researchers have therefore been utilizing ubiquitous computing that can serve these needs anywhere we go and build smarter cars for the future. In-car infotainment systems for instance, have comfortably weaved into our automobiles to support us with a variety of functionalities. Since communication while driving is addressed by mobile phones, researchers have also designed tools to ensure less distraction for in-car mobile phone usage while driving. MirrorLink (previously Terminal Node) for instance optimizes Smartphone content for in-car usage with minimal user distraction [19]. It mirrors Smartphone applications such as calls, maps & music for easy operability with in-car controls [5]. Furthermore, advanced cameras on smartphones have been used to alert drowsy drivers [27] and predict waiting time-windows during traffic signals [16]. These innovations show that cars can be potential avenues for next generation ubiquitous computers. Hence, in this paper we have presented our qualitative study on user's needs and challenges related to driving and the means of coping with them in urban India. Through this study, we intend to put forth certain design implications for future smart-cars.

© Springer International Publishing Switzerland 2015
P.L.P. Rau (Ed.): CCD 2015, Part II, LNCS 9181, pp. 161–173, 2015.
DOI: 10.1007/978-3-319-20934-0_16

2 Related Work

Researchers from varied domains have explored driving habits of users in different locations across the world. These studies highlight that cars are not mere transportation means. They are extensions of our identities, preferences and personal spaces, as is evident in Bell's study [4]. Users' identity is manifested through personal belongings held in a car and personalization made to it.

Heikkinen et al. in their contextual study have conducted pre and post-trip interviews corroborated by on trip observations [9]. Their study reveals the role of mobile phones while driving primarily for entertainment, driving support and even work-related tasks. Their study also explored the supportive role of co-passengers serving the needs for information and entertainment. Likewise, Haddington and Rauniomaa focus on driver's actions to attend a call inside the car [8]. A 100 car study at Virginia tech revealed that the use of mobile phones and hand held devices were distractions leading to accidents [25]. This study indicates that in-car ubiquitous technology should also account for possible distractions to the driver.

Researchers also compare driving behaviors and car usage patterns across different countries. One such study by Ozkan examines driving behavior differences across Britain, Netherlands, Greece, Turkey, and Iran using Manchester Driving Behavior Questionnaire (DBQ) [20]. Even though DBQ measures behavior only in terms of driving errors and violations, it does reveal differences in driving behaviors due to environmental situations and traffic regulations. Similarly, a large-scale survey [15] assessed preferential differences among Austrian, American and South Korean car owners. It revealed varied cultural perceptions towards personal vehicles as luxuries as against necessities. Yet, as quantitative surveys, they do not reveal much about users' environment and accompanying needs. A contextual study in this space is thus required to corroborate such surveys and highlight intrinsic user needs.

Through an in-depth ethnographic study, Zafirgolu et al. examined car usage in Brazil, China and Germany [28]. They reveal that infrastructural issues determine driving in Germany and that security threats were critical in Brazil. However, the need for socializing on the move was high in Brazil and China. Their study shows how socio-cultural differences determine driving behaviors. Their study also implies that a qualitative data of driving habits is required in addition to dynamic driving data in order to have more robust findings.

It is suggestive from the cross-cultural studies that a dedicated field immersion for specific countries is worthwhile. Nonetheless, there is a dearth of studies to explore this space in the India. According to a global study [6], 48 % of Indian car owners want to upgrade to 'connected' vehicles, as against 27 % in USA, 22 % in UK and 20 % in Germany. Likewise, It is anticipated that the Indian auto- market will be larger than most European Markets by 2020 [11]. On the other hand, India being highest in reported road accident deaths from traffic causalities also warrants a dedicated understanding of driving behavior in this region [12]. At the same time, with nearly 74 million users on internet, India is set to become the third largest web-consuming country [13]. Thus, a study in this region is worthwhile given the challenges related to traffic, urban planning, and infrastructure [14]. In this paper, we share our qualitative study to better understand driving behavior in India and identify design opportunities to contribute to the smart car space of the morrow.

3 Methodology

The following research questions were considered for the field immersion:

- What are users' quotidian driving practices?
- What are the challenging situations faced while driving?
- How do users respond to these challenges?

A team of two researchers gathered data in three-phases - open discussions, situational observations and guided interviews lasting 2 h. Discussions were undertaken to understand users' vehicle in general. Subsequently, for situational immersions, researchers were with users as they drove [3]. During the journey, researchers had open-ended conversations with users, where interview questions were conversationally weaved in. The focus was on actual events that users encountered as they drove, for e.g. traffic/road/driving condition.

Finally, one-on-one guided interviews were carried out with all participants, where participants clarified situational observations gathered by researchers. All interviews were undertaken in English, Hindi or Kannada, according to respondents' convenience. The extended interviews were carried out within a day of situational interviews to ensure easier recall of driving events [2]. Field study was undertaken in urban Bengaluru, which has seen burgeoning of population, poor planning and increasing traffic-related problems [21]. Users were selected according to following attributes: *vehicle owned, Smartphone used*; *expertise in driving*; *marital status*; and *gender*.

Twenty participants were interviewed as part of this qualitative study. They were recruited through snowball sampling and were between 20-40 years of age. All respondents owned a smart, media device. 12 participants were male and 8 were female. Of these, 8 male participants and 4 female participants were married and had at least one child. Out of 20 users, 14 owned both hatchbacks and SUVs, while 6 owned a sedan and a hatchback. Finally, 11 participants were local to Bangalore, while the rest had moved in with driving experiences from other places of India.

Data was gathered as field notes, audio and video captures. Data was analyzed through modified Grounded Theory method and affinity Analysis [7]. The latter exercise yielded 172-first level themes, which were abstracted into 66-second level and finally clustered into 5-third level themes. Findings from cluster analysis are described in subsequent sections.

4 Findings and Observations

4.1 The Car-A Personalized Shared Asset

Cars were more than means of transport for users. People affirmed that the vehicle lent them personal space and the means to socialize. They further enhanced their individual space by personalizing it with accessories to meet personal needs. Yet, respondents shared the wheel with their family and car-pooled with their friends.

The sociality in driving practices meant that driving decisions were not personal and often influenced by members of one's personal network. Still there was a critical need to personalize and undertake personalization to maximize social experiences. To enable personalized experiences, users fitted accessories. Some adorned their cars with religious symbols. Others fixed stereos, wide-angled mirrors and reverse sensors. Minimal personalization was for those who avoided "*spoiling by overdoing.*"

Despite the private space it afforded, a vehicle was often shared between respondents and their personal social networks. Sharing occurred most when households with one vehicle had multiple family members. An interviewee mentioned sharing in his household as follows, "*My wife, brother and I share these two cars. My wife and I go out on weekends. Weekdays, my brother and I go to work in the same direction.*" Highlighting comfort as a factor in choosing between multiple vehicles, a user said, "*Depending on who commutes longer, we decide on X over Y, because X is comfy. If Dad or I go nearby, we take Y.*" Urgency and easy access to vehicle determined users' choice of vehicles. Wheel sharing revealed a lack of personalization. In this regard, a respondent said, "*I manually adjust seat level and incline. It's never the same from what it's left at. My wife, dad and brother adjust it for themselves.*"

Carpooling occurred when people were routinely bound for the same destination; were keen to avoid traffic challenges; and wanted to save fuel. Respondents mentioned car-pooling with friends and colleagues as well. Routine and leisure driving decisions were influenced by children and elderly parents. The father of a 3 year-old said, "*My son gets cranky on the way to school. But music soothes him. My H car has a music system, but not the V sedan. So, I prefer H.*" For the sake of his motion-sick toddler, a user avoided long, leisure drives.

Driving ensured family time through socializing and extended conversations. To enable sociality, people undertook measures like renting vehicles and turning down media devices. To optimize on family time, people reduced speeds and adopting greater safety practices. With preferences of family members tied into their driving, it was natural for users to perceive the car as an extension of their home. It afforded space during commutes for storing children's toys, toiletries, food and pillows. Recreating a 'multi-utility space' was critical in long journeys. The intimacy of enclosed spaces was negotiated constantly by users. Most significantly, they carried the comfort bubble of their home. As technology providers, we must consider personalization of settings in this shared space through ubiquitous devices.

4.2 Activities Before Driving

People undertook planned and pre-emptive activities prior to turning the engine on. These would influence their drive and journey. In turn, activities undertaken prior to driving were determined by past experiences and learning of users. Measures for safety and route planning/navigation aid were the most common pre driving activities. There were some activities undertaken as soon as users entered the car, irrespective of whether they were drivers or passengers. Wearing the safety belt and ensuring the safety of their personal belongings were some of them. Many respondents preferred comfort and ensured that the rest of the journey required least effort for certain activities, including music listening, accessing the mobile from easy-to-reach locations in the car and basic controls [air conditioner, rearview mirrors and sun visor].

Pre-driving activities were also about pre-empting critical eventualities like lack of fuel. If it were near low, users would get a fuel recharge at the earliest opportunity. Some respondents ensured safety by relocking their doors and checking their belongings before restarting their vehicle after a traffic signal. Some of the factors that influenced people's choice of vehicles before heading out were infrastructural conditions of the city and destination planned. A participant, who owned a big and small vehicle, explained that his preferences to take a big sedan or a smaller hatchback for the day were driven by availability of parking space. Most tasks were undertaken to ensure smooth driving experience and seamless connectivity. Thus, the need for a smart car experience began even before users entered their car and continued after they stepped out.

4.3   Activities While Driving

Of all activities undertaken while driving, music, navigation support and communication on mobile were predominant. Music was considered ubiquitous to driving in most conditions, including while driving alone and with others. Activities related to safety and social conversations with co-passengers were common too. In fact, multitasking occurred when a parallel activity required less effort and did not interrupt the primary, or attention demanding activity of driving. Hence, even phone calls were deferred. However, priorities and activities changed when people became passive drivers. Switching on music or connecting the mobile device frequently occurred, whilst changing music playlists was less. The latter was time-consuming when on the move and was done before a journey. Other user activities were related to safety and comfort, for e.g. being alert for traffic-related visual cues, or adjusting the air conditioner.

Ensuring safe conditions in driving was critical. The dashboard was constantly monitored for 'warning' signs; i.e. fuel, odometer, oil/brake lights. Users multitasked between attending to car's functionalities and road requirements. People also undertook other activities as passive drivers or passengers, including socializing with friends/family, or playing 'antaakshari' [a musical game played between two or more people]. Some used the time to plan their work. Many undertook coordination for pre-planned journeys. A respondent, who often did long journeys with others said, "*Not all are familiar with the destination. Each of us drives on our own. So, I reset our Odometer and start. We call each other, as we drive to check how many kilometres we've done and guess our distance from each other.*"

Music listening while driving was a norm. Users felt that it provided relief from the task of handling road conditions/driving. It was also a continuous activity to accompany the primary job of driving. There were different choices to music. Few preferred radio. Others wanted their own content. Listening to the radio was a substitute for some, when the primary source of music [e.g. an iPod] was unavailable. For others, the choice was driven by easy accessibility of storage devices. Context, such as user's mood, preferences, driving challenges and need for comfort levels also determined music preferences. Explaining his preferences, a user said, "*When alone I listen to English. With family it's Hindi. With mom and dad it's safe, old Hindi. When I'm sleepy, or when I drive long, I like a mix of Old Bollywood and English.*" It was interesting how spouses managed music preferences on shared devices. A respondent, who shared the wheel with his wife said, "*Our music is dumped in one iPod. Whoever drives gets to hear their choice. It's the driver's prerogative.*"

Another primary activity was managing communication on the move. Users restricted it to situations, where communication could not be deferred. An entrepreneur who had to be in touch with clients, said he will pull up and answer only client calls. For another respondent, calls from his wife (who recently had a baby) were urgent, since "*She doesn't call when I'm driving. But when she does, I know it's important.*" Familiarity with each other's context prompted users to decide on answering calls/messages. Most users preferred calls, messages and checking e-mails at particular time-windows, i.e. traffic signals or when the car was stationary. People wanted to weave in communication with driving by having easy access to a mobile phone [switching on speakerphone, Bluetooth and placing it in easily reachable locations].

Thus, participants deferred and did not stop communication events. Unlike navigation support, which was seen as a break from driving, music/mobile media consumption was not. Despite the cognitive load, it allowed weave-ins during driving and media devices were hence kept accessible. Yet, safety and coordination activities when not done through mobile were seen as breaks. Our findings reaffirm opportunities for providing lightweight entertainment and information to users.

4.4   Context Determined the Use of Driving Support Systems

The use of features or facilities made available for driving was dependent on how well they fitted to people's present situation. It varied from conditions as dynamic as users' driving context, to something all-encompassing as their social roles and technology comfort. Usually, tried and tested workarounds were preferred to features bundled in vehicles, which users then considered as redundant. Preferences and expectations were greatly determined by users' social roles and technology exposure.

Participants mentioned not having used certain facilities in their vehicle, since there was nothing that necessitated it. There were other functions, which were not used unless prompted by an event. For instance, wipers and hazard lights were used only in rains, while the odometer was for out-of-town jaunts. The use of functions depended on how important it was for people's daily driving. Besides, as a user pointed out, they were workarounds, which made certain features redundant.

Needs and actions of users were always context driven. Present context determined the urgency of weaving communication into driving. In this regard, a respondent revealed, "*It depends on which call or message is important. If my boss calls, I answer. But tomorrow I will not.*" Context also determined the speed at which people drove. Respondents explained that they drove fast to work, but drove slowly with family to savor the moments spent with them.

Context also influenced the means adopted for navigation support. Navigation aid was minimal for straight stretches, or familiar routes, or in the presence of adequate road signage. Users mentioned not wanting GPS aid or planning for familiar destinations. However, on unfamiliar roads, people would call their social circle for navigation aid. Often they would even ask for landmark-based directions from strangers. An interviewee said, *"After I drive into a town from the highway, I must know where to turn. I promptly roll down my windows to ask the auto or truck drivers, tea-stall owners and corner shop guys. They point out landmarks and I follow that."*

People were particular about what they considered non-negotiable. If features did not address basic concerns, such as privacy, it was less likely they would use them. Connecting to in-car gadgets was avoided, if it intruded on privacy. A respondent recounted, *"Once, my boss dropped me back and his wife called. He answered via the car speaker and said he was with someone. She hung up. It was so embarrassing. Now, I will never connect my car-phone."* Similarly, users expressed displeasure over a recent law to remove window tints, since it compromised their privacy and safety. One of the contexts, particularly for women, was in the social roles they played. Driving signified self-reliance for some female respondents. For others, it was a sign of sharing equal responsibilities with male family members. Yet, there were many instances where women played a passive role. One of these was for car servicing. *"When the car is being serviced, I wait in the other car. I don't talk to the mechanic. My husband does,"* a respondent stated. There were also instances of gender interdependencies. For instance, an interviewee said, *"I drove all the way to Shimoga and my husband checked for directions on his GPS to guide me."*

4.5   Learned Responses from Driving Experiences

Driving was a series of learned responses in a loop. People had to constantly relearn their responses to effectively address the ever-changing road and traffic conditions in the city. Initial learning was by drawing upon learned responses and knowledge of members in one's social network and even from online, special interest groups. Over time, people drew on their own repository of experiences to respond to situations and even devise workarounds to them.

Learning was a continuous activity. It ranged from responding to cues about car diagnostics and mechanism, to information about routes and navigation support. In addition, users learned driving in a smaller vehicle and shifted later to larger ones. Initially, people sought support from friends and family while parking, entering a busy road from a by-lane, highway and night driving. Support was also sought for car diagnostics, because many feared appearing ignorant. With learning though, people believed that they were better equipped. Previously perceived challenges were not daunting anymore, for e.g. operating stick shift vehicles and dashboard controls.

Learning from experience also made people discern a vehicle's likely response to certain driving actions. Many respondents explained how they changed their driving style based on engine feedback. Users could also guess when there was a problem with their vehicle and would take pre-emptive steps. Experience also taught people how to respond to traffic/road challenges. For instance, a respondent stated, *"If I stay long in these intersections, I can never get out. So, I wait for an auto rickshaw like this to turn and I turn with it, using it as a cover, since autos can worm their way."*

Navigation though was not resolved, despite driving experience. Alignment of roads in familiar cities and unfamiliar towns was a challenge. Others mentioned challenges like incorrect directions from local people, improper road signs or signs written in local scripts. It was thus found that initial learning entailed understanding the user's immediate vicinity, i.e. the automobile; its controls and response mechanism. The next level of learning was to understand larger space, i.e. roads, traffic and navigation. Learning ensured that users became less risk averse.

5 Discussions and Research Implications

Our study reveals that the car was perceived as an extension of the self (identity) by users, than as mere transport as discussed in [4]. The need for easy communication was also felt across all the users, as highlighted by Heikkinen et al. [9]. Some of the widely discussed emerging economy problems such as infrastructural constraints, navigation problems and safety [28], were also strongly dominant in Indian driving context. It may imply that there are common problems faced across nations, which can be addressed to achieve ideal smart-cars with culture-specific adaptations.

However, there were some differences in our premise, which led us to certain findings. Zafiroglu et al. [28] and Jeon et al. [15] have discussed infrastructural problems that affect user's route planning and way-finding. However, our study revealed that route information in India was not just limited to directions but also to avoid mob-protests, potholes, road-blockages and similar other unpredictable events.

Several studies including Haddington and Raoniuomaa [8] have also pointed out the role user's social circles play in driving experience especially in terms navigation, safety and communication support. However, in our study, the social roles were not confined to user's closed social members. They also extended to members outside of the vehicle and local sources of information (such as Rikshaw pullers and passersby etc.). Most importantly, findings by Haddington & Raoniuomaa [8], Heikkenen et al. [9], Jeon et al. [15] and Lee et al. [17] focus mainly on in-car interactions on the go. Whereas, our open-ended approach towards understanding user's activities associated with driving led us to infer that pre-driving decisions critically affect driving. In other words, there is a strong need in users to stay connected with their driving experience, which starts even before they enter their cars. This clearly indicates that ubiquitous systems designed to build smart-cars, should also take into account pre-driving activities users undertake for a seamless driving experience. Figure 1 illustrates how activities before driving affect user's experience while driving.

Actions undertaken before and while driving support each other in a continuous loop. In fact, activities before driving enable users to devise workarounds to cope with challenges while driving. By virtue of learning from prior experience of driving, users devise better coping strategies and pre-emptive steps to deal with various challenges. Workarounds are determined by certain innate conditions, for e.g. users' social roles/identities and driving skills to name a few. The study findings have helped us realize a design space for smart-cars, which includes before and while-driving situations. In the following sections, we highlight some of these avenues for further design and research to build well-integrated smart-cars in the near future.

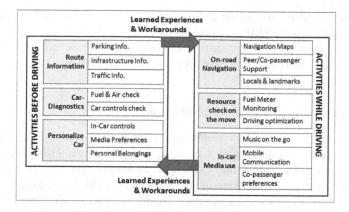

Fig. 1. Smart-Car design space: activities before and while driving

The study findings have helped us realize an overarching research and design space for smart-cars, which includes before and while-driving situations. The research opportunities also include harnessing users' social circles to offer seamless driving experiences. In this regard, we believe there is a strong need for an intelligent ubiquitous solution to keep us connected with our cars at all times. Such solutions can leverage on the advances in smart devices technology (e.g. smartphones, wearable devices etc.) and augment the experience via in-car controls and ambient technologies. In the following sections, we highlight some of these avenues for further design and research to build well-integrated smart-cars in the near future.

5.1   Weaving the Personal and Social Car

Influences from social/personal network greatly affected users' actions in navigation, personalization, in-car activities and safety related strategies. It was perhaps a cultural manifestation of preference for interdependence, unlike the individuality of Europe and North America [24]. In fact, to cope with varied familial needs, users had a smaller hatchback and a larger sedan/SUV. This strategy ensured personal and social space in changing contexts. Several decisions before entering the car such as media preferences, wheel sharing and car-pooling heavily involved people's social circles. Thus, it is reasonable to infer that the car constantly keeps switching its role as a personal and a shared asset.

Despite sociality of driving, there was the issue of personalizing features for those, who shared a vehicle. Few workarounds to the absence of personalized music device was to take turns to consume content within pre-designated time windows, or create different folders in the same device before starting the journey. In-car seating and other controls also needed adjusting. This highlights the need for an intelligent-solution that understands users personally and personalizes the vehicle based on their requirements. For instance, a shared car can have multiple profiles (akin to desktop computers with two accounts) for different users, which can be activated via smart devices.

While there have been solutions designed to engage co-passengers in monotonous drives, such as [12, 23], there is still an opportunity to utilize ambient technologies in cars to engage co-passengers in the driving experience. There is a similar opportunity for developing traditional games among people (e.g. *antakshari*), into an inter-device game, between multiple devices carried by occupants. These are certain research avenues to design solutions for people's social space in driving.

5.2   Enhanced Navigation – Beyond Maps and Routes

Route information was crucial to people before the journey. A factor that made navigating and route planning daunting was the presence of unpredictable road blocks in addition to infrastructural and traffic challenges. Solutions have already been tested to detect such challenges through Smartphone sensors [16, 18]. Thus, further examining the capabilities of sensors on smartphones for driving can be worthwhile. However, researchers should also consider how social roles can impact sharing of route related/navigation information with the community. There is an opportunity to integrate such technologies with social media (given its popularity in emerging markets) [26]. However, route planning is not always done real time given the practice of using printouts of online maps, or memorizing landmarks before getting inside the vehicle. In this regard, it would be worthwhile to further explore the capability of smart-cars, to learn from user's previous driving experiences and put forth the information for offline usage in upcoming drives.

Navigation has often been a challenge inside cities with dynamic road conditions, complex routes and lack of authentic information. People often seek directions to nearest landmarks from friends, passersby and online navigation tools. Leveraging this coping strategy, future smart-cars can have landmark-based incremental navigation for better visual judgments, apart from turn-by-turn contextual navigation [17]. It is also an opportunity to explore intelligent ways of integrating social, local and technological sources of navigation.

5.3   Intelligent and Ubiquitous Car Diagnostics

Checking for fuel and air before driving was essential for users to ensure smooth driving experience. Users were also concerned about any abnormal feedback from the car while driving and often depended on friends and family for support. Perhaps this can be an area for audio/voice based alerts or feedback while driving to ensure less distraction and allowing users to prepare for an action. Moreover, technologies such as 'automatic' [1] can be utilized to connect car to smart-devices for a ubiquitous car diagnostics. It is also an opportunity to investigate communication support systems during car breakdowns. A design direction can be to build intelligent systems that recommend driving optimizations, according to a vehicle's capabilities and user's skill levels.

5.4   Design for Safety and Social Support

Gender identities influenced how users coped with navigation challenges and safety, especially night-driving for female users. Our findings revealed that a close involvement by family and friends to ensure safety at such times was common. Map-based applications such as Safetipin utilize this factor [22]. Contacting close family members before the journey highlights the social roles played to ensure safety even before driving. Communication devices and sensors can be leveraged further to detect safety threats around the car and connect to appropriate authorities, as well as users' personal network during such threats. A crowd-sourcing approach can be taken here as well to enable people to broadcast route safety to others.

6   Conclusions

A primary implication of our study is that a smart car experience is not confined to driving alone, but begins even before a journey is undertaken. Activities before driving and the experience during a drive impact each other in continuous cycles. Besides, the presence and influence of users' social circles for informational and emotional support is critical to the driving and pre-driving experience. In all this, the car has to continually shift between personal and social spaces. Consequently, the design space for a smart-car has wide implications for pre-driving and post-driving situations. It also suggests that design avenues for next generation smart-cars should not be confined to users (drivers in this case) alone, but should also focus on members of social circles and other social information sources too. Thus, the findings and implications from this study lay the foundation for future research on smart-cars in India.

Acknowledgements. We are sincerely thankful to Dr. Ajit Bopardikar of SAIT-India and Dr. Debayan Dhar of MIT-ID for their critical reviews on the manuscript.

References

1. Automatic Link. https://www.automatic.com/. Accessed on 10th July 2014
2. Barriball, K.L., While, A.: Collecting data using a semi-structured interview: a discussion paper. J. Ad. Nurs. **19**(2), 328–335 (1994)
3. Becker, H.S., Geer, B.: Participant observation and interviewing. Hum. Organ. **16**(3), 28–32 (2009)
4. Bell, G.: Unpacking cars: doing anthropology at intel. Anthronotes **32**(2), 32 (2011)
5. Bose, R., Brakensiek, J., Park, K.: Terminal mode: transforming mobile devices into automotive application platforms. In: 2nd International Conference on Automotive User Interfaces and Interactive Vehicular Applications, AutomotiveUI 2010, pp. 148 – 155. ACM Press
6. Cars Online 12/13: My Car, My Way. http://www.capgemini.com/thought-leadership/capgeminicom-cars-online-1213-my-car-my-way. Accessed on 5th Jan 2014
7. Glaser, B.G., Strauss, A.L.: The Discovery of Grounded Theory: Strategies for Qualitative Research. Aldine Transaction, London (1999)

8. Haddington, P., Rauniomaa, M.: Technologies, multitasking, and driving: attending to and preparing for a mobile phone conversation in a car. J. Hum. Commun. Res. **37**, 223–254 (2011)
9. Heikkinen, J., Makinen, E., Lylykangas, J., Pakkanen, T., Vaananen, V., Raisamo, R.: Mobile devices as infotainment user interfaces in the car: contextual stufy and design implications. In: 15th International Conference on Human Computer Interactions on Mobile Devices and Services. MobileHCI 2013, pp. 137–146. ACM Press (2013)
10. Hoffman, G., Gal-Oz, A., David, S., Zuckerman, O.: In-Car game design for children: child vs. parent perspective. In: 12th International Conference on Interaction Design and Children. IDC 2013, pp. 112–119. ACM Press (2013)
11. India Automotive Market 2020, Booz&Co. (2011)
12. India has the highest number of road accidents in the world. Deutsche Welle, 29th April 2010.   http://www.dw.de/india-has-the-highest-number-of-road-accidents-in-the-world/a-5519345-1. Accessed on 15th December 2013
13. India is now the third largest internet user in the world after U.S, China. The Hindu. 24th Aug 2013. http://www.thehindu.com/sci-tech/technology/internet/india-is-now-worlds-third-largest-internet-user-after-us-china/article5053115.ece. Accessed on 10th Jul 2014
14. India's Urban Traffic is at Crossroads. The Economic Times, Oct 2011. http://economictimes.indiatimes.com/opinion/policy/indias-urban-traffic-is-at-crossroads/articleshow/10448787.cms. Accessed on 4th Jan 2014
15. Jeon, M., Riener, A., Lee, J., Schuett, J., Walker, B.N.: Cross-cultural differences in the use of in-vehicle technologies and vehicle area network services: Austria, USA and South Korea. In: 4th International Conference on Automotive User Interfaces and Interactive Vehicular Applications. AutomotiveUI 2012, pp. 163–170. ACM Press (2012)
16. Koukoumidis, E., Martonosi, M., Li-Shiuan, P.: Leveraging smartphone cameras for collaborative road advisories. IEEE Trans. Mob. Comput. **11**(5), 707–723 (2012)
17. Lee, J., Forlizzi, J., Hudson, S.E.: Studying the effectiveness of MOVE: a contextually optimized in-vehicle navigation system. In: International Conference on Human Factors in Computing Systems. CHI 2005, pp. 571–580. ACM Press (2005)
18. Mednis, A., Strazdins, G., Zviedris, R., Kanonirs, G., Selavo, L.: Real time pothole detection using android smartphones with accelerometers. In: International Conference on Distributed Computing in Sensory Systems and Workshops DCOSS 2011, pp. 1–6
19. Mirror Link Technology. http://www.mirrorlink.com/about-mirrorlink. Accessed on 1st March 2014
20. Ozkan, T., Lajunen, T., Chliaoutakis, J.E., Parker, D., Summala, H.: Cross-cultural differences in driving behaviors: a comparison of six countries. J. Transp. Res. Part F: Traffic Psychol. Behav. **9**(3), 227–242 (2006)
21. Ramachandra, T.V., Mujumdar, P.P.: Urban flood: case study of bangalore. J. National Inst. Disaster Manage. **3**(2), 1–98 (2009)
22. Safetipin. http://safetipin.com/. Accessed on 10th Jul 2014
23. Seeburger, J., Foth, M., Tjondronegoro, D.: Capital Music: personal expression with a public display of song choice. In: 6th Nordic Conference on Human Computer Interaction. NordiCHI 2010, pp. 777–780. ACM Press (2010)
24. The Hofstede Center. http://geert-hofstede.com/india.html. Accessed on 10th April 2014
25. The Impact of Driver Inattention on near-crash/crash risk: An analysis using 100-car naturilistic driving study data. National Highway Traffic Safety Administration (2006)
26. The Mobile Consumer: A global snapshot. Nielsen (2013)

27. You, C., Lane, N.D., Chen, F., Wang, R., Chen, Z., Bao, T.J., Montes-de-Oca, M., Cheng, Y., Lin, M., Torresani, L., Campbell, A.: CarSafe app: alerting drowsy and distracted drivers using dual cameras on smartphones. In: 11th Annual International Conference on Mobile Systems, Applications and Services. MobiSys 2013, pp. 461–462. ACM Press (2013)

28. Zafiroglu, A., Healey, J., Plowman, T.: Navigation to multiple local transportation futures: cross-interrogating remembered and recorded drives. In: 4th International Conference on Automotive User Interfaces and Interactive Vehicular Applications. AutomotiveUI 2012, pp. 139–146 ACM Press (2012)

Ask Local: Explore a New Place Like Locals

Cagri Hakan Zaman[✉], Federico Casalegno, Meng Sun,
and Kulpreet Chilana

Massachusetts Institute of Technology, Cambridge, MA 02139, USA
{zaman,casalegno,sunme,kulpreet}@mit.edu

Abstract. In this paper, we explore the ways of utilizing wearable technologies and social networking to cultivate a medium of cultural exchange between local communities and travelers in order to preserve and share local cultures. As wearable devices emerge and become a mainstream technology, a massive amount of potentials rises to empower micro-cultural habitats to present genuine characteristics of cities and neighborhoods to visitors through introducing contextualized and just-in-time communication. We introduce AskLocal, a novel location-based assisting system that mediates the communication between visitors and locals, allowing visitors to make real-time queries using Google Glass, and gather the user-generated information provided by the local network. We developed and tested a prototype that allows tourists to ask questions with our Google Glass application and receive local's answers on the device's display. Proposed system allows visitors to communicate a particular context that they encounter such as wayfinding in the city or making decisions on leisure activities. User testing demonstrated that the prototype adds a new level of freedom that allows tourists to traverse an unfamiliar place while providing them personalized information. We argue that proposed system encourages strangers to engage in more genuine communications that can be utilized in specific cultural contexts including culinary tourism, micro-history, and local merchandise.

Keywords: Wearable computing · Cultural interaction · Tourism experience

1 Introduction

The French term *'flanuer'* meaning 'stroller' in English, captures explicitly the exploration of the city through wandering around streets, paying attention to details of the urban life and engaging with the social context in a genuine and personalized way. Purified from intermediate facilitators and guides, *flanuer* initiates an uninterrupted conversation between the city and the travelers, enhanced by surprising encounters and unprecedented discoveries of micro-cultural habitats. In this paper we explore the possibility of utilizing wearable technologies and social networking to encourage *flaneur-like* explorations that enriches and empowers local cultures and allows travelers to enjoy a localized experience in the city.

© Springer International Publishing Switzerland 2015
P.L.P. Rau (Ed.): CCD 2015, Part II, LNCS 9181, pp. 174–183, 2015.
DOI:10.1007/978-3-319-20934-0_17

The proliferation of wearable technologies and universal connectivity has altered how people access information and interact with the other individuals and their environments [7]. The impact of mobile devices is particularly relevant to the field of human mobility and tourism since spontaneous and ad-hoc access to information is helpful for travelers [2]. Mobile device can provide instant information that enables travelers to more effectively solve situational problems [13]. Although tourists have access to a large amount of information that ranges from online resources to location-based data, filtering of this information often becomes a tedious task requiring a lot of time and planning. At the same time, mobile devices are consequently transforming the ability to access information while on the move [14]. More and more the wearable technologies improve their presences in daily practices, acquiring information concerning a particular context on mobile device becomes more relevant in assisting the decision-making process of urban exploration and tourism.

In 2013, Google released Google Glass, a wearable technology that displays information in a new mobile paradigm. Glass, which is a hands-free digital eyewear, enables interactions that take advantage of camera and voice recognition. We chose Google Glass to implement our prototype because of its non-invasive and non-disruptive addition to travel experience. Figure 1 depicts a tourist testing the prototype on Glass.

Fig. 1. A tourist tests the Google Glass prototype

This paper describes a wearable technology that is designed to help tourists explore a new place and find the crowd sourced answers to their questions. One can imagine exploring a city with a local guide next to them who is able to respond to questions wherever they go. A wearable interaction was designed to emulate such an experience by combining contextual data with human guidance. The proposed system, AskLocal, allows tourists to ask locals questions given the context, in this case, capturing the surrounding environment through camera using Google Glass. An assigned local or group of locals then answers in real-time and feedback is pushed to the tourists device. Because locals are fully aware of the context, they can provide information and suggestions accordingly as if they were in the same environment as the tourist.

The system was designed with regards the following four aspects: contextual awareness, just-in-time feedback, personalized experience, and non-invasiveness. The proposed system utilizes contextual awareness since, as previously pointed out, it is the key to assisting tourists to filter information and make decisions. Photographs are simple but powerful tools to communicate the contextual information between tourists and locals in addition to the textual query. The system is designed to give just-in-time feedback when the context is still relevant to the tourist. The goal is to allow tourists to consult the locals as if they are traveling together. Current applications such as TripAdvisor and Yelp provide reviews but do not create a personalized experience tailored specifically towards individual needs. By enabling tourists to make any inquiries directly, the system maximizes the possibility of receiving personalized context-aware recommendations. The system is also non-invasive for both tourists and locals. Tourists are in full control of when they opt to use the system. Locals receive the message through SMS on their phones and do not need to have a necessary commitment to participate.

2   Background

We present a survey of existing literature that informed our design process related to the following aspects: tourism, wearable technology and communication of local contextual information. A particular focus is revealing how local cultures would benefit from cutting edge technologies to preserve and communicate their authenticity. A recent cross-cultural study by Cheng et.al discusses how foreign visitors perceive the local cultural commodities [4]. The statistical measures over the recognition of different local cultural resources by tourist in Luoyang, China show that the majority of the interest is focused on local crafts and products, and the cultural and creative commodities in the area are substantially overlooked.

The key point to overcome superficiality of cultural exchange in local neighborhoods is to understand the nature of urban experience. The concept of understanding the city by strolling is primarily employed by the 19th-century French writers such as Charles Baudelaire, Emile Zola, and Balzac. The term influenced modernist and post-modernist studies in sociology, philosophy, literature and cinema. Walter Benjamin describes *flaneur* as "botanizing on the asphalt" [1]. De Certeau has followed Benjamin's footprints and explored the impression of experiencing the city by walking [3]. In his writing, we see the rise of pedestrian as an everyday practitioner of place who produce the space by organic mobility in the city. Similarly, in Lynch's work on city perception, he draws attention to motion awareness by stating that a city is perceived in motion with visual and kinesthetic senses [10]. The concept of moving is also associated with the fragmentation of urban perception.

Numerous tools have been developed to assist tourists in navigating through a new place. Kounavis *et al.* have previously explored the idea of utilizing augmented reality to enhance the tourist experience [8]. In a manner similar to how AskLocal aids in the decision-making process for tourists, they describe the idea of how contextual awareness can mitigate information overload. Ultimately, the benefits of such a highly portable AR application are that it can function as a tourist guide and delivers information upon request. AskLocal extends this idea to wearable devices, as the user is able to ask questions and get information on-demand. An added benefit is that the wearable device can seamlessly enter and leave the user's field of view as needed.

Tussyadiah evaluates the potential transformation of tourist experience by using Google Glass [12]. Applying a content analysis method over the tweets by the users who expressed their potential use if they had Google Glass, she revealed that the dominating use was exploration. Aforementioned tweets were part of a competition held by Google to win an early prototype of Google Glass. Her conclusion is that Google Glass introduce a new potential that would transform travelers to explorers, encouraging production of first person narratives, enriching spatial experiences with just-in-time information and removing the barrier between the visitors and locals by providing a feeling of safety and ease of interpreting local commodities.

Davies et al. that compares identifying landmarks by transmitting photos to a server or using a map [5]. The user research results include the counterintuitive observation that a significant class of users appears happy to use image recognition even when this is a more complex, lengthy and error-prone process than traditional solutions. More recent examples include the work by Fan et al. that use strangers as sensors and enable users to ask temporal and ego-sensitive questions, identifies promising strangers that are likely to know the answer and has been deployed in a larger setup [6]. Similarly, the work by Liu et al. enable geospatial query answering using a mobile crowd [9] These systems proved to be effective based on large user test. There are major differences between their works and the present study Ask Local. One difference is that Ask Local provides contextual information with images. Second significant difference is that it expands human sensor to the provide solutions to culture-sensitive questions.

3 Methodology

Our study comprises three consecutive parts: ethnographic immersion, conceptual design, and prototyping. In order to gain a deeper understanding of cultural interactions, we limited our study to a particular area of tourism and a local context. For the touristic context we focused on food considering the frequency of exchange around food and the diversity of food merchandise in local neighborhoods; and for the local context we have selected Istanbul, Turkey due to the rich cultural habitat it employs.

3.1 Ethnographic Immersion

An ethnographic study was conducted on tourists behaviors and usage of technology. The study primarily focused on food, considering that food is an important element of tourism [11]. Tourists were observed in restaurants and nearby public spaces. How they decided on where to eat and how they ordered food in a restaurant if they were unfamiliar with the area were among the questions that were explored. The result of the study showed that (1) very often people have trouble understanding the menu or are unable to quickly get a locals recommendation, (2) some tourists heavily relied on tourists reviews, which did not always reflect local taste and perspectives, and (3) mobile devices play a vital role in distracting people and limiting face-to-face interactions throughout dining, sightseeing, and many other experiences during a trip.

Fig. 2. A local guide answers questions about a restaurant in Istanbul

The concept was then validated in Istanbul, Turkey during the contextual inquiry study. Foreign to Istanbul, the authors were paired with a local as their guide to explore the city, during which they asked the guide different kinds of questions related to navigating Istanbul (Fig. 2). The goal was to understand the type of questions average tourists encounter in a new place and how locals can respond to these questions in a timely manner. For instance, some questions included Where shall we go to eat around here?, What is Simit? and What is this mosque called?. The result confirmed that unfamiliar geography makes it difficult to identify landmarks, and unfamiliar language makes it difficult to read signs, order food and use transportation etc. [15]. The local guide made it easy to get answers to all of these questions on the spot.

3.2   Conceptual Design

Based on the ethnographic study, an initial system was designed, which enables tourists to ask locals questions while on the move and to receive context-related answers in as close to real-time as possible. An attempt was made to alter how tourists traverse a city, by creating a Glass application that connects tourists and locals in real-time. Such a system needs to take into consideration contextual information and needs to be fully personalized. The following questions were considered:

- How can Glass be utilized to introduce a new layer of local communication for a tourist traversing a city?
- How can we improve a tourists experience in a non-invasive way?
- What kind of interactions can enrich the cultural and local experience for tourists?

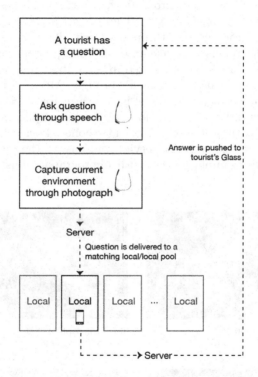

Fig. 3. System model and the communication flow.

To address these questions, the developed system captures contextual inquiries of the tourist and shares them with local networks. The system operates in real-time, given that the tourist expects an answer from a local within a few second while the context remains relevant. A group of locals committed to providing answers will be asked to respond to queries in time.

User Interface is designed to be simple and easy to reach for a traveler strolling the city. As it is also employed in the design of Google Glass, touch points with the system are limited to occupy small time-spans, providing required information as quick as possible.

3.3   Prototype Development

In the last phase, a functioning prototype was developed to test the proposed system on tourists and locals. Design evaluation was conducted based on a combination of Short Message Service (SMS) log files, semi-structured interviews and field observations.

For developing the prototype, the primary focus was on helping tourists find answers to their questions through communicating contextual information with locals. A simple Google Glass application was developed using the Glass SDK, which includes APIs to input text through speech and capture the environment with a built-in camera. The application starts once the user requests Glass: *"OK Glass, ask a local'* The interface prompts the user to ask questions with three given examples: *"What is good here?", "Where to get food?", "Pick one for me."* Once the user inputs the question through speech, the next viewport is a camera frame that allows the user to take and confirm a photograph. The questions along with the photos are sent and stored in a database and are time-stamped. The server then delivers this information, through SMS, to a matched local for a response. The complete system model is shown in Fig. 3. SMS was chosen as the delivery channel in favor of a stand-alone mobile application because of its simplicity and compatibility across different phones. Locals can see questions through their built-in text message service and answer the questions by replying the message. An example process with photographic illustrations is shown in Fig. 4.

(a) Ask local a question about what Turkish pastry to get

(b) Glass captures the environment of the pastry store

(c) Local replies to the question

(d) Suggestion is delivered to Glass

Fig. 4. Example Illustration of the prototype.

4   Design Evaluation and Results

After implementing the system, user research was conducted to evaluate the prototype and test its feasibility. Specifically, the average response speed, the quality of response, quantitative questions versus qualitative questions, and whether more than one local should to be matched with each tourist were evaluated. Quantitative data was gathered by logging the content of each message, the corresponding time stamp, and by whom the message was sent on what device (Fig. 5).

An initial user exploration was performed with two setups in order to gain perspectives from both tourists and locals. In the first setup, two locals were recruited from the area and assigned their phone numbers to the AskLocal server. One of the researchers pretended to be a tourist and used the system to ask questions. In total, 10 questions were asked over a testing period of two hours. Through this setup, the average response speed and the quality of response were tested. Log file analysis shows that the response was in average 1.5 min. An analysis of the quality of the answers showed that all answers were very informative and locals were genuinely interested in assisting tourists. The responses were easy to follow, and the advice allowed researchers to make decisions accordingly. Qualitative questions overall require longer response time but are generally more helpful than quantitative questions (yes/no questions).

In the second setup, Glass was given to tourists who came to visit a college campus. After being given Glass, tourists received a quick tutorial before they continued their trip using AskLocal. In this setup, the researchers served as locals, which ensured the response time and answered questions in a different environment with mobile phones. Field observations and follow-up interviews indicate that tourists sustained interest throughout the interaction and used

Body	Status	Sent Date	Image	Time
Thanks for the quick response!	sent	2014-05-04 09:37:58 PDT		
EECS / many other classes	received	2014-05-04 09:37:57 PDT		12 min
Hi! Ashley has a question for you: what is taught in this building? Here's what she's seeing.	sent	2014-05-04 09:23:41 PDT	http://bit.ly/1fHWYvI	
Thanks for the quick response!	sent	2014-05-04 09:17:06 PDT		
Walk straight until end of hallway, take left, walk down stairs, go straight until first door on left leads to a bridge to walk over	received	2014-05-04 09:17:06 PDT		3.5 min
Hi! Ashley has a question for you: how to get to start? Here's what she's seeing.	sent	2014-05-04 09:13:32 PDT	http://bit.ly/RhND1Y	
Thanks for the quick response!	sent	2014-05-04 09:12:27 PDT		
More commonly known as Killian Court	received	2014-05-04 09:12:27 PDT		1min
Thanks for the quick response!	sent	2014-05-04 09:11:57 PDT		
Overlooking the river from Lobby 10 under the big dome	received	2014-05-04 09:11:57 PDT		30 sec
Hi! Ashley has a question for you: what part of campus is this? Here's what she's seeing.	sent	2014-05-04 09:11:27 PDT	http://bit.ly/1fHVSjc	

Fig. 5. The log of communication between a student and a visitor in the college campus

locals feedback to make decisions. Response time is key in the AskLocal system. Since the analogy is to have a real local companion guiding the tourists and answer questions, tourists expect to receive immediate feedback. Failure of just-in-time response will result in (1) user is no longer in the relevant context as when the question was asked; (2) the feeling of having a local companion diminishes greatly and (3) the user loses interest in the service, finding it unreliable. A conclusion can be drawn that for AskLocal to work reliably, more than one local needs to be on-call to guarantee just-in-time responses.

5   Discussion and Future Work

The AskLocal system has been tested only on the individual scale. Future work for scaling up the system involves methods to identify and recruit locals. Potential solutions can be facilitating online community or using the tourists extended social network. Further research can be conducted on how many on-call locals are needed for each tourist to guarantee a timely response and keep tourists feeling like they are being accompanied.

6   Conclusions

By assessing the tourists experience in an unfamiliar place in the era of wearable technology, this paper describes a concept that enables tourists to experience a new place like a local using a combination of Google Glass and human intelligence. By creating a prototype that allows tourists to ask locals questions along with contextual information, and receive timely feedback, we demonstrated that wearable devices could provide tourists in a foreign place a new level of freedom and a more personalized experience. Ultimately, by merging augmented reality (Google Glass) with human intelligence (local perspective) the combined system brings in a human element to technology adding to the overall cultural experience for tourists.

References

1. Benjamin, W.: Charles Baudelaire: A Lyric Poet in the Era of High Capitalism. Verso Books, London (1977)
2. Berger, S., Lehmann, H., Lehner, F.: Location-based services in the tourist industry. Inf. Technol. Tourism 5(4), 243–256 (2003)
3. De Certeau, M.: The Practice of Everyday Life. University of California Press, Berkeley (1984)
4. Cheng, J., Xi, L., Ye, J., Xiao, W.: The research of regional culture characteristics of tourism commodities based on cross-cultural experience. In: Rau, P.L.P. (ed.) CCD 2014. LNCS, vol. 8528, pp. 24–34. Springer, Heidelberg (2014)
5. Davies, N., Cheverst, K., Dix, A., Hesse, A.: Understanding the role of image recognition in mobile tour guides. In: Proceedings of the 7th International Conference on Human Computer Interaction with Mobile Devices and Services, pp. 191–198. ACM (2005)

6. Fan, Y.C., Iam, C.T., Syu, G.H., Lee, W.H.: Using stranger as sensors: temporal and geo-sensitive question answering via social media. In: DCOSS, pp. 323–324 (2013)
7. Fuentetaja, I.G., Simon, I.Z., Aranzabal, A.R., Ariza, M.P., Lamsfus, C., Alzua-Sorzabal, A.: An analysis of mobile applications classification related to tourism destinations. In: Xiang, Z., Tussyadiah, I. (eds.) Information and Communication Technologies in Tourism 2014, pp. 31–44. Springer International Publishing, Switzerland (2014)
8. Kounavis, C.D., Kasimati, A.E., Zamani, E.D.: Enhancing the tourism experience through mobile augmented reality: challenges and prospects. Int. J. Eng. Bus. Manag. 4, 1–6 (2012)
9. Liu, Y., Alexandrova, T., Nakajima, T.: TeleEye: enabling real-time geospatial query answering with mobile crowd. In: Proceedings of the 22nd International Conference on World Wide Web, pp. 803–814 (2013)
10. Lynch, K.: Image of the City. MIT Press, Cambridge (1960)
11. Quan, S., Wang, N.: Towards a structural model of the tourist experience: an illustration from food experiences in tourism. Tourism Manag. 25(3), 297–305 (2004)
12. Tussyadiah, I.: Expectation of travel experiences with wearable computing devices. In: Xiang, Z., Tussyadiah, I. (eds.) Information and Communication Technologies in Tourism 2014. Springer International Publishing, Switzerland (2014)
13. Wang, D., Park, S., Fesenmaier, D.R.: The role of smartphones in mediating the touristic experience. J. Travel Res. 51(4), 371–387 (2012)
14. Want, R.: When cell phones become computers. IEEE Pervasive Comput. 8(2), 2–5 (2009)
15. Yang, J., Yang, W., Denecke, M., Waibel, A.: Smart sight: a tourist assistant system. In: The Third International Symposium on Wearable Computers, pp. 73–78 (1999)

Culture for Design and Design for Culture

Analysis of Emotional Design and Cultural Product Narrative Communication Model

Miao-Hsien Chuang[1(✉)] and Jui-Ping Ma[2]

[1] Department of Visual Communication Design,
Ming Chi University of Technology, New Taipei City, Taiwan
joyceblog@gmail.com
[2] Graduate School of Creative Industry Design,
National Taiwan University of Arts, New Taipei City 22058, Taiwan
artma2010@gmail.com

Abstract. Based on the product semantics model of Krippendorff (1989) and the design psychology concept of Norman (2004), we studied emotional design through narrative structures and Chinese characters. Employing case study and content analysis techniques, we found that designers can express creative ideas and product imagination using the form, sound and meaning of Chinese characters, as well as story elements (medium, role, interaction, spatial and temporal feel). We also made a case study of a designer in Taiwan who uses palmistry to illustrate business strategies for the cultural and creative industries. We adapted the product semantics model of Krippendorff into the cultural product narrative communication model by integrating narrative elements with form and meaning, as well as emphasizing the personal philosophies of designers and user participation. Designers pursuing innovation or promoting culture in product design can utilize this model as reference.

Keywords: Emotional design · Product semantics · Story narrative · Form and meaning

1 Introduction

Consumers in the 21st century, which has been characterized by excessive consumerism and the aesthetic economy, have many different reasons for purchasing products; function, utility, and price are no longer their primary considerations. As the artistic and emotional elements of products have taken precedence over their functionality, designers are facing the challenge of how to create product features that meet the affective requirements of consumers. Taipei City, in which the author resides, is set to become the 2016 World Design Capital. It is developing itself as an Adaptive City based on three design concepts: Use to User, Function to Feeling, and Hi-Tech to Hi-Touch, creating an outstanding environment, authenticity, and qualia (Lin 2011). Product design concepts are becoming more users-centric and focusing on how to allow users to experience the emotional meaning of products.

There have been a number of studies on product creativity and cultural design and marketing. In relation to design narratives, scholars have integrated the Barthes code

© Springer International Publishing Switzerland 2015
P.L.P. Rau (Ed.): CCD 2015, Part II, LNCS 9181, pp. 187–196, 2015.
DOI: 10.1007/978-3-319-20934-0_18

theory with semiotics and cultural studies to develop the concept of cultural codes. However, there are no studies that have integrated narrative elements with the design process of cultural products. This study combines the form and meaning of Chinese characters with storytelling elements, and analyzes the principles of emotional product design.

2 Literature Review

2.1 Product Semantics and Cultural Creativity

Rooted in semiotics, product semantics is the study of the meaningfulness of interaction between users and products. It emphasizes subjectivity and symbolic contexts rather than form and function. Krippendorff (1989) wrote that manufactured products have two key components - form and meaning - through which users understand the utility of the product (as shown in Fig. 1). Designers must consider the contexts in which users utilize products. Product semantics is not a merely trend or fashion; it is a discipline concerned with how users make sense of manufactured products, how these products are symbolically embedded in the fabric of society, and how they contribute to cultural autopiesis.

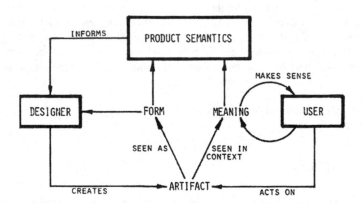

Fig. 1. Product semantics model of Krippendorff (1989)

McCoy (1989) saw product semantics as an interpretation of post-modernism. He believed that products must be meaningfully linked to constructs that satisfy diverse interpretations. We must pursue mystery and spirit in product design, rather than only material elements. According to McCoy, "products make myths tangible, either by reflecting a shared mythology or an individual vision." Mythology can be roughly defined as the common beliefs that humans create in their pursuit of social order, ethics, and morality. Norman (2004) pointed out that product design seeks to either improve or to create. Innovation means providing a completely different way of doing things or producing something that could not previously be achieved.

According to Lin (2005a), design covers cultural creativity, creative behavior, form, and economic behavior. Because culture is part of the everyday lives of consumers, the added value of cultural creativity makes a product unique and different. Cultural design can be divided into internal, external, and intermediate layers. Externally, products are designed directly from the form of cultural objects. In the intermediate plane, products are designed according to the functions of cultural customs or rituals. Finally, the internal dimension emphasizes the interaction and emotion between culture, product, and individual (Lin 2005b).

2.2 Narrative and Story Structure

As its name implies, narratology is a study of narratives and narrative structures. Even in a narrative with non-linguistic material, we can still use language-based narrative research methods to participate. Product design is just such an example. A narrative structure is like the skeleton of a high rise; you can't see it, but it determines the form and quality of the building (Lodge 1992). Using writing as an example, Yang (1998) expressed that before a writer puts pen to paper, he/she must first visualize the completed product and the aesthetic world that he/she intends to create. Writing is a life activity, and the product of writing is a kind of crystallization. He described the process between communicative writing and its objectives as a dynamic "structure".

A story is a set of characters and events that are linked together through time sequence and causal relationships, creating a potentially interesting narrative. The five elements to a story – the characters, the setting, the plot, the conflict, and the resolution- allow readers to clearly grasp the developing logic of the story. The product scenario approach is story-based, using people, times, places, and things (products) to describe a narrative and encourage participants to develop product contexts (Tang and Lin 2011).

2.3 Meaning of Form

Words are categorized as phonograms or ideograms. An alphabet system is used in most Western languages and words are phonetic notations that convey messages. Chinese language characters are both phonograms and ideograms, with each one having three elements: Shape, sound, and meaning. Shape refers to the appearance of the character, sound to how it is pronounced, and meaning to the idea or concept that it expresses. For example, the Chinese character ding (鼎) means an ancient Chinese vessel with three legs. The form of the character shows three legs and it is pronounced as ding. The character is interpreted as "tripartite" in meaning.

Chinese enjoy using homophonic elements to express their hopes or good wishes when giving gifts or engaging in religious worship. For example, the words for bottle (ping zi, 瓶子) and peace (ping an, 平安) both start with the same phonetic sound. Radish (cai tou, 菜頭) and fortune (cai tou, 彩頭) also share the same pronunciation. The characters for fish (yu, 魚) and surplus (yu, 餘) are homonyms, so a fish dish is seen to represent bounty (nian nian you yu, 年年有餘). The character for goat (羊)

forms part of the word for good fortune (吉祥). Bats represent good luck and crab represents gratitude because of the phonetic similarity between the word pairs.

Apart from understanding individual words, an author must also accomplish the following to produce a good piece of writing: Composition practice (word combinations, sentences, and different sentence structure); Writing techniques (expansion, abbreviation, sequels, and parodies); and narrative (theme, content, organization, modification, rhetoric) (Liao 2007).

2.4 Emotional Design

Emotions are the attitudes that people have towards their surroundings, themselves and their behaviors. Emotion is a subjective human reaction to an objective situation, an affirmative or non-affirmative psychological reaction to external stimuli (Gong and Duan 2007). Baudrillard et al. believed that instead of buying products for their functionality, people in our consumer society look to products for a sense of fun, an experience different from their everyday routines (Huang 2000). This is why emotional design, whether it aims to provide an imagined or experiential sense of fun, is a challenge encountered by a majority of modern designers.

Psychologist Donald A. Norman (2004) analyzed three levels of design using a teapot as a case study: visceral level (appearance-based), behavioral level (user-friendliness and satisfaction), and reflective level (rationalization of the product, its narrative and its link to self-image). He wrote that the last two dimensions are affected by the experiences, education level, and cultural perspectives of the individual.

As far as how products make a person feel, Goto (2008) explained that most designers use external appearance to bring about the initial surprise (first WOW). However, designers can create a stronger impression by consciously manipulating the psyche of consumers (later WOW). Russell (1980) combined physiological and psychological angles to produce the Circumplex model. The model employs a Cartesian coordinate system where the horizontal axis runs from pleasant to unpleasant (right to left) and the vertical axis runs from high stimulation to low stimulation (top to bottom). A product matching the coordinates for "pleasant" and "high stimulation" creates feelings of excitement, delight, and happiness in the user.

2.5 Summary

Based on form and meaning, as well as emotional design, this study explores the structural elements (form) and narrative elements (medium, role, interaction, spatial and temporal feel) of Chinese characters. We developed the product semantics model of Krippendorff into a communication model focused on cultural products. Lastly, we conducted an in-depth interview with an expert in cultural design, in order to gain an understanding of the individual vision and mythology of designers.

3 Methodology

We employed case study and content analysis techniques to research Stone Image Design Co. and its popular cultural products, particularly those with emotive design. Based on our results, we classed design techniques into categories and analyzed shared design principles.

3.1 Case Study: Stone Image Design Co

Founded by Cheng Xiang Ru, Stone Image Design Co. has researched and developed a range of products based on traditional Chinese culture. The company also formed a strategic alliance with Nova Design Co. Ltd to break into the product design industry. In 2007, the company officially re-launched itself as a design consultancy focused on helping traditional businesses to improve their products and operations through services such as brand and image development, marketing strategy, and product R&D. Its clients are mainly traditional craft businesses in the smaller towns and villages of Taiwan. We chose Stone Image as a case study because its products generally have unique narrative and semantic elements.

3.2 Content Analysis

We analyzed cultural products that have elements of emotive design. Product images were sourced from the Internet, printed media, and relevant events. The authors of these publications and designers of these products are all well-known professionals in their fields. Their works, which highlight local cultural features, are marketed on an international as well as local basis.

4 Discussion and Conclusions

Telling a compelling story through a product is an effective technique in the competitive design industry. Through storytelling, designers elicit an emotional response from consumers. Users construct, interpret, and assimilate the narrative, and even provide feedback useful to product design and manufacturing. This creates a cycle of design, ideas, and imagination (Chuang and Huang 2009). After categorizing the product images collected, we identified that products are designed to convey a sense of fun and uniqueness, as well as inspire users to associate the products with stories. The products in this study, which are analysed in the table below, express creativity through the form and meaning of Chinese characters, as well as structural narratives.

4.1 Product Design, and the Form and Meaning of Chinese Characters

Chinese characters comprise three elements: Appearance, sound, and meaning. Words are created through shape, pronunciation, and meaning. Product design operates through similar constructs. We analyze the sample products based on these three elements as well as the three layers of cultural design (Table 1).

Table 1. Comparing product design to the form and meaning of Chinese characters

Character	Technique	Product interpretation	Image	Layers of cultural design
Form	Appearance	Product: Red bean tart Appearance: Circular and split in the middle Meaningfulness: This product is named seppuku, which refers to the ancient Japanese custom of ritual suicide and implies apology and contrition.	(Source: http://mei.life101.com.tw/6536 71#ixzz3PiIs7lc1)	External (form): Split appearance Combined (cultural ritual): Seppuku ritual
Sound	Homophone	Product: CD case Appearance: Butterflies Meaningfulness: Homophonic sounds are used to allude to the Chinese word for good fortune.	(Source: from the designer Cheng Xiang Ru)	Intermediate (customs): Good wishes and blessings
Meaning	Collective meaningfulness	Product: Calendar Image: Daily life commodities traditionally used in Taiwan Meaningfulness: A collection of bygone memories	(Source: http://www.taaze.tw/sing.html?pid=61100001430)	Internal (emotion): Nostalgic memories

4.2   Association Between Product Design and Story Narratives

A story is a set of characters and events that are linked together through time sequence and causal relationships, creating a potentially interesting narrative. Marketing and promotional campaigns can of course tell a story, but so can the product itself, using a dynamic narrative structure. The products shown in Table 2 are designed using artistic or cultural elements and convey a sense of fun and creativity.

Table 2. Association between product design and story narrative

Story	Method	Product	Image (and product designer)
Carrier	The product is used to display a famous Chinese calligrapher's works	Pepper shaker (The individual components of the product can be freely manipulated)	By Cheng Xiang Ru (Source: from the designer)
Role	A role-playing doll	ART TOY (combining the work of Chinese contemporary artist Yue Minjun and graffiti king KAWS)	By Yue Minjun and KAWS (Source: http://www.hua-gallery.com/artist.html)
Interaction	Emotional interaction between product and user	Product: Mirror (Inspires the user to reflect)	By Eglė Stonkutė (Source: https://www.behance.net/gallery/17694711/Reflections-Narcis-suses-and-other-flowers-Mirrors)
		These chess bags are called "hope bags" (inside the bag is a woodcut chess set, which provides the user with an opportunity to visit with others while playing chess)	By Cheng Xiang Ru (Source: from the designer)
Spatial feel	Image are placed randomly on the products	Teaware designed in collaboration with Yue Minjun and Qingting Design Co (the black birds are placed at the top, middle, and bottom of the cups)	By Shi Dayu (Source: http://blog.artron.net/space-610077-do-blog-id-1026207.html)
Temporal feel	A futuristic or nostalgic sense	A conceptual display of containers and boxes named "Museum of Tomorrow"	By Mads Hagstom (Source: http://blog.yam.com/bal-ance1014/article/16982754)

4.3 Life Philosophies of Designers

Cheng Xiang Ru, founder of Stone Image Design Co, uses palmistry as a metaphor of the development of the cultural industry, calling it "a new gravity" (see Table 3).

The Need-hierarchy theory of Abraham Maslow is used to illustrate how life management principles can be applied to running a design company. In the short-term, the company must establish income sources and develop its role in the market. Next comes strengthening market position and image, and building a strong client base. The long-term goal is to realize the ultimate vision of the company directors. Stone Image Design Co. is operated with the aim of achieving a balance between its ideals and the market realities.

Table 3. Relationship between palmistry and cultural products

Palm line	Palm	Product	Business strategies
Life line		The personality and life of the product	Strategic alliances Specifications, copy models Extend product life
Head line		The soul of the product	Brand image, Brand story Product distribution channels
Health line		Quality of the product	Combination of media Family product line

A SWOT analysis showed that Stone Image Design Co. faces the same competition and pressures as any other company. Its strength is in its founder Cheng Xiang Ru and her extensive commercial experience, likeability, reputation, and interpersonal networks, as well as his experience in government consulting roles. A key turning point came when Stone Image re-launched itself as a cultural consultancy company, which allowed it to establish key alliances and progress in the integration of culture with technology. Cheng Xiang Ru still works closely with her colleagues to preserve Chinese culture and unique local features. This case study of Stone Image provides us with a good example of the mythology of designers.

5 Conclusions and Recommendations

This study discusses the psychological levels of emotional design, the form and meaning of Chinese characters, story narratives, and the life philosophies of product designers. Building on the product semantics model of Krippendorff, we developed a cultural product narrative communication model Fig. 2:

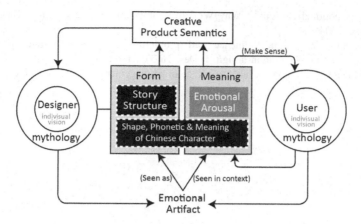

Fig. 2. Cultural product narrative communication model

This study provides references for researchers and academicians, as well as innovative design criteria that can be useful to designers in today's competitive environment. In future research, we will interview more designers and make a further study of the emotions that product design evokes in users.

Acknowledgements. Special thanks to Stone Image Design Co. for providing the images.

References

Chuang, M.H., Huang, C.: The analysis of product concept communication by story-telling. In: 14th Taiwan CID Annual Design Conference (2009)

Gong, Z.L., Duan, S.J.: Clairvoyance of emotion design in fortune in graphics. Packag. Eng. **28**, 136–137 (2007)

Goto, T., Sasaki, M., Fukasawa, N.: The Ecological Approach to Design (Huang, Y. M., Trans.). AzothBooks, Taipei (2008). (Original work published 2004)

Huang, R.C.: Modern and Postmodern. Liwen, Taipei (2000)

Krippendorff, K.: On the essential contexts of artifacts or on the proposition that "design is making sense (of things)". Des. Issues **5**(2), 9–39 (1989)

Krohn, L., McCoy, M.: Beyond beige, interpretive design for the post-industrial age. Des. Issues **5**(2), 112–123 (1989)

Liao, T.Y.: The Research of Enhance the Junior Hight Student's Capability of writing. (Unpublished master's thesis) Department of Chinese Teaching, National Kaohsiung Normal University, Kaoshiung (2007)

Lin, R.: Cultural creativity – combining technology and humanities. Sci. Dev., **396**, 68–75 (2005a) (in Chinese, semantic translation)

Lin, R.: Cultural creativity added design value. Art Apprec. **1**(7), 26–32 (2005b). (in Chinese, semantic translation)

Lin, R.: Environment, Authenticity, Qualia –Taipei as a World Design Capital, Taipei Economic Quarterly No.7 (2011) (in Chinese, semantic translation)

Lodge, D.: The Art of Fiction. Secker & Warburg, London (1992)

Norman, D.: Emotional Design — Why We Love (or Hate) Everyday Things. Basic Books, New York (2004)

Tang, H.H., Lin, Y.Q.: The influence and problems of scenario design approach on multi-disciplinary collaboration design. J. Des. **16**(3), 21–44 (2011)

Yang, Y.: Chinese Narratology. ChiaYi: College of Management of Nanhua University (1998)

From Design to Humanity - A Case Study of Costumer Value Toward Dechnology Products

Chi-Ying Hung[✉], Pei-Hua Hung, Wen-Zhong Su, and Hsi-Yen Lin

Graduate School of Creative Industry Design,
National Taiwan University of Arts, Ban Ciao District,
New Taipei City 22058, Taiwan
{yumeeiren, paywhathome, orpheussu, p3yann}@gmail.com

Abstract. This study explores customer value using 13 dechnology products, and discusses differences in customers' preferences with regard to use of advanced technology, display of design aesthetics, and expression of human care. The experiment comprises two parts, elementary school students and netizens, in each group subjects are asked about their preference for and evaluation of product design attributes. Results show that the two independent samples were consistent when choosing the product they liked most, and that the only significant difference was their evaluation of the product's concern for humanity. This study uses a means-end chain to construct a customer value model for dechnology products, and further analyzes their attitude towards and preference for the products, thereby providing a basis for enterprises to evaluate the value they deliver to target customers.

Keywords: Dechnology · Aesthetic perception · Customer value · Means-end chain model

1 Introduction

All products and services in the market must contain customer value, to what extent, however, is an important consideration of consumers when deciding whether or not purchase it at the price it is offered. Hence, it is important to consider customer value when designing products or developing services. Although enterprises can use mature technologies, such as surveys or product trials, to test the market's reaction and reduce the risk of failure, in a competitive market where information is easily accessible, new products and services are constantly emerging, and there are diverse channels for advertisement, the ability to seek out customer value and make breakthroughs in value-added designs are keys to maintain a competitive advantage. How to customers perceive these products? What are the attributes of these products? How do these products deliver value to customers? These are important issues that this study will explore.

© Springer International Publishing Switzerland 2015
P.L.P. Rau (Ed.): CCD 2015, Part II, LNCS 9181, pp. 197–208, 2015.
DOI: 10.1007/978-3-319-20934-0_19

2 Communication and Customer Value

Based on previous studies (Lin 2007; Lin and Kreifeldt 2014), a three-level design model was proposed as shown in Fig. 1. A successful communication must satisfy three aspects: the first is a technical aspect that must allow the person receiving a message to see, hear, touch, and even feel; it involves precisely conveying a message. The second is a semantic aspect that must allow the person receiving a message to understand its meaning; it involves precisely conveying the original intention of the message without causing any misunderstanding. The third aspect is the effect of a message, how to let the person receiving the message take the correct course of action; it involves how to effectively influence expected behavior. This study divides design attributes based on this concept of communication into use of advanced technology, display of design aesthetics, and expression of human care (Hsu et al. 2011, 2013, 2014).

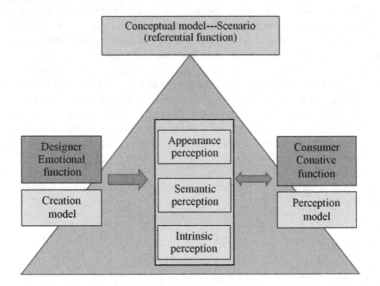

Fig. 1. Three levels of a design model

Use of advanced technology refers to the systematic evaluation of techno-logical development trends that may influence competition in the industry, wealth creation, and quality of life. Advanced technology originates from anticipations of future technology, but emphasizes an open attitude using conscientious and creative approaches of science for predictions, hoping to explore long-term development opportunities and feedback future vision to current objectives and topics (Ko 2011). Product design is founded on the use of advanced technology, which can increase the product's value-added or create an excellent user experience. It is an effective competition strategy for developing market demand and increasing customer value.

Aesthetics is a set of principles for perceiving or appreciating beauty, and is the science of perceiving things with our senses. In traditional fields of design, e.g. architectural design, product design, graphic design, and fashion design, aesthetics has long been an important subject. Even though the interactive aesthetics conveyed by industrial designers in the form of products is somewhat different from other fields, aesthetic elements that are explored are all based on the con-tent and form of interaction between people and things (Ma 2012). Hence, integrating aesthetic designs into technology products, so that the products may con-vey aesthetics and further interact with people is an important task of product designers.

Humanity is what drives design, if we use Maslow's hierarchy of needs: (1) physiological needs, (2) safety needs, (3) social needs, (4) esteem needs and (5) self-actualization needs in the technology aspect of product design, as well as the historical development of aesthetics, it corresponds to the functionality, friendliness, fun, uniqueness, and experience of perceptual technology (Lin and Kreifeldt 2014). When people satisfy high level needs, they begin to enrich their lives through experiences. This explains why the design of any product should be based on human care.

2.1   Customer Value

Studies on customer value adopt two main perspectives, one is the traditional rational perspective and the other is an experiential perspective. The experiential perspective evaluates the intrinsic pleasure symbols of a product, as well as the customer value of an aesthetic and enjoyable experience. Woodruff (1997) defined customer value as a customer perceived preference for and evaluation of those products attributes, attribute performances, and consequences arising from use that facilitate (or block) achieving the customer's goals and purposes in use situations. Product attributes can by a symbolic meaning, hedonic response, or aesthetic standard. On the other hand, the rational perspective evaluates products based on their utility or effectiveness, which is also referred to as rational consumption value. Kotler (2003) defined it as an offering, including combinations of options, and evaluated the potential difference between overall customer benefits and cost, e.g. problem solving and satisfying demand. Hence, Huang (2001) believed that scholars who define value by its effectiveness, cost-benefit ratio or difference take on a rational perspective, while scholars who emphasize emotions and preferences take on an experiential perspective.

Holbrook (1994) further divided customer value into three aspects, namely extrinsic value and intrinsic value, self-oriented value and other-oriented value, and active value and reactive value. The categories of customer value, namely efficiency, excellence, status, esteem, play, aesthetics, ethics and spirituality, based on these three aspects are shown in Table 1 (Holbrook 1999) quoted from (Yao 2009).

Table 1. Categories of customer value

		Extrinsic	**Intrinsic**
Self-oriented	Active	Efficiency (O/I, Convenience)	Play(Fun)
	Reactive	Excellence(Quality)	Aesthetics(Beauty)
Other-oriented	Active	Status(Success, Impression Management)	Ethics(Virtue, Justice, Morality)
	Reactive	Esteem (Reputation, Materialism, Possessions)	Spirituality (Faith, Magic, Ecstasy)

2.2 Means-End Chain Model

The basic concept of the means-end chain model can be traced back to an approach proposed by psychology researchers in studies on human behavior in the 1930s. This model believes that customers' purchase motivation is not for the object itself, but a connection with the object created through a series of value evaluations and choices. This connection is meaningful and is an exploration of the relationship between the object and customers' abstract values. Ladder analysis is employed to analyze how customers form meaningful connections between product attributes, results and goals, and further explain the hierarchical relationship between value perception and customer behavior (Yang 2012). In short, the means-end chain model is used to explore how customers choose products, and which results serve the purpose of which values held by consumers.

Hence, the main purpose of the means-end chain model is to construct and explain the connection made by customers between product attributes, results and values (Gutman 1982). Figure 2 shows that attributes-results and results-values form a two stage means-end chain, in which results are a means and also an end. Olson (1983) (quoted from Huang (2001)) derived six levels from this model (see Fig. 2), in which products have concrete and abstract attributes, customers that purchase the products gain functional or social results, at which time results transforms from an end to a means to satisfy customers' goals, and further realizes utility and the ultimate value. This is how the attribute-results-values chain operates.

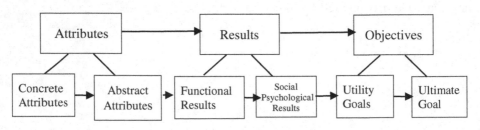

Fig. 2. Means-end chain model

3 Research Methodology

Based on the exploration of design attributes and customer value in chapter two, the three levels of the means-end chain model can be used. Content analysis showed that in the three levels of the design model, appearance perception corresponds to attributes, semantic perception corresponds to results, and intrinsic perception corresponds to goals. Hence, this study divides customer value of dechnology into three stages: stage one is the literature review and theoretical foundation above; stage two uses a sample of dechnology products and designs a questionnaire survey based on three categories of design attributes; stage three comprises data organization, statistical analysis, research on customer value theories and perception, explores research results, constructs a new design model for dechnology products, and obtains possible conclusions and recommendations.

Technology is rational while aesthetics is perceptual. The two are like two sides of a scale, but if they can be combined, the results will be worth looking further into. Dechnology is one approach to finding a solution.

Dechnology stands for Design + Technology. Its main purpose is to channel Taiwan's rich design energy into value-added aesthetic design of technology products, hoping to combine the ration left brain of scientists with the sensitive right brain of designers, allow technology to breakthrough its constraints, and transform technology into moving products in the market (Zhang 2012). This study uses the innovative products of Dechnology 2014 New Collection shown in Table 2 as the research sample, and explores the relationship between design attributes and customer value from the perspective of customers Hung and Huang (2013).

Table 2. Products in the sample

1(A)	2(B)	3(C)	4(D)	5(E)	6(F)	7(G)
Sheathing Fabric Pot	Cake Steamer	Low Temp.	Portal	Purification Bag	Beauty Mirror	Sit Properly
8(H)	9(I)	10(J)	11(K)	12(L)	13(M)	
Flip IRB	Water 911	Health Travel	Ultrasound Monitor	Medical HMD	Touch Handlebar	

Based on the discussion on communication and customer value in chapter two, a questionnaire survey consisting of two parts is conducted. Subjects of the first group are 72 elementary school students (41 boys and 31 girls, ages 10–11) of grade 5 and products shown in Table 2 are printed out on the questionnaire. Subjects of the second group are netizens of a model making blog and an online questionnaire survey is conducted; 120 effective samples were collected, the majority are in the ages 21 ~ 25 (31 %), followed by 20 years and younger (24 %). The items are measured on a 5 point Likert scale, in which 1 indicates strongly disagree and 5 indicates strongly agree. The questionnaire displays images of the products, and subjects are asked to choose their preference with regard to use of advanced technology, display of design aesthetics, and expression of human care. This is used to analyze whether if the value conveyed by the designer and the product is significantly correlated with customer value. It is also used to verify the hypothesis that design attributes are intrinsic customer values, and that customers use the perception model to determine their preference for a product.

4   Results and Discussion

4.1   Experiment Results

Table 3 shows test one and test two subjects' preference and compatibility with the three design attributes, in which the average preference was 3.6 in test one and 3.7 in test two. Subjects of test one and two both preferred products (E) and (I) the most with an average score of 4; their scores for the three design attributes were also above 4. This shows that subjects' preference is in direct ratio to the three design attributes. Products (E) and (I) have bright colors, vanguard design, and their use satisfy human needs, which makes them the most popular among different groups.

Table 3. Average scores for compatibility with product attributes in tests one and two

Test 1: Evaluation by elementary school students					Test 2: Evaluation by Netizen				
Attribute Product	Preference	Technology	Design Aesthetic	Human Care	Attribute Product	Preference	Technology	Design Aesthetic	Human Care
1(A)	3.2	3.4	3.2	3.3	1(A)	3.3	3.7	3.3	3.6
2(B)	3.8	3.9	3.5	3.4	2(B)	3.3	3.7	3.8	3.3
3(C)	3.5	3.7	3.4	3.3	3(C)	3.7	3.8	3.7	3.6
4(D)	3.9	4.0	3.9	3.7	4(D)	3.8	4.0	4.0	4.0
5(E)	3.9	4.2	3.9	3.9	5(E)	4.0	4.1	3.9	4.2
6(F)	3.3	3.5	3.6	3.5	6(F)	3.5	4.1	3.3	4.1
7(G)	3.8	3.8	3.7	3.7	7(G)	4.0	3.9	3.9	4.3
8(H)	3.7	4.1	3.8	3.9	8(H)	3.5	3.9	3.3	3.9
9(I)	4.1	4.3	4.1	4.0	9(I)	4.0	4.1	4.0	4.1
10(J)	3.9	4.1	3.9	4.0	10(J)	3.8	4.0	3.7	4.3
11(K)	3.4	3.8	3.6	3.9	11(K)	3.6	4.1	3.6	4.1
12(L)	3.3	3.7	3.4	3.9	12(L)	3.7	4.2	3.4	4.1
13(M)	3.8	4.2	3.9	4.1	13(M)	3.6	3.9	3.3	4.1

4.2   Elementary School Students

Correlation analysis of the preference, technology, design aesthetics, and human care scores of elementary school students are shown in Table 4. All four are significantly positively related (p < 0.001), and the correlation coefficient all reached a certain level. Preference is then used as the dependent variable and technology, design aesthetics, and human care are used as independent variables in multiple regression analysis. The regression model constructed is shown below:

Product preference $= 0.08 + 0.65$(Technology) $+ 0.67$(Design aesthetics) $- 0.39$(Human care)

Adj.$R^2 = 0.92, P < 0.01$

The model shows that product preference is affected by technology, design aesthetics, and human care with standardized regression coefficients of 0.65, 0.67 and -0.39, respectively. This shows that use of advanced technology and display of aesthetic design have a relatively strong influence on elementary school students' preference for products, while human care does not. We can reason that elementary school students gain a more direct perception from the appearance and symbols of products, or the utility and aesthetics of products, but gain less from intrinsic emotions of human care. This is possibly related to their incomplete socialization and education.

Table 4. Correlation analysis results for elementary school students

	Preference	Technology	Design aesthetics	Human care
Preference	1			
Technology	0.91***	1		
Design aesthetics	0.92***	0.89***	1	
Human care	0.71***	0.85***	0.81***	1

***p<0.001

4.3   Netizens

Correlation analysis of the preference, technology, design aesthetics, and human care scores of netizens are shown in Table 5. All four are significantly positively correlated (p < 0.001) and their correlation coefficient reach a certain level. The model generated from multiple regression analysis is shown below:

Product preference $= -.15 + 0.46$(Design aesthetics) $+ 0.54$(Human care)

Adj.$R^2 = 0.90$ P < 0.01

The standardized regression coefficients of design aesthetics and human care are 0.46 and 0.54, respectively, showing that the influence of human care on preference is higher than design aesthetics. Technology did not have a significant effect on the preference of Netizens, which may be due to subjects frequently receiving technology related information and are more exact when evaluating products' use of advanced technology. This result indicates that online consumers not only require dechnology products have an aesthetic appearance, but also offer intrinsic values as well.

Table 5. Correlation analysis results for Netizenss

	Preference	Technology	Design aesthetics	Human care
Preference	1			
Technology	0.63***	1		
Design aesthetics	0.65***	0.17***	1	
Human care	0.77***	0.77***	0.2***	1

***$p<0.001$

4.4 Comparison of Elementary School Students and Netizens

Independent t-test is employed to evaluate the influence of elementary school students and netizens' preference on the three design attributes. A significant difference was found between the opinions of elementary school students and netizens regarding products' human care ($t = 3.21$, $p < 0.05$), but there was no significant difference in terms of preference, technology, and design aesthetics. This shows that age will affect subjects' intrinsic perception of products, and further result in different evaluations of the expression of human care.

4.5 Customer Value Design Model for Dechnology Products

The statistical analysis above shows that customers' perception of product attributes will influence their preference for products, and we can further infer that design attributes are highly correlated with customer value. Therefore, after combining the pyramid-shaped perception model of design communication with the means-end chain model and customer values table, the resulting customer value design model for dechnology products is shown in Fig. 3.

Figure 3 shows that the values delivered by design attributes are closely related to customer values. The relationship between different design elements used by designers and the values desired by target customers are a crucial factor in the design process Chen (2012). Although the entire design process is strongly subjective, the customer value table can be used to analyze and evaluate if customers know the design elements that deliver value, and allow developers to find a balance between design elements and customer value, making products closer to customers' expectations and deliver values desired by customers.

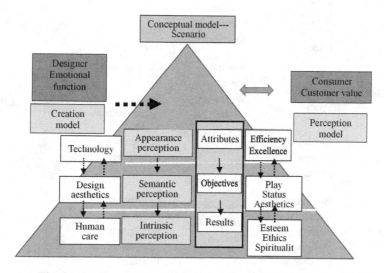

Fig. 3. Customer value design model for dechnology products

Design communication of dechnology involves a vast scope. Besides the efficiency offered by the technology, it also includes rational values such as utility, price, taste and status, and experiential values such as profound aesthetic content and symbols and spiritual value. Based on the model displayed in Fig. 3, this study uses content analysis on the customer values in the sample and combines it with the customer value table of Huang (2001) into Table 6.

Based on the model in Fig. 3 and analysis in Table 6, products in the sample of this study, whether it may be for living, sports, travel, medical devices, multimedia, home appliances, or lighting, the main characteristic is they are used by customers as a habit, hobby or interest, and most importantly they satisfy customers' intrinsic needs. This study found that every product contains the eight customer values of Holbrook (1999), only that the ratio of each customer value varies with the product's purpose. This is consistent with the fact that age or other factors of the two groups will result in significant correlation with the design attributes, especially the expression of human care.

Table 6. Customer values for dechnology products

MEC	Attributes	Results	Objectives	Sample
Design modal *Customer Value*	**Appearance**	**Semantic**	**Intrinsic**	
Efficiency	Easy to use Simple Search Physiological Price utility	Save time Comfortable Save/Health	Free Pleasure Meet Achievement	
Excellence	Achieve Professional Specific store	Worth it Taste Satisfactory service	Comfortable life Security Achievement	
Status	Luxury Impression Management	Status upgrade Confidence Success Interpersonal	Recognition Belonging Achievement	
Esteem	Brand owners Particular type Service Wearing appropriate	Reputation Self-expression Position Affirmative	Get respect Achievement Strengthen self-esteem Pleasure	
Play	With Diversity Voluntary Creative	Growing up Importance Relief Save	Meet/Free Accomplishment Pleasure	
Aesthetics	Color Pattern Modeling Cultural Fashion	Pleasing Craving Confidence Popular	Pleasure Achievement Comfortable life	
Ethics	Boycott Expose Charitable	Justice Ethics Virtue	Responsibility Helping sense of achievement	
Spirituality	Style Gregarious Divine Faithful	Identity Fascinated Magic Safe	Spiritual freedom Heaven Pleasure	

5 Conclusion

Customers receive information of design attributes conveyed by the product using their perception model, generate a connection with the product, and further develop a subjective evaluation of the product. This study found that elementary school students and Netizens both preferred the same products. A good product must be able to continuously past the tests of its customers, and the products that were preferred contained customer values that satisfied the needs of most people. There are eight customer values that form the core values of customers, and products that deliver these values will gain unmatched competitiveness.

This study also found that there was no significant difference between scores given by the two groups for technology and design aesthetics, but there was a significant difference in human care. Observing based on the customer value theory, the former are rational perspectives that emphasize effectiveness and utility, and thus generally result in the same opinions between groups. The latter is an experiential perspective that emphasizes intrinsic pleasure, emotions and preference, and there are thus greater differences between age groups and individuals. Hence, product design can target the needs of different groups to find a niche market.

Therefore, whether enterprises embrace several customer values or focus on a single customer value, communicating through products and satisfying customers' needs is the one and only way to run a business. Before beginning the design of a new product, studying the connection between design attributes and customer value in the planning process, and understanding values of target customers will increase the product's success rate. Future studies may look into different products or groups to strengthen the theoretical foundation, or develop a more exact means-end chain model for design communication, and help evaluate customer value before products enter the market.

Acknowledgements. The authors gratefully acknowledge the support for this research provided by the Ministry of Science and Technology under Grant No.MOSY-103-2410-H-144-003 and MOST-103-2221-E-144-001. The authors also wishes to thank Prof. Jhon. G. Kreifeldt and Po-Hsien Lin, especially, Prof. Rungtai Lin.

References

Chen, J.-Y.: Exploring the principle of the product design. J. Calligraphy **12**, 217–231 (2012)

Gutman, J.: A means-end chain model based on consumer categorization processes. J. Mark. Spring **46**, 60–72 (1982)

Holbrook, M.B.: The nature of customer value: an axiology of services in the consumption experience. Serv. Qual. New Dir. Theory Pract. **21**, 21–71 (1994)

Holbrook, M.B.: Introduction to consumer value. In: Holbrook, M.B. (ed.) Consumer Value: A Framework for Analysis and Research. Routledge, New York (1999)

Hsu, C.H., Chang, S.H., Lin, R.: A design strategy for turning local culture into global market products. Int. J. Affect. Eng. (Kansei Eng. Int. J.) **12**(2), 275–283 (2013)

Hsu, C.H., Fan, C.H., Lin, J.Y., Lin, R.: An investigation on consumer cognition of cultural design products. Bull. Jpn. Soc. Sci. Des. **60**(5), 39–48 (2014)

Hsu, C.-H., Lin, C.-L., Lin, R.: A study of framework and process development for cultural product design. In: Rau, P. (ed.) IDGD 2011. LNCS, vol. 6775, pp. 55–64. Springer, Heidelberg (2011)

Huang, Y.-Y.: A means-end chain analysis of customer value–consumption experience of children's clothes. Ph.D, National Sun Yat-sen University, Kaohsiung City (2001)

Hung, W.K., Huang, W.: Creating value for technology by design: a case study of Technology project. J. Des. **18**(1), 41–64 (2013)

Ko, C.-E.: Technology foresight and S&T policy formation: a case study of Taiwan agricultural technology foresight 2025. J. Technol. Manag. **16**(3), 1–28 (2011)

Kotler, P.: Marketing Management, 11th edn. Prentice Hall International, Englewood Cliffs (2003)

Lin, R.: Transforming Taiwan aboriginal cultural features into modern product design: a case study of a cross-cultural product design model. Int. J. Des. **1**(2), 45–53 (2007)

Lin, R., Kreifeldt, G.J.: Do Not Touch: The conversation between Dechnology and Humart, Taipei (2014)

Lin, R., Lin, C.L.: From digital archives to E-business: A case study on turning "art" into "business". In: e-Business (ICE-B). Paper presented at the Proceedings of the 2010 International Conference (2010)

Lin, R., Yen, C.-C., Chen, R.: From adaptive design to adaptive city-design in motion for taipei city. In: Rau, P. (ed.) CCD 2014. LNCS, vol. 8528, pp. 643–649. Springer, Heidelberg (2014)

Ma, Y.-P.: Aesthetics of Interaction Design for Environmental Awareness. (Ph.D), National Cheng Kung University (2012)

Olson, J.C., R, T.J.: Understanding Consumers' Cognitive Structures, Implications for Marketing Strategy. Lawrence Erlbaum Associates, Mahwah (1983)

Woodruff, R.B.: Customer Value: The Nest Sourse for competitive Advantage. J. Acad. Mark. Sci. **25**(2), 139–153 (1997)

Yang, C.-C.: Exploring consumer values toward the functional clothing from means-end chain analysis. J. Hum. Develop. Family **14**(1), 67 (2012)

Yao, W.-C.: Exploring Customer Value of Culture Creative Product-A Case Study of NewChi. (Master). Ming Chuan University, Taipei City (2009)

Zhang, Y.W.: The value of technology and humanity. Ind. Technol. (2012)

From Design to Technology

A Case Study of Children's Perception
Toward the Dechnology Products

Pei-Hua Hung[✉], Chi-Ying Hung, Hsi-Yen Lin, and Wen-Zhong Su

Graduate School of Creative Industry Design,
National Taiwan University of Arts, Daguan Rd., Banqiao District,
New Taipei City 22058, Taiwan
{paywhathome,yumeeiren,p3yann,orpheussu}@gmail.com

Abstract. Children as future adults are the oncoming high-tech user population; they live in this new-tech epoch with great variety and rapid change and their perception towards the world already changed accordingly. However, they rarely are considered to be participants in the experimental period of technology and design development. In an attempt to understand children's interests and their perception or even aesthetic perception/preference under this high-tech tendency, this research adopted the "Dechnology 2014 New Collection" products as stimuli to investigate elementary school-age children's insights and to explore any gender differences. Results are found that gender variations indeed exist on children's perception and aesthetic preference toward new Dechnology (Design + Technology) products. And the variation often happens when the object is a simile or metaphor of the opposite gender. This study is intended to reveal the ways in which children sense and perceive new Dechnology products and to provide information of children's concern and viewpoint to technologists, designers, and educators.

Keywords: Dechnology · Perception · Aesthetic perception · Aesthetic judgment · Aesthetic preference · Aesthetic impression

1 Introduction

Children have their own interests, curiosities, beliefs and demands that are quite different from adults. Those born in this highly visual and high-tech world have experienced and been heavily influenced by digital and new technologies, and the ways they sense and learn are changed accordingly. However, Druin (2002) indicated that there was a short but rich history of developing shared paths for communication between diverse users and technologists, but there were merely rare instances where children had more direct involvement as users, testers, informants with technology developers, and rarely actually tested experimental technology before release. Yet, with the emergence of children as an important new consumer group and user population of technology, knowing children's concerns about new-tech is becoming more critical than ever.

© Springer International Publishing Switzerland 2015
P.L.P. Rau (Ed.): CCD 2015, Part II, LNCS 9181, pp. 209–221, 2015.
DOI: 10.1007/978-3-319-20934-0_20

A recent research on the interaction between children and screen-viewing announced that this transform already influenced children's concepts about digital products, consciousness and life (Jago et al. 2014). Indeed, children's perceptions about this world are constructed by the interaction among the environmental factors. Their perceptions however are not merely built on the aspect of cognition but also on emotions. Hence, under the influences of this era, what does this generation value or what is it interested in? What kinds of technological products would catch their eyes? And furthermore, in what ways do they view current high-technology as future users? And whether the ways they use are based on their perceptions toward the products or even their aesthetic perceptions?

With the aim to investigate above concerns, the research objectives therefore are listed as follows:

1. To explore children's interests under these high-tech effects and to determine whether or not differences between genders exist: and if so, what they could be?
2. To reveal children's perceptions regarding the technological products as well as to determine any gender differences.

2 Framework of Children's Perception to Aesthetic Preference

2.1 Perception

Children who grew up in this digital and new-tech epoch are forced to live with electronic products and become imperceptibly used to them. Under this influence, are their structures of perception being changed? Or in what ways do they recognize and feel high-tech products? According to Piaget's theory, children's perception toward the objective world is based on their knowledge about it. Children select and comprehend their experiences upon their psychological structure, and they modulate these structures to understand more detailed realities. The reality is not isolated but is built on their previous experiences and cognitive bases (Yin 2006).

From Piaget's cognitive development theory, two of the specific characteristics in Concrete Operational Stage as are loss of egocentrism and logical thinking, which means that elementary-school-age children can already have logical thinking in certain concrete situations and can value or judge conditions based on multiple points of view (Jhu 1997). Meanwhile, children's cognition toward reality is a positive, dynamic, and constructive process based on the interaction of the subjects and objects. Their cognition in every stage is different from adults; it varies on the ways of information handling and representation. From Piaget's theory, children assimilate and accommodate stimuli through interaction with their surroundings, and their cognition is consequently changed by it (Piaget 1969).

On the other hand, from Erikson's psychosocial theory of development, he believed that the elementary-school children of the ages in 6–12 have the hope of "industrious" association and with it face their challenges outside. They attain the sense of competence by the interaction among peers, social participation, and academic performance.

They value the relationship of peers, and if they fail on these challenges, feelings of inferiority occur instead (Jhu 1997; Kivnick and Wells 2014). On the other hand, according to Bruner's systems of representation theory, three stages of representation were claimed to exist: enactive, iconic, and symbolic. These three stages of cognitive development occur gradually and also could coexist and are complementary to each other. Any perception could be earned by the learning process of enactive representation (concrete), iconic representation (icon) and to symbolic representation (abstract). Comparing to Piaget's natural readiness of cognitive development, Bruner believed that accelerated readiness is possible for a child through the educational format (Jhu 1997).

Furthermore, Vygotsky, from his viewpoint of cognitive development, emphasized that social context and culture are the important factors affecting children's cognitive development (Wozniak and Fischer 2014). He also proposed the Zone of Proximal Development (ZDP) which means that children can solve problems by implication given from adults or by cooperation with elder peers, when their cognitive function is on the transition period of maturing (Jhu 1997). Namely, that the basis for psychological development generally is not merely in individual cognition, but also in interpersonal relations, communication, and cooperation within sociocultural environment.

2.2 Aesthetic Perception

The concept of "Aesthetic" originated from the Greek "Aisthetika" with the meaning of "things perceptible through the senses". Its related verb "aisthe" denoted "to feel, to apprehend (Abbs 1987). That is, the experiences of aesthetics emerge from perceptions, rather than from concepts (Abb 1989; Kant 1987).

Abb (1987) described that aesthetic is a distinct category of understanding, a both sensual and cognitive mode of knowing. Consistent with children's cognitive development, aesthetic perception was also expected to vary by age, i.e. adults perform better than children and elder children perform better than younger children as well. Over and above age, however, aesthetic perception was predicted to be linked to their experiences (Parsons 1987). Freedman (2001) further asserted that children's aesthetic perceptions needed to be built on meaningful connections within the real world.

Meanwhile, although little is known about the aesthetic developmental mechanisms, there is evidence to suggest that sociocultural factors influence its course. Greenwood (2010) described that aesthetic is culture-based and also a complex and dynamic process. Parsons (1994) argued that in a society that is relatively homogenous and changed slowly, people may come to understand their art without needing aesthetics. But our world today is not only with multiplicity, but also where there is no one stream of thought dominates others. He also claimed that children do in fact think in characteristic ways about the arts and have implicit philosophies of it which are shaped by the development of important underlying cognitive abilities. And the development of abilities with respect to aesthetics is closely related to the development of the more general abilities required for mature aesthetic responses.

2.3   Related Researches on Aesthetic Judgment, Aesthetic Preference, and Aesthetics Impression

Of Parsons' five developmental stages of aesthetic judgment, elementary school-age children are in the second stage of Beauty and Realism. They prefer realistic styles work. And they judge art works merely by beauty and proficient skill of realism (Parsons 1987). Researches also have elaborated upon the finding that traditional paintings are chosen or preferred more often than abstract or revolutionary pieces of work. Katz (1942) claimed that elementary-school-aged children preferred traditional paintings to modern paintings in a ratio of about three to two (Salkind and Salkind 1973). Dietrich and Hunnicutt (1948) further explored the findings that landscapes were more preferred than interiors, and still lives were preferred over portraits by children (Salkind and Salkind 1973). Stallings and Anderson investigated the aesthetic preference of children to reproductions of paintings by requiring the children to rank the stimuli in order of preference, and the resulting introspective responses relating to the followings: (a) subject matter such as details, (b) sensory impressions such as color, and (c) formal qualities such as arrangement (Salkind and Salkind 1973).

Moreover, the research conducted by Valentine (1962) showed that the "revolutionary" or "avant-garde" type pictures obtained lower scores on a scale of preference in contrast to "conventional" ones. On the other hand, 8 to 10 year old children prefer subject, colors, realism, skills and emotion in art work in that order. And the interests in art works of 11 to13 year old children listed from most to least preferred are: subject, skills, colors, realism and emotion (Lark-Horovitz et al. 1967). They gradually pursue the appreciation of logicality. Their ability of aesthetic judgment increases at this stage and they value the experience of visual appreciation as well (Wu 1989).

From the researches above, there were many studies concentrating on children's aesthetic judgment towards art works or art reproductions, but there was less concern focused on design products. Even in the school curriculum, the subject "Arts and Humanities" in Taiwan seldom introduces design products or design appreciation Table 1.

Table 1. The Process of Perception - Aesthetic Preference (Based on the Literature Research)

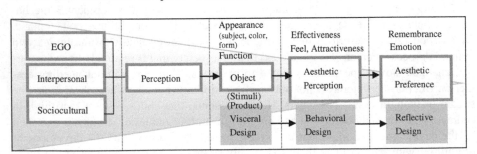

As the concept of "Aesthetic" with the meaning of "things perceptible through the senses" already mentioned in the literature, the term "product aesthetics" may relate to what the product presents to the senses (Lawalski 1988). Aesthetic impression is the context similar to aesthetic perception and aesthetic experience that may relate to the perception of how sensing the process of regarding an object is (Csilkszentmihalyi and Robinson 1990) and as the sensation that results from the perception of attractiveness or unattractiveness in products (Crilly et al. 2004). In comparison with Norman's three stages of design as visceral, behavioral, and reflective (Norman 2002), this study concluded the process of perception to aesthetic preference and tried to visualize this process as children's perception and aesthetic preference towards technology and design products.

3 Methodologies

A survey was made in order to study children's perceptions toward technological products and also their interests. The survey comprised the following two stages. (1) Choosing the stimuli: the 41dechnology products as known as Dechnology 2014 New Collection (www.dechnology.com.tw) are the target dechnology products in this stage. A web-based questionnaire was administered to 13 experts as a pilot study, and by choosing their favorable top 20 dechnology products plus the worst favorable one as the stimuli for the second stage. (2) Questionnaire research: the second stage administered a questionnaire to 72 elementary school students (41 boys and 31 girls, ages 10–11) of grade 5. They were from three different classes of an urban area elementary school and of normal distribution of academic performance.

"Dechnology" here is defined as "Design + Technology", which describes a complete product design cycle that starts from the raw materials, to manufacturing, and to crucial technology developments. Beginnings in 2009, the Department of Industrial Technology with other eight high-tech institutes have made a great effort towards animating technology into product design cycles. They are trying to provide a field for cooperating research institutes and the industry designers to explore a new dimension and to earn more commercial opportunities in the paring of "Technology R&D" and "Industrial Design" (Hung and Huang 2013).

The 41 "Dechnology 2014 New Collection" products therefore were designed by the eight institutes mentioned above. The web questionnaire displayed pictures of 41 products with the description of their functions and characteristic. The experts in this stage were doctoral students at design graduate schools. They were asked to choose 20 favorable products from the 41without ranking them. Based on a frequency distribution of the choices, the favorable top 20 dechnology products plus the worst favorable one are illustrated in Table 2.

The survey questionnaire was distributed in a one-period class and the examiner used the same descriptions and terms to all the students. The questions were grouped into three main parts: (1) Interests; (2) The attributes of dechnology products; (3) Preferences on the products. The quantitative findings of the three parts were on the five-point Likert Scale (5 = most agreeable (favorable), 1 = totally un-agreeable (unfavorable)).

According to Lin and Lin (2010), Lin (2012), Lin et al. (2014), the tendency of Taiwan design development already changed from technology innovation to user experiences, and this evolution can be viewed as a process of adaptive design which is a fusion of Dechnology (Design-Technology) and Humart (Humanity-Art). Therefore, the attributes of technology products here are categorized into three parts as "the Application of Advanced Technology", "The Display of Aesthetic & Design", and "The Expression of Human Caring".

Table 2. The top 20 faborable dechnology products and the worst one elected by the experts

Preferred 1	Preferred 2	Preferred 3	Preferred4	Preferred	Preferred 6	Preferred 7
Preferred 8	Preferred 9	Preferred10	Preferred11	Preferred12	Preferred13	Preferred14
Preferred15	Preferred16	Preferred17	Preferred18	Preferred19	Preferred20	Preferred41

4 Results

4.1 Children's Preferences/Interests

From the quantitative survey of the first part, a frequency distribution was used to analyze the interests of the 72 student participants. According to the results, the aspects "Manga and Games" interested the students the most (mean = 4.34) and "Political Issues" the least (mean = 2.04). The variety of interests between the participants exist on the aspect "Model and Toys" as the most different one (variance = 2.507), and "Manga and Games" is the aspect earned identical agreement (variance = 1.170) (Fig. 1).

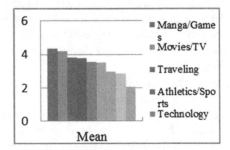

Fig. 1. The chart of mean of children's interests

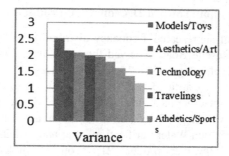

Fig. 2. The chart of variance between children's interests

4.2   Gender Variation in Preference/Interests

And from the result through the Independent Sample T-test, the interests on the aspects as "Aesthetics and Art" (t = −3.682, P < .001), "Manga and Games" (t = 3.726, P < .001), "Traveling" (t = −2.427, P < .05), and "Models and Toys" (t = 3.002, P < .05) have significant differences between genders. Girls have more interests on "Aesthetics and Art" (mean = 3.65) and "Traveling" (mean = 4.23) as opposed to boys (mean = 2.46; mean = 3.48) Tables 3 and 4. And boys pay more attentions to "Manga and Game" (mean = 4.72) and "Models and Toys" (mean = 3.98) compared to girls (mean = 3.84; mean = 2.90) (Fig. 2).

Table 3. The statistic analysis of the interests between genders

Aspect	Gender	N	Mean	SD	SEM
Aesthetics and art	M	41	2.46	1.380	.216
	F	31	3.65	1.305	.234
Manga and games	M	40	4.72	.905	.143
	F	31	3.84	1.098	.197
Traveling	M	40	3.48	1.601	.253
	F	31	4.23	.990	.178
Models and toys	M	41	3.98	1.557	.243
	F	31	2.90	1.423	.255

Table 4. The Independent Sample T-test of the interests between genders

Aspect	N	MD	SE	DF	t	Sig. (2-tailed)
Aesthetics and art	72	−1.182	.321	70	−3.682	.000**
Manga and games	71	.886	.238	69	3.726	.000**
Traveling	71	−.751	.309	69	2.427	.018*
Models and toys	72	1.072	.357	70	3.002	.004*

*p < .05; **p < .01

4.3   Children's Perception Toward Dechonology Products

From the second stage of the research, frequency distribution analysis revealed that the product 16 as "Water Rescue Boat" received the most high appreciation on the two attributes "Advanced Technology" and "Aesthetic & Design" (mean = 4.28; 4.14). Oppositely, product 06 -"Cardio Care" -was the worst on those two aspects (mean = 3.19; 2.83). On the other hand, the product 10 as "Beauty Mirror" hed the most variation of agreement (variance = 2.365) on the attribute as "Advanced Technology", and so did the product 05 "Fun Water Purification" (variance = 2.225) on the attribute as "Aesthetic & Design". However, product 21, "Touch Handlebar", was the worst favorable product judged by the experts in the pilot study and here it is the product with the least variation (variance = 1.284) among school-age participants on the attributes both of "Advanced Technology" and "Aesthetic & Design". Meanwhile, product 21 on the attribute "Human Caring" attained the most appreciation (mean = 4.07), and the product 01, "Dual Ray Desk Lamp", gained the worst appraisal on this attribute (mean = 3.21). On the variations of agreement, the product 10 "Beauty Mirror" was the one with the most different opinions on this attribute between the participants, and the product 15, "Un-flip IRB", was the one earning identical agreement.

4.4   Gender Variation in Dechnology Perception/Aesthetic Perception

According to the Independent Sample T-test, products 01 (p < .016), 07(p < .013), 08 (p < .031), 09(p < .031), 10(p < .001), 12(p < .007), 13(p < .045), 20(p < .025) have significant differences between genders on the attribute of "Advanced Technology". And the differences exist on the girl participants giving higher agreement to the eight products on this attribute.

From the result displayed, product 10 "Beauty Mirror" (t = −2.763, p < .007), 11 "Float Lamp" (t = −2.089, p < .040), 12 "Sit Properly" (t = −2.977, p < .004), 13 "3D Printer" (t = −2.265, p < .027), 20 "Curve Warning Auxiliary Equipment" (t = −2.123, p < .037) have significant differences between genders on the attribute of "Aesthetics & Design" (Table 5).

Table 5. The statistic analysis of the agreement on "Aesthetic/Art" between genders

Product	Gender	N	Mean	SD	SEM
10	M	41	3.17	1.564	.244
	F	31	4.06	1.181	.212
11	M	41	3.39	1.498	.234
	F	31	4.03	1.110	.199
12	M	41	3.34	1.460	.228
	F	31	4.16	.860	.154
13	M	39	3.51	1.449	.232
	F	31	4.16	.934	.168
20	M	41	3.29	1.487	.232
	F	31	3.90	.944	.169

And also products 09 "Personal Water Purification Bag" (t = −3.024, p < .004), 10 "Beauty Mirror" (t = −3.029, p < .003), 12 "Sit Properly" (t = −2.846, p < .006), 14 "Electric Cart" (t = −2.735, p < .008), 20 "Curve Warning Auxiliary Equipment" (t = −2.388, p < .020) were found as the products with significant differences between genders on the attribute of "Human Caring". The survey result also revealed that the product 10 "Beauty Mirror", product 12 "Sit Properly" and product20 "Curve Warning Auxiliary Equipment" are the ones without agreement between genders neither on the attribute of "Advanced Technology", nor of "Aesthetic & Design" and "Human Caring" (Fig. 3).

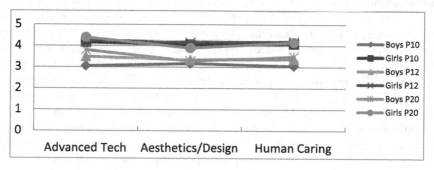

Fig. 3. Gender variation in perception on Product 10, 12, and 20

4.5   Gender Variation in Dechnology Preference/Aesthetic Preference

For the preferences, the top three preferred products elected by elementary-school-aged children are product 16 "Water Rescue Boat" (mean = 4.11), product 17 "Health Travel Band" (mean = 3.94), and product 09 "Personal Water Purification Bag" (mean = 3.93). Compared to these positive results, the worst three products "Cardio Care" product 06 (mean = 2.81), "Electric Cart" product 14 (mean = 3.15), and "Sheathing Fabric Pot" product 02 (mean = 3.18) achieved the least preferences. However, the difference of preference between genders still occurs among the products. Significantly, product10 "Beauty Mirror" attained extreme significant difference (p < 0.001) between genders (Table 6).

Table 6. Gender variation in dechnology product preference

Product	N	MD	SE	DF	t	Sig. (2-tailed)
2	72	−.759	.307	70	−2.473	.016*
3	72	−.666	.286	70	−2.327	.023*
10	72	−1.341	.308	70	−4.349	.000**
20	72	−.562	.276	70	−2.038	.045*
*p < .05; **p < .01						

5 Discussion

5.1 The Possible Factor of Gender Variation in Dechnology Perception

Although there is no obvious difference on intelligence of genders among elementary-school age, the varieties do exist on the aptitude and their academic performance. And the factors underneath could be explained include: the objective factors (e.g. the effect of traditional culture and education), the subjective factors (e.g. stereotypes of gender characteristics), and the physical factor (e.g. body maturation) (Chang, 1996). From the research of Qiu (2007), it indicated that elementary-school-aged girls have higher achievement than boys on the concept of art. And also it appears on the ability of aesthetic analysis. Oppositely to the boys, girls from the results indeed pay more attention on the aspect of "Aesthetic and Art" and mostly, their preference on every dechnology product is higher than boys. Namely, girls in this age can accept more varieties and possibilities of new-dech products and as well as give more their appreciation on it. On the other hand, compared to the attributes of "Aesthetic & Design" and "Human Caring", there are more products existing wider differences on agreement of "Advanced Technology". It might indicate that identification of technology is more difficult to define in their age. Moreover, before the questionnaire survey, the researcher asked children verbally predicted the functions of each product. Most boys predict it far away from the recent technology possibility while girls predicted it based on their known reality instead. Also, from the class observation, the student who has more related knowledge or experience on certain product would predict the product more accurately. On the attitude towards the dechnology products, students pay high attention on them, but when the real function was revealed, boys showed their disappointment and came to reject the product. It might be because children of elementary-school-age are not as socialized as adults, and they, especially the boy participants, individuals directly respond their thoughts relied on their intuitions.

5.2 The Possible Factor of Gender Variation in Aesthetic Preference

Students of test age have their own aesthetic judgment. They focus on the subject and skills of realism, and have the ability to distinguish between aesthetics and non-aesthetics. They strongly prefer the picture which has a familiar subject and with bright colors. From this view of point, comparing back to the result, we can recognize that the top three preferred products all have bright colors and the subject matter is easily understood by children and also have a close connection to their real life. In opposition, the subject matter of the worst three products is unfamiliar to children of this age and is beyond their life experiences. Also the colors of these three products are pale to catch children's eyes.

The other fact found is that products with too familiar appearance to children's eyes are hard to earn appreciation and gain identical agreement on "Aesthetic & Design". It might be because the outer form of the technology product is not as same as the realism of art works; they don't admire the skills upon it, instead, they prefer technological products with creative appearance. On the other hand, the product "Touch Handlebar" which is the worst choice by the experts but is the product with high appreciation on all the three attributes to children. Considering the possible reasons for this, it might be because the product is symbolic of mature man and therefore successfully touches a boy's heart. Oppositely, the product "Beauty Mirror" least favored by most boys because they might consider it symbolic of the female. This might reveal some hidden information, i.e. while the product obtains children's immediate preference, it earns his/her heart, and vice versa.

5.3   The Oncoming Threat to Future Adults

From the study results, elementary school children rarely concern about human caring. In addition, they do not pay much attention on technological products which only focused on human care, especially focused on the elders. However, according to the Population Projections for R.O.C. (Taiwan): 2012–2060 and the statistics data released by the National Development Council, the percentage of old-age population (65+) of the total population was 10.9 % in 2011, which defined Taiwan as an aging society under the delimitation of the World Health Organization. As the percentage of the old-age population in 2018 is predicted to be 14 %, Taiwan therefore will be defined as an aged society; furthermore, the super-aged society with 20 % old-age population ratio will soon arrive in 2025. Simultaneously, when the respondents of 10–11 year-of-age today (2015) grow up as adults in 2036, the potential support ratio of agers 15–64 years old to the elders above 65 years old will be 2.2:1. Namely, almost two persons of 15–64 year-of-age should take care of one old person above 65 year-of-age at that time. Even more, the median age of population in 2036 is going to be 51 years old (Ministry of the Interior, 2013).

Aiming to decrease the social pressure under both the trend of fewer children and an increasingly aging society, technology focused on human care is earning higher and higher attention than ever. According to the literature review on children's perception and cognitive development, children are able to be educated on it. Since they are naturally and intangibly educated by the circumstances among them, educators possibly could provide or build for them appropriate and challengeable surroundings to enhance their learning possibilities.

6   Conclusions and Suggestions

Based on the results of this study, conclusions follow:

1. Gender variation indeed exists on children's dechnology perception and aesthetic preference, and the variation often happens when the object is a simile or metaphor of the opposite gender.
2. Children's perceptions and preferences are intuitive and grounded on their experiences, and can also easily be affected by peers and surroundings.
3. Children of this age seldom concern about human caring. And their interests are actually affected by high-tech tendency.

Therefore, on the basis of previous studies, aesthetic education could be suggested and positioned to instruct children how to experience and value beauty and its relation with human life (Madeja 1971). Namely, instead of generating concepts about the aesthetic, releasing the practical function from the products and focusing directly on what makes it unique might assist children's appreciation of new-tech design.

On the other hand, in order to assist future adults to confront their coming aged society, the concepts about universal or user-centered design and the concerns about human caring must be more involved in their daily life from now on. Therefore, in which ways could be practicable to educate our future adults the concepts of design toward a sustainable world and the attitude toward the coexistence of both organisms and the environment, might be the following concerns and further research issues or even the social responsibilities of technologists, designers, and educators.

Acknowledgements. The authors gratefully acknowledge the support for this research provided by the Ministry of Science and Technology under Grant No. MOSY-103-2410-H-144-003 and MOST-103-2221-E-144-001. The authors also wish to thank Prof. Jhon. G. Kreifeldt and Po-Hsien Lin, especially, Prof. Rungtai Lin.

References

Abbs, P.: Living Powers: The Arts in Education. Falmer Press, London (1987)

Abbs, P.: Aesthetic education: an opening manifesto. In: Abbs, P. (ed.) The Symbolic Order: A Contemporary Reader on the Arts Debate. Falmer Press, London (1989)

Chang, C.S.: Educational psychology. Tunghua Press, Taipei (1996)

Chang-Peng, W.: Instructing appreciation of chinese painting to elementary school children. Inf. Res. **51**, 14–18 (1989)

Crilly, N., Moultrie, J., Clarkson, P.J.: Seeing things: consumer response to the visual domain in product design. Des. Stud. **25**, 547–577 (2004)

Csikszentmihalyi, M., Robinson, R.E.: The Art of Seeing: An Interpretation of the Aesthetic Experience. J. Paul Getty Museum, Los Angeles (1990)

Dietrich, G.L., Hunnicutt, C.W.: Art content preferred by primary grade children. Elementary Sch. J. **48**, 557–559 (1948)

Druin, A.: The role of children in the design of new technology. Behav. Inf. Technol. **21**(1), 1–25 (2002). http://hcil2.cs.umd.edu/trs/99-23/99-23.html

Freedman, K.: How do we understand art? Aesthetics and the problem of meaning in the curriculum. In: Duncum, P., Bracey, T. (eds.) On Knowing Art and Visual Culture, pp. 34–46. Canterbury University Press, Christchurch (2001)

Greenwood, J.: Aesthetic learning, and learning through the aesthetic. In: Schonmann, S. (ed.) Key Concepts in Theatre/Drama Education, pp. 47–52. Sense Publishers, Rotherdam (2010)

Hung, W.K., Huang, W.: Creating value for technology by design: a case study of dechnology project. J. Des. **18**(1), 41–64 (2013)

Jago, R., Thompson, J.L., Sebire, S.J., Wood, L., Pool, L., Zahra, J., Lawlor, D.A.: Cross-sectional associations between the screen-time of parents and young children: differences by parent and child gender and day of the week. Int. J. Behav. Nutr. Phys. Act. **11**(54), 29 (2014). http://www.ijbnpa.org/content/11/1/54

Jhu, J.-S.: Education Psychology. Wanan Press, Taipei (1997)

Kant, I.: Critique of Judgment (trans. W. Pluhar). Indianapolis, Hackett (1987)

Katz, E.: A test for preferences for traditional and modern paintings. J. Educ. Psychol. **33**, 668–677 (1942)

Kivnick, H.Q., Wells, C.K.: Untapped richness in Erik H. Erikson's rootstock. The Gerontologist **54**(1), 40–50 (2014)

Lark-Horovitz, B., Lewis, H.P., Luca, M.: Understanding Children's Art for Better Teaching. Charles E. Merrill, Columbus (1967)

Salkind, L., Salkind, N.: A measure of aesthetic preference. Stud. Art. Educ. **15**(1), 21–27 (1973). National Art Education Association

Lewalski, Z.M.: Product Esthetics: An Interpretation for Designers. Design and Development Engineering Press, Carson (1988)

Qiu, L.-L.: The Study of Elementary School Senior Graders' Aesthetic Ability in Art Appreciation Education. Unpublished master's thesis, National Hsinchu University of Education, Hsinchu, Taiwan (2007)

Lin, R., Lin, C.L.: From digital archives to E-business: A case study on turning "art" into "business". In: Proceedings of the 2010 International Conference on e-Business (ICE-B), pp. 1–8. IEEE, July 2010

Lin, R.: From Dechnology to Humart in Taiwan Design Development. Research Project Supported by Taiwan National Science Council (2012)

Lin, R., Yen, C.-C., Chen, R.: From adaptive design to adaptive city-design in motion for taipei city. In: Rau, P.L.P. (ed.) CCD 2014. LNCS, vol. 8528, pp. 643–649. Springer, Heidelberg (2014)

Madeja, S.S.: Aesthetic education: an area of study. Art Educ. **24**(8), 16–19 (1971)

Ministry of the Interior: 2013 Demographic Fact Book R.O.C

National Development Council: Population Projections for R.O.C. (Taiwan): 2014∼2060

Norman, D.A.: Emotional design. Basic Books, NY (2002)

Parsons, M.J.: How We Understand Art. Cambridge University Press, London (1987)

Parsons, M.J.: Can children do aesthetics? a developmental account. J. Aesthet. Educ. **28**(3), 33–45 (1994). Special Issue: Aesthetics for Young People, University of Illinois Press

Valentine, J.: The Psychology of Beauty. E. Puffer, New York (1962)

Piaget, J., Inhelder, B.: The psychology of the child. Basic Books, New York (1969)

Wozniak, R.H., Fischer, K.W. (eds.): Development in Context: Acting and Thinking in Specific Environments. Psychology Press, NY (2014)

Su, Y.-H.: What kind of aesthetic education we need? Aesthetic education in opposition to art education. J. Aesthet. Educ. **165**, 58–68 (2008). National Taiwan Arts Education Center

Yang, C.F., Wu, C.S., Gong, Y., Sung, T.J.: Transformative service design: from technology to dechnology. In: Advances in The Human Side of Service Engineering, vol. 1, p. 210 (2014)

Yin, Z.-Z.: On dialectics in the theory of children's cognitive development by jeam piaget. J. Shanxi Normal University **33**(3), 136–138 (2006). (Social Science Edition)

Monster Design and Classifier Cognition

Larry Hong-lin Li[(⊠)]

General Education Center, National Taiwan University of Arts,
No. 59, Sect. 1, Banqiao District, New Taipei City 22058, Taiwan
larryli@ntua.edu.tw

Abstract. This study aims to explore the interpretation and comprehension of mythical creatures in human mind. We focused on mythical living forms that were created out of body parts of different animals. Fictional creatures like these have two potential interpretations. First, they may be viewed as a synthesis of distinct animals. By contrast, they may be conceptualized as a totally novel, bizarre entity. In order to solve the puzzle, we conducted a picture-phrase matching task, where subjects selected from the classifiers *zhi* versus *ge* for these mythical creatures. The choice of classifiers helped us determine the conceptual status of the mythical living entities under discussion.

Keywords: Mythical creatures · Chinese classifiers · Analogy

1 Introduction

Monsters are imaginary or legendary creatures invented in science fictions, fantasy stories, comic books, and video games. They are objects with abnormal structures or physical deformities, which have not been envisioned previously. Some of them are so famous and appealing that they keep people intrigued.

Many of the mythological monsters or beasts were created out of the body parts of varying animals. As illustration, the Pegasus is a horse with wings of a bird, and a griffin is a creature combing an eagle and a lion. These fantastic mythical creatures have appeared in human beliefs, storytelling, music, literature and art for thousands of years. Let us take centaurs for example. A centaur is a legendary creature in ancient Greek stories that has a human's upper body and the lower body and legs of a horse. Many people think that they can imagine what a centaur is like. However, as Hull cautions, they can only do this in a very superficial way [10]. Too many questions are waiting to be answered, and no means are available for answering them. How many pairs of lungs does a centaur have? How many hearts and stomachs does a centaur have? How are the circulatory and pulmonary systems of these creatures connected? Or, what happens to food that has been digested in the human half of the centaur? Does it move into the stomach of the horse half? In Hull's words, these questions are unanswerable since they are imaginary, unreal entities.

Designing monsters and fictional creatures is a great challenge because their unusual appearances and structures call for creativity, imagination, and inventiveness. Especially, these mythological living entities are noteworthy since they are a synthesis of common life forms on one hand, and they are newly coined objects on the other

© Springer International Publishing Switzerland 2015
P.L.P. Rau (Ed.): CCD 2015, Part II, LNCS 9181, pp. 222–229, 2015.
DOI: 10.1007/978-3-319-20934-0_21

hand. What is intriguing to us is, given the two potential interpretations, how they are construed and conceptualized in human mind. In order to obtain deeper insight into the mental construal of these legendary creatures, we suggest that we should adopt an experimental approach that examines the interrelation of these fictional creatures to Chinese classifiers. By means of this investigation, we are able to gain a better picture of the creatures at issue, which will shed light on the research of creativity and design.

Familiarity or Novelty? If it is the right case that the design of imaginary creatures is build on real world knowledge, the question that is immediately raised is how the fictional creatures are construed and understood in the eyes of perceivers. Specifically, from the perspective of comprehension, it still remains a puzzle as to whether the invention of legendary and fantasized creatures is profiled with reference to our perception of animals.

We propose that we should explore the imaginary life forms created out of parts of animals. Invented creatures like these are worthy of investigation for they are ambiguous between "familiar" and "novel". They are familiar objects in the sense that their bodies comprise parts of various common animals. Studies on creativity have pointed out that the process of design may invoke many strategies. One of the strategies is combination. Combining different things, as Li and Riedl note, is a great source of inspiration for gadgets [11]. This can be well illustrated by many mythological creatures. The Pegasus is a horse combined with wings of a bird. A griffin is an eagle plus a lion. So to speak, the components of these mythical creatures are drawn from pre-established species. Therefore, it makes sense to say that the physical forms of these invented objects are a combination of existing animals.

On the other hand, these monstrous creatures are novel and bizarre in the sense of human cognition. Human beings are able to categorize objects because they know the attribute structures that are specific to classes and categories [8]. As Garner stresses, real world entities are perceived to possess high correlational structure [7]. That is, attributes of real word objects always appear in combination with one another. Given the complex attributes of feathers, fur, and wings, our encyclopedic knowledge informs us that wings co-occur with feathers more than with fur [18]. Such an interrelation helps define an entity in the network of human categorization. In terms of human categorization, the fictional creatures under discussion comprise body parts that are not constructed and structured like any other common life forms. Therefore, it is also reasonable to say that these creatures are odd and bizarre things.

Mythical Creatures and Classifier Cognition. It is crucial to explore the above-mentioned creatures since their images have a two-fold interpretation. In terms of internal structure, they are an aggregation of animal parts. By contrast, from a holistic perspective, they are non-existing, bizarre objects. Before an informed decision can be made regarding this issue, empirical evidence is required. Therefore, we aim to inspect the conceptual status of legendary creatures using an experimental approach. In order to explore this issue, we focus on illustrations of fictional creatures that are made up of parts of distinct animals, and probe how they are construed and encoded in the cognitive domain. To this end, we inspect the choice of Chinese classifiers for them. Chinese classifiers play a critical role in the study of human cognition because they serve as a reflex of how the world is interpreted and profiled in mind. Therefore, the survey as to the classifier selection for the invented mythological living objects serves to provide a solution to the puzzle.

2 Literature Review

Although the creation and generation of fictional living entities have been addressed, how mythical living things are perceived and construed in human mind has scarcely been discussed. Very luckily, studies have been extensively conducted as to human's (in-)/ability to detect emergent structures in visual images. They are crucial to our discussion for they help us approach our research question. They can be subsumed in two contrasting views as elucidated below.

Structured Creativity View. In the structured creativity view, when representing unreal, non-existing entities, human beings bring their knowledge of reality to bear. Studies such as Ward and Ward and Sifonis point out that the real world knowledge tends to constrain creativity and imagination [19, 20]. Ward invited college students to draw aliens from other planets by imagination. They were instructed to be as imaginative as possible to design creatures. Most of their creations preserved the main features of animals found on earth. What is more, when they were required to draw creatures with feathers, they inclined to add wings and beaks. What these studies demonstrate is that human beings tended to preserve the co-occurring features of real creatures even when they were required to design a novel living object.

Akin to the production and generation of fictional creatures, it has been proposed that human beings evaluate fictional information using real world knowledge [21]. This view holds that all entities are comprehended by what we have seen, what we have experienced, and what we have learned. Along this thread of thinking, fictitious creatures are encoded with reference to our understanding of real life forms. Specifically, on the assumption that our perception of the world is shaped and structured by existing knowledge, the mythical creatures under discussion should be conceptualized as a synthesis of different animal parts.

Unstructured Creativity View. In contrast to the structured creativity view, it has been claimed that creative thinking reveals spontaneous, unstructured characteristics. Closely related to this proposal is the notion "chaotic thinking". Chaotic thinking refers to the tendency to view the world as a basically unpredictable place that is filled with complicated relations and meaningful connections [6]. Chaotic thinkers are generally impulsive, spontaneous, and metaphorical, and they focus their attention on what is happening in the moment. Their thoughts and actions typically promote creativity that is original as well as innovative.

Due to the unconstrained nature of creativity, chaotic thinkers are able to detect less accessible associations and connections, particularly those that cross over conceptual boundaries. They are experts at divergent thinking, being capable of exploring fascinating possibilities without any plan beforehand [12]. Gibson adds that most chaotic thinkers do not refute the existence of structure, but prefer to let the structure emerge naturally and spontaneously [9]. Well-ordered thinkers, in contrast, are inclined to reduce complication and complexity and impose structure on things. If human beings can be freed from the existing knowledge framework, the legendary living things being discussed should not be regarded as merely a composition of different animal body parts. Instead, they should be interpreted as brand new objects existing outside human cognition.

3   Theoretical Basis

Since we aim to examine the classifier selection for mythical creatures, it is necessary to introduce Chinese classifier systems. We illuminate how classifiers are used with objects in what follows.

Chinese Classifiers. Chinese speakers always have to pick a classifier when they want to refer to a number or an amount of something. As illustration, consider (1) and (2) as follows.

(1)   yi ben shu
        one CL book
        'one book'

(2)   yi qun gou
        one MW dog
        'one pack of dogs'

As in (1), the classifier *ben* is selected for the noun *shu* 'book'. In (2), the measure word *qun* denotes a pack of animals. Pink notes that each Chinese classifier tends to go with a class of entities [16]. There are classifiers for people, animals, round things, long things, tiny things, and so on. However, the association between classifiers and nouns is not always transparent. They cannot be generalized by rules, and thus must be memorized. Take the classifier *tiao* for example. It is often used for long flexible objects like fish and pants. But it can also be used for shorts and news items, which are not long and flexible. In Pinker's view, Chinese speakers store the nouns that go with each classifier in an associative memory. When Chinese speakers have not memorized the classifier for an object, they use the classifier for a similar object.

Analogy and Chinese Classifiers. What is of interest to our study is the use of the classifier *zhi*. Myers pinpoints that *zhi* is required for animals [13]. It was first used for individual birds, showing one bird in a hand. By then, the use of *zhi* contrasted with *shuang*, which showed two birds. Later, the use of *zhi* was extended to all animals.

In addition to *zhi*, the use of another classifier *ge* needs to be addressed as well. Myers stresses that *ge* is different from other classifiers. It is used in situations that have nothing in common but an inability of the speaker to draw on memory or an analogy with something in memory. In other words, it kicks in when the size and shape of the object does not fit with any classifier. People use *ge* when they cannot remember a noun or cannot remember its classifier. This explains why the combination of *ge* with a noun tends to be lower in relatively frequency than those of other classifiers with their nouns.

These two classifiers are useful to our research since they help us discriminate whether the legendary beasts in focus are conceived of as a synthesis of animals versus a novel object.

4   Methodology

We adopted the picture-phrase matching task [15] to examine the selection of classifiers between *zhi* and *ge* for the mythical creatures. We collected images of mythological creatures[1], and tested whether subjects preferred the use of the classifier *zhi* or the classifier *ge* for them. Our experimental method is outlined as follows.

4.1   Subjects

Sixteen students from a university in northern Taiwan volunteered to participate in this survey. They were randomly selected native Chinese speakers, and were naïve as to the purpose of our study. Three of them were male, and 13 of them were female. Their average age was 20.4.

4.2   Material

We employed a pencil-and-paper questionnaire survey on 11 images collected from a webpage online. The webpage contains images of legendary creatures from different cultures. They are coined by combining body parts of different animals. We excluded the creatures comprising human bodies since *zhi* does not denote human beings. One of the images is shown in Fig. 1.

We devised two conditions for this survey, where subjects were required to report whether the entity being portrayed went with the "one + classifier" phrases *yi zhi* and *yi ge* respectively. If they considered the classifier (either *zhi* or *ge*) to fit with the target object, they gave a yes-response; otherwise, they gave a no-response. Since it was a within-subject design, each subject would have to judge images across the two conditions. In other words, they would have to judge 22 items in total, the presentation

Fig. 1. A mythical creature-"Pegasus"

---

[1] The images were obtained online at http://jesteppi.deviantart.com/art/Mythical-Creatures-158221063.

order of which was randomized. What is worth noting is that no linguistic label for the creature was provided since we intended to explore the relation of the fictional creature itself with the classifier.

4.3   Procedures

The survey was executed in a quite classroom. It took approximately 5 to 10 min to complete the questionnaire. They were instructed to answer the questions by intuition. Additionally, they were reminded to judge each question independently.

4.4   Results and Discussion

Following up on Baayen [2] and Myers [14], we analyzed the data by the Mixed-Effects Logistic Regression Model. This model is employed to model binary outcome variables. In the Mixed-Effects context, we can analyze binary responses across both subjects and items in a statistical model. Also, since the model cope with the raw data, not averages across subjects or items, the sample size is defined in terms of the total number of observations, which can be sufficient for small experiments [14].

With one missing data points, the study yielded 351 observations in total. All the observations were processed using R [17], the R package lme4 [4], and languageR [1]. In our analysis, we defined the variables of subjects and items as SUBJECT and ITEM. We used both subjects and items as random effects [3] in order to avoid the language-as-a-fixed-effect fallacy [5].

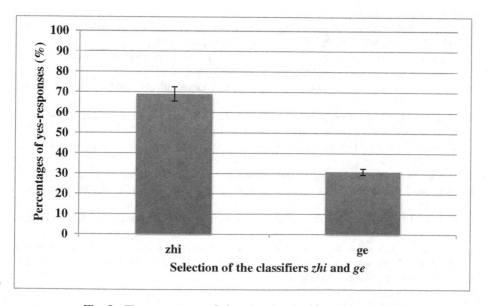

Fig. 2. The percentages of choosing the classifiers *zhi* versus *ge*

The results showed that the classifier *zhi* was selected 69 % across all data points. By contrast, the classifier *ge* was chosen 31 % across all data points. This means that the selection of the classifier *zhi* for the target objects produced an impact with a significant difference relative to the classifier *ge* ($B = -3.71$, $SE = 0.39$, $z = -9.50$, $p < .05$). The percentages are sketched as in Fig. 2.

Our analysis demonstrated that the classifier *zhi* was the preferable choice for the mythical creatures being discussed. Since *zhi* is a classifier commonly used for animals, the outcome of our experiment indicated that the mythical creatures were construed akin to animals. In contrast to *zhi*, the classifier *ge* is used when no category exemplar is accessed or when no specific classifier is available in use. The relatively low percentage of choosing *ge* for the target objects illustrated that they still patterned with animals in human mind.

5 Conclusion

The finding sheds light on the study of arts creation and design. We suggest that experimental approaches provide an alternative to evaluate the products of creativity. As in this study, the picture-phrase matching task demonstrated that a psycholinguistic experiment gave us a clearer picture of visual images. For future research, we should use open-answer questions so as to elicit unconstrained responses. By so doing, we can take a further step to confirm the effect obtained in the current study.

References

1. Baayen, R.H.: LanguageR. R package (2009)
2. Baayen, R.H.: Statistics in psycholinguistics: a critique of some current gold standards. In: Mental Lexicon Working Papers, vol. 1, no. 1, pp. 1–47 (2004)
3. Baayen, R.H., Davidson, D.J., Bates, D.M.: Mixed-effects modeling with crossed random effects for subjects and items. J. Mem. Lang. **59**(4), 390–412 (2008)
4. Bates, D., Maechler, M., Bolker, B.: lme4: Linear mixed-effects models using S4 classes (2012)
5. Clark, H.H.: The language-as-fixed-effect fallacy: a critique of language statistics in psychological research. J. Verbal Learn. Verbal Behav. **12**(4), 335–359 (1973)
6. Finke, R.A., Bettle, J.: Chaotic Cognition: Principles and Applications. Psychology Press, East Sussex (1996)
7. Garner, W.R.: The Processing of Information and Structure. Erlbaum, Potomac (1974)
8. Gelman, S.A., Meyer, M.: Child categorization. Wiley Interdisciplinary Rev. Cogn. Sci. **2**(1), 95–105 (2011)
9. Gibson, J.J.: The Ecological Approach to Visual Perception. Houghton Mifflin, Boston (1979)
10. Hull, D.L.: A function for actual examples in philosophy of science. In: Ruse, M. (eds.) What the Philosophy of Biology Is. Nijhoff International Philosophy Series, vol. 32, pp. 309–321. Springer, Netherlands

11. Li, B., Riedl, M.O.: Creative gadget design in fictions: generalized planning in analogical spaces. In: Proceedings of the 8th ACM Conference on Creativity and Cognition, pp. 41–50. ACM, November 2011
12. Mednick, M.T.: Research creativity in psychology graduate students. J. Consult. Psychol. **27**(3), 265 (1963)
13. Myers, J.: Rules vs. analogy in Mandarin classifier selection. Lang. linguist. **1**(2), 187–209 (2000)
14. Myers, J.: MiniJudge: software for small-scale experimental syntax. Int. J. Comput. Linguist. Chin. Lang. Process. **12**(2), 175–194 (2007)
15. Pike, M., Swank, P., Taylor, H., Landry, S., Barnes, M.A.: Effect of preschool working memory, language, and narrative abilities on inferential comprehension at school-age in children with spina bifida myelomeningocele and typically developing children. J. Int. Neuropsychol. Soc. **19**(04), 390–399 (2013)
16. Pinker, S.: Words and Rules: The Ingredients of Language. Basic Books, New York (2015)
17. R Development Core Team: R: A Language and Environment for Statistical Computing. R Foundation for Statistical Computing, Vienna (2009)
18. Rosch, E., Lloyd, B.B.: Cognition and Categorization. Erlbaum, Hillsdale (1978)
19. Ward, T.B.: Structured imagination: the role of category structure in exemplar generation. Cogn. Psychol. **27**(1), 1–40 (1994)
20. Ward, T.B., Sifonis, C.M.: Tosh demands and generative thinking: what changes and what remains the same? J. Creative Behav. **31**(4), 245–259 (1997)
21. Weisberg, D.S., Goodstein, J.: What belongs in a fictional world? J. Cogn. Cult. **9**(1–2), 1–2 (2009)

Design of Literature Management Tool

Xiaojing Liao[✉]

National University of Singapore, Singapore, Singapore
liaoxj0809@gmail.com

Abstract. This study aimed to design a literature management tool which can support the use and management of literature during the entire research project. In the design process, user requirement of literature management tool is collected through interviews. The functional framework of the tool is proposed based on the interview results and relevant literature. Function design and interface design are represented in the prototype, and the prototype is used for testing usability and user satisfaction. The test results shows subjects' acceptance of the tool. Further development of the tool is discussed.

Keywords: User-centered design · Literature management tool

1 Introduction

Research process can be divided into six stages, namely choosing a topic, literature research, constructing research framework, data collection, data analysis, writing and publishing. Literature related information is essential throughout the research process since researchers need to clarify research topic and build methodology by studying existing literature. In different stages, literature related activities can be different, and these activities can be classified as literature acquisition, literature organization, literature reading and literature retrieval. Currently there are reference management tools, readers and note-taking tools which can support research work. However, most of these tools can only support one or two stages of research process. The objective of this research is to design a literature management tool (denote with "Tool") to provide users with help and convenient operation as far as possible in the stages of research process which literatures are involved. Hence, the function of Tool is constructed based on research process, and aimed to support literature related activities in one tool.

2 Literature Review

Existing studies regarding personal knowledge management provide implications for functional design of Tool. The implications include the following:

- Personal knowledge management tool should provide task space which is related to the research topic: if a research project is considered as task, the information space which includes all task-related information will become a task space [1].
- It is necessary to establish a tasked-focused set of files to facilitate management of these files [2]. Some researchers believed that the personal file management systems

© Springer International Publishing Switzerland 2015
P.L.P. Rau (Ed.): CCD 2015, Part II, LNCS 9181, pp. 230–240, 2015.
DOI: 10.1007/978-3-319-20934-0_22

should simulate the file management in the physical environment, in which task-related paper documents are put together to form an overview of the task, and the placement of paper documents can reveal the importance and progress of the task [2].

- Research information management systems should be able to support knowledge management activities, and establish an organized, searchable and editable knowledge base. Using different directories for the files can make information retrieval easier. Different directories give the file multiple attributes [3].
- Name of files should be meaningful, concise and be able to allow users to identify content of files [4].
- Folders which contain project-related file can serve as a reminder and plan [7]. Folder can be regarded as a tool for classification.
- Screen reading tool should allow user to annotate on the file, but the annotations will be stored separately, provide various telegraphic annotations such as highlights and underlines, make sure that annotating will not influence reading [5].

3   User Requirement Gathering

3.1   Method

Research forms an important part of daily life of college teachers, postgraduates and research assistants. Therefore, they are regarded as potential users of Tool. Face-to-face interviews were conducted. There are fifteen interviewees attending the interview. All the subjects are from department of Industrial Engineering, Tsinghua University. Five of the interviewees are teachers, and they all have engaged in research work for more than seven years. There are nine postgraduates participating in the interview, which all have published their research results in journals or conference. One research assistant attended the interview, and she has been doing research for five years. All these interviewees have research experience. They are familiar with research process, and they need to read a lot of literatures in their work. Therefore, they are the target subjects of the interviews.

They were asked a few questions in the interviews, including:

- Methods and tools that interviewees used for literature management, such as how they categorize and retrieve literature, how they read and annotate literature, and how they use literature information.
- Problem regarding literature management that interviewees encountered in research process.
- Interviewees' requirement of an ideal literature management tool.

3.2   Results

Methods of Literature Management. Interviewees described their three-step research process: problem clarification, problem solving and results interpretation. Their research process and relevant activities are summarized in Table 1.

Table 1. Literature-related activities

Research process	Literature related activities	Activity description
Clarify problems and target (choosing topic and searching relevant literature)	Search literatures	Search via web-browser
	Collect literatures	14 interviewees download manually
		1 interviewees download via literature management tool (Zotero)
	Organize literatures	Organize literatures by using folders
		Organize literatures in literature management tool
	Read literatures	Annotate
		Take notes in separate file
Solve problems (construct research framework, data collection, data analysis)	Find literatures they already read for reference	Scan in the folder
		Search in the folder
		Search on the internet again
	Search new literature to support the result	Search via web-browser
Report the result (writing & publishing)	Find literatures they already read for reference	
	Read notes	
	Insert citations and bibliography	Use literature management tools
		Insert manually

Some interviewees built their own ways to organize literature systematically. One PhD candidate renamed literature using "Author-Year-Journal-Title" format. Interviewees are willing to rename literature because a unified format can facilitate later retrieval and provides important literature information.

Different interviewees used different ways to classify literature. Project, research themes and time are their major criteria to categorize literature. When a literature is related to several categories, interviewees will put the file or shortcut in different folders.

When reading on screen, all interviewees annotate the text. One PhD candidate uses a rigorous method to annotate. He uses yellow highlight to mark important points, green underline to mark definitions, red underline to mark conclusions, and purple underline to mark important references. Visual cues may be useful to help user recall the context and meaning of the annotations. Most of interviewees organize important annotations in separate editable file.

Tools of Literature Management. There are ten interviewees using EndNote. They use it to insert citations and bibliography, and they are not satisfied some functions of

EndNote, such as notes, inconvenient reading PDF in the tool and search. One teacher uses Zotero in the Windows platform to download literatures classify literatures. She uses Sente in Mac client to annotate literature, and she likes the function that the annotations can be quoted and copied into documents easily.

Calls for Innovative Function. Interviewer proposed some imaginary functions and discussed with interviewees. They thought unified interface, using tags to management literature, picking out annotations automatically, setting reading status and setting interlinks between literatures and notes were good.

Interviewees also talked about their own requirement of an ideal literature management tool, including:

- View or edit literature relationship in the tool.
- Tool should provide introduction pages of every category, the introduction pages include description of the category and literatures related to the category.
- Customize bibliography format easily.
- Share is necessary.

4   Functional Framework

4.1   Literature Acquisition

In the stage of literature searching and downloading, user can use Tool to complete the following operations:

- Download literatures by using web-browser add-on.
- Import PDF files from local disk. Tool will automatically read and record the literature information, including references.
- Edit literature information.
- Search references. References of the literature will be read and presented as a list, users can select the reference which they want to know more and search the selected reference by simply clicking the search button.

4.2   Literature Organization

After importing literature information and downloading PDF files, researchers usually need to organize and manage PDF files for convenient search and use. Tool can help users manage their literature as follows:

- Set PDF file rename formats. Tool can read metadata of the literature, such as title, author, publication time and journal. When importing literature information and download full text for the first time, Tool will pop up a window in which user can choose rename format of the PDF file from several formats offered by the tool, such as "Author-Title-Publication time", and user can also customize rename format.
- Use tags to classify literatures. Tags are divided into three categories: theme, projects and research methods. Tags are personalized literature information. Users can edit or add tags to literatures when viewing literature information.

- Manage tags. When creating a tag, users can write a description for the tag. Tags can be created, merged and moved. In the page of tags management, users can add associated literatures to the tag as a batch.
- Synchronize personal library on different devices.

4.3   Literature Reading

In the process of literature reading, Tool will provide several features to ensure a convenient and pleasant reading experience:

- Set reading status and degree of importance. There will be visual cues of read status on the list of literatures. That is, unread literatures are marked in bold, read literature are displayed by using normal font, and green color will fill half of the grid of literature title to indicate reading unfinished (see Fig. 1). When opening reading-unfinished literature, Tool will ask whether to continue the reading.
- Provide a variety of annotation formats and annotations can be easily picked out. The tool has its own PDF viewer, which offers a variety of annotation formats, including different color highlight and underline. User can customize the meaning of the annotation formats. For example, when a sentence is marked as definition, the sentence will be picked out as annotation and classified as definition.
- Provide function of literature summary editing.
- Take notes. The notes can be independent of literature. And the notes can be classified by using tags, and be associated with several literatures.

4.4   Literature Retrieval

- Filter literature. Literature information such as title, author, journal, publication time, read status and importance, can be used as filter, which can facilitate narrowing the search range, and user can read a specific range of literature optionally.
- Search literatures. The tool provides two search methods: quick search and advanced search. Quick search is keyword search. When using advanced search, user can input or select several search criteria, including metadata of literature, and personalized literature information, such as tags.

4.5   Facilitate Writing

The tool also provides functions to support writing:

- Export annotations and notes. Annotations and notes can be exported as the form of a PDF or editable documents. Users can export annotations of a single literature, and can also export annotations of literatures classified by tags.
- Establish outline for writing. User can create outline in the tool before writing, and add knowledge items (such as literature, annotations and notes) to the points in the outline. Outline can be exported to facilitate writing.
- Provide add-on of text editor to generate references.

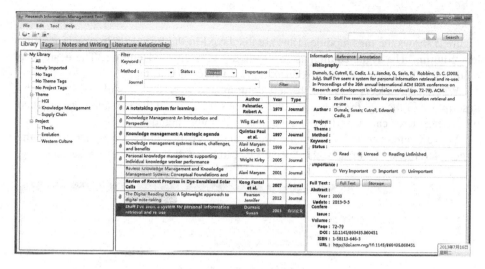

Fig. 1. Library

4.6   View Relationship Between Literatures

The tool will calculated the relationships between literatures based on literature information, user's reading status and use of literatures, and the tool will graphically demonstrate the relationships. It will help users to see literature relationship clearer.

5   Interface Design

There are four modules of the tool, library, tags, notes and writing, and literature relationships. Tabs are used to present these modules. The high-fidelity prototype is developed using VB.NET.

5.1   Library

The library module is shown as Fig. 1. The left column displays classifications of literatures. When users select a kind of category in the left column, the middle column will show a list of literature related to the category. Users can use filters presented in the middle column to narrow the literature range. After selecting a literature in the middle column, the literature information will appear in the right column. The right column is the edit area. There are three function modules, namely literature information, references and annotations. In literature information module, user can view and edit literature information, type in tags for article, and open PDF viewer to read the full text. User can edit and search references in the reference module. The annotation module is used for managing and exporting annotations.

5.2 Tags

Figure 2 shows the tags module. Tags are displayed in the form of tree structure in the left column. The right column is the area for viewing and editing. There are two modules in the right column, overview and add reference to tag.

When user selects a tag in the left column, the overview module will show the description of the tag, the literatures and sub-tags included in the tag, and notes marked by the tag. User can export the annotations and notes included in the tag.

In Add reference to tag module, user can search literatures first, then select the target literatures. As a result, the selected literatures will be added to the selected tag.

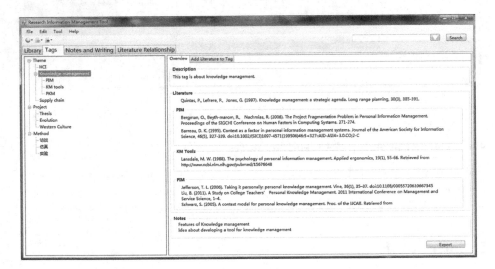

Fig. 2. Tags

5.3 Notes and Writing

Notes and Writing module is used for managing outlines and notes. The outlines and notes are presented in the form of tree structure in the left column. There are three modules in the edit area (i.e. the right column), overview, edit and create new outline.

When selecting an outline in the left column, user can view and edit description of the outline, and view content of the outline, including points and knowledge items related to the outline. Outline can be exported.

In Edit module, the outline is presented in the form of mind map. User can rename, add and remove points. If users want to add a knowledge item to a point, they can simply drag the knowledge item from the right column to the appropriate position. User can add points by clicking button or pressing hotkeys (Fig. 3).

5.4 Literature Relationship

User can see the literature relationship in the literature relationship module. The tool provides five literature relationships, namely reference, co-author, time axis, project

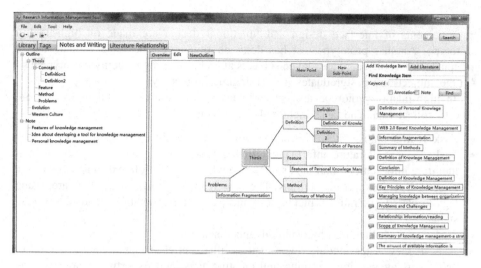

Fig. 3. Notes and writing

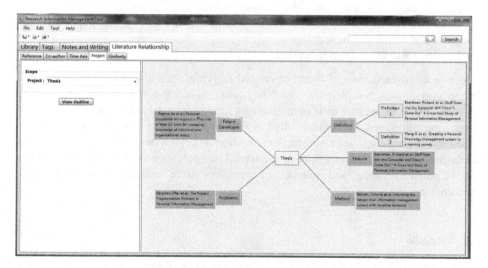

Fig. 4. Literature relationship

and literature similarity. For example, Project Module shows the relationship between the points of outline and literatures (Fig. 4).

6 High-Fidelity Prototype Test

6.1 Test Design

There are two prototype tests. Low-fidelity prototype is designed on the platform of Microsoft Visio 2010, and prototype test is conducted to figure out problem of usability and interface design. Five postgraduates from Tsinghua University attended the test. Improvements of interface design and functional design are made on high-fidelity prototype. Another prototype test has done on this prototype to investigate user's acceptance of Tool. There are eleven subjects attending the high-fidelity prototype test. All the subjects are postgraduates from Tsinghua University.

In high-fidelity prototype test, scenario tasks, questionnaires and interviews are used to collect data. The tasks include the following:

- Task 1: import PDF files. This shows how to create library by using Tool.
- Task 2: view literature information. In the task, participants will view and edit literature information, mark and summarize when reading full text, search a specific reference, and export annotations. The new features shown in the task are: using tags to classify literatures, picking out and exporting annotations, and setting read status.
- Task 3: search literature by using advanced search.
- Task 4: view Tags module. Participants will experience classification method of using tags by viewing, merging and creating tags, and exporting annotation and notes included in the tags.
- Task 5: view outlines. Notes and Writing module is involved in this task. Participants will see how Tool contributes to writing through editing and exporting outlines, and creating a new outline.
- Task 6: view literature relationship.

These tasks covered most of literature-related activities, and also shown new features. When participants completed a task, they were asked the reason why they made mistakes in the tasks, and their opinion about functions involved in the task. After all tasks were completed, participants filled in Post-Study System Usability Questionnaire (PSSUQ) [6] to assess user satisfaction. A short interview was conducted to collect participants' subjective evaluation of the tool. User behavior was recorded during the test. Completion time and number of mistakes were calculated to assess task performance.

6.2 Results

Participants were asked to explain their process of decision making for the wrong actions when completing tasks. Their explanations suggest that they made mistakes because of the limitation of the prototype. There should be several ways to complete tasks, but the prototype provides only one way that user can get feedback.

In PSSUQ, Question 1 to Question 8 test the Systems Usefulness, Question 10 to Question 15 suggest the Information Quality, and Question 16 to Question 19 indicate the Interface Quality [6]. Question 9 is not included since prototype did not show error recovery function. These questions are used to assess system usability satisfaction. Figure 5 suggests that the average scores of interface quality are higher, and average score of Question 18 ("This system has all the functions and capabilities I expect it to have." [6]) is the highest. This will indicate that, Tool designed from the perspective of research workflow, and it can meet users' requirements of literature management.

The average scores of information quality are relatively lower. Some participants thought that some expressions in the tool are confusing, so it is not easy to find the information they want.

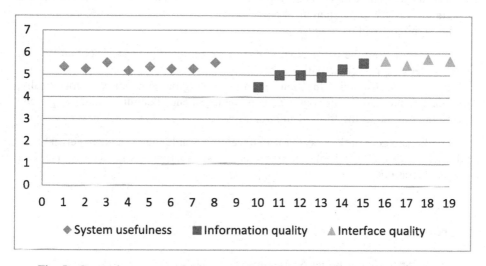

Fig. 5. Comparison scores of systems usefulness, information and interface quality

According to interview, methods and functions presented in task 1, task 2, task 4 and task 5 gain high degree of acceptance, and the function of exporting annotations and outlines is popular. The usability of library module, tags module and notes and writing module get positive feedback. The function shown in task 6 is a new, so the subjects are not sure whether they have the requirement of viewing literature relationships.

6.3 Improvement of Prototype

High-fidelity prototype has demonstrated complete functions and interfaces of Tool, and the design of functions and interface has been recognized through usability test. However, subjects thought the tool is complicated when they use it for the first time. To help user adapt to the interface quickly and get information they want timely, improvements should be made in the perspective of guidance and information presentation:

- When the cursor is moved into edit areas, Tool should remind users by changing the color of edit areas.
- Provide shortcuts to switch between pages easily.
- For some special expressions, the tool should provide clear explanation in the tutorial, and use bubble tips in the tool.
- Tutorial should be attractive, clearly and easy to understand. The distinctive functions and key operation methods should be shown in the tutorial.

7 Conclusion

The User Centered Design approach is used in this research, and the potential users are involved in every stage of Tool development. The functional framework is built based on literature review and requirement analysis.

The highlights of this research are listed as follows:

- Design Tool from the perspective of the whole research process. Tool can support most literature-related activities in the research process.
- Propose some distinctive functions, such as picking out annotations automatically, exporting annotations and outlines, tags management, literature relationships, and creating outline in the form of mind map.

The ultimate goal of the research is to develop a usable literature management tool. And it will be desirable if Tool can bring users good experience when they manage and use their literatures.

References

1. Abela, C., Staff, C., Handschuh, S.: Task-based user modelling for knowledge work support. In: De Bra, P., Kobsa, A., Chin, D. (eds.) UMAP 2010. LNCS, vol. 6075, pp. 419–422. Springer, Heidelberg (2010). http://www.springerlink.com/index/6Q876282UR556213.pdf
2. Bondarenko, O., Janssen, R., Driessen, S.: Requirements for the design of a personal document-management system. J. Am. Soc. Inform. Sci. Technol. **61**(3), 468–482 (2010). doi:10.1002/asi.21280
3. Chang, K., Perdana, I.W.T., Ramadhana, B., Sethuraman, K., Le, T.V., Chachra, N.: Knowledge file system – a principled approach to personal information management. In: 2010 IEEE International Conference on Data Mining Workshops, pp. 1037–1044 (2010). doi:10. 1109/ICDMW.2010.119
4. Frand, J., Hixon, C.: Personal Knowledge Management: Who, What, Why, When, Where, How? (1999). http://www.anderson.ucla.edu/faculty/jason.frand/researcher/speeches/PKM. htm
5. Marshall, C.C.: Annotation: from paper books to the digital library. In: Proceedings of the Second ACM International Conference on Digital libraries, pp. 131–140 (1997)
6. Lewis, J.R.: Psychometric evaluation of the PSSUQ using data from five years of usability studies. Int. J. Hum. Comput. Interact. **14**(3–4), 463–488 (2002)
7. Völkel, M., Schaffert, S., Oren, E.: Personal knowledge management with semantic technologies. In: Emerging Technologies for Semantic Work Environments, pp. 138–153 (2008)

Emotion and Perception: A Case Study of Aesthetic Response to Frith's Narrative Painting "The Railway Station"

Po-Hsien Lin[1(✉)], Mo-Li Yeh[2], and Jao-Hsun Tseng[3]

[1] Graduate School of Creative Industry Design, National Taiwan University of Arts, Daguan Rd., Banqiao District, New Taipei City 22058, Taiwan
t0131@ntua.edu.tw, rtlin@mail.ntua.edu.tw
[2] Department of Fashion Design, Hsing Wu University, Linkou, New Taipei City 24452, Taiwan
1101moli@gmail.com
[3] Department of Dance, National Taiwan University of Arts, Daguan Rd., Banqiao District, New Taipei City 22058, Taiwan
t0190@ntua.edu.tw

Abstract. This study intends to exam Clive Bell's theory of significant form. For Bell, a painting could not be a work of art if line and color were used to recount anecdotes, express ideas, and indicate the lifestyle of an age. In his influential book *Art*, Bell claimed that William Powell Frith's famous narrative painting *The Railway Station* was not a work of art. This paper used Frith's painting as the subject to explore whether viewers' aesthetic responses to a narrative painting would be affected by their perceptive awareness of image. Statistical data showed that, contrary to Bell's criticism, the artistic value of the work was confirmed by viewers' responses, demonstrating that he underestimated the attractiveness of representational painting. The results of this study partly supported Bell's argument. Comparing with artist's achievement of realistic representation, the viewers were indeed unmoved by the effects of idea communication and emotional expression in the painting. No significant association was found between viewers' perceptive awareness and their aesthetic judgments, suggesting that visual attraction could be more critical than cognitive information for viewers' aesthetic responses to a work of art.

Keywords: Emotion · Perception · Aesthetics response

1 Introduction

Located in London, Paddington Station was built in 1838 and started to operate in 1845, seven years earlier than that of King's Cross Station which featured in J. K. Rowling's famous novel of Harry Potter. Paddington Station was reconstructed as an underground station complex after 1863 and became the terminus of central London railway.

As shown in Fig. 1, the painting entitled *The Railway Station* was created by a British genre painter William Powell Frith (1819-1909). The work was completed in

© Springer International Publishing Switzerland 2015
P.L.P. Rau (Ed.): CCD 2015, Part II, LNCS 9181, pp. 241–251, 2015.
DOI: 10.1007/978-3-319-20934-0_23

1862, 101 inch long and 46 inch wide. Through a Victorian scene of 19th century Paddington Station, the artist depicted a virtual reality of lifestyle in London after the industrial revolution. Most viewers would agree that this painting is a work of art. However, in his influential book *Art*, the famous British aesthetician and art critic Clive Bell (1881–1964) proclaimed that Frith's *The Railway Station* is not a work of art [1].

Fig. 1. The Railway Station, W. P. Frith, 1862, Royal Holloway College, Surrey, UK

One of the most important issues raised by Bell was the difference of artistic significance evoked by emotion and perception. Bell believed that the aesthetic value of a work of art derived from viewers' emotional pleasure derived instinctively when gazing at the abstract elements of its composition. He argued that if forms and the relations of forms are employed to achieve the purpose of suggesting emotion and conveying ideas, they are created for visual perception rather than aesthetic emotion [1].

In this study we intend to examine Bell's theory of significant form. Using the image of Frith's *The Railway Station* as the study object, we attempted to explore whether viewers' aesthetic responses to a narrative painting would affected by their perceptive awareness of image.

The purpose of this study was to construct an accessible criticism model of art appreciation. An aesthetic paragon connected to mental function was addressed based on viewers' response to different level of perceptive awareness. The output of the study was expected to enhance aesthetic literacy of the public.

2   Literature Review

Before the sixteenth century, the concept that art imitates nature underlay representational theory. Even in the eighteenth century, Immanuel Kant still claimed that art can only be called beautiful if we are aware that it is art and yet it looks to us like nature [2]. However, the invention of photography resulted in a revolutionary development.

Now that the machine could easily imitate reality in nature even better than humans could, what was the value of a representational painting? In his theory of significant form, Clive Bell rejected representation as the essence of art. He praised primitive art for its absence of representation and description.

From a psychological point of view, human perception is significantly effected by emotion. In a study on the impact of emotion on perception, Zeelenberg, Wagenmakers, & Rotteveel claimed that emotionally significant stimuli were better identified than neutral stimuli [10]. Weierich and Barrett in their article discussing visual attention also suggested that the affective value would enhance visual sensitivity [9]. The conclusion that emotional content of the pictures effected perceptual encoding of outer stimuli could be drawn from the results of many experiments [8]. However, Bell suggested that aesthetic emotion derived from pure sensational stimuli but not cognitive awareness of a work of art.

According to Bell, human aesthetic experience derives from a particular composition of lines, colors, and forms. He claimed that in each masterpiece, lines and color combined in a particular way, certain forms and relations of forms, stir our aesthetic emotion. These relations and combinations of lines and colors, these aesthetically moving forms, Bell called "Signification Form" [1]. For Bell, a painting could not be a work of art if line and color are used to recount anecdotes, express ideas, and indicate the lifestyle of an age. Accordingly, Bell claimed that William Powell Frith's painting *The Railway Station* is not a work of art.

Frith specialized in genre subjects and narrative panorama. The painting represented a lively scene of London Paddington station. Every detail on the canvas was an imitation of the real world. The engine of the locomotive was drawn based on a photograph. The structural elements such as pillars, arches, and girders, which occupying almost the entire upper half of the canvas, still looks the same after one and a half century. The most dramatic effect of the painting is nearly a hundred figures separating on the lower part of the canvas in which the artist set up several scenarios happening in different groups of people. In an age without motion picture this painting represented a marvelous pictorial spectacle. However, according to Bell, this work is merely an interesting and amusing historical document. He argued that line and color in this painting are used to recount anecdotes, suggest ideas, and indicate the manners and customs of an age; they are not used to provoke aesthetic emotion [1].

It is interesting that the same comment of "historical document" was employed by another art critic to argue that Frith's painting became one of the most important contemporary works of art. In a biographical and critical essay written in 1978, Aubrey Noakes used "Extraordinary Victorian Painter" as the title, highly recommended Frith's *The Railway Station*. Noakes claimed that the artist accurately represented the fashion of in the 1860s. He argued that the artistic value of this painting derived from its documentary significance through which social historians were inspired over a century [6].

Bell's notion sustained the theory of several modern art movements, including abstractionism and minimalism. Noël Carroll argued that Bell intended to exclude photography from the art world because he was writing in the shadow of this new technology [3]. Bell foresaw the challenge of photography. His theory of significant form influenced art creation, and as an influential art critic his theory influence major museum collections in Britain, France, and the United States in the early twentieth century. By the end of the 20th century, the development of computer technology enabled artists to master more powerful media and to create visual images that look real. Once again, Bell's argument about significant form inspires us to reconsider the value of representative paintings.

3   Methodology

3.1   Research Instrument

In order to examine whether viewers' aesthetic responses to a narrative painting would be effected by their perceptive awareness of the image, a questionnaire was developed to obtain participants' aesthetic response after completing their appreciation of the work.

Participants were divided into two groups. An interpretation of the work was introduced in detail to the experimental group. In contrast, participants in the control group were not offered any information about the work before answering the questionnaire.

3.2   Framework of the Study

Participants' educational background and their awareness of the creation motifs of the painting were used as independent variables. An aesthetic judgment connecting to mental function was examined based on viewers' response to different levels of perceptive awareness. A framework for the research design is shown in Fig. 2.

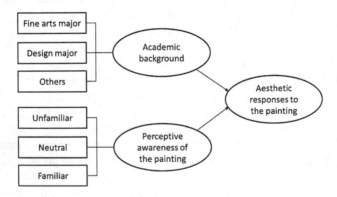

Fig. 2. Framework of the research design

Educational background was divided into three categories of (1) Fine arts major, (2) Design major, and (3) Others. Perceptive awareness included three levels of (1) Unfamiliar, (2) Neutral, and (3) Familiar. There are two sets of dependent variables.

The first is a multi-choice question about how the painting attracted the viewer including six categorical items: (1) Integrated and compact composition, (2) Detailed and fluid contours, (3) Vivid and vigorous colors, (4) Lively figures and scenery, (5) Clear idea communication, and (6) Abundant emotional expression. The second is a group of questions using the format of 5 points Likert scales to examine participants' criticism of the painting:

(1) This is a work with high artistic value.
(2) This work is more like a historical document.
(3) This work demonstrates the zeitgeist of artist's time.
(4) This work rigidly adheres to the skill of realistic depiction.
(5) This work seems to narrate an interesting story.
(6) The visual expression is better than content narration in this work.
(7) Taken as a whole, I highly appreciate this work.

4 Data Analysis

The study completed 119 effective questionnaires, covering three different educational backgrounds (Fine arts major 28, Design major 40, and Others 51) and three diverse levels of perceptive awareness (Unfamiliar 33, Neutral 43, and Familiar 43). The significant outcomes and discoveries are as below.

4.1 Descriptive Statistics

Descriptive statistics of mean score and standard deviation were used in this study to demonstrate participants' criticisms evaluated by 5 points Likert scales.

Table 1 shows that the mean scores of questions "This is a work with high artistic value" and "Taken as a whole, I highly appreciate this work" were significantly greater than the assumed mean of 3, suggesting participants' positive attitudes toward this panting. Among all items, the question "This work demonstrates the zeitgeist of artist's time" got the best rates, the question "This work adheres to the skill of realistic depiction" obtained the lowest score.

Table 1. Mean scores and standard deviation of participants' evaluation of the painting

Items	Mean	SD
1.This is a work with high artistic value	3.82	.747
2.This work is more like a historical document	3.73	.972
3.This work demonstrates the zeitgeist of artist's time	4.17	.847
4.This work adheres to the skill of realistic depiction	2.86	.945
5.This work seems to narrate an interesting story	3.75	1.043
6.The visual expression is better than content narration	3.46	1.080
7.Taken as a whole, I highly appreciate this work	3.87	.853

4.2 Chi-Square Test and Correspondence Analysis

Chi-square test was manipulated in this study to examine the association between two independent variables and the categorical dependent variable of aesthetic judgments.

Table 2 shows that two sets of Chi-square score were less than the critical values, suggesting that participants' educational background and perceptive awareness of the painting did not result in significant differences in their aesthetic judgments. Most of the participants selected item 4 "Lively figures and scenery". The second was item 1 "Integrated and compact composition". The final was "Detailed and fluid contours".

Table 2. Chi-square tests for aesthetic judgments by educational background and perceptive awareness.

	1	2	3	4	5	6	X^2 (df)
Fine art major	6	3	2	11	4	2	**12.57**
	21.4 %	10.7 %	7.1 %	39.3 %	14.3 %	7.1 %	**(10)**
Design major	9	2	4	20	1	4	
	22.5 %	5.0 %	10.0 %	50.0 %	2.5 %	10.0 %	
Other major	5	1	11	26	4	4	
	9.8 %	2.0 %	21.6 %	51.0 %	7.8 %	7.8 %	
Unfamiliar	7	1	6	15	0	4	**7.60**
	21.2 %	3.0 %	18.2 %	45.5 %	.0 %	12.1 %	**(10)**
Neutral	8	3	6	18	5	3	
	18.6 %	7.0 %	14.0 %	41.9 %	11.6 %	7.0 %	
Familiar	5	2	5	24	4	3	
	11.6 %	4.7 %	11.6 %	55.8 %	9.3 %	7.0 %	
Total	20	6	17	57	9	10	119
	16.8 %	5.0 %	14.3 %	47.9 %	7.6 %	8.4 %	100.0 %

A technique of correspondence analysis was employed in this study to identify systematic relations between two sets of categorical variables. Through two-dimensional graphics, the data demonstrated how participants' aesthetic responses to the painting were related to their educational backgrounds and their cognitive awareness of the painting.

Figure 3 shows that as regards the attractiveness of the painting, participants of fine arts major distinctly put their focus on detailed and fluid contours and clear idea communication. Participants of design major stressed the significance of integrated and compact composition and abundant emotional expression. Non-art and non-design major participants preferred vivid and vigorous colors and lively figures and scenery.

Figure 4 suggests that the participants who are unfamiliar with the painting drew their attention to colors and emotional expression. The participants well acquainted with the painting preferred lively figures and scenery. The participants who knew a little about the painting tended to give weight to composition, contours, and idea communication.

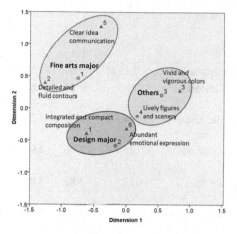

Fig. 3. The relation between educational backgrounds and aesthetic responses

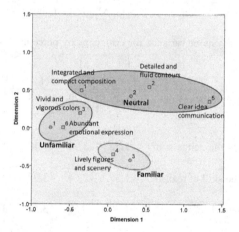

Fig. 4. The relation between cognitive awareness and aesthetic responses

4.3   Analysis of Variance

An analysis of variance (ANOVA) was conducted to explore how participants' criticism were effected by independent variables of educational background and conceptive awareness of the work.

Table 3 shows that the mean scores for "This is a work with high artistic value" and "Taken as a whole, I highly appreciate this work" demonstrated significant variance due to educational background differences. Results of Scheffe's post hoc analysis suggested that in these two questions, scores of fine arts and design major participants were significantly less than that of other majors.

Table 4 shows that participants' perceptive awareness of the work did not result in significant differences in their criticisms.

Table 3. Analysis of variance for criticisms by educational background

Items	F	M			Scheffe's post hoc
		FA	D	O	
1.This is a work with high artistic value	7.13**	3.64	3.58	4.10	O>FA, O>D
2.This work is more like a historical document	1.83	4.04	3.63	3.65	
3.This work demonstrates the zeitgeist of artist's time	.74	4.00	4.20	4.24	
4.This work adheres to the skill of realistic depiction	.45	2.96	2.90	2.76	
5.This work seems to narrate an interesting story	.27	3.82	3.80	3.67	
6.The visual expression is better than content narration	.04	3.43	3.50	3.45	
7.Taken as a whole, I highly appreciate this work	5.61*	3.64	3.65	4.16	O>FA, O>D

*$p<.05$, **$p<.01$, FA: Fine Arts Major, D: Design Major, O: Others

Table 4. Analysis of variance for criticisms by perceptive awareness

Works	F	M			Scheffe's post hoc
		U	N	F	
1.This is a work with high artistic value	.29	3.79	3.88	3.77	
2.This work is more like a historical document	.43	3.61	3.81	3.74	
3.This work demonstrates the zeitgeist of artist's time	2.92	3.94	4.40	4.12	
4.This work adheres to the skill of realistic depiction	1.57	2.64	3.02	2.86	
5.This work seems to narrate an interesting story	1.70	3.67	3.58	3.98	
6.The visual expression is better than content narration	1.90	3.58	3.63	3.21	
7.Taken as a whole, I highly appreciate this work	.87	3.82	3.77	4.00	

U: Unfamiliar, N: Neutral, F: Familiar

4.4   Correlation Analysis

Correlation coefficients were calculated in this study to examine the relationship between every pair of items of participants' criticism. Table 5 shows that the score of "this is a work with high artistic value" is significantly correlated with that of "this work demonstrates the zeitgeist of artist's time" and "taken as a whole, I highly appreciate this work". The correlation between the score of "this work is more like a historical document" and "this work rigidly adheres to the skill of realistic depiction" is significant. Participant's responses to "this work seems to narrate an interesting story" and "taken as a whole, I highly appreciate this work" are also significantly correlated.

Table 5 Correlation Matrix for Seven Items of Criticism

	1	2	3	4	5	6	7
1	–						
2	−.162	–					
3	**.277****	−.027	–				
4	−.110	**.245****	−.033				
5	.092	−.151	−.019	−.072	–		
6	−.019	−.018	−.021	.132	−.061	–	
7	**.359****	.007	.020	−.077	**.247****	−.015	–

**p<.01

5   Findings and Discussion

This study attempted to explore whether viewers' aesthetic responses to a narrative painting would be effected by their perceptive awareness of the work. Based on statistical analysis of data, some important findings are discussed below.

5.1   Regarding the Attractiveness of the Painting

In responses to the question about the attractiveness of the painting, most of the viewers selected "lively figures and scenery" and "integrated and compact composition". According to Bell, human aesthetic experience derives from a particular composition of lines, colors, and forms. He rejected representation as the essence of art. From this point of view, Bell underestimated the attractiveness of representational painting.

To Bell, line and color in Frith's *The Railway Station* were used to recount anecdotes, suggest ideas, and indicate the manners and customs of an age; they are not used to provoke aesthetic emotion. The results of this study partly supported Bell's argument. Compared with the artist's achievement of realistic representation, the viewers were indeed cared less about the effects of idea communication and emotional expression in the painting.

5.2   Regarding Viewers' Criticisms on the Painting

Seven questions were conceived by using 5 points Likert scales to explore participants' aesthetic judgments on the painting. Statistical data showed that, contrary to Bell's criticism, the artistic value of the work was highly confirmed. Participants also express their appreciation to this panting. Among all questions, the comment "This work demonstrates the zeitgeist of artist's time" got the best rates and this judgment was significantly correlated with the artistic value of the work. The feature of story narration was also significantly correlated with participants' appreciation of the work.

In summary, the viewers accepted Frith's work as a historical document and narrating an interesting story. Though the visual expression could be better than content narration in this work, they opposed the idea that this work rigidly adhered to the skill of realistic depiction. Bell's theory was not sustained by participants' criticisms of the painting.

5.3 Regarding the Influence of Viewers' Perceptive Awareness of the Painting

The results of both Chi-square or ANOVA showed that there was no significant association between viewers' perceptive awareness and aesthetic judgments, suggesting that visual attraction could be more critical than cognitive information for viewers' aesthetic responses to a work of art.

The outcome of further correspondence analysis suggested that the participants who are unfamiliar with the painting drew their attention to colors and emotional expression. The participants well acquainted with the painting preferred lively figures and scenery. To provide the viewers with prior knowledge of the work would influence their attitude toward the arts.

5.4 Regarding the Influence of Viewers' Educational Background

When rating artistic value of the painting and participants' appreciation of the work, educational background was a critical factor resulting in significant differences. It is understandable that participants of fine arts major and design major had higher standard of than participants of other majors. However, there were no significant differences within three groups of participants in response to the other five questions about qualitative descriptions of the painting.

6 Conclusions

This study intended to examine Bell's theory of significant form. He rejected representation as the essence of art. According to Bell, all systems of aesthetics must be based on personal experience of a peculiar emotion. Thus, aesthetic experience is not cognitive and not a judgment involving objective concepts. Bell proposed that there must be some qualities which are the essence of art. He believed that significant form is exactly that essence to evoke viewers' aesthetic emotion and without which an object cannot really be regarded as a work of art.

When Bell explicitly pointed out that Frith's *The Railway Station* is not a work of art, he attempted to convince us the skills applied in this painting were used to recite anecdotes, suggest ideas, and indicate the lifestyle of an age, they were not used to provoke aesthetic emotion. However, the result of this study showed that the viewers appreciated artist's representational style of painting. We may conclude from this study that people did get aesthetic emotion from the significant form of this painting, but they also enjoyed the pleasure derived from perceptive awareness of the work.

Did we amplify an artist's achievement? After all, the original motive for Frith was commercial appeal. Andy Warhol, the hottest American Pop artist, claimed that "Why do people think artists are special? It's just another job". [7] In fact, Frith had been enjoying considerable popularity as a narrative painter in the Victorian age. *The Railway Station* was commissioned by Louis Victor Flatow, an art dealer and financier, who invested £4,500 in this deal. It took Frith two years to complete the work. The commission was described as an entirely new departure according to the press at that time. Flatow's accurate judgment on art market was manifested by the grand total of £30,000 income after the exhibition [6].

The artistic value of Frith's painting was not recognized by Bell. Ironically, the public love this painting no matter whether in Victorian times or nowadays. The audiences were deeply attracted by artist's way of narration and his delicate representation of the manners and customs of an age. Today, this skill can be easily replaced by the functions of a camera. Carroll was right when he argued that Bell intended to exclude photography from the realm of the arts. Bell never denied his intention of fighting against narrative paintings. He believed that this sort of works would be spared because of the development of photography and motion picture [2].

Though Bell confessed that "the representative element in a work of art may or may not be harmful; always it is irrelevant," nevertheless, he insisted that "to appreciate a work of art we need bring with us nothing from life, no knowledge of its ideas and affairs". [2] The result of this study shows that many people were profoundly moved by this painting because it demonstrates the zeitgeist of artist's time. This is a perceptive interest to the work. We would like to argue that whether or not a painting is a work of art is no more the critical issue. In his *On the Genealogy of Morals*, Nietzsche quoted from Stendhal, claimed that Beautiful is a promise of happiness [5]. People lined up and paid to see Frith's exhibition. They involved themselves in an art event and got enjoyment from a narrative painting, and that might be the answer.

References

1. Barthes, R.: Camera Lucida: Reflections On Photography. Hill and Wang, NY (1981)
2. Bell, C.: Art. Chatto and Windus, London (1924). (Original work published 1914)
3. Carroll, N.: Clive bell's aesthetic hypothesis. In: Dickie, G., et al. (eds.) Aesthetic: A critical anthology, pp. 84–95. St. Martin's Press, NY (1989)
4. Kant, I. . Critique of the power of judgment. In: Guyer, P. (ed.), Guyer, P., Matthews, E. (Trans.). Cambridge University Press, UK (2000). (Original work published in 1790)
5. Nietzsche, F.: On the genealogy of morals. In: Kaufmann, W., Hollingdale, R.J. (Trans.). Random House, Inc., NY (1967). (Original work published 1887.)
6. Noakes, A.: William Frith: Extraordinary Victorian painter: A Biographical And Critical Essay. Jupiter Books Limited, London (1978)
7. Warhol, A.: The Philosophy of Andy Warhol. Harcourt Brace Jovanovich, NY (1975)
8. Schupp, H.T., Junghofer, M., Weike, A.I., Hamm, A.: Emotional facilitation of sensory processing in the visual cortex. Psychol. Sci. **14**, 7–13 (2003)
9. Weierich, M., Barrett, L.F.: Affect as a source of visual attention. In: Balcetis, E., Lassiter, G.D. (eds.) Social psychology of visual perception, pp. 125–148. Psychology Press, NY (2010)
10. Zeelenberg, R., Wagenmakers, E.J., Rotteveel, M.: The impact of emotion on perception: bias or enhanced processing? Psychol. Sci. **17**(4), 287–291 (2006)

Traditional Western Art Elements in Disney Animations, Elite Influence in Mass Culture Through the Prism of the Frankfurt School

Nai-Hsuan Lin[1](✉) and Shwu-Huoy Tzou[2]

[1] Sociology Department, National Cheng Chi University,
NO.64 Sec.2, ZhiNan Rd., Wenshan District, Taipei City 11605, Taiwan, R.O.C
99502004@nccu.edu.tw
[2] Department of Art and Design, Yuan Ze University,
135 Yuan-Tung Road, Chung-Li 32003, Taiwan, R.O.C
sophiet@saturn.yzu.edu.tw

Abstract. Thanks to the development of the media and internet, American mass culture has been spread worldwide. Above all, Disney animation is one of the most successful in its industry. However, the success of the Disney Corporation appears not only due to the prosperity of the company but also the wide dissemination of American mass culture. While our children are watching their films they are learning the American culture and values at the same time, which will shape their ways of thinking and habits of consumption in future. This is the most important criticism of the "culture industry" from the Frankfort School. Even though Disney animations were classified as mass culture, the themes which have been used in Disney animations often contain numerous elements of western traditional culture and arts: when audiences watch these cartoons, those elements are also beginning to be implanted in their mind. In this study I intend to analyze how Disney animation uses elite culture to enhance the quality of their films, and how elite culture can be introduced to the world through an approach free of ambiguity. Most importantly, I attempt to explore how the successful experience of Disney could transfer to Taiwanese animation industry.

Keywords: Mass culture · Elite culture · Disney · Culture industry · The Frankfort School · Taiwan animation industry

1 Introduction

What is "culture industry"? The term "culture industry" first appeared in "Dialectic of Enlightenment" by Max Horkheimer and Theodor W. Adorndorno, which is widely considered the most important book of The Frankfort School. The term 'Culture industry' refers to the fact that cultural artifacts have been produced through industrial methods, and eventually cause the deception effect toward consumers. The standards that determine the production of artworks and cultural activities are no longer the inspirations of artists but the the logic of industrial technology. The consequences of culture industry would be a trend towards standardization, with entrepreneurs small differences on each products to create the illusion of personalization which would

P.L.P. Rau (Ed.): CCD 2015, Part II, LNCS 9181, pp. 252–262, 2015.
DOI: 10.1007/978-3-319-20934-0_24

increase the willingness to purchase amongst consumers. Yet, the result of culture industry was the birth of mass culture. "Mass culture" refer to the new term of cultural performance in industrial society from the 20th century. It's most famous features are 1. consumerism 2. reproduction. In the point of view of The Frankfort School's scholars, the needs that we are purchasing to satisfy these days are actually not our real needs but the one that been created by capitalism. This is the reason why they tend to use the term "culture industry" instead of "mass culture", in "Dialektik der Aufklarung: Philosophische Fragmente" they claimed that the word " mass culture" would mislead the public. The phrase "mass culture" implies grassroots origin but, it actually controls and shapes the needs as well as ideology of the audience [1, 7].

However, are mass culture and culture industry the only cause of negative effects? W. Benjamin, a scholar of The Frankfort School, held a different point of view. In Benjamin's opinion, art is variable, and can be changed into distinct terms in different times and environments. In the industrial era, the ceremonial value of arts has been gradually replaced by its commercial or exhibited value, which also means the aura of art has disappeared. Yet, due to the development of camera and video, each photo or film can be reproduced, and each copy will identical to the original: in this case, is the aura still a necessarily element of arts? Furthermore, the ready availability of copies allows master pieces to be spread worldwide, giving more chances for the public to approach the classical or elite culture. Under this approach, does mass culture and culture industry still only lead into negative effect? [9].

2   Literatures Review

2.1   Mass and Elite Culture Elements in Disney Animations

Through the development of the media and internet, American mass culture is spread worldwide. Above all, Disney animation is the most successful enterprise (Fig. 1).

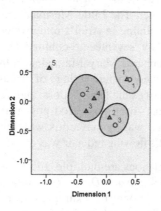

Fig. 1. The willing of audiences to rewatch the Little mermaid after knowing *Repenting Magdalene* was in the film.

Thanks to the development of the media and internet, American mass culture has been spread worldwide. Above all, Disney animation is one of the most successful in its industry. However, the success of the Disney Corporation appears not only due to the prosperity of the company but also the wide dissemination of American mass culture. Most children nowadays are familiar with the big-eared black mouse who wears red shorts and yellow shoes and talks with abnormal high pitch. While our children are watching their films they are learning the American culture and values at the same time, which will shape their ways of thinking and habits of consumption in future. This is what Zbigniew Kazimierz Brzeziński had mention in his book " Between two ages: America's role in the technetronic Era", "As a sweeping generalization, it can be said that Rome exported law; England, parliamentary party democracy; France, culture and republican nationalism; the contemporary United States, technological scientific innovation and mass culture derived from high consumption" [4].

2.2   Mass and Elite Culture Elements in Disney Animations

Even though Disney animations are classified as mass culture, the themes which have been used in Disney animations often contain numerous elements from the western tradition of culture and arts. By the time an audience watch these cartoons, those elements are also beginning to implant in their minds. The book "Da Vinci code", which was published in 2009, has these two following paragraphs:

> Most of Disney's hidden messages dealt with religion, pagan myth, and stories of the subjugated goddess. It was no mistake that Disney retold tales like Cinderella, Sleeping Beauty, and Snow White—all of which dealt with the incarceration of the sacred feminine. Nor did one need a background in symbolism to understand that Snow White—a princess who fell from grace after partaking of a poisoned apple— was a clear allusion to the downfall of Eve in the Garden of Eden. Or that Sleeping Beauty's Princess Aurora—code-named "Rose" and hidden deep in the forest to protect her from the clutches of the evil *witch—was the Grail story for* children.
> When Langdon had first seen The Little Mermaid, he had actually gasped aloud when he noticed that the painting in Ariel's underwater home was none other than The Penitent Magdalene by seventeenth-century artist Georges de la Tour—a famous homage to the banished Mary Magdalene—fitting decor considering the movie turned out to be a ninety-minute collage of blatant symbolic references to the lost sanctity of Isis, Eve, Pisces the fish goddess, and, repeatedly, Mary Magdalene. The Little Mermaid's name, Ariel, possessed powerful ties to the sacred feminine and, in the Book of Isaiah, was synonymous with "the Holy City besieged". Of course, the Little Mermaid's flowing red hair was certainly no coincidence either [3].

The topics of Disney animations are multiple. Either they adapt classical literatures into films, (e.g. *The Hunchback of Notre Dame, Hercules and Beauty and the Beast,*) or directly use art works in the cartoon, for example, Georges de La Tour's *Repenting Magdalene* as above. Inside Disney's films we can usually catch a glimpse of traditional western culture elements. Compared to mass culture, elite culture usually represents a world which is not familiar to the public. Yet, would it be easier for the public to approach elite culture if it were hidden under the surface of mass culture? While Disney animations became more and more popular all around the world, has it successfully introduce western traditional culture to Taiwanese? Could it be possible for Taiwanese animation industry to spread our traditional culture to the public by the same means? (Fig. 2).

2.3 Animations in Taiwan

The first Disney animation shown in Taiwan cinemas was the Little Mermaid in 1989. Disney authorized the copyright to Taiwan in 1991 for VHS and soundtrack, and in 1995 the Disney channel started to appear on TV, which was also a turning point for Disney walking into Taiwanese homes (Fig. 3).

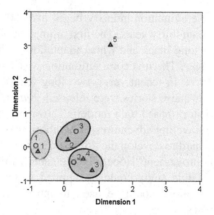

Fig. 2. The willing of audiences to rewatch the Little mermaid after knowing the film was adapted from *Little mermaid.*

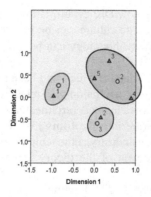

Fig. 3. The willing of audiences to rewatch the lion king after knowing the story was enlightened from Hamlet.

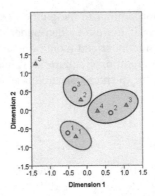

Fig. 4. The willing of audiences to rewatch Beauty and the beast after knowing *Girl with a Pearl Earring* was in the film.

The domestic Taiwanese animation industry begin in 1950s, which was later than Disney company by more than thirty years. The first animation released by a Taiwanese company was a ten minute long black and white adaptation of the classic Chinese folk tale *Wu Song Fights the Tiger*. The first color animation was *The Race Between Turtle And Rabbit*, released in 1969. In recent years, two long feature animations, based on traditional Chinese and Taiwanese stories were released: *Butterfly lovers* and *Kavalan*. The latter was an adapted story based on a modern Taiwanese novel, the main plot of which was about the time traveling adventures of an aboriginal teenager. Even though Taiwanese animators tried hard to develop the domestic industry, box office receipts are yet to show substantial improvement. Hopefully the successful experience of Disney company and the result of this study could be applied to the Taiwanese animation industry and one day animations could be used to introduce Taiwanese traditional culture to the public (Fig. 4).

3   Research Methods

In this study I intend to analyze how Disney animation use elite culture to enhance the quality of their films, and how elite culture can be introduced to the world through a free of ambiguity approach. My methodology can be divided into three main stages as below:

First, I chose five Disney animations which had been released in Taiwan after 1989 (The year in which the first Disney animation was released in Taiwan) to analyze how they put the three main visual arts elements (architectures, painting and sculpture) and the origin of the story – literature into the films [5]. At the same time, I will study existing research on the culture industry, elite culture and The Frankfort School to deeply understand the development of the theory and the status it holds in society nowadays (Fig. 5).

Second, I used the knowledge that I gained from the above stage to make a questionnaire presented to college students from Taiwanese universities. The reason

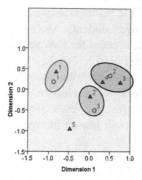

Fig. 5. The willing of audiences to rewatch Beauty and the beast after knowing the story was adapted from *Beauty and the beast.*

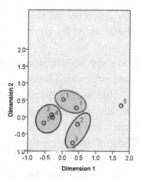

Fig. 6. The willing of audiences to rewatch Hercules after knowing the wide differences between the original story and the cartoon.

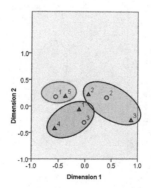

Fig. 7. The willing of audiences to rewatch The Hercules the film was adapted from the Greek legend.

why I chose college students as the participants was their wider knowledge of western traditional culture than the younger students. Moreover, since all the Taiwanese universities prepare a school e -mail account for their students, it will be more effective for me to approach the participants (Fig. 6).

Last, I will use SPSS to analyze the questionnaire results and a draw conclusions on how Taiwanese audiences respond to western traditional culture elements in Disney animations. Moreover, I will compare the result of the students from different subjects to see if the study background would impact the reactions of the audiences (Fig. 7).

4   Results and Discussions

The five animations that I chose were all adapted from classical western literature :*The Little Mermaid*(adapted from Hans Christian Andersen's *The little Mermaid*), *Beauty and the beast*(adapted from traditional French fairy tale which written by Jeanne-Marie Leprince de Beaumont and published in 1756), *The lion king* (the story was inspired by Shakespeare's *Hamlet*), Hercules(adapted by the story of Hercules from Greek legend) and *The Hunchback of Notre Dame*(adapted by *Notre-Dame de Paris* which written by Victor, Marie Hugo) (Fig. 8).

My questionnaire was completed by 133 subjects, most of them from arts related departments or social science related subjects. The questionnaire includes 42 questions. Except for the background of the subjects, the questions can be sorted into four types: 1. If the subjects had seen the animations and the original literatures 2. If they noticed the classical elements that had been used in the films. 3. Would the knowledge of the element's presence affect the willing of watching the animations 4. What are the main methods that subjects usually use to see the films (Fig. 9).

According to the results below, we can see that the number of respondents who had seen the animation was higher than those who had read the original literature (Fig. 10).

In the questionnaire, there were 13 questions which pointed out the classical elements that had been used in the animation. According to the data, the subjects who

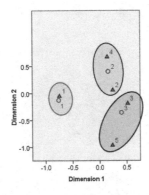

Fig. 8. The willing of audiences to rewatch The Hunchback of Nortre Dame after knowing the wide differences between original literature and the cartoon.

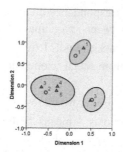

Fig. 9. The willing of audiences to rewatch The Hunchback of Nortre Dame after knowing the real use of Gargoyles.

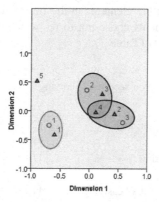

Fig. 10. The willing of audiences to rewatch The Hunchback of Notre Dame after knowing the story was adapted from *Notre-Dame de Paris.*

recognized them are mostly from arts related subjects, but a majority of the subjects, no matter what study back ground were they from, didn't noticed the appearance of the elite culture's elements (Fig. 11).

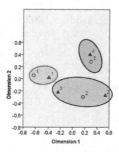

Fig. 11. The reasons for audiences from different education background to watch Disney animations.

In addition, a technique of correspondence analysis was employed in this study to identify systematic relations between participants' study background and their responses. ● refers to study background. 1 refers to subjects from arts related departments, 2 refers to subjects from social science departments, and 3 refers to others (Table 1).

▲ refers to the subjects willing to re -watch the films after knowing the appearance of the elite culture elements. 1 means "will watch again", 2 means "perhaps will watch again", 3 means "perhaps will not watch again", 4 means "will not watch again", and 5 means the subjects had already known the existed of the elements so it makes no difference to them (Table 2).

Through two-dimensional graphics, the data demonstrated that, subjects from arts related department tend to have more willing to watch the animations again after they have been told of the elite culture elements in the films. In the contrary, subjects from social science related departments chose not to re- watch the movies even they know the existence of these elements (Table 3).

Table 1. Have you seen the following Disney animations?

Items	Yes	No
The little mermaid	121	12
	91.0 %	9.0 %
The lion king	119	22
	84.4 %	15.6 %
Beauty and the beast	110	22
	83.3 %	16.7 %
Hercules	66	65
	50.4 %	49.6 %
The Hunchback of Notre Dame	50	84
	37.3 %	62.7 %

Table 2. Have you read the following literatures?

Items	Yes	No
The little mermaid	1067	27
	9.7 %	20.3 %
Hamlet	46	87
	34.6 %	65.4 %
Beauty and the beast	44	89
	33.1 %	66.9 %
Hercules	76	57
	57.1 %	42.9 %
Notre-Dame de Paris	16	117
	12.0 %	88.0 %

Table 3. Would you buy the media products of animations?

	Yes	No
Experiences of purchasing media products of animations	43	80
	35.0 %	65.0 %

Table 4. The reason you do not buy the media products of animations?

	Too expensive	Not worthy to collect	Can be downloaded on line
Reason of not buying	18	41	42
	17.8 %	40.6 %	41.6 %

Table 5. What kind of media products of animations you buy most?

	DVD	Blue -Ray	Soundtrack
Types of media products bought	33	10	20
	52.4 %	15.9 %	31.7 %

The following figure shows the reasons for watching Disney films amongst subjects from different education backgrounds. Subjects from art related majors tend to watch Disney animations because of the story's plot, while those from social science department's subjects see the movies due to the subjects of the stories and the painting styles (Table 4).

Lastly, according to the data, more subjects tend not to buy the media products related to the animations (DVD, blue ray, soundtracks etc.). The reason is because they think they are not worthy to keep and people can download them on line instead (Table 5).

Yet, for those who still willing to buy the media products of animations, their most favorite choice would be DVD, and then soundtracks. If Taiwan animation industries want to release media products to approach to the market, following the consumer's preferences would give them more chances.

5 Conclusion and Recommendation

Based on the previous study, we find that people are more likely to gain their knowledge of the story from the film than from the original literature. Yet, the appearance of the elite cultural elements can increase the willingness of specific groups to re-watch the film.

Since to the emergence of the internet, the willingness of people to purchase media products has decreased due to their online availability. On the bright sight, it means that inside films containing elite elements are more attractive to audiences, however, in contrast, if those who watch the films online are getting the animations for free, then it will lower the income of animations industry, which may cause the risks in long term. Nevertheless, I also discovered that people would not notice the classic cultural elements which were hidden in the films unless others point them out. This means that even though using the elements in the animation can expand the population that become more familiar with, how to present them effectively to the audience will be another task.

Additionally, the questionnaire results reveal that people nowadays prefer to watch the films on TV or on the internet (the number was over 70 % of the subjects). In this case, I think Taiwan animations industry, may start their work from the small screen, which can lower the manufacturing budget and also make for more effective access to public attention. After Taiwan's audiences are familiar enough with Taiwan-domestic animations films, they may be more willing to pay for the movie tickets to see the cartoons in a theater.

Lastly, the plot and subjects of the animations are the two main elements which could affect the willingness of the audience to watch, so if Taiwanese animations industry wants to develop the quality of the cartoons, these are the two parts that animators should be working on, and accompany them with a unique painting style that can attract the audience.

References

1. Adorno, T.W., Horkheimer, M.: Dialectic of Enlightenment. Stanford University Press, Redwood City (2007)
2. Allan, R.: Walt Disney And Europe: European Influences on the Animated Features Films of Walt Disney. John Libbey and Company Ltd, London (1999)
3. Brown, D.: Da Vinci Code. Anchor, NY (2009)
4. Brzeziński, Z.K.: Between Two Ages: America's Role in the Technetronic Era. Praeger, CA (1982)
5. Eliot, T.S.: Notes Towards a Definition of Culture. Faber and Faber, London (1973)
6. Gabler, N.: Walt Disney: The Triumph of the American Imagination. Knopf, NY (2008)
7. Jay, M.: Adorno. Harvard University Press, Cambridge (1984)
8. Booker, K.M.: Disney, Pixas and the Hidden Messages of Children's Films. Praeger, CA (2010)
9. Benjamin, W.: The work of art in the age of mechanical reproduction. In: Kearney, R., Rasmussen, D. (eds.) Continental Aesthetics: Romanticism to Postmodernism, an Anthology, pp. 182–211. Blackwell Publishers Ltd., Malden, MA (2001). Original work published in 1935

From Dechnology to Humart – A Case Study of Taiwan Design Development

Rungtai Lin[1]([✉]), John Kreifeldt[2], Pei-Hua Hung[1],
and Jun-Liang Chen[1]

[1] Graduate School of Creative Industry Design,
National Taiwan University of Arts,
Ban Ciao City 22058, Taipei, Taiwan
rtlin@mail.ntua.edu.tw
[2] Tufts University, Medford, MA, USA
John.Kreifeldt@tufts.edu

Abstract. Taiwan economic development is a fusion of Dechnology (Design-Technology) and Humart (Humanity-Art) which could be represented as a smile curve, from OEM (Original Equipment Manufacture), ODM (Original Design Manufacture), to OBM (Original Brand Manufacture). The three stages also reflect the tendency of Taiwan design development, from "use" to "user", from "function" to "feeling", and from "hi-tech" to "hi-touch". Based on the Taiwan experience, this paper is intended to study the relationship between Dechnology and Humart which were merged into design thinking to explore Taiwan design development. Hence, the purpose of this paper is to provide designers, companies, and organizations with an idea for how to direct their efforts to meet the requirements of a new proposed design strategy by applying design thinking. Results of this study are also intended to illustrate the interwoven experience of local design and global market in Taiwan's economy, industry and design development as well to provide a framework for looking at Taiwan's cross-cultural design development.

Keywords: Taiwan design development · Localization · Globalization · Glocalization · Design strategy · Cross-cultural

1 Introduction

With increasing global competition, connections between local culture and global market have become increasingly close. Recently, the increasing emphasis on localized cultural development in Taiwan demonstrates an ambition to promote Taiwan design in the global market. As the Taiwan design hub, the Taiwan Design Center (TDC, http://www.tdc.org.tw/) should take the opportunity to propose a "Design Thinking" approach for Taiwan to formulate the global design strategy for the future. Taiwan economic development is a fusion of Dechnology (Design-Technology) and Humart (Humanity-Art): from OEM (Original Equipment Manufacture) to ODM (Original Design Manufacture) to OBM (Original Brand Manufacture). These three stages of OEM, ODM and OBM also reflect the tendency of Taiwan design development as moving from "use" to "user", from "function" to "feeling", and from "hi-tech" to

© Springer International Publishing Switzerland 2015
P.L.P. Rau (Ed.): CCD 2015, Part II, LNCS 9181, pp. 263–273, 2015.
DOI: 10.1007/978-3-319-20934-0_25

"hi-touch": a process of design evolution showing an adaptive design in Taiwan design development (Lin, 2012).

Furthermore, the factors affecting the concept of marketing in Taiwan design development include: (1) from global market to local design, (2) from globalization to localization to glocalization (global-localization), and (3) from business model to life style. There are three dimensions identified which influenced Taiwan's cultural and creative industry, namely: (1) from digital archive to E-business, (2) from user-centered to user experience, and (3) from content to context. There are four factors affecting manufacture: (1) from quality to qualia which is a term that is used to denote the more subjective properties of our own personal existences which refers to what it is like to have an experience (Lin, 2011), (2) from hardware to software, (3) from market share to customer share, and (4) from value-added to core value respectively (Chen et al., 2014; Chen et al., 2013; Lin & Chen, 2012).

Based on the Taiwan experience, the concept of Dechnology and Humart was indentified to investigate the Taiwan design development (Hsu et al., 2014; Hsu et al., 2013; Lin, 2012). This study also explores other implications through the Dechnology and Humart perspectives for design strategy. The study results attempt to provide an interface for looking back at how Taiwan design development crosses over Dechnology and Humart as well as illustrating the interwoven experience of local design and global market in Taiwan's economy, industry and design development. This study then proposes an approach for establishing glocalization (global-local) design strategy for Taiwan design development with an idea for how to direct these efforts in design fields (Yeh et al., 2014; Yen et al., 2014; Lin, 2009, Lin 2007).

2 Adaptive Design in Taiwan Design Development

Taiwan's companies have seen a recent shift from technological innovation to cultural product design based on discovering new opportunities in the global marketplace. Companies are more focused on adapting new technologies and combining them in ways that create new experiences and value for customers. With the process of Taiwan design development, most companies gradually realized that the keys to product innovation are not only aspects of market and technology but also local design. The evolution of Taiwan design development is a process of adaptive design which is a fusion of Dechnology and Humart. Thus, Taiwan's economic development was identified as progressing from OEM to ODM to OBM and represented as a smile curve (Hsu et al., 2014; Hsu et al., 2013; Lin, 2012) as shown in Fig. 1.

Before 1980, OEM vendors in Taiwan reduced costs to produce "cheap and fine" products to be successful in the global market. With the OEM style of having "cost" but without a concept of "price" in mind, or just by knowing "cost down" but not knowing "value up", these vendors created Taiwan's economic miracle by earning a low profit from manufacturing. Those dependent upon hard-working patterns from the OEM pattern became obstacles in developing their own designs. These vendors were extremely busy producing products to meet manufacturing deadlines; there was no time to develop design capabilities so that this situation could not nurture design talents (Hsu et al., 2014; Hsu et al., 2013; Lin, 2012).

After 1980, Taiwan enterprises began to develop ODM patterns to extend their advantages in OEM manufacturing. Taiwan's government promoted a series of policies to stimulate the nation's economic growth including the "Production Automation Skill Guidance Plan", and the "Assisting Domestic Traditional Industrial Skill Plan" (IDB, 2012). These plans were to guide vendors to make production improvements, to lower costs and to increase competition. Starting from 1989, the industry Bureau pushed the "Plan for Total Upgrading of Industrial Design Capability" over three consecutive five-year plans. The scheme established working models by experienced design scholars and students from universities for the purpose of working on design. The design students worked with the enterprises on specific projects to set up a working pattern of industrial design based on enterprises' real needs. Especially starting from 1989, adapting the local marketing concept of "One Town One Product (OTOP)" had started to integrate local culture with innovations and to explore the development of distinctive local industry (Rana, 2008; Scott, 2004). All those started from localization as the longitude and local feature as the latitude not only to promote more people and more investment but also to draw new business opportunity (Huang, Shyu, & Tzeng, 2007).

Recently, product design in Taiwan has stepped into the OBM era. In addition, cultural and creative industries have already been incorporated into the "National Development Grand Plan", demonstrating the government's eagerness to transform Taiwan's economic development by "Branding Taiwan" using "Taiwan Design" based on Taiwanese culture (MOEA, 2012). For example, in 2005 the National Palace Museum (NPM) in Taiwan made an agreement with Aleesi in Italy to use The Chin Family series as the basis for a joint project - "A Third Culture: East meets West" - that is the essence of the NPM's "Old is New" campaign. Through the globalization strategy the NPM and Aleesi, while bridging Taipei and Milan, have cultivated this modern culture; that is "from localization to globalization". (Hsu et al., 2014; Hsu et al., 2013).

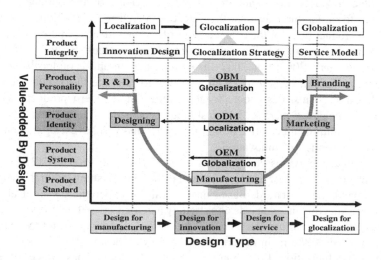

Fig. 1. Taiwan's economy and design development

However, we now live in a small world with a large global market. While the market heads toward "globalization", design tends toward "localization". So we must "think globally" for the market, but "act locally" for design. While the cultural product is under tough competitive pressure from the developing global market, it seems that local design should be focused on the global market to adapt innovation to product design.

3   From Globalization to Glocalization

One can take Taiwan's economic development from OEM to ODM to OBM as shown in Fig. 1 as an example. In the OEM phase, Taiwan's manufacturers reduced costs to produce "cheap and fine" products to be successful in the global manufacturing industry which is typical "Globalization". After 1980, Taiwan enterprises began to extend their advantages in OEM manufacturing and drew on local culture to develop ODM patterns which focused on designing local features into modern products which is typical "Localization". NPM's "Old is New" project is a typical example showing the process from "Globalization" to "Localization". Recently, Taiwan's economic development is to be furthered by "Branding Taiwan" using "Taiwan Design" based on Taiwanese culture (Hsu et al., 2014; Hsu et al., 2013; Lin, 2012). Obviously, product design in Taiwan has stepped into the OBM era which integrates "globalization" and "localization" into "glocalization". The change of Taiwan economy development from globalization to glocalization is also shown Fig. 1.

Glocalization blends global(ization) and local(ization). The process of glocalization is used to describe a product or service that is designed to be distributed globally but also attractive and accommodated locally (Boztepe, 2007a). For a long-term view of globalization, local culture is a consequence of globalization. Local cultures cannot be isolated or unconnected from the global processes (Bell & Jayne, 2003). Designing local features into a product appears to be more and more important in the global market where products are losing their identity because of the similarity in their function and form. Cultural features then are considered to be a unique character to embed into a product both for the enhancement of product identity in the global market and for the fulfillment of the individual consumer's experiences (Boztepe, 2007b; Lee, 2011; Leong & Clark, 2003; Lin, 2007). The increasing emphasis on localized cultural development in Taiwan demonstrates an ambition to promote the Taiwanese style in the global market. Thus, designing "local culture" into modern products will be a design trend in the global market. Design strategy is considered to be one of the pivotal components in cultural and creative design industries and will have a significant impact on consumer perception of innovation.

After reviewing previous studies (Hsu et al., 2014; Hsu et al., 2013; Lin, 2012; Moalosi et al. 2010), it is clear that local culture is the force pushing cultural and creative industries development forward. Based on the Taiwan experience, Hsu et al. (2013) studied factors affecting the glocal design strategy and focused on how to extract cultural features from the local culture and then transfer them to designing the innovate product. Based on the studies, the main factors affecting Taiwan design development could be identified as: Globalization, Localization and Glocalzilation. These three dimensions provide an index for looking at Taiwan design development crossing over cultures as well as illustrating the interwoven experience of local design and the global market in the cultural creativity industry. The three factors also reflect the development of Taiwan design from "Function" to "Feeling" (OEM, globalization), from "Use" to "User" (ODM, localization) and from "Hi-Tech" to "Hi-Touch" (OBM, glocalization).

4 Taiwan Design Development

In Fig. 1, in the OEM era, the "function" of the product will come first when designing a product. Then in the ODM era, what the "use" should be in the "function" will come next. Thus, the function focuses on the specification for the manufacturer, and the use concerns usability for the users. Finally, the designer will seek to produce a "Hi-Tech" product. In the OBM era, user-centered plays an important role in the product design. Who the users are always come first while designing a product. Then, how to design "Feeling" into products becomes an important issue. Finally, designers will consider "Hi-Touch" beyond "Hi-Tech".

4.1 From "Function" to "Feeling"

In the early 20th century when users thought about "design", "form follows function" often came to mind. Today, technological progress has shifted dramatically and provides platforms for completely new forms of "design" and "service" delivery. Now, we communicate with our friends using a cell phone (design) or plan and buy a trip around the world using the internet (service).

From a design point of view, we could use five "Fs" to describe the change from designing "function" for the user's need to servicing "feeling" for the user's pleasure as shown in Fig. 2. These five F's are: (1) 1930's – design for "Function", (2) 1950's - design for "Friendly", (3) 1970's - design for "Fun", (4) 1990's - design for "Fancy", and (5) 2001's - design for "Feeling" (Hsu et al., 2014; Hsu et al., 2013; Lin, 2012). These five "Fs" also reflect the process of Taiwan design development.

Along with technological progress, we may examine the history of design of the last century. In the 1930's, we find that "form follows function"; that is, the appropriate pleasing product form will follow if the product is appropriately designed for its function. This philosophy dominated design concept. In the 1950's after World War II, the new discipline of human factors was introduced and the concept of "design for human use" applied to product design. The concept of "user friendly" became common sense with the popularity of the PC in the commercial market. In 1970's, designing for "function" and "friendly" was not seen as sufficient so some designers tried designing "Fun" into the product. The application of post-modernism in the design field is a typical example of designing for fun. Then, in the 1990 s, designers tried designing "fancy" into their design based on advance technology such as concurrent engineering or RPT (Rapid Prototyping Technology) and the concept of product personality became a tool for differentiating the market. Finally, designing "Feeling" into products to present the emotional communication of user experiences became a design trend in the 21st century. As a result, "design for feeling" became the key factor for innovative

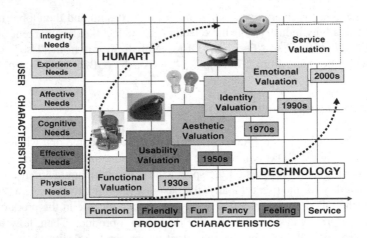

Fig. 2. Taiwan design development from "Function" to "Feeling"

products. In other words, the product must be endowed with an immediate attraction and this therefore renders user perception of innovative product form an important issue for "pleasure" (Gobe, 2011; Heskett 2009; Norman, 2004). In Fig. 2, we use a pencil sharpener as an example to demonstrate the change from "design for function" to "design for feeling", respectively (Hsu et al., 2014; Hsu et al., 2013; Lin, 2012).

This change of design history with five "Fs" is similar to Taiwan's design development from OEM to ODM to OBM. The users need not only the 5 Fs but also innovation service for their integrity needs. The only way to deal with this complexity is to keep user needs and desires central to any design strategy. Indeed, service innovation design is part of the solution to this challenge with its deep user involvement throughout the creative process and a keen view of the functional and emotional details that enable people to enjoy the services that are important in their lives. On the other hand, a powerful if risky strategy is to develop a product for a purpose that people do not originally realize that they "need". Like the Polaroid camera, Xerox copy machine, Apple computer, Walkman, etc., etc. Then the "need" must be created through promotion, advertising, adoption by status figures, etc. which is a job for marketing and advertising experts. Of course, a strategy for new product development must include experts in all phases of creation, production, distribution, marketing and advertising. This still requires what designers must realize above in terms of making the product appealing to people, especially when there is competition to consider.

4.2   From Use to User

As mentioned previously, in the OEM era when designers thought about "design", use of the product often came to mind first. Today, technological progress has shifted dramatically and provides platforms for completely new forms of "design (use)" and "service (user)" delivery. For example, we communicate with our friends using the iPhone (design) or Facebook using the internet (service) (Sangiorgi, 2011). In the

ODM era, the new discipline of human factors was introduced and the concept of "design for human use" applied to product design. The concept of "user friendly" became common sense with the popularity of the PC in the commercial market. Finally, designing "Feeling" into products to present the emotional communication of user experiences became a design trend in the OBM era. As a result, "design for feeling" became the key factor for innovative products. Figure 3 demonstrates the change from "use" to "user" in Taiwan economic development.

Based on the previous analysis, "from use to user" could describe the change of Taiwan design development from designing "function" for the user's need to servicing "feeling" for the user's pleasure. In other words, the product must be endowed with an immediate attraction and this therefore renders user perception of innovative product form an important issue for "pleasure" (Gobe 2010; Kreifeldt, Lin & Chuang, 2011; Heskett 2008; Norman, 2004).

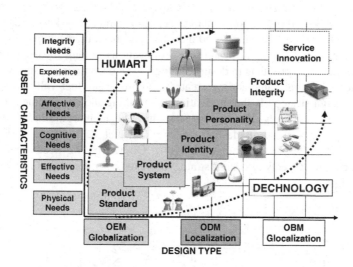

Fig. 3. Taiwan design development from "Use" to "User"

In order to reach the purpose of branding Taiwan, some changes need to be made in Taiwan's industry structure. If we can mix cultural concepts with diverse service innovation design to make art livable, then we can create a new design strategy of cultural and creative design industries and become culturally industrialized to highlight Taiwan's international image. This design strategy also verifies the change of Taiwan design development from globalization/localization to glocalization.

4.3   From "Hi-Tech" to "Hi-Touch" – Cultural Branding

In the past, Taiwan developed information technology to produce "Hi-Tech" 3Cs products as "Computer", "Communication", and "Consumer" electronic products and many related accessories. As mentioned previously, Taiwan's economic miracle was promoted by small enterprises through the hardworking spirit and cheap labor of the people. But all these advantages have been seized by China in recent years. If Taiwan still wants to play a role in the global economy, it should establish a Taiwanese cultural brand. Besides its skill leverage, it has to cover both ODM and OBM, which is the purpose of promoting cultural and creative industries from the service innovation design point of view. Therefore, the required change in Taiwan's design industry structure is to: (1) maintain its cost down advantage; (2) reinforce design value up, and; (3) seek service innovation design in cultural and creative design industries (Segall, 2012; Chang, Lin, Wea & Sheu, 2002).

Cultural and creative design industries are the "4Cs" industries: "Cultural", "Collective", "Cheerful" and "Creative". The 4Cs will be a design evaluation key point of "Hi-Touch" products as shown in Fig. 4. Many countries that are highly prominent in design popularity are promoting service as design as part of cultural and creative design industries. Taking England as an example, service design has been the second highest output value of their creativity industry (Roberta & Marco, 2010; Sangiorgi, 2011; Spohrer and Maglio 2008). The potential market is quite large. In the knowledge economy era, the connections between culture and industry have been increasingly close.

In the global market - local design era, connections among local culture, global market and innovative products in design strategy have become increasingly close. For design strategy, cultural value-adding creates the core of product value. It's the same for culture; design strategy is the motivation for pushing the development of creative industries forward. Recently, creative industries have been emerging in the design field and providing a key trend in design strategy (Desmet & Hekkert, 2007; Kim & Mauborgne, 2005; Lee, 2011; Redstrom 2006). Obviously, we need a better understanding of cultural aspects in design strategy; not only for the global market but also for local design.

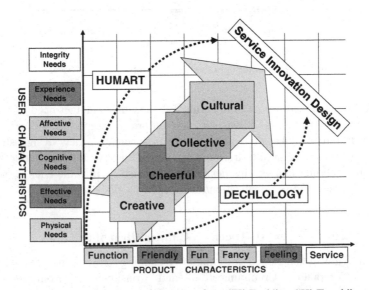

Fig. 4. Taiwan design development from "Hi-Tech" to "Hi-Touch"

5   A Conceptual Framework for the Glocal Design Strategy

Based on Taiwan design development and Solomon's study, the following framework is proposed for defining, classifying, assessing, and modeling the glocal design strategy for turning "local features" to "global market" as shown in Fig. 5 (Solomon et al., 2002; Solomon, 2003).

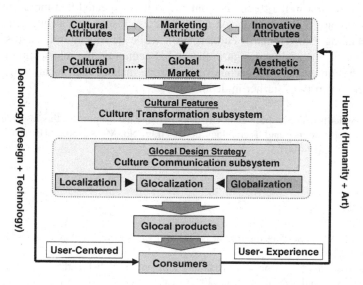

Fig. 5. A conceptual framework for the glocal design strategy

The conceptual framework which integrates the local features and innovative products into the glocal design strategy comprises the attribute subsystem, the cultural transformation subsystem, the culture communication subsystem, and lastly, consumers. The attribute subsystem is responsible for generating and filtering new ideas. The cultural transformation subsystem is responsible for selecting new ideas based on design strategy, making them tangible, mass producing these ideas, and then managing their distribution. The culture communications subsystem is responsible for giving meaning to the new "glocal products" and providing them with symbolic sets of attributes that are communicated to consumers (Teng 2000; Zafarmand, 2007).

6   Summary

Based on the previous studies and Taiwan experience, this paper studied the relationships between Dechnology and Humarts which were merged into design thinking to explore Taiwan design development. Firstly, this paper explored Taiwan design development and identified the three stages of OEM, ODM and OBM for illustrating how to transform "local culture" into "global market" through a process of design evolution showing an "Adaptive Design" in Taiwan design development. Then, a conceptual frame work was used to study the tendency of Taiwan design development, from "use" to "user", from "function" to "feeling", and from "hi-tech" to "hi-touch". This paper also analyzed the factors affecting local design and global market to understand Taiwan design development. A conceptual framework was established to provide companies, organizations, and designers with a valuable reference for using design thinking to build a glocal design strategy. There are some tendencies for subjective interpretation in the foregoing context, so it is expected that more specific and rigid methodology will be conducted to verify these results in the future, especially, from Dechnology to Humart. Furthermore, while cross-cultural factors become important issues for product design in the global economy, the intersection of service innovation design and culture becomes a key issue making both local design and the global market worthy of further in-depth study.

Acknowledgements. The authors gratefully acknowledge the support for this research provided by the Ministry of Science and Technology under Grant No. MOSY-103-2410-H-144-003 and MOST-103-2221-E-144-001.

References

Bell, D., Jayne, M.: Assessing the role of design in local and regional economies. Int. J. Cult. Policy **9**(3), 265–284 (2003)

Boztepe, S.: Toward a framework of product development for global markets: a user-value-based approach. Des. Stud. **28**(5), 513–533 (2007a)

Boztepe, S.: User value: Competing theories and models. Int. J. Des. **1**(2), 55–63 (2007b)

Chang, S.C., Lin, N.P., Wea, C.L., Sheu, C.: Aligning manufacturing capabilities with business strategy: an empirical study in high-tech industry. J. Technol. Manage. **24**(1), 70–87 (2002)

Chen, C.C., Lin, R., Zhang, A.F.: Constructing a service innovation model for creative industrial parks. Int. J. Arts Commer. **2**(6), 151–165 (2013)

Chen, C.-L., Lin, R., Chen, S., Zhang, A.-F.: Exploring a SEE-based service innovation for the fast fashion apparel industry - a case study of the fashion institute of Taipei in Taiwan. Int. J. Inf. Technol. Bus. Manag. **30**(1), 1–14 (2014)

Desmet, P.M.A., Hekkert, P.: Framework of product experience. Int. J. Des. **1**(1), 57–66 (2007)

Gobe, M.: Emotional Branding: The New Paradigm for Connecting Brands to People. Allworth Press Pages, New York, NY (2010)

Heskett, J.: Creating economic value by design. Int. J. Des. **3**(1), 71–84 (2009)

Hsu, C.H., Fan, C.H., Lin, J.Y., Lin, R.: An investigation on consumer cognition of cultural design products. Bull. Jpn. Soc. Sci. Des. **60**(5), 39–48 (2014)

Hsu, C.H., Chang, S.H., Lin, R.: A design strategy for turning local culture into global market products. Int. J. Affect. Eng. (Kansei Eng. Int. J.) **12**(2), 275–283 (2013)

Huang, C.-Y., Shyu, J.Z., Tzeng, G.-H.: Reconfiguring the innovation policy portfolios for Taiwan's SIP mall industry. Technovation **27**, 744–765 (2007)

IDB: 2012 Annual report of Taiwan's cultural & creative industries. Industrial Development Bureau (IDB) of Ministry of Economic Affairs, Taipei (2012)

Kim, W.C., Mauborgne, R.A.: Blue ocean strategy: from theory to practice. Calif. Manag. Rev. **47**(3), 105–121 (2005)

Kreifeldt, J., Lin, R., Chuang, M.-C.: The importance of "Feel" in product design feel, the neglected aesthetic "Do Not Touch". In: Rau, P. (ed.) IDGD 2011. LNCS, vol. 6775, pp. 312–321. Springer, Heidelberg (2011)

Lee, K.: Looking back, to look forward: using traditional cultural examples to explain contemporary ideas in technology education. J. Technol. Educ. **22**(2), 42–52 (2011)

Leong, D., Clark, H.: Culture -based knowledge towards new design thinking and practice - a dialogue. Des. Issues **19**(3), 48–58 (2003)

Lin, R.: From Dechnology to Humartss in Taiwan Design Development. Research project supported by Taiwan National Science Council (2012)

Lin, R.: Designing friendship into modern products. In: Toller, J.C. (ed.) Friendships: Types, Cultural, Psychological and Social, pp. 1–24. Nova Science Publishers, New York (2009)

Lin, R.: Transforming Taiwan aboriginal cultural features into modern product design: a case study of a cross-cultural product design model. Int. J. Des. **1**(2), 47–55 (2007)

Lin, R., Chen, C.T.: A discourse on the construction of a service innovation model: focus on the cultural and creative industry park. In: Ifinedo, P. (ed.) E-BUSINESS – Application and Global Acceptance, pp. 119–136. InTech, Croatia (2012)

Moalosi, R., Popovic, V., Hickling-Hudson, A.: Culture-orientated product design. Int. J. Technol. Des. Educ. **20**, 175–190 (2010)

Norman, D.A.: Emotional Design: Why We Love (or Hate) Everyday Things. Basic Books, New York (2004)

MOEA: Taiwan annual report: Cultural and creative industries. Ministry of Economic Affairs, Taiwan, Republic of China (2012)

Rana, E.C.: Sustainable local development through one town one product (OTOP): the case of OTOP movement in Mindanao, Philippines. J. OVOP Policy **1**, 31–38 (2008)

Redstrom, J.: Towards user design? on the shift from object to user as the subject of design. Des. Stud. **27**(2), 123–139 (2006)

Roberta, S., Marco, P.: Rethinking service innovation: four pathways to evolution. Int. J. Qual. Serv. Sci. **2**(1), 79–94 (2010)

Sangiorgi, D.: Transformative services and transformation design. Int. J. Des. **5**(2), 29–40 (2011)

Scott, A.J.: Cultural-products industries and urban economic development - prospects for growth and market contestation in global context. Urban Aff. Rev. **39**(4), 461–490 (2004)

Segall, K.: Insanely simple: The obsession that drives Apple's success. Penguin Group, New York (2012)

Solomon, M.R., Bamossy, G., Askegaard, S.: Consumer Behavior – A European Perspective, 2nd edn, pp. 471–475. Prentice-Hall, Upper Saddle River (2002)

Solomon, M.R.: Consumer Behavior: Buying, Having and Being. Prentice Hall, Saddleback, NJ (2003)

Spohrer, J., Maglio, P.P.: The emergence of service science: toward systematic service innovations to accelerate co-creation of value. Prod. Oper. Manage. **17**(3), 238–246 (2008)

Teng, C.L.: Comments on design strategy. Des. J. **5**(2), 54–61 (2000)

Yeh, M.L., Lin, R.T., Wang, M.S., Lin, P.H.: Transforming the hair color design industry by using paintings: From art to e-business. Int. J. E-Bus. Dev. **4**(1), 12–20 (2014)

Yen, H.Y., Lin, P.H., Lin, R.: Emotional product design and perceived brand emotion. Int. J. Adv. Psychol. (IJAP) **3**(2), 59–66 (2014)

Zafarmand, A.Y.: Glocal product design: A sustainable solution for global companies in regional and/or local markets. In: International Association of Societies of Design Research, IASDR 2007. The Hong Kong Polytechnic University School of Design, Hong Kong (2007)

Human Factors Perspective of Dancing Props Design: A Case Study of "Feiyan's Dancing on Palms"

Jao-Hsun Tseng[1(✉)] and Po-Hsien Lin[2]

[1] Department of Dance, National Taiwan University of Arts, Daguan Rd., Banqiao Dist, New Taipei City 22058, Taiwan
t0190@ntua.edu.tw
[2] Graduate School of Creative Industry Design, National Taiwan University of Arts, Daguan Rd., Banqiao Dist, New Taipei City 22058, Taiwan
t0131@ntua.edu.tw

Abstract. "As light as a swallow" is considered as a standard of aesthetic interpretation in female body figure in contemporary world. What the "swallow" really represent is the famous dancer Zhao Feiyan in Han dynasty in China. According to the literature, she is good at a kind of chinese Kung Fu. She was able to dance on the palms of man. Two dancing pieces "Dancing on palms" (1996) and "Feiyan's dancing on palms" (2010) were created by the author previously. In order to reshape a historical character being so familiar to the general public, how to profile a vivid appearance and personality was the main concern. The fulfilment of this task relied on a profound exploration of the scenario including historical background, social context, and cultural phenomenon. The costume further played an additive role in the process of choreography. According to the historical record, the Emperor Chen of Han (51-7 BC) also made a special "crystal plate". The dancer Zhao Feiyan can dance on the crystal plate which the assistants held. To have a better performance and safety concern, several human factors about the costume including material quality, make-up method and surface area are another important issues. In order to present the images in artwork "Feiyan's dancing on palms," many factors should be considered in the process of choreography. For example, the material quality of "crystal plate" including its thickness, weight and surface area; the choice of dancers to fulfill the character (the type of build, ability of dance, stage manner); an appropriate music for the dance (form, rhythm, style). After considering the human factors in the design of "crystal plate", it also solved the problems in the make-up of dancing props. The original idea and design of the author could be well presented on the stage.

Keywords: Zhao Feiyan · Dancing on palms · Props design

1 Introduction

The Han dynasty is a critical era that contributed to the development of Chinese dance, and one that laid a solid foundation for related developments and achievements in later generations. Zhao Feiyan, a talented and well-known elite dancer during the Han dynasty,

© Springer International Publishing Switzerland 2015
P.L.P. Rau (Ed.): CCD 2015, Part II, LNCS 9181, pp. 274–284, 2015.
DOI: 10.1007/978-3-319-20934-0_26

was able to become a queen by using her superb dancing skills. Her achievements, particularly the one in which she was able to dance "as lightly as a swallow," has had a profound influence on the development of dance performed by people in later generations.

In 1996 and 2010, the researcher of this study participated in the choreography for annual dance performances, *Record of Chinese Dance Styles* and *40 Years of Chinese Dance*, delivered by the Department of Dance, National Taiwan University of Arts. The dances in the two performances were designed in an attempt to pass the art of traditional Chinese dance, one that embodies a wealth of Chinese culture, onto the public. The historical record of Zhao Faiyan dancing on palms (Fig. 1) was selected as the theme of the choreography to display Zhao Feiyan's graceful, bird-like gestures to pay tribute to this ancient dance. Therefore, the dance works for the two annual dance performances were named *Dancing on Palms* in 1996 and *Feiyan's dancing on palms* in 2010. In addition, new aesthetic interpretations of the dances were introduced to showcase a modern version of a female dancer in Han dynasty.

Fig. 1. Dancing on Palms. Source of data: *A Story of Ancient Dancers*, by Wang Ke-fen (1986: p. 60) [10]

2   Research Objectives

In the present study, an ex post facto method was adopted to analyze the process of choreography, in which stories of historical figures were used as themes for dance creation and dancing props were used. This study was grounded on hermeneutics and visual culture theories [1–5, 7]. The focus was on the dancing prop design that adopted human factors engineering for the choreography of *Feiyan's Dancing on Palms*.

Specifically, this study investigated the design and production of "crystal plates" and the choreographic practices in which these special dancing props were used.

The techniques for performers to control the crystal plates (which included dancers dancing on the crystal plates, as well as performers holding the crystal plates) were also examined, to highlight the theme of the dance work. Subsequently, efforts were made to discover methods for realizing the aesthetic imagery of the dance in the performance of *Feiyan's Dancing on Palms*. The objectives of this study are as follows:

1. To conceive a human factors perspective for unique dancing prop design to allow dancers to display their body movements and deliver flawless performances while their safety is protected;
2. To represent the artistic talents of ancient Chinese dancers by using historical records as themes for the creation of dance performances;
3. To enrich the artistic expressions of dances and transform classic, historical stories into dance performances, as well as to transmit and promote Chinese culture by using contemporary art and aesthetic theories; and
4. To supplement professional dance theory-related courses (e.g., history of Chinese dance, appreciation of the art of dance, and dance criticism) with visual mediums (e.g., dance videos) to facilitate learning effectiveness.

3 Unique Characteristics of the Dance Work

The unique part of *Feiyan's Dancing on Palms* was how Zhao Feiyan (portrayed by the dancer) was able to dance and walk gracefully between the crystal plates suspended in the air. However, the dance should not be viewed as a type of stunt; the beauty of the dance lies in the themes and human emotions being conveyed, as opposed to a special type of dancing skills being shown off. Therefore, as Zhao Feiyan was absorbed in the graceful movements of the body, the performers holding the crystal plates was fixated on the process of coordinating with one another (e.g., movements of the feet and controlling the part of their arms that was carrying the weight of the crystal plates); both parties were faced with an enormous amount of psychological pressure.

For the dance choreography that used Zhao Feiyan and the crystal plates as themes, the focus was put on creating clear images and a personality for Zhao Feiyan, obtaining and using the crystal plates, and creating onstage dance performances by using information found in historical records.

4 Factors to Consider in Dance Choreography

The growing popularity of visual culture research in recent years has expanded visual culture from popular culture to the fields of art history and everyday life [3]. According to English scholar Rogoff (1998), the purpose of visual culture is to develop the eye of a critic to reexamine the approaches by which people see their world and the history that is represented [9].

In the interpretation of *Feiyan's Dancing on Palms* centering on the main character of Zhao Feiyan, in addition to examining the refined and aesthetic qualities of the dance, this study sought to adopt the visual culture perspective, particularly focusing on the role of women that generates conflicts and confrontations in social class consciousness, to analyze the original meanings and the implications of the visual signs presented in this dance work.

Jacques Maquet (1988) in his book *The Aesthetic Experience* indicated that the following four secondary signs take on visual forms: referents (signs by reference), indicators, images, and symbols. In particular, images refer to visual duplicates of people, objects, sceneries, and anything with a form that can be observed [8]. To better understand the images of Zhao Feiyan as "being as light as a swallow and able to dance on the palms of man," historical books were studied to learn about objective factors related to her; these included the historical background, living environment, her personality traits, and her thoughts and feelings.

Portraits of Han dynasty women drawn by painters were also collected to enrich the knowledge of the choreographer in the creation of the dance, who was enabled to construct images identical to those produced in the past. Another crucial topic of concern involved the search for crystal plates made from suitable materials, on which performers could showcase their dancing skills, followed by the selection of appropriate styles of music to create an atmosphere that effectively depict the mood of the dance. The objective was to construct images, a sign described by Maquet, which are composed of visual duplicates including Zhao Feiyan (people), crystal plates (objects), music (sceneries), and tangible objects that can be observed in the external world.

In the performance of *Feiyan's Dancing on Palms*, crystal plates were held high on stage by performers with a strong physique and superior muscular endurance. During the 1996 performance (*Dancing on Palms*), four male dancers were chosen from the Department of Dance, National Taiwan University of Arts to hold the crystal plats. For the 2010 performance, a new, modern visual culture perspective was adopted for the choreography of *Feiyan's Dancing on Palms*, in which a total of eight male dancers were selected to hold two crystal plates that differed in size.

The interdependence between the male dancers and the crystal plates, and the way that they complemented each other, further enriched the role of crystal plates as dancing props and metaphors. In addition, the body performance of the male dancers holding the crystal plates (Fig. 2) was deliberately showcased to exhibit their masculinity, which created a stark contrast with the submissive and graceful gestures of Zhao Feiyan (Fig. 3), to highlight the difference in gender roles between men and women.

Concerning the setup and use of the two crystal plates (Fig. 4), they were used to create a fourth dimension on the stage. In general, dancers performing on stage deliver 2D performances; by having dancers stand on the crystal plates and dance, a 3D performance can be delivered. The reason why another crystal plate was added in the 2010 performance of *Feiyan's Dancing on Palms* was to enable Zhao Feiyan to change her locations on stage, thereby constructing a 4D performance. The two crystal plates were separated, united, stacked, placed in various layers and at various heights to engender an illusory effect, symbolizing that Zhao Feiyan attempted to break free from the existing temporal and spatial confinement but was still unable to escape from the crystal plate prison built by the king (Fig. 5).

Fig. 2. Display of masculinity

Fig. 3. Image of female submissive and graceful

Fig. 4. Use of the two crystal plates

To display the imagery of *Feiyan's Dancing on Palms* in actual forms, numerous factors must be considered during the art creation process, such as selecting props with appropriate properties (i.e., thickness, weight, and surface area) as the crystal plates, dancers with appropriate attributes (i.e., type of build, ability to dance, and stage manner) for Zhao Feiyan, and dance music with appropriate qualities (i.e., form, rhythm, and style). These three factors must be able to work together and supplement each other to drive the performance. Moreover, the human factors were considered for the design of the crystal plates as they play a pivotal role in *Feiyan's Dancing on*

Fig. 5. Crystal plates symbolizing the prison

Palms. By adopting human factors engineering, problems relating to dancing props were resolved, and the original ideas and design concepts were realized.

5 Human Factors Considered in Props Making

Dances were created primarily to convey themes, express emotions, and engage the senses. The crystal plates, as described in historical records, served as a pivotal subject in *Feiyan's Dancing on Palms*, because the images of the crystal plates were one of the key factors contributing to Zhao Feiyan's prominence in the development history of Chinese dance. To ensure the safety of the performers holding the crystal plates, human factors had to be considered when designing such props to achieve performances that were complete and flawless.

In general, for objects to achieve the predetermined effect, they must rely on the actions of the people operating them (i.e., movements made by the joints, strength exerted by the muscles, and feelings perceived by the senses) [11]. The same principle applies to props used in the field of dance. In human factors engineering, the subject of object control is studied in the domain of biomechanics research. The control of dancing props is limited by the physical limits of the dancers, the weight of the props, and the width of handles for grabbing, which are key factors that influence dancers' control of objects. Therefore, the biomechanics (i.e., the physical limits of humans), the weight of the props, and the width of the handle were crucial factors that must be simultaneously considered in the dancing prop design. Regarding the critical factors that influenced the display of the imagery of "Feiyan's Dancing on Palms" in actual forms, dancer selection and props selection, which were mutually influenced, were proposed and are explicated in the following sections.

5.1 Selection of Dancers

To present the imagery of *Feiyan's Dancing on Palms* in actual forms and to bring life to the dancing scenes as recorded in historical sources, the dancer portraying Zhao Feiyan must have the appropriate type of build, ability to dance, and stage manner. These were the criteria considered during the dancer selection process.

5.1.1   Suitable Type of Build

Because the diameter of the crystal plate measured only 150 cm, maintaining balance on the small surface area was challenging. In addition, the psychological fear of falling that prevented dancers' central nervous systems from effectively maintaining their balance severely jeopardized the results of the performance. Therefore, dancers measuring approximately 150 cm in height and 45 kg in weight were the best candidates to play Zhao Feiyan (Fig. 6).

Fig. 6. Zhao Feiyan dancing gracefully on the crystal plates

5.1.2   Strong Ability to Dance

The ability to dance gracefully is a skill that cannot be quickly learned; it is acquired through years of practice. To become an outstanding dancer with a solid dancing foundation, a person needs to possess basic dancing abilities, undergo substantial training, invest great efforts into acquiring related professional knowledge, and maximize their creative potential (Fig. 7).

5.1.3   Superior Stage Manner

Dancers who participate in performances are inevitably subjected to pressure, which leads to psychological anxiety. This pressure is also a byproduct of them demanding the best from themselves. Therefore, dancers must possess a calm and stable mind to be able to deliver superior performances on stage.

Fig. 7. Zhao Feiyan showcasing her solid dancing ability and excellent stage manner

5.2   Selection of Props   •

The crystal plates were the primary props used in the dance. The materials used to make the crystal plates, the hardness and sizes of the props, and the design and production processes are described as follows:

5.2.1   Materials

Although crystals give people the impression of something that is crystal clear and glitters, they are expensive and difficult to obtain. Considering the high cost and poor practicality of crystals, acrylics (an item that is also transparent) were used as a replacement.

5.2.2   Hardness

Although crystal is hard regardless of thickness, they are brittle; in contrast, acrylics are more resilient. However, the hardness of acrylics is directly proportional to its thickness, and it is heavier than crystal. Therefore, when assessing the hardness and weight of the acrylics to be used, the weight of the dancer playing Zhao Feiyan must also be considered to ensure that the sum of their weight is one that can be sustained by the performers holding the crystal plates (each crystal plate is held by four performers). The thickness of the acrylics thus was determined after considering the safety of the performers.

5.2.3   Size

Because the crystal plates were a minimized version of the actual stage, to enable the dancers to dance gracefully on them, the surface area of the crystal plates must be sufficient. This was because crystal plates suspended in the air and featuring an overly small dancing area would lead to difficulty in maintaining balance and that the psychological fear of falling would jeopardize the performance.

Although an increase in the surface area of the crystal plates would allow dancers to have more room to operate, the added weight would create an additional burden on the performers holding the crystal plates. Therefore, the sizes of the crystal plates were determined after the demands of the two parties were carefully considered, providing dancers with enough room to move and change positions.

After taking into account the factors involved in the choreography, the safety of the dancers, and various aspects of concern, two crystal plates made from acrylics of varying sizes were used. The first crystal plate measured 1.8 cm in thickness and 150 cm in diameter; the second crystal plate measured 1.5 cm in thickness and 100 cm in diameter. These crystal plates featured a surface area and weight that were deemed to be appropriate and safe, and they enabled Zhao Feiyan to showcase a graceful dance performance. The two crystal plates were separated, misplaced, and stacked to create a variety of images and to make movements and dances on the crystal plates visually pleasing to watch.

6 Analysis and Review   •

For the performance of *Dancing on Palms* choreographed in 1996, only one crystal plate was used. The original idea was to employ three performers to hold the crystal plates to create a more visually pleasing view. However, after considering the safety of the female dancers, as well as the physical conditions of the performers holding the crystal plates (i.e., to prevent them from shoulder injuries and pushing beyond their physical limits), an additional performer was added.

For the performance of *Feiyan's Dancing on Palms* choreographed in 2010, two crystal plates that varied in size were used. The skillful control of the crystal plates and the elegant body movements of the performers successfully supplemented each other and enhanced the richness and tension of the performance, in terms of both the external presentation of the dance and the implications hidden within.

As stated by Susann Langer (1957), a renowned American scholar who studied semiotics and aesthetics, art is created in the form of symbols to express human emotions [6]. Props are stationary objects and only come to life when beautiful dances come together with skillful prop control. These props work in harmony with the dancers, supplementing each other to create enriched and colorful dance images. They allow the creation of dances to achieve new heights and enable the audience to be satisfied with the magnificent visual performances and the interpretation of the connotations involved in the dance work.

7 Conclusions and Recommendations

Dance is a form of expression in which the body moves to create postures; it is also a way of expressing thoughts and emotions through rhythmic movements. Dances are a space-oriented art, as well as a time-oriented art. They must be performed in front of an audience, in which the audience experiences the emotions depicted and then comprehends and appreciates the art embedded in the performance.

7.1 Conclusion

During the choreography process for *Feiyan's Dancing on Palms*, to ensure the effective display of the refined and aesthetic qualities of the art work, artifact records and historical data from the Han dynasty were carefully studied. The records and data were abundant, from which the life stories of Zhao Feiyan were examined to find ideas for creating the dance.

Dancers are the subjects in dance performances; therefore, the dancer with appropriate dance skills and who matched the appropriate image of Zhao Feiyan was selected. The usage of the dancing prop, the historically renowned crystal plates, was also integral to the dance. The making and use of the crystal plates presented challenges to the choreographers and the performers (including the female dancer standing on the suspended crystal plates and the male performers holding the crystal plates) during the dance creation and performance processes.

In addition, appropriate music had to be chosen from a large selection of available music. These were the factors that must be considered to produce the dancing images of Zhao Feiyan, for these images to be imprinted in the minds of the audience, and to enable choreography theories to be applied in practice.

7.2   Recommendations

Traditional dances in Taiwan are characterized by the repeated use of props. The wide variety of props available has resulted in various usage methods and operational skills. Choreographers use their artistic prowess to connect dancing props to dancers, which therefore can work in harmony with each other to create enriched and colorful dance images. Thus, the creation of dances can achieve new heights, enabling the audience to enjoy the magnificent visual performances and to interpret the connotations implied in the dance work.

An ex post facto self-interpretation methodology was adopted in which an objective perspective was employed to perform an in-depth analysis and self-reflection on *Feiyan's Dancing on Palms*. The result may be used as a reference for subsequent choreography of dance works in an attempt to perfect the performances. The recommendations are as follows:

1. The use of dancing props as symbols primarily focuses on the successful presentation of the dance content. Choreographers concerned with results of the performances must first pay attention to the props (i.e., the crystal plates), as well as the psychological state of the performers (i.e., female dancer standing on the suspended crystal plates and male dancers holding the crystal plates). The ability of dancers to convey emotions through props relies on their mastery of prop control and how well they can dance on and with the crystal plates. Because no shortcuts exist for dancers to become skilled at their craft, they must constantly practice;
2. Concerning the use of the crystal plates, male dancers must possess sufficient physical strength and determination to support the plates; female dancers must overcome the fear of falling and maintain balance on the narrow platform; and choreographers must consider the safety of the dancers in the design of dances; and
3. To produce good dance performances, dancers must not only possess perfect dancing skills but also have a thorough understanding of Chinese culture and the ability to express emotions. To enrich the performance skills of dancers, choreographers must educate dancers on the aesthetics of culture and arts, which should not be ignored in dance education.

References

1. Bi, H.D.: Research Methods of Interpretation and Quality Study. Ju Liu Publishing, Taipei (1996)
2. Bryson, N.: Vision and painting: The logic of the gaze. Yale University Press, New Haven (1983)

3. Chen, Y.Y.: Visual Culture Theory. Wei Bo Culture Publishing, Taipei (2004)
4. Gadamer, H.: Truth and Method. Continuum International Publishing Group, New York (2004). Original work published in 1975
5. Hong, H.D.: Modern Philosophy Interpretation. Wu Nan Bookstore, Taipei (2008)
6. Langer, S.K.: Problems of Art. Charles Scribner's Sons, New York (1957)
7. Liang, F.Z.: The methods of interpretation and its use on educational research. Li Wen, Kaohsiung (2000)
8. Maquet, M.: The Aesthetic Experience: An Anthropologist Looks at the Visual Arts. Yale University Press, London (1986)
9. Rogoff, I.: Studying visual culture. In: Mirzoeff, N. (ed.) Visual Culture Reader, pp. 14–26. Routledge, New York (1998)
10. Wang, K.F.: The story of ancient Chinese dancer. Lan Ting Publishing, Taipei (1986)
11. Xu, S.X.: Ergonomics. Young Ze Culture Publishing, Taipei (1991)

The Application of Chinese Poem
"*Yu Mei Ren*" in Design

Mo-Li Yeh[1]([⊠]), Hsi-Yen Lin[2], Ming-shean Wang[3], and Rungtai Lin[2]

[1] Department of Fashion Design, Hsing Wu University,
Linkou, New Taipei City 24452, Taiwan
1101moli@gmail.com
[2] Graduate School of Creative Industry Design,
National Taiwan University of Arts,
Daguan Rd., Banqiao Dist, New Taipei City 22058, Taiwan
p3yann@gmail.com, rtlin@mail.ntua.edu.tw
[3] Digital and Design Department, Mingdao University, Changhua City, Taiwan
wangms0730@gmail.com

Abstract. The purpose of this study, alternatively, is taking inspiration for culture creative design from an invisible culture element, the Chinese poetry. With its external form and internal meaning, poetry is applied and transferred to design, using their common structural features. This study developed a model for transforming poetry into creative basic design and Art. The procedures require three essential phases of visualizing abstract concepts, concretizing visual components, and utilizing 3D products. Implementation steps include selecting themes, analyzing application types, transferring design elements, concretizing design elements, enforcing external functionality, utilizing for everyday life, experiencing design aesthetics, and achieving goals for cultural creative design. In conclusion, this study contributes to academic study, education for cultural creative design, development of cultural creative industries, and culture preservation. With a well-established research framework, this study integrates relevant theories, research methodology, and implemented case studies to turn the originally "emotional" poetic content to a "rational" and logical step-by-step process, and thus acquires its academic significance. Following the concrete transfer design model, design students will be effectively instructed and inspired in applying cultural creativity for expressing abstract poetic concepts. As for cultural creative industries, this model derived from theories of transfer design and supplemented with illustrative implemented cases, will provide them a specific and feasible reference for practical applications in highlighting emotional experience and cultural elements in their products. After a thorough investigation of the "traditional" poetry, cultural elements are now transferred to poetry-related "modern" creative design in this study. Hereafter, with active participation of the new-generation designers inspired by this implementation model, the glorious traditional Chinese culture elements will be carried on and extended.

Keywords: Poetry · Cultural creative · Design application

© Springer International Publishing Switzerland 2015
P.L.P. Rau (Ed.): CCD 2015, Part II, LNCS 9181, pp. 285–293, 2015.
DOI: 10.1007/978-3-319-20934-0_27

1 Introduction

This study investigated the origins of traditional Chinese culture, one characterized as deep and profound, through elements found in its poetry. The meaning of the poetry, whether explicitly or implicitly expressed, was used as the design concept of cultural creative products in the field of creative design as well as the impetus for Taiwanese designers to create cultural creative designs. Traditional poetry and literary composition in rhyme reflect the cultural wisdom of ancient Chinese poets and serve as great inspirations for contemporary creative designs. Regarding related studies on the design application of elements found in poetry, Beatty (2011) published articles such as "The Intersection of Poetry and Design" and "Similarities Between the Design Process of Poetry and Design," in which the perspective of "writing poetry" was used to examine the sources of inspiration, problems encountered and resolved, and works revised during the poetry-writing process. The relationship between poetry and design was examined by comparing the principles that governed them. By contrast, in the current study, the objective was to investigate how creative ideas found in poetry were applied to creative designs. A series of studies from 2011 onward has revealed that designs made by applying cultural concepts found in poetry differ when the "transformation of cultural concepts" differs. The "shape" and "essence" of poetry were used to analyze key imageries in the poetry, in which shape was defined as real and tangible forms, whereas essence was defined as abstract ideas. The shape and essence of poetry were subsequently used to decide the color, texture, and shape of the design works. The transformation of cultural concepts was divided into four types, namely "from shape (in poetry) to shape (in design works)," "from shape to essence," "from essence to shape," and "from essence to essence." The six viewpoints of poetry were based on the six viewpoints principle proposed in The Literary Mind and the Carving of Dragons (Chapter: Companion) and were used to evaluate the six aspects of poetry, namely weiti (poets' use of explicit expressions), tongbian (whether poets can use the methods passed down from the past as well as innovate such methods in their poetry), qizheng (whether poets can produce diversified works and maintain their unity), shiyi (whether the people or things depicted in the works are vivid and able to reflect real life situations or transmit ideas), gongshang (the flow of the language in the poetry), and zhici (the meaning and characteristics of the poetry and whether they can reproduce the imageries that have been formulated in the mind). The six viewpoints served the following functions when poetry was transformed into design works: (i) showed the shapes, patterns, and structure to be used; (ii) provided design principles; (iii) innovative use of emotions and implied meanings; (iii) accentuated texture and colors; (iv) engendered a dynamic atmosphere; and (6) illustrated key characteristics. In this study, Yu Mei Ren, written by Li Yu, was used to demonstrate the aforementioned transformation.

2 Concepts Adopted in the Application of Elements Found in Poetry

Poetry and design are a form of communication. According to Jakobson, six elements must be present for communication to transpire. These six elements are "addresser," "context," "message," "contact," "code," and "addressee." Poets are unique addressers. They are emotionally affected by the world (the context), and the experience leads to their affections (the message). They use contacts transmitted through sound or light (e.g., air, speakers, book pages, and audiovisual equipment) as well as words of poetry (the code) to send messages to people who can appreciate the poetry (the addressee). All six dimensions must be in place to produce a favorable communication process. Without great poets, spatiotemporal environments, ideas, tools, languages, and audiences, the communication cannot be comprehensively understood. Similarly, designers are affected by their environments (the context), and the experience leads to their creative works (the message). They use colors, shapes, and materials (the contact) as well as design methods (the code) to produce design works for consumers (the addressee). The comparison shows that poetry and design share similar methods of communication.

Regarding poetry content, in addition to investigating explicit expressions or implied meanings, selecting appropriate implications as the key implication is crucial to successful transformation. The use of the key implication method was inspired primarily by the keyword method. In 1978, Pressly and Levin adopted the concept of mental image to examine the effect of the keyword method on learning. The term *mental image* signifies the image that appears in the mind of people when reading an article and an image that enables them to experience the feeling of virtually being in the environment depicted by the article. Pressly and Levin proved that the use of keywords to produce mental images can help improve memories and that concrete words are more effective at generating mental images and more easily remembered compared with abstract words. This finding indicates that the use of the keyword method depends on the mental images to be generated. Furthermore, if the learning content is on specific fields, abstract forms, or subjects of which learners have no prior knowledge, the keyword method becomes even more critical during the early stages of transformation learning. This is because keywords expand the imagination of learners regarding the content and because they imperceptibly enables the interactions between old and new messages. In this study, the keyword method was used to develop key implications that were subsequently used to transform poetry. The key implications improved the readers' memories of poetry, facilitated the continuity of poetic culture, and rendered the abstract words of poetry concrete, which enabled them to be manifested in actual design works (Fig. 2).

Yuan (1996) proposed that imageries in poetry can be divided into five categories: nature (e.g., astronomy, geography, animals, and plants), society (e.g., war, serving as officials, hunting and fishing, and weddings and funerals), humans (e.g., the four limbs, facial features, organs, and psychology), artificial objects (e.g., buildings, artifacts, clothing, and cities), and imaginary things (e.g., immortals, ghosts, the supernatural, and the underworld). In addition, Yuan stated that "an object can create many interesting and charming imageries." Images can be used to transmit and present objective knowledge or elicit and convey subjective feelings. Objective knowledge can be described by nonverbal media, whereas subjective feelings create imageries because writers incorporate feelings into the images. Poets use concrete images as the medium to convey feelings, and readers experience these images through vision, hearing, smell, taste, and touch, which triggers associative thinking and enables them to resonate with the poets. Therefore, by analyzing the five senses and the mental images created in the minds of readers by applying the five imagery categories (e.g., nature, artificial objects, and imaginary things), they facilitate the visualization of abstract concepts and enable these concepts to be transformed into designs.

3   Theories and Steps to Transforming Poetry into Designs

Regarding the theories for transforming poetry into designs (Ye, 2014; Joseph, 1996; Chen, 2004; You, 1997; Chen, 2010; Lin, 2007), in addition to studying creation theories, those on the cognitive process in educational psychology must be examined. These theories facilitate the understanding of the process involving the transformation of abstract ideas to concrete objects. Regarding the design method, theories pertaining to design procedures and design operations were adopted to facilitate the visualization of abstract poetry-related concepts, concretization of visual design elements, and introduction of design elements for daily use. Related theories are organized and described in Fig. 1 as follows:

Design Theories for Poetry Transformation	Visualization of Abstract Concepts	Concretization of Visual Design Elements	Introducing design elements for daily use
Procedural model of the design process (Joseph)	Concept stage	Implementation stage	Detail modification stage
Model of design and creative operation (Chen)	Operation stage	Design-related references	Create creative works
Design representation method (You et al.)	Associative thinking: artists describing and presenting concepts that they have in their mind	Transformation: imageries transformed into vocabularies of basic shapes	Implementation: the finalization of designs and completion of associative thinking
Visual thinking stages (Chiu)	Senses at work stage	Symbol representation stage	Integrated and concrete operation stage
Literature-based creation thinking (Chen)	Basic skills: observation skills, abilities to relate and imagination	Special abilities: identify the theme and gather materials, develop a literary structure, and establish a style	Integration ability: the ability to enable the three types of skill to "interact" with each other and the mastery of these abilities
Procedures to designing poetry education (Lin)	Sharpening the perception ability senses	Strengthening the ability to relate the objective with the subjective	Breaking through the wall of common sense

Fig. 1.   Theories and procedures for transforming poetry to design (organized in this study)

The process in which designers are inspired and engage in creative thinking is a crucial topic in the field of design research. As described in the general procedural model of the design process (Joseph, 1996), the process of creative operation, in essence, follows a stage-by-stage procedure, which includes a concept stage, implementation (concretization) stage, and detail modification stage. Chen (2004) combined the concepts of circularity of Hegel (1770–1831) and Plato's anodos to develop the model of design and creative operation. The model showed that designers use the interactions between variables, such as design operation, design-related references, and creating creative works, to make artworks more refined, mature, and complete. In a study on design representation, You et al. (1997) investigated the method by which imageries of products can be transformed to design representation and subsequently proposed a three-stage design method that involved associative thinking, transformation, and implementation (concretization). Associative thinking refers to experiences, ideas, memories, or perceptions that audiences can directly "feel," which designers describe and present ideal and meaningful concepts (imageries) that they have in their mind. Poets' use of imagery transformation is often attributed to the associative thinking effect. During the process of creation, associative thinking is a key psychological activity. Hegel believed that all artworks are a product of the mind and that a "subjective force" is required to push the creative activity. Such a creative activity is commonly referred to as an artist's "imagination." The key words of the imageries serve as the basis for converting symbols dimensionally. Transformation is one of the key steps during the process of design transformation, which "concretizes" the associative thinking elicited by imageries so that it can be visualized. Associative thinking is transformed from abstract ideas to having basic shapes, and from having basic shapes to three-dimensional (3D) designs (i.e., a model). Implementation (concretization) is the finalization of designs, which indicates the completion of the associative thinking transformation process. After the modified works have been transformed, designers must review and revise related steps used to control the rationality of design elements, the processing of design-related details and the ratio of design elements, and design-related color schemes.

Regarding literature creation, Chen (2010) indicated that people must have basic, special, integration, and various skills to be able to read, write, and engage in various types of learning. Basic skills include thinking abilities, observation skills, ability to memorize, ability to relate, and imagination. Special abilities include the ability to establish a style, select a style, decide the theme and gather materials, use vocabularies, modify phrases, and develop a literary structure. Integration ability includes creativity. By enabling the three types of skill to "interact" with each other, these abilities are subsequently mastered, and step by step they become a thinking system, leading to literature creation. Lin (2007) asserted that the steps to teaching new poetry begin with the perception of objects followed by the formation of inspirations so that the objects and inspirations become one and are reflected in the design of poetry education. Education on poetry transformation is subsequently divided into various stages, such as "sharpening the perception ability senses" to help students be more easily inspired, "strengthening the ability to relate to things" to improve the ability of students to relate the subjective with the objective, and "breaking through the wall of common sense" to induce the poetic thinking skills of students. Related theories pertaining to literature creations, design procedures, and design operations were used as the preliminary ideas to form the implementation stage of our transformation design. This implementation stage was developed according to the characteristics of poetry, which were divided into three stages comprising visualization of abstract concepts, concretization of visual design elements, and introducing design elements for daily use. The procedures were selecting key implications for the topics to be discussed, analyzing the types of imagery, transforming and summarizing design elements, presenting concrete design elements, employing elements to strengthen design appearance and functions, introducing design elements for daily use, experiencing the aesthetics of emotional designs, and achieving cultural and creative design objectives.

4   Experiencing the Aesthetics of Emotional Designs and Achieving Cultural and Creative Design Objectives

For the visualization of abstract concepts stage, the theories of methods to transform designs described in the previous section were employed to produce a concepts in operation stage. By using methods such as observations, associative thinking, and imagination as well as selecting appropriate poetry, poets trigger the readers' senses of perception, from which imageries in the minds of poets are described and presented. Therefore, when studying poetic culture, related abstract elements, such as senses and imageries, are collected and analyzed to investigate the transformation from poetry to visual designs. Yue (2005) indicated that when attempting to improve the ability of students to remember images, the concept mapping method may be used. This method enables students to use their imagination to create images for abstract knowledge that has no images. When reading text, readers can remember only keywords or concepts before placing them together. The same principle applies to abstract images. For the transformation from poetry to design, the aforementioned methods are used to enable designers to provide additional approaches to inspire the creativity of readers along with the visualization of abstract concepts. Moreover, by using methods such as observation, associative thinking, and imagination, readers are able to understand the environment in which the poetry was written, which enhances the depth of their understanding when visualizing abstract concepts.

For the concretization of visual design elements stage, key implications and imageries obtained from the analysis during the previous stage were transformed using a transformation index. The index differed between varying poetry types. Imageries were transformed into concrete 2D or 3D images with colors, texture, and shapes. These imageries were used as the elements to construct the designs. The characteristics of the poetry were included into the design of objects to help strengthen the ability of the viewers to relate to things. Liou (2012) examined the emotions of designers during the image abstraction process and discovered that they used shapes, texture, colors, environments, and characteristics of elements to depict imageries. Lin indicated that poetic thinking is characterized by writers regarding themselves as observers who transfer their subjective emotions to objective objects. The objects become a manifestation of their emotions, and the two subsequently become one, which enables poetry (a reflection of the mind) to transform into products (an object). By deciphering the codes hidden in the poetry, readers are able to identify elements of concretization as the proof of concretization of visual design elements, showing how poetry has been effectively transformed into designs and how it strengthens the ability of viewers to relate to things.

For the introducing design elements for daily use stage, designers were encouraged to engage in poetic thinking and enable mental images to "interact" with each other so that ideas were fully mastered and became motivations for creating designs for daily use. These design creations were to transcend the limitations and development imposed by rationality and enhance the effectiveness of the design elements. The types and properties of the designs were to be ensured, and detailed design modifications were to be made to complete the poetry-design transformation process to enable the product designs to fully depict the emotions of the poets. In addition, designers had to consider whether the products were convenient to use, easy to operate, pleasing to look at, and truly suitable for daily use. For example, regarding the various household items (e.g., items for use, to be looked at, and to feel), using appropriate designs will make them more pleasing to use, to be looked at, or to feel, which increases the quality of life and enables cultural traditions to be deep-rooted in people's daily activities, thus achieving the goal of introducing design elements for daily use.

Implementation stage	Implementation procedure	Content of implementation (*Yu Mei Ren*, written by Li Yu)
I. Visualization of abstract concepts	1. Selecting key implications for the topics to be discussed	"When had the spring flowers and autumn moon end? How much of the past is still known? The Easterly wind swept across the small attic last night; but I couldn't bear recalling my lost kingdom under the clear moonlight! The carved balustrades and jade ornaments should still have survived; changed only are the crimson faces fair. You ask how much sorrow can one ever unleash? As much as the spring river flowing east!"
	2. Analyzing the types of imagery	The "spring river flowing east" was selected as the key implication for analysis. In the analysis of the imageries, "river" and "flowing" were used to form concrete objects.
II. Concretization of visual design elements	3. Transforming and summarizing of design elements	The "sense of movement" was used to display the flowing of the spring river and crystallized, transparent materials were employed. For the "shape" of the design elements, scenery of the spring river was used.
	4. Presenting concretely the design elements	Regarding the presentation of concrete elements, transparent glasses were used. The phrases "When had ... end" and "how much of the past is still known" were manifested in glasses with multilayered curves and sequentially emerging lights to illustrate a sense of movement, indicating the ebbing of the tide.
III. Introducing design elements for daily use	5. Employing elements to strengthen design appearance and functions	The performance of the design elements was improved and the design categories were identified.
	6. Introducing design elements for daily use:	The various aspects pertaining to the design product was considered; that is, whether they would be convenient to use, easy to operate, and pleasing to look at.
	7. Experiencing the aesthetics of emotional designs	The aesthetic experience in which poetry was transformed into practical design was appreciated.
	8. Achieving cultural and creative design objectives	Deep-rooted traditional culture was used in the creation of contemporary designs.

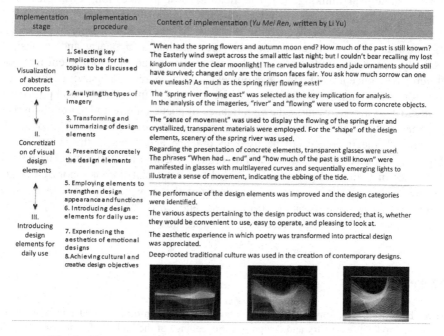

Fig. 2. Example of transforming the poem (*Yu Mei Ren*) into designs

Regarding the key implications to be selected for the topics to be discussed, "spring river rushing east" was selected as the key implication for analysis. An analysis of the imageries showed that movements depicted in the poetry were transformed into the colors, texture, and shapes of the design products. Regarding the analysis of the imageries, "river" and "flowing" were used to form concrete objects. The "sense of movement" and crystallized, transparent materials were used to display the flowing of the spring river. For the "shape" of the design elements, scenery of the spring river was used. The "river" and "flowing" depicted in the poem were used to form concrete objects with curved shapes. The phrases "When had ... end" and "how much ... is still known" were manifested in glasses with multilayered curves and sequentially emerging lights to illustrate a sense of movement, indicating the ebbing of the tide.

5   Conclusions

In this study, the topics of poetic culture as well as the design and application of poetic culture were studied. The design and application of poetic culture in various areas such as the fields of academic research, design education, and the creative industry as well as in cultural continuity were investigated. The results for the four areas are described presented as follows: (1) The field of academic research: In a systematic and logical research framework, academic research methods and tools are combined with poetry-related theories and case studies to transform emotions depicted in poetry into rational and logical thinking. (2) The field of design education: Concrete poetry transformation design is used to convey abstract emotions to introduce various culture into people's lives, such as by enabling people to re-embrace the beauty of poetry and forge an awareness of the connection between aesthetics in poetry and in designs, effectively motivating students to use abstract elements and transform them into concrete creative concepts. (3) The development of the creative industry: Theories proposed for poetry transformation designs are employed in actual design projects to encourage designers to examine the significance of poetic culture and to enlighten them about the mental cognitive experience from poetry. The experiences will provide the industry with the references to be used in practice and enhance the emotions and cultural significance conveyed in the artworks. (4) Cultural continuity: The cultural significance of traditional poetry is examined to create related contemporary designs, inducing the active participation of people from the new generation, which subsequently stimulates their creative inspirations and wins their approval of Chinese culture, achieving the goal of preserving Chinese culture.

References

Beatty, E.L., Ball, L.J.: Investigating exceptional poets to inform an understanding of the relationship between poetry and design. In: Proceedings of the 2nd Conference on Creativity and Innovation in Design (DESIRE 2011), pp. 157–165. ACM, New York (2011)

Beatty, E.L.: The intersection of poetry and design. In: Proceedings of the 8th ACM Conference on Creativity and Cognition (C&C 2011), pp. 449-450. ACM, New York (2011)

Hegel, G.W.F.: Aesthetics: Lectures on Fine Art (i) (T. M. Knox, Trans.). Oxford University Press, New York (1975)

Jakobson, R.: Language in Literature. The Belknap Press of Harvard University Press, Cambridge (1987)

Joseph, S.: Design systems and paradigms. Des. Stud. **17**, 227–239 (1996)

Pressley, M., Levin, J.R.: Developmental constraints associated with children's use of the keyword method of foreign language vocabulary learning. J. Exp. Child Psychol. **26**, 359–372 (1978)

Plato: Symposium (A. Nehamas & P. Woodruff, Trans.). Hackett Publishing Company Inc., Indianapolis (1989)

Yeh, M.L., Chien, C.W., Lin, R.T.: Employing poetry culture for creative design with six-standpoints. In: 2014 Conference on Design Research Society 2014. Sweden, Ume (2014a)

Yeh, M.-L., Wang, M., Lin, P.-C.: Applying the time and space forms of poetry to creative design. In: Rau, P.L.P. (ed.) CCD 2014. LNCS, vol. 8528, pp. 798–807. Springer, Heidelberg (2014)

Lin, X.L.: Designing the teaching of new poetry by using inspiration-oriented thinking and analysis of implementation results. In: First Annual Thinking and Creation Symposium. National University of Tainan, Tainan (2007)

Lin, R.T.: From service innovation to qualia product design. J. Des. Sci. **14**(S), 13–31 (2010)

Yueh, H.P.: E-Learning and Teachers' Professional Development: A National Taiwan University Experience. The National Taiwan University Teaching and Learning Electronic Newsletter, p. 36 (2005). http://edtech.ntu.edu.tw/epaper/940610/prof/prof_2.asp

You, M.L., Kao, Y.C., Yeh, P.H.: A study on product image and its representation design—with radio design as a case study. J. Des. **2**(1), 31–45 (1997)

Yuan, X.P.: Art of Chinese Poetry. The Peking University, Beijing (1996)

Chen, M.M.: Thinking system and literary creation. Sun Yat-sen J. Humanit., p. 29 (2010)

Chen, C.H., Chen, Y.P.: A study on the relation of interaction between the model of design-creating-thinking and variations. J. Des. **9**(2), 71–86 (2004)

Yeh, M.L.: Creative Design and Application of Poetic Culture (unpublished doctoral dissertation). Graduate School of Creative Industry Design. National Taiwan University of Arts, Taipei (2014)

Yeh, M.L., Lin, P.H., Hsu, C.H.: Applying poetic techniques of shape–spirit transformation in cultural creative design. J. Des. **16**(4), 91–106 (2011)

Liou, C.L.: A Study on Thinking Context and Design Techniques of Abstractly Process in Visual Design (unpublished master's thesis). Department and Graduate School of Visual Communication Design. The National Yunlin University of Science & Technology, Yunlin (2012)

Cultural Identification and Innovation–A Study on the Design of Exhibition and Dissemination System for a City's Cultural Heritage Under the New Media Context

Lie Zhang[✉] and Wen Zhang

Department of Information Art and Design, Academy of Arts and Design, Tsinghua University, Beijing 100084, People's Republic of China
zhlie@tsinghua.edu.cn, ww53371023@163.com

Abstract. A city's cultural heritage is a unique symbol of the city's identity. It is a valuable basis for the modern city to trace the cultural origins, look for their own position, restore urban identity, and get public recognition. In-depth study and excavation of urban heritage and the effective use and dissemination of cultural wealth of the city are regarded as necessary measures to highlight the city's character and promote the development of urban culture. In combination with art and technology, exhibition, dissemination and service tools of new media being used in the field of cultural heritage, will help to achieve cultural heritage protection and mutual promotion between development and innovation, thus it has important practical significance for the sustainable development of urban culture and economic. This article introduces ideas and experience based on new media exhibition system of the Pingdingshan Museum.

Keywords: Cultural heritage · Urban culture · New media art · Exhibition and dissemination · Interactive exhibition design

1 Introduction

City refers to the convergence of population, resources, public facilities, industry commerce and culture. No matter historic or new blooming, the development of urban requires not only both political and economic powers for the city's maintenance and promotion, but also the gathering and inheritance of culture which beard the soul of the city. Cultural heritage reflects the life trajectory of the city. It is the concentrated expression and interpretation of urban characteristics, as a real existence of the memory of the city. Scientific and in-depth understanding and mining of city's cultural heritage, restoring and enriching the connotation of urban identity, and positioning urban qualities reasonably are the foundation for the construction of urban culture. Accurate grasp of the cultural identity of the city helps to lay a good foundation for obtaining wide spread recognition of the public and positioning of urban cultural development direction. The "recognition" plays an important role to establish a good image of urban culture and expand urban culture externally, and gather public consensus internally, safeguards a strong spiritual motivation and intellectual support for the city's economic and social development.

© Springer International Publishing Switzerland 2015
P.L.P. Rau (Ed.): CCD 2015, Part II, LNCS 9181, pp. 294–303, 2015.
DOI: 10.1007/978-3-319-20934-0_28

Combined with new concepts and technologies, exhibition, dissemination and service means of new media being used in the field of cultural heritage have broad and important application prospects. The use of technical means and concept methods of new media, and mining, development and dissemination of the spirit of the city make cultural heritage become active construction of urban identity for promoting urban cultural development and innovation. In one word, it is one of possible ideas that are worth trying to promote comprehensive and sustainable urban development.

2   Related Work

In recent years, as a new means of communication, new media art has spread to a certain application in the field of cultural heritage at home and abroad. For example, recently, the Cleveland Museum of Art of the United States makes extensive use of new media art and technology, a large touch wall, matching action recognition, etc. (Fig. 1), which make people understand the contemporary museum with a new look. In China, the Nanjing Museum builds a Digital Experience Center (Fig. 2), as a consequence, new media tools have received centralized applications. New Media Art, which has a new and attractive entertainment features with its sound and light means,

Fig. 1. New media exhibition items of the cleveland museum of art of the united states (http://www.clevelandart.org/gallery-one)

Fig. 2. Digital experience center of the nanjing museum (http://www.njmuseum.com/Antique)

brings to the viewers a strong visual, appeal, and immersive experience. It is regarded as its unique communication advantage, different from other artistic means. More importantly, the new media art brings a new narrative mode; its rich, vivid, interactive, nonlinear characteristics might change the discourse system of traditional museum and bring new urban cultural experience.

3   New Media Exhibition and Dissemination System Design of the Pingdingshan Museum

3.1   Trinity Analysis Method for Cultural Heritage: "Origin", "Evolution", and "Characteristics"

The basis of culture communication is accurate analysis, awareness and positioning. For understanding its own values and positioning the core spirit of its character of each city, it is necessary to explore its own life trajectory and grasp the pulse of sustainable development from the city origin and development context. System analysis and reconstruction of "origin", "evolution", and "characteristics" of the city's cultural heritage, is an effective way to recognize and develop the city's cultural heritage and shape urban identities. The trinity analysis method of "origin", "evolution", and "characteristics" (Fig. 3), in short, is to pursue the "origin" of urban culture from the origin of the city and geopolitical environment, the "evolution" of urban culture from the historical changes, and the "characteristics" of urban culture from the major historical events.

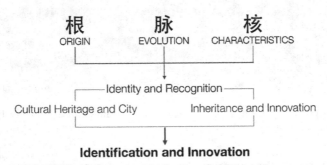

Fig. 3. Trinity analysis method of "origin", "evolution", "characteristics"

3.2   New Media Narrative System Construction of the Pingdingshan Museum

New media exhibition and dissemination design of the Pingdingshan Museum is one of our most recent cases. Pingdingshan, as a new city of coal industry in modern China, is well known, but its urban culture is slightly dim. Recent archaeological excavations have opened a door for the history and culture of the city. The finding of town site and a large area of cemetery of the Zhou Dynasty, helps to make a substantial advance of the civilized era of Pingdingshan city. Moreover, the inscriptions of unearthed jades and bronzes can further confirm, the ancient state with "Eagle" as totem – the existence of the Ying State (In Chinese classical literary, "Ying" means "Eagle"). (Figures 4, 5, 6) The pursuit of "Eagle" culture fits the people's feelings of finding origin, adding to the cultural advantages of Pingdingshan. Eagle's image and characteristics are also in line with enterprising spirit and local character of the industrial city, therefore, "Eagle" as the theme of the spiritual heritage has opened up new horizons for cultural development of Pingdingshan.

Fig. 4. Unearthed white eagle carved by lines in Pingdingshan

Fig. 5. "Ying" in chinese classical literary

Fig. 6. Unearthed bronzes in Pingdingshan and the inscriptions

In the construction of the new urban museum of the Pingdengshan Museum, along the trinity analysis of ideas of "origin", "evolution", and "characteristics", we've combed the narrative system of Pingdingshan cultural context together with museum researchers and experts in various aspects. In the combination of traditional culture and innovative technology, with the use of the internet and new technology for digital new media as the important content of core nodes, we focus on narrating, plan a new media narrative system of interactive media projects, including *New media sound and light relief of the origin of the Eagle City,*[1] *Virtual space and time roaming in ancient city by Vehicles and Horses,*[2] and *Chime-bells Interaction,*[3] interactively narrate historical origins, cultural context and hot stories of the Eagle City, so that viewers can be deeply immersive with interactive experience, and feel ancient culture and unique charm of the Eagle City (Fig. 7).

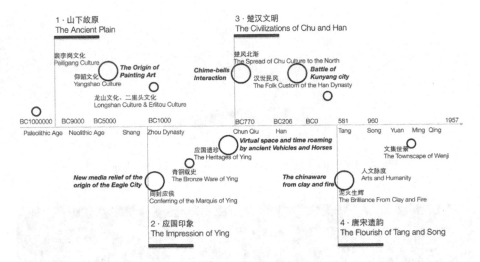

Fig. 7. Pingdingshan's cultural context and new media narrative system

3.3   New Media Art Works of the Pingdingshan Museum

New Media Relief of the Origin of the Eagle City. "Finding origin" seems to be a natural human feeling. The consciousness of culture of "origin", makes people find their own foothold point and identity recognition in the complex world and society. The starting point of diverse cultural nature explains the fundamental problems of urban existence, and largely influences the development direction of the city.

In Western Zhou Dynasty, Pingdingshan area was vassal state controlled by the fourth son of the King Wu of Zhou (also known as the ancient Ying State historically). During the long-term excavation process, in the cemetery of the Ying State, there are up to million pieces of unearthed copper, pottery, jade, stone and other types of artifacts, and over two hundred pieces of bronzes with inscriptions, thus opening a long-submerged mystery of ancient central plains. In 1986, an important cultural relics with the

---

[1] Designer: Lie Zhang, Zhi-Gang Wang, Zhi-Jun Zheng.

[2] Designer: Lie Zhang, Feng Xian, Jun-Yu Chen, Bo-Hang Pan, Jin Huang, Li-Wen Gong, Hai-Yong Sun, Chun-Yu Xu.

[3] Designer: Lie Zhang, Ye-Qing Deng, Yi-Xi Zhong, Bai-Zhuang Ye.

significance of family emblem – the Jade Eagle, was unearthed from the 1st tomb of the Ying State cemetery. The eagle is the most representative of the limitless sky, broad-minded birds, and can tell an enthusiastic spirit of fighting the sky. It is also the origin of Pingdingshan's alias – the Ying City. With the Jade Eagle, the Ying State, inscriptions, and the modern spirit of Pingdingshan, these different elements are integrated together to tell the story of the origin of the Eagle City, as an important new media works of the Pingdingshan Museum. We use superimposed projection in artistic creation of relief, through meticulously arranged narrative script and imaging and lighting with precision control, in this way, the seemingly traditional static relief appears to be "alive", which presents a vivid and detailed dynamic sound and light new media relief works (Fig. 8).

Fig. 8. New media relief of the origin of the eagle city

Virtual Space and Time Roaming in Ancient City by Vehicles and Horses. Cultural heritage on the interpretation of urban identity also reflects the inheritance in the context of the city's culture. Thanks to historical documents and recent excavation research of cultural relics, historical development of the ancient city of Pingdingshan gradually become clear. The findings of stacked cultural layers make the city's heritage thicker and calmer, regardless of the time change, cultural diversity is always accommodated and gathered with a broad-mind.

In order to fully experience the geospatial features and the context of development of times of Pingdingshan region, we combine kinect sensing equipment to design the *Virtual space and time roaming in ancient city by Vehicles and Horse*. In front of the big immersive screen, viewers only make a gesture of pulling the reins by waving their hands, and then horses in the screen will lead them to travel the ancient cities of Pingdingshan in a specific period. Ancient topography and geomorphology and customs are demonstrated in front of eyes of viewers. The shape of vehicles and horses, different decoration, and the surrounding scene, are all on the basis of rigorous archaeological research with artistic creation. As shown in Fig. 7, the scene is by now completed, which can present the period of ancient Ying State of the Western Zhou Dynasty. Next, we will incorporate information from different historical periods, so that people can further travel through the different times, such as the Spring and Autumn Period, Han, Song and Yuan Dynasties and so on in Pingdingshan by vehicles and horses (Fig. 9).

Chime-bells Interaction. Major archaeological discoveries and major historical society events are one kind of marks of urban identity of cultural heritage. As witness of the historical changes and a milestone in social development, a city can become very charming. Pingdingshan was located in the northern border of the Chu State during the

Fig. 9. Virtual space and time roaming in ancient city by vehicles and horses

Eastern Zhou Dynasty, as an important north-south traffic road and important military powerhouse in the disputing period of vassal states. The Xu State as the state with surname Jiang in the Zhou Dynasty, it moved the capital to here in the Spring and Autumn Period. In March 2002, the monarch of the Xu State, XuGongning tomb of the Spring and Autumn Period in Ye County in Pingdingshan was found. A set of unique Chu bells is the most impressive among the unearthed artifacts in tomb. The chime-bells are divided into 5 groups with 37 pieces, including Yong bells, Niu bells and Bo, which can help to fill the missing link from small bells in the Spring and Autumn Period to the large ZengHouyi Chime Bells in the history of the development of the Bronze Bells in China, being called the first sign of large portfolio belles in the Spring and Autumn Period. Meanwhile, the group of bells is regarded as the bells, which are currently known in the same period, with maximum size, the largest number of pieces, the best sound quality, and the most unique and complex combinations. The bells are the result of blending a variety of cultural factors, thus they provide a rare kind of information on the study of exchange and fusion of Central Plains culture and Chu culture.

For such a major archaeological discovery and its unique features of social and historical changes of the Spring and Autumn Period, we design a new media interactive entertainment works – Chime-bells Interaction. We take the traditional spatial design technique of opposite scenery, using spatial modeling to create a semi-independent open space. One side is a group of real unearthed chime-bells; the other side is completely digital interactive virtual chime-bells. But both are almost identical in shape, texture and appearance, and size. People can understand the characteristics of the group of chime-bells and its social and historical background through interactive images. The bells can be struck, so that people can hear the wonderful sound of real chime-bells. In addition, with natural guide of screen, it plays a melodious music of chime-bells. People can be immersed in the space with the change of real world and virtual world, listening to classical and novel music of Pre-Qin Dynasty (Fig. 10).

Based on the above works, We look the rich cultural heritage of our city as a target resource, excavate its cultural value, and refine some factors which can symbolize and summarize the history, culture, personality of city. The city's origin, evolution, Characteristics will highlight the culture of the city. Under the New Media Context, we

Fig. 10. Chime-bells interaction

arrange and decorate the representative narrative thread and the typical scene using art and technology forms, develop and utilize innovative digital communication and display technology, to find the most suitable and best art presentation. Finally, we take the city's cultural heritage resources into digital display dissemination system to achieve the goal (Fig. 11).Requirement analysis and implementation

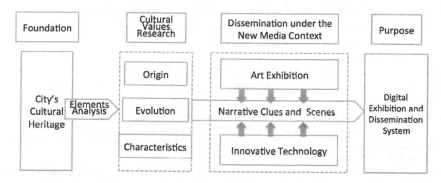

Fig. 11. The framework map of digital exhibition and dissemination system construction about city's cultural heritage

4   Conclusion

Cultural evolution is continuing forward in the ongoing process of innovation and tradition. Without innovation, culture loses its vitality. Today, the colorful cultural heritage that is presented in front of us is bred from ancestors in innovation and tireless exploration. To achieve inheritance and innovation of the city's cultural heritage, it is necessary to examine and explore, realize and develop its wisdom and achievements along the clues of historical evolution. Meanwhile, the combination of advanced technology and artistic means, attractive, innovative, and appealing exhibition and dissemination methods in full of the spirit of the times, are widely accepted, and the city's position and advantages by highlighting the cultural characteristics give people who reside in the city the spirit of enlightenment and emotional attribution, so that cultural identity and innovation can become spiritual power and inexhaustible culture source to maintain sustainable urban development.

Acknowledgement. This article was supported by the National Social Science Fund Project in Arts - *Development Status and Construction of Interaction Design Discipline* (Ministry of Culture 13CB113) and Promotion fund research project of Humanities and Social Sciences of Tsinghua University-*Information Design Methods and Teaching* (Ministry of Education 2011WKYB010).

References

Marstine, J.: New Museum Theory and Practice: An Introduction. Wiley Blackwell Publication, Hoboken (2006)

Shan, J.-X.: Keep the Origin and Soul of City's Culture. Science Press, Beijing (2010)

Macdonald, S.: A Companion to Museum Studies. Blackwell Publication, Oxford (2006)

Sauter, J.: Sensitive skins in media art and design. In: ITS 2014 Proceedings of the Ninth ACM International Conference on Interactive Tabletops and Surfaces (2014)

Hung, Y.-P.: An image-based approach to interactive 3d virtual exhibition. In: Mery, D., Rueda, L. (eds.) PSIVT 2007. LNCS, vol. 4872, p. 1. Springer, Heidelberg (2007)

Watkins, J.: Social media, participatory design and cultural engagement. In: OZCHI 2007 Proceedings of the 19th Australasian Conference on Computer-Human Interaction: Entertaining User Interfaces (2007)

Kortbek, K.J., Grønbæk, K.: Interactive spatial multimedia for communication of art in the physical museum space. In: MM 2008 Proceeding of the 16th ACM international Conference on Multimedia (2008)

de Toledo, M.B.F., Capretz, M.A.M., Allison, D.S.: Recovering brazilian indigenous cultural heritage using new information and communication technologies. In: WI-IAT 2009 Proceedings of the 2009 IEEE/WIC/ACM International Joint Conference on Web Intelligence and Intelligent Agent Technology, vol. 03 (2009)

Casella, G., Coelho, M.: Augmented heritage: situating augmented reality mobile apps in cultural heritage communication. In: ISDOC 2013 Proceedings of the 2013 International Conference on Information Systems and Design of Communication (2013)

Dodsworth, C., Mayer, J.: Cultural heritage and digital experience design: presentation, adaptation and competitive evolution. In: VAST 2001 Proceedings of the 2001 Conference on Virtual reality, Archeology, and Cultural heritage (2001)

Antoniou, A., Lepouras, G., Bampatzia, S., Almpanoudi, H.: An approach for serious game development for cultural heritage: case study for an archaeological site and museum. J. Comput. Cult. Heritage (JOCCH) 6(4) (2013)

Ciula, A., Eide, Ø.: Reflections on cultural heritage and digital humanities: modelling in practice and theory. In: DATeCH 2014 Proceedings of the First International Conference on Digital Access to Textual Cultural Heritage (2014)

Li-Der, C., Chia-Hsieh, W., Shih-Pang, H., et al.: Requirement analysis and implementation of palm-based multimedia museum guide systems. In: AINA 2004 Advanced Information Networking and Applications, 18th International Conference (2004)

Burgard W., Cremers, A.B., Fox, D., et al.: The interactive museum tour-guide robot. In: AAAI, pp. 11–18 (1998)

Miyashita, T., Meier, P., Tachikawa, T., et al.: an augmented reality museum guide: mixed and augmented reality. ISMAR 2008 7th IEEE/ACM International Symposium (2008)

Suominen, J., Sivula, A.: Gaming legacy? four approaches to the relation between cultural heritage and digital technology. J. Comput. Cult. Heritage (JOCCH) 6(3) (2013)

Owen, R., Buhalis, D., Pletinckx, D.: Identifying technologies used in cultural heritage. In: VAST 2004 Proceedings of the 5th International conference on Virtual Reality, Archaeology and Intelligent Cultural Heritage (2004)

Culture for Health, Learning and Games

Paper Catalog and Digital Catalog - Reading Behaviors of College Students in Taiwan

Yu-Ju Lin[1]([⊠]), Hui-Yun Yen[2], Chiui Hsu[3], Yige Jin[4],
and Po-Hsien Lin[3]

[1] Department of Visual Communication Design,
Taipei College of Maritime Technology, Taipei 25172, Taiwan
naralin@mail.tcmt.edu.com
[2] Department of Advertising, Chinese Culture University, Taipei 11114, Taiwan
pccu.yhy@gmail.com
[3] Graduate School of Creative Industry Design,
National Taiwan University of Arts Ban Ciao City, Taipei 22058, Taiwan
hsu.chiui@msa.hinet.net, t0131@ntua.edu.tw
[4] Shanghai Art and Design Academy, Shanghai, China
yigeqll@sina.com

Abstract. This study focused on undergraduates with varying reading habits and investigated their behavioral differences as well as the structural relationships between their attitude toward reading paper and digital catalogs, their digital usage behavior, and their paper and on-screen reading literacy. Fifty undergraduate students from Northern Taiwan comprised the sample population and were interviewed in depth. Comparative analysis was conducted on the behaviors between reading paper and digital catalogs. The results show that paper catalogs emphasized (a) richness of content messages, (b) viewing comfort of graphics editing, (c) convenience of storage, (d) connectivity of data search, and (e) influence of applied operations, whereas digital catalogs focused on (a) interactivity of media exchange, (b) immediacy of feedback sharing, (c) authenticity of audio–video transmission, (d) interoperability of service platform, and (e) potential of diverse internationality. Based on these qualities, the reading behaviors of undergraduate students who read using paper and digital catalogs were investigated and compared to determine the influence of paper and on-screen reading on the students. Finally, strategic recommendations for promoting digital catalogs are proposed through inductive analysis.

Keywords: Paper catalog · Digital catalog · Reading behavior

1 Introduction

In the digital age, the widespread applications and public knowledge of computers and the introduction of mobile reading technologies along with iPad and iPhone devices in 2010 have gradually expanded the use of tablet computers and smart phones. Digitization has become an integral part of peoples' lives. People traditionally acquire and accumulate knowledge by reading printed materials. As technologies progress, reading

© Springer International Publishing Switzerland 2015
P.L.P. Rau (Ed.): CCD 2015, Part II, LNCS 9181, pp. 307–317, 2015.
DOI: 10.1007/978-3-319-20934-0_29

behaviors have rapidly changed from linear paper reading to nonlinear on-screen reading.

Catalogs frequently assist leaders in transmitting, reading, and comprehending messages and ultimately completing purchase behaviors. Catalog contents exhibit the functions of displaying corporate image, manifesting product attraction, and enhancing emotional associations, which are means of conveying commercial messages. Because the on-screen reading industry and relevant technologies have seen rapid development, catalogs no longer convey strictly visual knowledge but adopt digital multisensory stimulations through surface representation. Contrary to traditional paper catalogs, digital catalogs provide readers with a brand-new audience experience, which has revolutionized paper reading patterns and integrated graphics, audio, and video in nonlinear reading patterns, stimulating readers' interests through innovative, charming presentations. This has led to a revolutionary age since the advent of printed mass media and has transformed advertiser marketing, media pricing, and consumer behaviors. However, the effects of these revolutionary features and whether they meet reader expectations thereof remain unclear.

The purpose of this study is to determine participants' level of acceptance of reading catalogs presented in various media formats, their usual text reading habits and behaviors for various media formats, and their opinions on text presented in various media formats.

Based on the research purpose, the specific objectives are described as follows:

- Investigate differences in the reading behaviors of undergraduate students who read using digital or printed text formats.
- Investigate the selection motive and usage condition of undergraduate's students who read using digital or printed text formats.
- Investigate the roles of digital and printed text formats in the reading activities of undergraduate's students.

2 Literature Review

2.1 Reading Properties Associated with Paper Catalogs and Digital Catalogs

Previously, businesses were required to publish numerous planar catalogs for marketing products. However, products are often phased out or upgraded before all the catalogs have been distributed because of fierce market competition. This is no longer the case in the digital age because digital business has become a market expansion channel through the emergence of the Internet. In addition, this change has facilitated the development of paper catalogs into digital catalogs. Online reading has emerged because of the increase digital information, constant development of digital technology, and ever-changing digital content and media technologies. These facets complete the Internet at present and have prompted the diverse applications of on-screen reading, digital catalogs, digital magazines, digital picture books, and multimedia books. As the national economy and per capita income rise, the formation and development of the logistics system prompt a market of approximately NT\$4–5 billion on catalogs per year. Since the Internet emerged, digital business has become a channel for seeking marketing opportunities and has promoted the development of catalogs. The Internet has become a crucial channel for business marketing, and the World Wide Web has been deemed to become a focal point of prospective lifestyles and mainstream commercial exchange [1]. Digital catalogs are free from stock problems and can be revised and viewed online at any time. This application has gradually received increasing attention from business operators. An increasing number of companies has committed to developing digital catalogs and has gradually replaced costly planar printed versions. The emergence of digital publishing has diversified potential electronic book developments. Digital contents can be stored, and readers can upload or download and read preferential online content on their computers or personal readers. This provides a brand-new and convenient approach to reading [2]. Therefore, prospective developments of paper and digital materials and readers' preferential reading properties are worth investigating.

2.2   Textual Presentation and Reading Behaviors

Reading is a complex cognitive process influenced by individuals' perceptual skills, decoding abilities, experience, language background, and reasoning abilities. Reading can be separated into two components, which are word identification and verbal comprehension [3]. Reading behavior refers to the conditions of readers in reading activities and their level of preference and is typically limited to analyses on reading frequencies and breadth [4]. Gary Hartzell considered that reading comfort is a crucial factor that encourages reading activities. A study showed that reading digital materials is 30% slower than reading printed hardcopies and asserted that on-screen reading comfort plays a pivotal role in the potential replacement of paper reading [5]. Wang et al. adopted an interview survey method to analyze the reading behaviors of people who read using paper and digital materials and found that the results were mostly independent of the content, time, and location. However, regarding reading frequencies, most readers preferred paper reading [6]. HarperCollins Publishers, Hachette Livre, Scholastic and MCT Consulting and Training have stated that people prefer reading digital materials in crowded subways and paper materials at home. On-screen reading is no longer characterized by generation-based division but rather scenario-based division. New reading patterns provided publishers with restructuring opportunities, which are expected to take place over the Internet. These opportunities include new marketing methods for digital business, network marketing, and social community manipulation [7].

Rosenbaum (1999) adopted Taylor's Information Use Environment concept and Giddens' Structuration theory and proposed the digital information environment theoretical framework to determine how readers use information and communication technology as well as digital information to influence situational and information behaviors [8]. Schcolink (2001) investigated on-screen reading strategies and determined that readers presented positive attitudes toward digital readers. Digital books provide mostly either real-time information or leisure and entertainment contents.

The most common reading strategy or behavior is paging. Most leisure and entertainment materials adopt linear navigation methods and favor image display and paging methods instead of scrolling methods. Navigation methods are more common than study-based reading [9]. These results suggest that situational behaviors substantially influence personal information behaviors. Figure 1 shows that paper and digital information environments consist of users and providers. Providers comprise various sources, such as Websites, newspapers, catalogs, and libraries. Crucial behaviors must be considered during the interactive process between users and providers, namely retrieving, sharing, communicating, interacting, presenting, managing, and storing.

2.3   Prospects of Paper- and Digital-Based Reading

The publishing industry has changed drastically in the past two decades. The State of the News Media 2013, published by the Pew Research Center, indicated that the number of digital media readers increased by 7.2% between 2011 and 2012, when relevant advertising revenue increased by 16.6%. Therefore, the development of digital publishing in Taiwan, where the penetration of the World Wide Web has reached 74.18%, is anticipated to duplicate that of the United States [8]. In the Taiwan Digital Publishing Forum, Shih mentioned that the additional increase in the on-screen reading population is anticipated following the introduction of 4G services. The largest reading material provider in Taiwan, books, formally announced that they would be entering the on-screen reading market in 2015 [10]. Carr considered that digital-based reading is expected to occupy a certain market share, but a complete replacement of paper-based reading is unlikely. Thus, reading is expected to assume numerous forms. Consumers can select among digital-based reading, audio reading, and multimedia reading. Each of these options presents a unique reading format and therefore has no risk of being replaced [11].

3   Research Methods

Surveys and interviews are the most commonly adopted methods in studies on reading behaviors and both have their merits. However, because of the unique properties of this study, to prevent misunderstanding by participants as well as to obtain specific results on reading behaviors and relevant influences, an objective in-depth interview method was adopted. Moreover, this study focused on readers who read both paper and digital catalogs to collect their opinions on reading behaviors associated with digital and printed text formats. The samples selected comprised the Dechnology new-aesthetics (paper) catalog and the corresponding Dechnology Website (digital catalog).The participants were 50 undergraduate students from a design institute in Northern Taiwan with experience in reading both paper and digital catalogs. The study was divided into three implementation stages. At the first stage, a relevant literature review was conducted and the 50 undergraduates were interviewed to determine their reading behaviors. At the second stage, the 50 undergraduate participants were tested and interviewed using the paper catalog. At the third stage, the same participants were

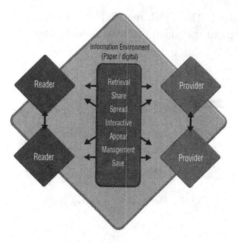

Fig. 1. User–provider interaction in an information environment (Revised in this Study)

tested and interviewed using the digital catalog in 2weeks' time to determine the behavioral differences and structural relationships between their attitude toward reading paper and digital catalogs, their digital usage behavior, and their paper and on-screen reading literacy.

4 Research Results and Discussion

4.1 The Industrial Technology Research Institute Dechnology Project on Readers' Textual Interpretation of Paper and Digital Catalogs

Dechnology refers to the integration of design and technology to achieve a new technology that is aesthetic and innovative. Since 2009, the Department of Industrial Technology, Ministry of Economic Affairs has initiated the Dechnology project, which focuses on technological aesthetics and integrates the eight legal entities comprising the Industrial Technology Research Institute (ITRI), the Institute for Information Industry, the Taiwan Textile Research Institute, the Food Industry Research and Development Institute, the Development Center for Biotechnology, the Metal Industries Research and Development Centre, the Automotive Research and Testing Center, and the Ship and Ocean Industries Research and Development Center to jointly implement the Dechnology project. The research and development (R&D) value derived from the joint efforts of the technology and design industries is expected to increase the technological competency of Taiwan, thereby instilling technology–design aesthetics, living experience, and design energy into the lives of the general public. This project was initiated to adapt to innovative global industries and market change in which prospects and manufacturing of technology are not priorities. The creation of emotional products through the techno-logical commercialization process has become the key to dominating markets. Thus, the Department of Industrial Technology, Ministry of Economic Affairs promoted the Dechnology project, introduced technology into design work, and enabled innovative technological applications. The ITRI released the Dechnology catalog (paper) and Website (digital catalog) to introduce potential products and commercial opportunities (Figs. 2 and 3).

Fig. 2. Dechnology catalog (paper)

Fig. 3. Dechnology website (digital catalog)

4.2   Textual Analysis on the Information Environment

According to the provider–user interaction in the information environment proposed by Chen, the textual analysis of the paper and online Dechnology catalogs are shown as follows:

The analysis revealed that the paper catalog displayed functions such as communicating messages and can be conveniently stored. However, the continuous cost of printing traditional paper catalogs and limited paper quantities affected the number of readers. Therefore, the paper catalog exhibited inadequacy in retrieving, sharing, interacting, and managing properties (Tables 1 and 2).

The analysis showed that using Rich Site Summary as a medium can substantially increase the portability of an electronic catalog. Furthermore, the medium enables quick and comfortable viewing on various devices. A service-oriented framework was adopted to provide various concepts by incorporating multiple sources. In addition, the Internet was used to clearly introduce various product specifications and content information for convenient access. Messages can be actively transmitted to readers automatically from the server side. Information is integrated in high security through interactive communication channels to complete matching processes.

Table 1. Textual analysis of the information environment of the paper dechnology catalog

Item	Content	Feature
Retrieving	Only 22 pages long; table of contents not provided for retrieval.	X
Sharing	Must be printed to share.	X
Communi- cating	Designated message transmission or quick response (QR) code connections.	O
Interacting	Introduces strictly 41 innovative goodies; no interactive functions.	X
Presenting	Comprises Chinese–English bilingual presentation, designer, technical departments, and product identification pictures.	O
Managing	Printed distributions are free of subsequent management problems.	X
Storing	The catalog measures 18 × 14.5 (cm) for convenient storage.	O

4.3   Differences in the Reading Behaviors of Undergraduate Students Who Read Using Paper Catalog or Digital Catalogs

Stage 1: Sample description The interview participants' experience in reading both paper and digital catalogs were first confirmed. Among the 50 undergraduate students, 34 were male and 16 were female, yielding a male-to-female ratio of approximately 7:3. This study focused on participants who read at least one digital catalog per month; therefore, the slightly higher male population can be explained by their comparatively higher familiarity with technological products. Consequently, more male students than female students read the digital catalog. The participants mostly used desktop or laptop computers for reading digital materials (58%), followed by other devices such as cell phones (34%) and tablet computers (8%). The percentage of owning tablet computers was below the overall average of 90%, indicating that tablet computers remained comparatively expensive and were uncommon among students. The contents, ranked from highest to lowest preference, were lifestyles and hobbies (31.3%), fashion and entertainment (29.5%), and crammers' companions (16.8%). The male participants preferred reading materials on lifestyle and hobbies, whereas the female participants favored those on fashion and entertainment. After the participants' reading devices and material contents were identified, their reading attitudes, digital-based usage behavior, and critical paper and digital catalog functions toward reading paper and digital

Table 2. Textual analysis of the information environment of the dechnology web site (digital catalog).

Item	Content	Text	Feature
Retrieving	The digital catalog features a navigation page for data retrieval		o
Sharing	Messages from the digital catalog can be shared with friends on Facebook, Twitter, or Google+		o
Communicating	The digital catalog can be browsed on other digital readers by using the QR Code		o
Interacting	The digital catalog provides a platform for manufacturers to submit business partnership proposals and product reviews		o
Presenting	In addition to Chinese–English bilingual descriptions and designer and technical departmental information, multi perspective product pictures are provided		o
Managing	The knowledge bank of the digital catalog is constantly updated; product listing and correction managements can be instantly performed		o
Storing	The digital catalog can be added to My Favorites or downloaded and saved on digital readers for offline viewing		o

catalogs as well as their level of satisfaction with the digital catalog platform were analyzed.

Stage 2: Reading attitude and behaviors of undergraduate students who read using paper catalogs The results showed that 16%, 64%, and 20% of the participants completed reading the paper catalog in less than 10 min, between 12 and 20 min, and between 20 and 30 min, respectively. No users expended more than 30 min reading the catalog, suggesting that the participants could not read excess information because of the length of the catalog.

> "The contents of the Dechnology catalog (paper) were extremely attractive and showcased 41 innovative products that inspire design and creative thinking processes. However, further product information would be of great help for relevant learning."

> "[The catalog] demonstrates a global perspective. Not a lot of catalogs present Chinese–English bilingual contents. Product design concepts are well detailed but lack additional product images. The products are shown in single pictures without actual sample operating diagrams. The operating methods or correlation between internal and external structures are sometimes unclear."

> "The catalog features appropriate dimensions, a handy design and portability, high-quality printed texture, well-executed layout, sound viewing comfort, and contemporary appearance. The only drawback is that most of the images were synthetically simulated. Structural diagrams would aid in the interpretation of product operation methods and structures."

> "Such refined catalogs are rarely seen. In addition to learning from them, I would like to keep them as part of my collection."

> "The title is attractive.[I] would have wished for more elaborate content information as the introduction was concise but insufficient. The QR code is too small. The Website cannot be successfully connected to using a cell phone."

Regarding paper catalog-based reading behaviors, the undergraduate participants mostly emphasized on the following contents: (a)richness of content message (instructional aspects; attractive contents increase readers' willingness to learn); (b) viewing comfort of graphics editing(graphic layout also influences readers' willingness to read); (c)convenience of storage(dimensions and paper selections, appearance design, and texture quality leave marked impressions in readers); (d)connectivity of data search(in addition to existing content data, the importance of extended reading is emphasized); and (e)influence of applied operations(readers voluntarily participate and select the messages of interest).

Stage 3: Reading attitude and behaviors of undergraduate students who read using digital catalog The digital catalog was tested by the same participants in 2 weeks' time after Stage 2.Observations were made during the test, and the participants were interviewed. The results showed that 2%, 42%, 50%, and 6% of the participants completed reading the digital catalog in less than 15 min, between 16 and 30 min, between 31 and 60 min, and more than60 min, respectively. Only less than 10% of the users completed reading the catalog within 15 min, suggesting that the participants did not skim through the digital catalog but rather developed an interest in the material.

> "The Website features a clean navigation layout in which a title list accelerated search processes. In addition, the Website contains rich product themes and has a product search function that accelerates processes for finding relevant product information. However, multilevel buttons tend to cause confusion during user operation, which is considerably inconvenient."

"Interactive structures strengthen connections between users and designers and consist of professional design matching capability and mechanisms. However, the instant feedback feature was weak and lacked adequate management."

"[The Website] contains numerous pictures that present various angles and structures of the products and elaborate on product operation and usability. However, most of the products are in development stages, and most of the pictures were illustrated using 3D-simulated diagrams. As digital media continue to develop, 360° or virtual reality product presentation options can be added."

"The online platform presents increased information contents, technology descriptions, and design concepts but lacks the English translation function and thus lacks global development potential. In addition, providing external connections to designers (teams), technological terms, and technical legal entities substantially expands and completes the spectrum of database information."

"The products consist of numerous items. Data variety should be enhanced. Products lacked adequate classification and were difficult to search for."

In addition to the five reading behaviors that were similar to those toward reading the paper catalog, the undergraduate students reported several crucial items regarding the digital catalog: (a) interactivity of media exchange (readers can often express opinions or exchange experiences online through interaction with others), (b) immediacy of feedback sharing (information can be shared with friends through built-in social functions; this provides tagging functions in on-screen reading), (c) authenticity of audio–video transmission (in addition to image and text product descriptions, multimedia or virtual reality dynamic presentations can be incorporated), (d) interoperability of service platforms (provide external connection services by connecting to other cloud computing services to complete the spectrum of viewing services), and (e) potential of diverse internationality (provide multilingual options and potential global perspectives and control information services and application opportunities).

5 Conclusion

How do readers decide between paper and on-screen reading on identical catalog content? This study showed that the selection was determined according to the properties of the text contents. Readers select the digital catalog when they want a quick overview or to acquire in-depth information of the contents. The diverse properties of the media provider increased relevant links and enhance accessible information. To seek convenient data or portability features, readers select paper catalogs. The paper catalog in this study featured a QR code that integrates cloud services in traditional paper-based publicity and marketing models, which strengthens the marketing advantage through complementary effects. Therefore, the potential development of a new media carrier among the traditional counterparts remains to be observed.

The undergraduate participants interviewed in this study preferred an on-screen reading environment. This was primarily due to the rapid and convenient properties of technological instruments and the richness of the text contents (including relevant contents and topics). For the undergraduate online users, the digital catalog provided diverse reading channels and material options, increased content richness, and facilitated immediate interactions. The present advantageous influence of the on-screen reading interface enabled the undergraduate participants to access data sources and employ diversified text processing methods instead of merely accessing information during the reading process. The World Wide Web is changing the information behaviors and reading habits of people. This study provided ITRI recommendations for enhancing the Dechnology Website (digital catalog) design:

- Presentation of audio–video technology (construct an interactive space for new media to increase technological presentation)
- Strategy on the core construct (guided search–retrieval operations; present orderly messages)
- Integration of the business platform(diversified corporate Website links; provide comprehensive services)
- Service on information tagging (readers can browse tagged content, which strengthens functional data retrieval)
- Aesthetics of the Windows environment (administrators may manage the display interface and provide a professional experience)

The ITRI has promoted an information-based catalog construct, which profits from selling existing content to readers, to provide service to innovative technological R&D institutions, industrial designers, and readers. The digital catalog emphasized the property of the contents and the development and operation of knowledge properties. Therefore, this technology and the applications thereof must be emphasized to revolutionize reading conventions.

References

1. Chen, S.C.: A Research on the behavior of catalogue Consumers—based on a catalogue company. Graduate School of Management Institute, Asian University (2005)
2. Tseng, M.L.: Non-book—eBook. Soochow Univ. Libr. Newslett. **14**, 1–30 (2002)
3. Lin, Y.C.: The Effect of Integrating Picture Books into Reading Instruction on Children's Reading Motivation and Word Recognition Ability. Graduate School of Speech and Hearing Disorders and Sciences, National Taipei University of Nursing and Health Science (2011)
4. Huang, H.C.: A Study of the relationship between reading behavior and writing attitude. Graduate School of Education, National Pingtung University of Education (2012)
5. Lin, C.M.: A survey on e-reading habits and behaviors of elementary school students in taiwan. National Central Libr. Bull. **100**(2), 30–59 (2011)
6. Wang, C.Y., Liu, S.Y., Chen, P.T., Yang, C.C.: The reader reading motivation: reading behavior and market share. J. Graph. Commun. Technol. **4**, 47–64 (1998)
7. Chou, Y.L.: Reading era: digital publishing trend of social networking site. Learn. Dev. **703**, 48–55 (2014)
8. Lin, S.J.: An exploratory study on e-reading behaviors of academic faculty. J. Libr. Inf. Stud. **1**(1), 75–92 (2003)
9. Schcolnik, M.: A Study of Reading with Dedicated E-Readers. Graduate School of Computer and Information Sciences, Nova Southeastern University (2001)
10. Pew Research Center for the People & the Press. In changing news landscape, even television is vulnerable (2012)
11. Nicholas, C.: The Shallows: What the Internet Is Doing to Our Brains. W W Norton & Co Inc., New York (2010)

"Break the Language Great Wall" (RedClay): The Language Learning Application

Ting-Yu Tony Lin, Benoit Serot, Maxime Verlhac, Marie Maniglier, Na Sun, and Pei-Luen Patrick Rau[✉]

Department of Industrial Engineering, Tsinghua University, Beijing 100084, China
{tony507yu,bntserot,maxime.verlhac}@gmail.com, marie.maniglier@ecl2015.ec-lyon.fr, sunna_15@163.com, rpl@mail.tsinghua.edu.cn

Abstract. There are more and more people moving to China for Chinese-learning. We applied the concept of "language partner" to build a language learning application for two groups of people – foreigners in China eager to discover their host language and culture and Chinese citizens wanting to improve their foreign tongues. This language-learning application is called "RedClay", a reference to the color of China and the material used in building the Great Wall. As a mobile-web application, RedClay provides social networking and learning functions (including cultural support and preference-based vocabulary lists) to help people who want to improve their foreign language abilities meet each other in real life.

Keywords: Chinese learning · Learning application · Social network · Language learning and culture · Language partner

1 Introduction

In 2010, there were more than 40 million people studying Chinese [1], and 750,000 people took the HSK Chinese proficiency test [2]. Learning Mandarin Chinese has become a pervasive need for people from different societies to get familiar with both the Chinese language and culture [3].

The utilization of information technology such as mobile devices has become an emerging trend. It is promoted by some researchers of Computer-Assisted Language Learning. For example, Chen and Li [4] describe a project which combines context/location awareness with a rudimentary kind of intelligent tutoring system. The delivery of content is based on both the user's profile, learning history and current location, taking advantage of mobility and making the learning process more interesting and contextual. Robert [5] supports the notion that language educators should encourage and assist learners' autonomy, as well as enable and provide means for learners to combine formal and informal learning. Learning becomes more efficient and permanent when tied to learners' lives outside the academic environment. Mobile devices are a great way to build this tie between users.

© Springer International Publishing Switzerland 2015
P.L.P. Rau (Ed.): CCD 2015, Part II, LNCS 9181, pp. 318–327, 2015.
DOI: 10.1007/978-3-319-20934-0_30

The use of multimedia tools can also enhance the motivation and the range of education. Sweller [6] argued that instructional design can be used to reduce the cognitive load of learners. Language self-learning could be more effective with multimedia tools, such as animations, flash cards or digital dictionaries. The motivation for learning can also be enhanced [7].

A lot of applications have been developed to teach Chinese. Many of them are simple dictionaries, but there are also more complex ones that involve innovative features. Table 1 compares seven popular Chinese learning applications of which we tried to identify their specificity. Flashcards are the most commonly used learning process. Some mobile applications such as *Hello Talk* already focus on an interaction and exchange between users. It connects two individuals eager to learn each other's language. However, the resulting relationships are not meant to develop outside the virtual world.

The aim of this study is to develop a language learning application of which the focus is set on social networking, motivation and cultural support. The application will be called "RedClay", a reference to two Chinese symbols: the red color, and clay, a material used for constructions and referring to the Great Wall of China.

2 Survey of User Needs

2.1 Target User

The university environment is conducive to finding eager-to-learn and available people. Therefore, for the first version of RedClay, we decided to limit the scope of our user-base to a student population. The target users of RedClay could thus be described as follows:

1. 20 to 30 years old university students interested in learning more about foreign cultures
2. People ready to interact through an English-Chinese relationship and make new acquaintances.

Eventually, our aim would be to extend our target population to all foreigners in China and all Chinese people wanting to find a language partner.

RedClay will be developed in two versions: one for foreign students wanting to learn Chinese, and one for Chinese students wanting to learn another language and more specifically English. Those two versions shall also enable the app to identify the type of user in order to suggest a contact only between a foreign and a Chinese student. In order to figure out what would be the main functions offered by RedClay to its users, a survey was conducted.

As this survey was meant to identify the needs of the whole target population, we made two versions of it: one for international students and another for Chinese students. We got answers from 63 Chinese students and 45 international students.

Table 1. Comparison of popular Chinese learning applications

Pleco	• Great dictionaries -- It offers many input possibilities: English, Pinyin, Chinese characters, voice and pictures (OCR). • Flashcard System -- It provides flashcards to help the user memorize vocabulary. • Advanced function -- It has developed and now offers sentence propositions and an apprenticeship module. The most basic version is free but some options are not.
Anki Flashcards	• Flashcard System & community -- Ankidroid is based on "cards" and "decks" which you can download freely through the internet. These decks are created and evaluated by members, so there is an Ankidroid community. • SRS algorithm – Spaced repetition software, test users based on memorization. • Memory card -- Ankidroid is not only for languages learners, but also for anything that can require the creation of a flashcard deck. • Exercise -- Users can define the amount of card they want to study. The cards are mostly used to enable people to learn new vocabulary and they have the form of small exercises.
Hello Talk	• Online communication -- It basically works like an international "whatsapp". The user can write and send vocal messages to people whose mother tongue is the one he wishes to learn. • Record -- Hello Talk gives one the possibility to listen, write, and translate messages automatically. Users can save messages they wish to revisit later, and record themselves. • Localization -- Users can freely decide to activate localization so that they can meet each other in real life.
Skritter	• Chinese characters writing -- It is meant to make the user review specific words and characters, their tones (through audio samples) and how to write them (in the right order). It also includes a translating function for single words. • SRS algorithm -- test users based on memorization. • Fee -- Around 15 US dollars per month.
Hello HSK	• HSK test -- Helping users progress in HSK Chinese test norms and evaluations is the main purpose of Hello HSK. • Training -- It has 6 training levels, and each of them is again subdivided in the different exam parts (Writing, Listening Comprehension, and Reading). The user can evaluate his level (and hence his progression) through exercises and training. It also provides corresponding lessons consisting of vocabulary, grammar points and common expressions. • Simulation test -- It provides the simulation test in order to understand the scores.
Chinese Character	• Culture-transmitting -- It focuses on Chinese characters and their evolution (from the original representation to present-day simplified symbols). It gives the meaning of the characters in 8 languages including Chinese and English. It is interesting for users who want to discover more about Chinese symbols.
Chinese Writer	• Chinese characters writing -- The learning process uses character packs. There are several difficulties, some are for casual use and others are designed for the HSK test. • Personalization & sharing -- Users can create new packs. Moreover, these packs can be shared with friends online.

2.2   Result

2.2.1   Students and Languages

Most of the international students that were surveyed would like or strongly wish to learn Chinese. 40 % of international students even ticked "I came here to learn Chinese". In addition to this, 62 % of the international students currently use a Chinese learning app (mainly the ones tested in Table 1: Pleco and Ankidroid).

Chinese students are interested in English (75 %), German (33 %), Japanese (32 %) and French (27 %) and 41 % of them use learning applications to learn foreign languages.

2.2.2   Friendships

20 % of international students estimate they have 10 or more Chinese friends. 42 % of them have 3 or less, and the remaining 38 % declare they have around 5. The Chinese students' repartition is more extreme as 25 % of them don't have any international student friends while 35 % have 10 or more.

84 % of the international students would like to meet more Chinese students and 9 out of 10 would like to meet them as friends rather than "Chinese teacher only" (7 %) or "Chinese guide" (4 %). Results are similar for Chinese students as 92 % of them would like to meet more international students, mostly as friends (in a same proportion: 90 %). 73 % of the international students and 68 % of Chinese students are eager to meet new students through an app.

2.2.3   Joint Activities

More than half of the international students are interested by most the activities we suggested in the questionnaire, especially learning Chinese (73 %), cultural activities (64 %), traveling and playing games (62 %), playing sports and visiting places around Beijing (60 %). Having lunch or dinner on campus (58 %), cooking (56 %) and going out to eat (51 %). The repartition is almost the same among Chinese students, although they ticked on average less boxes, so that the percentages are lower overall. The order as also differs: learning a foreign language ranks first (62 %), then traveling (56 %), doing sports (44 %), playing games (40 %), having lunch or dinner on campus (37 %), going out to eat (33 %), visiting places around Beijing (33 %), cooking (32 %) and cultural activities (27 %).

3   Development

3.1   Main Idea

RedClay is a mobile-web language learning application, coded in HTML5 and PHP. RedClay aims at motivating language learners to master a foreign language. The design of RedClay is based on the creation of strong "language partner" relationships. A "language partner" relationship involves real contact and intellectual enrichment through everyday life situations and activities.

As a complex language, Chinese consists of distinct aspects: Reading, Writing and Speaking. Linking written and oral Chinese requires practice because it is not phonetically intuitive [8]. The objective of RedClay is not to provide full lists of vocabulary and lessons to users learning a foreign language. Its aim is to give them few key words in relation with different fields in order to start a conversation with their language partner about a subject and learn from him/her directly.

Such interactions involve various assets RedClay relied on during the development process: social networking, motivation and cultural support.

Social networking is an upcoming trend in language learning. It has been found that social networks significantly influence learners' performance [9, 10]. According to Benson and Avery [11], the digital generation is more willing to access information and interact with others through the internet. Motivation has a major effect in learning efficiency [12]. Therefore, RedClay tries to raise the level of involvement by giving users the possibility of doing common activities according to their interests. It is impossible to ignore the relationship between language and culture. Second language acquisition is bound to second culture assimilation [13]. According to Kuo [14], culture and language affect each other. Language is the epitome of the speaker's culture, and culture relies on the philosophy, religion, economic and social position of the individual.

A language learning application with cultural support can benefit from the features of Social Network Sites (SNS) and the importance of culture. It provides a new learning process where users can interact and learn from each other.

3.2   Information Architecture

Figure 1 is the information architecture of RedClay. The red borders represent the main functions of the application.

Every page is in Chinese or in English depending on the choice of the user during the registration phase. The welcome page has to be bilingual.

A user viewpoint is going to be used in order to explain the information architecture. First, the user arrives on the welcome page (Fig. 2). He/she then has two choices: whether to log in or to register. If he/she does not have an account, the user has to register which can be done in two steps. The first step is to fill in personal information (left side of Fig. 3). The second step consists of setting user preferences (right side of Fig. 3). Once the user finishes the registration, the account is created. The user is then able to log in on the welcome page and access to the homepage.

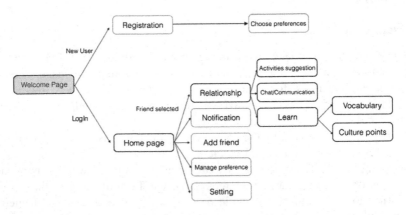

Fig. 1. Information architecture of the application

In the homepage, several relationships are available and are sorted according to frequency of interaction. The user can select one of his/her language partners and manage their relationship. Some activities are suggested according to the common interests of the user and his/her language partner. Users can also chat with their friends

Fig. 2. Welcome page

Fig. 3. Registration pages: registration info on the left and Interests on the right.

and access to the learning section of the application. On the learning page, the topics they both are interested in are shown in priority. Users can find some useful vocabulary words and interesting cultural points to discuss with their language partners.

3.3 Social Network

Social Network Sites provide new ways for language learners to interact and connect with one another. According to Harrison [15], SNS can help language learners to explore new relationships. By implementing the concept of "pedagogy 2.0" and "language partner", RedClay tries to build a platform for language learners with common interests meet each other. RedClay mainly provides:

(1) **Preference-based recommendations.** RedClay is trying to help users find language partners who share common interests to raise their motivation for learning.

(2) **Suggestions.** RedClay provides activity suggestions to "language couples" based on their common interests – such as doing sport or trying traditional food together – to help them interact from online to offline and enhance the cultural understanding.

(3) **Learning support.** RedClay offers specific topics, vocabulary lists, and related culture points for each "language couple" to help them have a profound and contextual interaction.

3.4   Interest

The design of the two-steps registration procedure (personal information form and preferences choice), is shown on Fig. 3. After registration, users can start searching for language partners with common interests and receive invitations from other users. For example, Amber is a female exchange student from the U.K currently in China. During her registration on RedClay, she chooses Chinese cooking, Athletics, playing Mahjong, and visiting Beijing as her preferences. In the "Add friend" page, she can find some language partners with similar preferences and send them invitations. She can accept or cancel invitations by checking the notifications, as shown on Fig. 4.

Fig. 4. From Left to Right: Notification tab, Home Page, and a Relationship Page

In the sidebar, "Add interests" and "Setting" allow the user to change his/her interests and password. In the homepage, users can check their language partner lists and manage their relationships.

3.5   Friendship

The core of the application is the management of relationships between language partners. In the relationship page, RedClay provides each "language couple" with activity suggestions based on their common interests. For example, as Amber and Tony both like Athletics, Chinese cooking, playing Mahjong and Visiting Beijing, they both can see suggestions related to these preferences in their relationship page. RedClay also provides a chat function that allows users to communicate and discuss their availabilities. There are 34 categories of vocabulary provided in the learning section. They follow an order based on the preferences both friends choose. As an illustration, for Amber and Tony: Athletics, Chinese cooking, playing Mahjong, and visiting Beijing will consist of the top four ranking, so that they can quickly access vocabulary and cultural information in these subjects.

3.6 Vocabulary/Cultural Support

In the learning page, the user can select one topic that he/she wants to learn about. The topics shared with his/her friend are suggested in priority. The board where the user can choose a topic is shown on the left side of Fig. 5.

Fig. 5. From Left to right: Learning page, Chinese cooking page where "dumpling" has been selected, Cultural point page.

After selecting a topic, the user arrives to the screen in the middle of Fig. 5 (Chinese cooking, in this example). The vocabulary lists display within three levels and the user can choose one of them. By clicking on a word, the user can make the pinyin and the English word appear. This part is useful for those who want to learn some new words or have a discussion with their friends.

The cultural exchange in the language partner relationship is also a priority. The user can access cultural points from the vocabulary page. All the cultural points of the topic are shown on the screen with a title and a description as seen on right side of Fig. 5. This part is useful for users who want to deeply understand culture differences through in-depth communication modes.

4 Contents of RedClay

4.1 Categories

The categories and subcategories come from the results of the survey. RedClay includes the following categories: Basic (to enable users to actually learn the basics of Chinese or a foreign language), Sports, Cooking, Playing Games, Going out (including cultural activities), Travelling (including traveling and visiting places around Beijing), Miscellaneous (including other subcategories that seemed relevant to us).

4.2 Sub-categories/Topics

All subcategories included various subcategories detailed in Table 2. In each subcategory, we decided to sort the vocabulary we provided according to 3 different levels of language. It would enable users to improve their level with new words of vocabulary.

To these words of vocabulary were added cultural points for both Chinese and international students related to each subcategories.

Table 2. Categories and subcategories

BASICS	Greetings, Numbers, Moving around
SPORTS	Football, Basketball, Martial Arts, Racquet Sports, Athletics, Water Sports, Mountain Sports, Others
COOKING	French, Chinese, Japanese, Moroccan, Italian, Mexican, Ingredients, Utensils
PLAYING GAMES	Mahjong, Chess, Cards, Other Games
GOING OUT	Visit Beijing restaurants & bar, Karaoke, Others
TRAVELLING	Transport, Beijing, Accommodation
MISCELLANEOUS	Western festivals, Chinese Festivals, University, Politics

5 Conclusion

RedClay is a mobile-web application aiming at motivating learners to master a foreign language. By implementing the concept of language partners, RedClay offers a new source of motivation and tries to help each "language couple" interact from online to offline. In real-live interactions, each "language couple" may do activities suggested by RedClay and have language and culture exchanges.

Acknowledgment. This study was funded by a Natural Science Foundation China grant 71188001 and State Key Lab of Automobile Safety and Energy.

References

1. Confucius Institute Headquarters (2010)

2. Liu, L.: "Chinese language proficiency test becoming popular in Mexico", 27 June 2011. Accessed 12 September 2013

3. Bianco, L.J.: Advantage plus identity: neat discourse, loose connection: singapore's medium of instruction policy. In: Vaish, V., Gopinathan, S., Liu, Y. (eds.) Language, Capital, Culture: Critical Studies of Language and Education in Singapore, pp. 5–22. Sense Publishers, Rotterdam (2007)

4. Chen, C.-M., Li, Y.-L.: Personalized context-aware ubiquitous learning system for supporting effective English vocabulary learning. Interact. Learn. Environ. 18(4), 341–364 (2010)

5. Godwin-Jones, R.: Emerging technologies: mobile apps for language learning. Lang. Learn. Technol. 15(2), 2–11 (2011)

6. Sweller, J.: Cognitive load during problem solving: effects on learning. Cogn. Sci. 12(2), 257–285 (1988). doi:10.1016/0364-0213(88)90023-7

7. Chuang, H.Y., Ku, H.Y.: The effect of computer-based multimedia instruction with Chinese character recognition. Educ. Media Int. 48(1), 27–41 (2011)

8. Krashen, S.D.: Second Language Acquisition and Second Language Learning. Pergamon Press, Oxford (1981)

9. Cho, H., Gay, G., Davidson, B., Ingraffea, A.: Social networks, communication styles, and learning performance in a CSCL community. Comput. Educ. 49(2), 309–329 (2007)

10. De Jorge Moreno, J.: Using social network and dropbox in blended learning: an application to university education. Bus. Manage. Educ. 2, 220–231 (2012)

11. Benson, V., Avery, B.: Embedding web 2.0 strategies in learning and teaching. In: Lytras, M.D., Damiani, E., Pablos, P.O. (eds.) Web 2.0 , pp. 1–12. Springer, USA (2007)

12. Mondahl, M., Razmerita, L.: Social media, collaboration and social learning – a case-study of foreign language learning. Electron. J. E-Learn. 12(4), 339–352 (2014)

13. Spackman, C.L.: Culture and Second Language Acquisition (2009)

14. Kuo, M.M., Lai, C.C.: Linguistics across cultures: the impact of culture on second language learning. Online Submission, 1(1) (2006)

15. Harrison, R., Thomas, M.: Identity in online communities: social networking sites and language learning. Int. J. Emerg. Technol. Soc. 7(2), 109–124 (2009)

Interact Through Your Data: Collective Immersive Experience Design for Indoor Exercises

Xu Lin, Linkai Tao, Bin Yu, Yongyan Guo, and Jun Hu[✉]

Eindhoven University of Technology,
Den Dolech 2, 5612AZ Eindhoven, Netherlands
{X.Lin, L.Tao, B.Yu, Y.Guo, J.Hu}@tue.nl

Abstract. This paper presents an explorative design for improving indoor exercising experience, through real-time data visualization and social connection in an immersive environment. A prototype was designed and implemented based on the review of related research on cognitive and mental models. Facing existing design challenges, the project aims to find potential opportunities for future indoor exercises, and explore the relationship between the immersive user experience and users' intention of exercising.

Keywords: Immersive experience · Data visualization · Social interaction · Indoor exercising

1 Introduction

1.1 Background

Regular exercising in daily life, such as running, cycling and swimming, is considered to be beneficial for people in both physical and mental health.

To increase the efficiency of exercise, large numbers of professional fitness machines have been invented to help in controlling the quality of posture and movement, improving the pertinence of individuals' fitness plans, and saving our time.

However, besides the benefits brought by the machines, there are also varieties of drawbacks, especially from the perspective of user experience, such as being stuck indoor with unchanged environment, getting abstract and confusing data as feedback, and feeling being isolated by the machines.

These disadvantages could gradually drive regular exercising in recent days into a lonely, boring and repeated process. It is hard for many to carrying on doing the exercises for a longer period of time. Boredom, loneliness and no obvious progress are common excuses for many to quit their exercises for fitness.

A better context for people to keep regular exercising is to experience an enjoyable or interesting process with their friends together at the same place, which is usually difficult to accomplish in real life. It gives opportunities for research and design practice to explore new concepts and solutions to improve current situations.

© Springer International Publishing Switzerland 2015
P.L.P. Rau (Ed.): CCD 2015, Part II, LNCS 9181, pp. 328–337, 2015.
DOI: 10.1007/978-3-319-20934-0_31

1.2   Related Work

A lot of studies have been done to improve the indoor exercising experience. Currently, there are two typical research directions: one is to simulate the real sports environment or create virtual immersive environment [1, 2]; the other is to combine the exercises with (online) gaming elements [3]. There are also improvements on extended service like long-term data recording and analysis.

Simulation of the real environment helps to build up an immersive experience with familiar outdoor scenes in exercising, and enriches the experience by adding natural factors onto indoor training. For example, some cycling machines provide different exercising modes to simulate outdoor contexts like climbing a mountain or riding along a road.[1] The creation of virtual immersive environment can provide people with more engaged and fresh experience that they may not have indoor in real life. However, these research directions seldom focus on creating social connection for users.

The direction to combine indoor exercising with game factors, especially online game modes, focuses more on facilitating social interaction and creating playful experience through gaming mechanics,[2] while the exercising quality is no longer a core of the sporting process.

With the maturity of sensing technology and social media, applications and services have been implemented to motivate people to do exercises through making use of psychological factors in competitions. These products and systems also provide users new approaches to record and share their achievements with others, and are becoming increasingly intelligent in giving appropriate advices based on the analysis of long-term exercising records.[3] Yet, these design concepts suit more in providing support services rather than improving the real-time experience during the exercises.

Based on observation on related work, it indicates that there is still a need to explore more possibilities for improving indoor exercising experience and evoking users' intention of exercising in places like gymnasium and sports center.

Compared with existing solutions, the design project presented here pays more attention to creating a real-time and immersive experience in digitally augmented indoor environment. It focuses on two major design problems: one is how to create an immersive but functional exercising experience, which can transform the abstract numbers from the sensors into understandable information or intuitive feelings to help users improve their exercising quality; the other is how to facilitate the sense of being accompanied through social connection and collective exercising with others.

In order to deal with the design challenges, we conducted a theoretical review to obtain a better understanding of potential methods and tools. A design framework was created and followed, aiming at bringing users a new indoor exercising experience, in order to evoke and strengthen users' intention of exercising and improve the quality of

---

[1] How to Ride Inside: Indoor Trainer Workouts for Cyclists, http://www.bicycling.com/training-nutrition/training-fitness/how-ride-inside-indoor-trainer-workouts-cyclists.

[2] Play It: Soccer Becomes a Virtual Sport in Barcelona, http://www.moodmedia.se/newsdetail.asp?catid=2&id=3084.

[3] Six running apps to keep you fit for 2012, http://www.phonesreview.co.uk/2012/05/24/6-running-apps-to-keep-you-fit-for-2012/.

their exercises. A prototype was implemented based on the design framework during the hackathon event in Eindhoven, called SPRINT14.[4]

2 Collective Immersive Experience

Usually, indoor places for exercising are public, except personal environment (e.g. living room or bedroom at home), and there are lots of people in exercising, which shows potentials to provide them with a collective and immersive experience. A common method is to facilitate the immersive experience in the surrounding environment by enhancing the atmosphere around with visual or multi-modal augmentation.

2.1 Immersive Environment for Indoor Exercises

Immersive virtual environment (IVE) technology shows the potential in improving indoor exercising experience and enhancing the enjoyment of using. Taking advantages of virtual reality (VR), extrinsic and intrinsic motivations can be applied to evoke users' intention of exercising.

Immersion and presence are two important properties of virtual environments [4]. Since the feeling of presence is positively correlated to enjoyment [5], IVE usually emphasizes the feeling of "being there", which "requires a self-representation in the virtual environment - a virtual body" [4], according to Slater and Wilbur (1997).

While in the context of indoor exercising, users need to focus on their physical bodies, rather than the virtual body, which indicates that only digitally augmenting the environment is not enough for users who exercise regularly, as they need to pay attention to the quality of their physical exercises as well.

It is also related to users' understanding of the abstract data presented on equipment's dashboard panels. It is not so easy for people to transform the data into an intuitional feeling of how well they are doing. Even if they can understand the data after getting familiar to the functions, the reading and transforming process is still a distraction from exercising. There is a need to provide more direct or intuitive feedback to help them in real-time self-evaluation and adjustment.

Moreover, although a higher sense of presence does associate with a stronger feeling of enjoyment, it also brings possibilities in blocking social interactions and isolating users in the same indoor space.

Thus, in this context, instead of creating an immersive virtual reality environment, we tried to keep users immersed by enhancing the interplay between their exercising status and the visualization of physiological data, and to provide opportunities for social interaction. The abstract physiological data was transformed into intuitively understandable feedback through vivid and metaphorical data visualization, and projected into the physical environment, changing along with users' real-time exercising status.

---

[4] The website of SPRINT14, http://www.sprint14.nl/.

2.2   Related Study on Cognition and Mental Models

In order to facilitate the immersive experience through visualization of the physiological data, a design framework is created based on the literature review on related notions and models, including the model of users' intention, the cognitive hierarchy, and mental model in data visualization.

Users' intention of doing exercises. Literature review on user acceptance model showed the potential of explaining the user's intention of exercising and providing a guideline for design.

Figure 1 shows the basic model that explains the relation between users' intention and their actual behaviour. It is based on the theory of planned behaviour model (TPB) [6], which is an extension of the most widely used model called theory of reasoned action (TRA) [7]. The upper blue area shows the TRA and the entire figure shows the TPB. The main difference between two models is Perceived Behavioural Control.

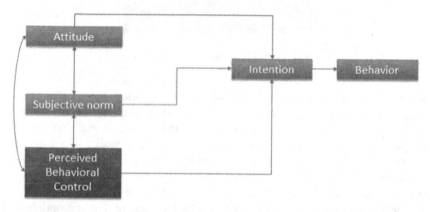

Fig. 1. Theory of reasoned action and theory of planned behaviour

Ajzen indicates that the combination of attitude towards the behaviour, subjective norms, and perception of behavioural control (Fig. 1) plays an important role in the actual behaviour execution [8]. People's subjective norms, which can be considered as "a kind of grammar of social interaction", change slowly through the social behaviour [9]. Furthermore, the easier users perceive that they can control the behaviour, the stronger their intention to perform the behaviour becomes [8].

In our context of indoor exercising, we mainly explored two design problems based on this model: (1) whether a better understanding of users' exercising status gives users a stronger perceived behaviour control, and results in stronger intention of taking the action; (2) whether the social interaction during the exercise will positively influence user's subjective norms and intention of taking the action.

Cognitive Hierarchy. Figure 2 shows the hierarchy of cognition [10], which indicates the process of knowledge generation in intelligence systems. It can be used to explain not only the process in computing system (e.g. the exercising assistance system), but also the process in human mind.

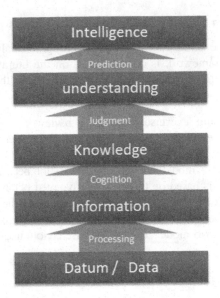

Fig. 2. The cognitive hierarchy [10]

At the bottom of Fig. 2, in the context of indoor exercising, the internal exercising data (e.g. users' physiological data) and external data (e.g. the environment data) basically present the facts, and are processed into information in the next step.

To gain knowledge from information, users' cognition works as an interpreter, translating information into knowledge, with which users can recognize the situation in a general context. When there is enough knowledge about the exercise, users can achieve an understanding of the exercising status by judging the knowledge. The final step is intelligence, which is used to support decision-making. An appropriate understanding gained from former steps will help users predict their exercising status and adjust their performance.

The cognitive hierarchy shows the process of how the external and internal data being transformed into knowledge that can help users to evaluate and adjust their performance in exercising process. And it indicates that the step of transforming information into knowledge through cognition plays an important role in obtaining good understanding to influence users' intention of exercising.

Mental models for data visualization. Considering the cognitive hierarchy mentioned above, current information presentation applied by many existing indoor exercising systems leaves a gap between information and knowledge. Most data cannot be made full use of in a smooth and continuous process. While it is suggested in many related studies that mental models can work as a joint in between [11, 12].

Mental models have been defined as an internal representation of concepts, which is considered to be critical for cognition theories. Since they are mental structures, they are used to infer novel knowledge, which is the deeper understanding of presented information [13], and have strong influences on users' knowledge construction. In visual analytics process [11], abstract knowledge is generated from information by users' mental models. In the case of indoor exercising system design, mental models will be engaged for ensuring that understandable knowledge is provided to users.

2.3   Design Framework

Based on the combination of mentioned models, we propose a design framework for indoor exercising (Fig. 3). In this framework, data has been divided into two categories, and information will be processed into different potential knowledge.

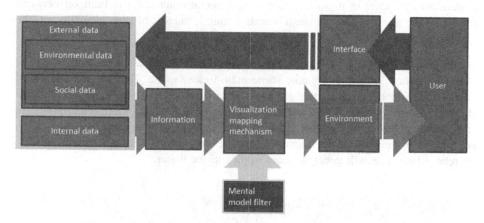

Fig. 3. Design framework for indoor exercises

Internal data will be collected to present the exercising status, such as users' heart rate and the calories burned during the exercises. External data, including both the indoor environmental data and users' social data, will also be collected to help project visualized information into the physical space and create potential social connection between users.

Users' mental models are used to create a mental model filter, and a visualization mapping mechanism is designed for more appropriate data transformation and knowledge generation based on this filter. The generated knowledge will be projected into the physical environment to create an immersive experience. Since the knowledge is generated by the mapping mechanism, based on users' mental models, the understanding should be more suitable and accurate. After obtaining a better understanding of the exercising status, users can better adjust their performance and interact with others though the visualization in the environment.

3   Project RIPPLE

3.1   Concept Implementation

Concept for prototype. The concept "RIPPLE" entails an interactive immersive environment for cycling exercises. The goal of the project is to offer a better user experience by creating an immersive environment and an interactive visualization. The prototype was initially constructed during a two-day hackathon event, called SPRINT14 in Eindhoven, and became one of the winning concepts to be further developed, due to the novel immersive experience and the delighting social connection it might bring to users.

The metaphorical data visualization is employed to present users' exercising status and exercise-related physiological data (e.g. heart rate and calories). Compared to the traditional graphic or numeric display, the interactive visualization is assumed to feedback the sport and bodily information to the users in a more intuitional and understandable way. In multi-user contexts, a social connection is built up between users in the same space through the dynamic changes of the elements in the visualization.

Visualization Design. As shown in Fig. 4, we selected the 'sea' as the background of the visualization; it renders a nature scene in an indoor space. The size and amount of waves under the cycling machine are mapped from the cycling speed, which creates a dramatic effect, as if the user is riding across the surface of the water. The ripples are triggered by the user's heartbeats. The idea here is to present a sweat-breaking process of cycling exercises. As the intensity and the duration of the exercise increasing, increased heart rate will generate more ripples in the water.

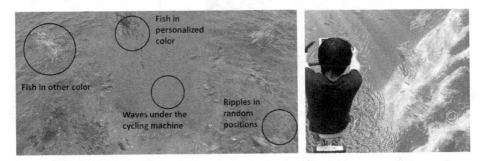

Fig. 4. Visualization design in the project

To promote social bonding or connections in a 'light-weight' way with little extra operation and distraction from exercising, we use the "abstract fish" as the symbol of users; the amount of the fish of one user will be mapped to the calories she burnt in the exercise. The fish appear around the user initially, and as the exercising time passes by, the fish will swim outside to 'communicate' with the fish of other users. This process is designed to create a social bonding and a collective exercising experience, breaking the individuals' isolated status and providing users with more fun and motivation.

Data collection. In this prototype, a phytoplethysmograph (PPG) sensor is used to measure pulse signals from the participant's index finger. Compared to ECG electrode, the biggest advantage of the optimal PPG is being easy to use. Participants do not need to attach gel-coated electrodes on their chest. Heart rate data is calculated from pulse signal and used in in real-time. The calories burned during the exercise session are estimated by using the following formula: $C = (0.4472 \times H - 0.05741 \times W + 0.074 \times A - 20.4022) \times T/4.184$ [14]. C is the number of calories burned, H is the average heart rate, W is the weight, A is the user' age and T is the length of the exercise session in minutes.

Set-up. In order not to interrupt the exercise process, the visualization is projected on the floor, under the cycling machine (Fig. 5). A projector is fixed on a frame above and in front of the cycling machine. A cycling machine is placed on a white curtain tiled on the ground. The visualization program is developed in Processing.

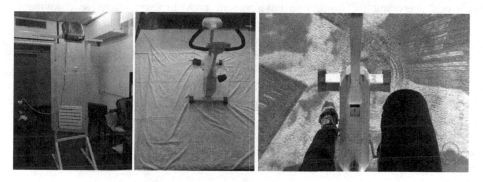

Fig. 5. The set-up of the 'Ripple'

3.2 Social Interaction Through Exercising Data

Besides the real-time interplay between users and the visualized data, the potential social connection between users is also explored, in order to create a collective exercising experience, breaking the individuals' isolated status and providing users with more fun and motivation.

Since the context of doing regular exercises with friends together is hard to realize for many in daily life, design concepts are explored, for example, facilitating interaction between people who are doing exercise at the same place.

The indoor exercising space holds the potential to provide users with a social environment, while it is usually hard for strangers to break the ice and socially interact with each other. There is a need to help them create the connection that will neither make them feel embarrassed nor interrupt their exercises.

Compared with the solutions that connect friends online for gaming or communication, we prefer to enhance the connection at same indoor places, based on the physiological data visualization.

The social interaction in this context is to connect users by facilitating cooperation through the visualization, raising social awareness between people via its lively movements and changes [15], and providing a collective feeling of being accompanied or appreciated in exercising. When people are connected, the interaction between their data and the impact brought towards the whole augmented environment will change along with the cooperation. For example, if all the users are exercising in a standard or high-quality status, the collective visualization may transform into a more harmonic presentation as a reward or general feedback for their efforts.

3.3 Next Steps

The design concept introduced in this paper tries to transform the indoor space into an immersive environment for exercising people through ambient projection. The whole design aims to help users concentrate on their exercising while being aware of their exercising status (e.g. standard or not).

In addition, instead of connecting with friends online to socially interact through avatars or images, we explore the possibilities to highlight or create social connection between the people who are doing co-located exercising. The social interaction between users and the immersive environment provide users intensive enjoyment, which can be considered as an intrinsic motivation for taking regular exercises.

For the next steps, iterations of the design framework and the prototype will be conducted, in order to deploy further design research on the relation between the immersive experience and users' engagement and motivation towards indoor exercising.

The mechanism of mental models needs to be further developed and tested, in order to work as an instrument for knowledge selection and visualization mapping in a certain context.

The long-term data recording may be added into the system for a better self-evaluation and real-time analysis of users' exercising status. The recording can also be used for socially motivating users by combining it with current social service.

4 Conclusion

In the presented project, we focus on creating an immersive experience through data visualization, creating and enhancing social interactions between co-located exercising people.

To evoke and strengthen users' intention of exercising, literature study on cognitive psychology, immersive virtual reality, and user acceptance was conducted. A design framework was used to guide the visualization design process for indoor exercising context, such as gymnasium and sport center. A prototype was implemented based on the design framework, using the sea and fish as metaphor to create an interactive immersive environment for indoor cycling context.

Through this design, we hope to create an interesting, motivating and unique experience for indoor exercising through data visualization and ambient projection in physical space.

Acknowledgments. We would like to thank China Scholarship Council for the support on the design research. We also thank MADspace Eindhoven and InnoSportLab Sport en Beweeg and all the sponsors of SPRINT14 for the support on the event.

References

1. Poussard, B., et al.: 3DLive: a multi-modal sensing platform allowing tele-immersive sports applications. In: 22nd Signal Processing Conference (EUSIPCO), pp. 356–360. IEEE: Lisbon, Portugal (2014)

2. Pallot, M., et al.: Augmented sport: exploring collective user experience. In: Virtual Reality International Conference: Laval Virtual, pp. 1–8. ACM: Laval, France (2013)
3. Mueller, F., Agamanolis, S., Picard, R.: Exertion interfaces: sports over a distance for social bonding and fun. In: SIGCHI Conference on Human Factors in Computing Systems, pp. 561–568. ACM: Ft. Lauderdale, Florida, USA (2003)
4. Slater, M., Wilbur, S.: A framework for immersive virtual environments (FIVE): speculations on the role of presence in virtual environments. Teleoperators Virtual Environ. 6, 603–616 (1997)
5. Ijsselsteijn, W.A., de Kort, Y.A.W., Westerink, J., de Jage, M.: Virtual fitness: stimulating exercise behavior through media technology. Presence Teleoperators Virtual Environ. 15(6), 688–698 (2006). MIT Press
6. Ajzen, I.: The theory of planned behavior. Organ. Behav. Hum. Decis. Process. 50(2), 179–211 (1991)
7. Fishbein, M., Ajzen, I.: Belief, Attitude, Intention and Behavior: An Introduction to Theory and Research. Addison-Wesley, Reading (1975)
8. Ajzen, I.: Constructing a theory of planned behavior questionnaire (2014). http://www.researchgate.net/publication/235913732_Constructing_a_Theory_of_Planned_Behavior_Questionnaire
9. Bicchieri, C., Muldoon, R.: Social Norms, Stanford Encyclopedia of Philosophy. http://plato.stanford.edu/entries/social-norms/#Con
10. Cox, J.: Intelligence: Definitions, Concepts and Governance. Parliamentary Information and Research Service, Library of Parliament (2009)
11. Liu, Z., Stasko, J.T.: Mental models, visual reasoning and interaction in information visualization: a top-down perspective. Vis. Comput. Graph. 16(6), 999–1008 (2010). IEEE
12. Mueller, K., Garg, S., et al.: Can computers master the art of communication? a focus on visual analytics. IEEE Comput. Graph. Appl. 3(31), 14–21 (2011). IEEE
13. Rapp, D.N.: Mental Models: Theoretical Issues for Visualizations in Science Education. Models and Modeling in Science Education, pp. 43–60. Springer, Netherlands (2005)
14. Keytel, L.R., et al.: Prediction of energy expenditure from heart rate monitoring during submaximal exercise. J. Sports Sci. 23(3), 289–297 (2005)
15. Hu, J., Le, D., Funk, M., Wang, F., Rauterberg, M.: Attractiveness of an interactive public art installation. In: Streitz, N., Stephanidis, C. (eds.) DAPI 2013. LNCS, vol. 8028, pp. 430–438. Springer, Heidelberg (2013)

Leap-Motion Based Online Interactive System for Hand Rehabilitation

Zhe Liu[1(✉)], Yingzhi Zhang[1], Pei-Luen Patrick Rau[1], Pilsung Choe[2], and Tauseef Gulrez[2]

[1] Department of Industrial Engineering, Tsinghua University, Beijing, China
{zheliu1992,zhangyz.0208}@gmail.com,
rpl@mail.tsinghua.edu.cn
[2] Department of Mechanical and Industrial Engineering,
Qatar University, Doha, Qatar
pschoe@gmail.com, gtauseef@qu.edu.qa

Abstract. Insufficient recognition to hand afunction caused by overwork, injury and geratic complications leads to inadequate auxiliary for hand rehabilitation. Patients' rehabilitative training is usually limited to rehabilitation center in hospitals, leaving their time at home inefficient for precise recovery.

In this paper, we introduced an online interactive system for hand rehabilitation based on Leap Motion controller. We established this system for doctor, on which they can prescribe patient to imitate standard exercise motion and get automatic feedback, such as score, according to similarity, thus enhance rehabilitation effect. In pilot study, we recruited 4 rehabilitation doctors and 8 patients to investigate core requirements for rehabilitation and then developed this system based on their expectation. After briefly presentation of the first version prototype to doctors, we got evaluation showing that the Leap-Motion-Based interactive system for hand rehabilitation can be effective for better independent training, and designating a direction for future work as well.

Keywords: Hand rehabilitation · Natural Free-Hand interaction · Leap motion controller · Hand tracking

1 Introduction

Hands, as the most dexterous part of our body, are of vital importance to our everyday life. However, since hands are extensively used in nearly all tasks, they are exposed in more dangerous environment than any other parts. Overwork, injury and geratic complications, such as stroke can all cause hand afunction, totally or partially, which directly diminish the quality of life. According to the statistics from World Health Organization (WHO) 2014, rehabilitation and palliative care has not been given enough attention and essential basic equipment is still not available everywhere, not only in most developing countries, but also in some developed countries [1], thus many patients of hand afunction cannot be provided prevention, diagnosis or treatment.

In addition, unlike other diseases, hand impairment and afunction require sufficient patient's exercise besides doctor's treatment. Exact motion exercise can profoundly help with patient's rehabilitation [2]. However, currently there is no other method than

P.L.P. Rau (Ed.): CCD 2015, Part II, LNCS 9181, pp. 338–347, 2015.
DOI: 10.1007/978-3-319-20934-0_32

doctor's judgment telling patients what to exercise and how they exercise, and patients only exercise their finger and thumb by repeatedly fisting or picking up small items during their long time staying at home, without doctor's instructions. Thus, there is a potential demand of designing a hand rehabilitation system to utilize patients' time at home to exercise accurate motion training.

The key procedure of designing such an exercising system is to reproduce the training atmosphere in hospital for patients who need hand rehabilitation [3]. Previous studies [4, 5] have shown that following and imitating are effective in motivating training and increasing exercising accuracy. We used the user-centered design approach to innovate an interactive rehabilitation system for patients to encourage their exercises at home and meanwhile provide them with direct instructions. Their finger movements above the Leap Motion sensor are tracked and projected to a computer screen where they can see standard motions and their own motions at the same time. The Leap Motion-based rehabilitation system, both easy and efficient to exercise, is considered to be very helpful in motivating patients to exercise at home as well as correcting their inaccurate motions.

This article firstly introduces an analysis of interviews we conducted with patients, doctors. We collected their opinions and preferences for both real and interactive exercise to generate a list of requirements which is used in the later design of the system. Shortcomings of current indoor sports equipment are summarized with a brief introduction of the Leap Motion-based system in Sect. 4. A detailed illustration of the design of the rehabilitation system is then presented. Some improvements based on a usability test are suggested. Discussion and conclusions are summarized in the last section.

2 Background and Related Work

Generally, hand rehabilitation, which focuses on recovery of both strength and nimbleness [2, 3], causes for professional training in rehabilitation center and long-term persistent self-exercise. According to present medical care situation in China, most patient can only afford one or two treatments in hospitals per week, which is considerably insufficient for rehabilitation. Improving the efficiency of patients' self-exercise at home is a key method to reduce rehabilitation time and increase rehabilitation effect.

The human-computer interaction community has made attempts and carried out researches to enhance hand rehabilitation with HCI technologies. Khademi, M. et al. [6] modified the game "Fruit Ninja" with Leap Motion controller for patients with stroke to practice arm and hand. Boulanger et al. [8] built a game, as well, using Microsoft Surface's hand position. These games and researches involve new or existing interaction games and adapt them into hand control mode to encourage rehabilitation. Another example of hand rehabilitation is an interactive glove proposed by Hallam et al. [9] to help patients with stroke with hand reuniting. There is also another glove-based treatment system called HandTutor [10] focusing on finger rehabilitation. The above researches show examples about tangible and intangible interaction rehabilitation designs. Yet, rehabilitation system using free-hand interaction for patients' self-exercise and introducing doctor's instruction still remains to be investigated.

3 User Requirement Gathering: Interview

System design was started by an interview of 4 doctors and 8 patients, who need hand rehabilitation, in a Grade III-A Hospital in Beijing, China, which is a top grade hospital according to Chinese grading system and runs fully functional rehabilitation center.

3.1 Interview with Doctors

To study the general procedure of hand rehabilitation and know better about hospital's demand for interactive system, we conducted a series of interviews with 4 doctors of rehabilitation in January 2014. 3 diagnosticians and 1 physical therapist participated to answer a list of 8 questions about their current treatment procedure and concerns they had when carrying out therapeutic scheme. They are each in charge of diagnosing injured parts and severity, designing rehabilitation project, and assisting rehabilitation training.

During the interviews, we mainly investigated their common cases, general procedure, usual training motions and equipment, and opinions about self-exercise at home. Since doctors' instructions will be introduced into this rehabilitation system, we also surveyed their preference about operation process and interface about online system. Additional concerns about rehabilitation they had were also included in generating a list of requirements we need to consider in designing the system.

They introduced the whole process of rehabilitation and gave their ideas about in what stage they hope auxiliaries can help. They also showed around the rehabilitation center about the common equipment and standard training plans. Besides, they stated that, according to their clinical experience, flexibility recovery was far more important than strength recovery, which most rehabilitation equipment failed to help, and that they regarded patients' time at home was not effectively used for rehabilitation, because they could only repeat simple motions, such as clenching fist, for fear that they exercised wrong without professional instructions and feedback. As for the system design, they mentioned the existing prescription system since they were quite familiar to that and suggested the rehabilitation system to follow that procedure and be added to the existing system.

3.2 Interview with Patients

We also randomly recruited 8 patients in the rehabilitation center who were under treatment of those doctors. The 8 patients—consisted of two elderly people suffering from geratic complications and six other patients who injured their hands.

During the investigation, we asked about their rehabilitation circumstances, including the duration and frequency they came to hospital, their exercise at home, and their attitude towards independent training and assisting auxiliary. This investigation consists of more than 16 open-ended questions. Since the online system requires user to operate by gestures, we also surveyed their IT background and experience of using computers and interactive devices. Additional concerns about rehabilitation they had were also included in generating a list of requirements we need to consider in designing the system.

As identified, most patients regard their exercise at home useless and usually cannot maintain a tight and long-term exercise schedule because they do not set regular time for simple training and often forget to exercise daily. Instead of exercise at home, they trust doctors much more, but most of them cannot afford a whole course with doctor's instruction. Generally, they spent the first few weeks at hospital, having professional training every day, yet after they rehabilitate to some degree, they move back home and visit hospital one or two times every week considering time and expense. All of them take positive attitude towards self-exercise equipment, saying that they would like to try such system if doctor permits. As for the type of training, they claimed that they prefer a series of training lessons which each focus on one part of hand, so that they can pertinently exercise according to their disease. When the interface and operation design was mentioned, they worried about whether their IT background could handle the system, since they may cannot use their finger flexibly and operate the mouse. They further added a requirement to play some similar game because they hope to increase entertainment.

3.3   User Requirements

Results from the interview shed light on the demand of a new system for online hand rehabilitation with doctors' instructions. All subjects showed interests in the idea we put forward about a series motions for exercises at home and were willing to have a try. They expected to have an interaction device of good usability, great efficiency, high safety, and social connectivity at an affordable price. A list of user requirements for the hand rehabilitation is summarized as below.

- The system should have adequate but accurate exercises to be effective, but the duration of each exercise motion should be limited to avoid overtiredness.
- The system should be easy to start with and self-explainable. It should be easy for elderly people and people without abundant IT knowledge to understand.
- The system should apply gesture to interaction with computers considering the patients' low level of control to their fingers.
- The system should provide specific training motions for exercise need for different parts of hand. Different motions should enable patients to exercise different hand parts, especially their fingers.
- The system should encourage patients to maintain a clear schedule by doing hand rehabilitation every day. And if patients fail to follow the schedule, the system should remind them and contact doctors to adjust their rehabilitation plan.
- The system should give clear feedbacks to patients for them to correct their gestures and improve, and record their performance for themselves and their doctors to check.
- The system would be better if social connectivity is provided between patients.
- The system should allow doctors to check their patients' performance and give instructions easily and synchronously.

- The system should provide convenient access for doctors to manage and monitor their patients.

4   Improvement of Existing Hand Rehabilitation Equipment

There are a large number of patients who need hand rehabilitation in the word today according to status from WHO, and attentions on equipment for that are still inadequate. Currently, products designed for hand rehabilitation are limited, which we proposed that with the help of some well-designed device and systems, patients can be instructed and encouraged to rehabilitate safely, correctly and, most important, efficiently by themselves.

4.1   Shortcomings of Existing Equipment

Current hand rehabilitation equipment, which consists of two types: wearable devices and interactive video games, both have their own focuses. Thus when used by doctors for assistance, they could have several inherent drawbacks as follows.

- Wearable devices, such as hand dynamometer, and gloves (e.g. MusicGlove [12], Gloreha [11] as shown in Fig. 1) consist of mechanical parts and are fixed on hands by elasticity or else, which may all add extra compression and cause reinjury.
- Interactive video games, for example Khademi's Ninja game with Leap Motion controller, focus only on encouraging users to exercise their hand, paying no attentions on precise training motions, while nimbleness recovery which is of equal importance causes for precise exercise.
- Both of these products are designed for patients to exercise all by themselves. However, doctors' opinions and instructions may give much help for rehabilitation, which should be taken into account.

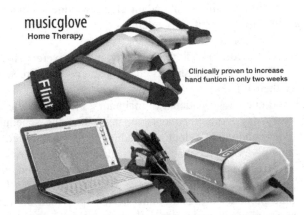

Fig. 1. Product demos of musicglove snd gloreha

4.2   Improvement Using Leap Motion Controller

The Leap Motion controller is an excellent sensor which can tracking hands and fingers with high speed and precision [13]. It enables a series of operation in interaction with computers. These unique advantages could improve current hand rehabilitation products in following points.

- The Leap Motion Controller enables doctors to record standard exercise motion beforehand by tracking their example motions through its camera and IR sensors without contact, which can be shown to patients and instruct their self-training.
- Besides beforehand recording, the Leap Motion controller could also real-time process the data it tracks. By comparing real-time data with recorded data, users' motions can be judged whether matching with the standard motions or not.

As a result, the Leap Motion controller has been chosen to realize most of the requirements doctors and patients proposed, because of its well performance in tracking users' hand, as well as sending and processing real-time hand data. Users only need to move their fingers above the Leap Motion controller. The prototype system refers a set if sample codes in Leap Motion SDK, with 3D hands modeling and displaying.

5   Prototype Design and Development

5.1   Prototype Apparatus

The online hand rehabilitation system consists of four parts: users (include patients and doctors), a Leap Motion controller, a personal computer and a display screen. Connecting with the Leap Motion controller and display screen, the PC processes the real-time data of hands obtained from the Leap Motion controller and displays on the screen when the system is running. Patients only needs to sit in front of the PC and hold hand above the Leap Motion controller in order that his or her hands can be captured and tracked. Patients are able to wave his or her hands to select and click on the buttons presented on the screen and operate the system, as shown in Fig. 2.

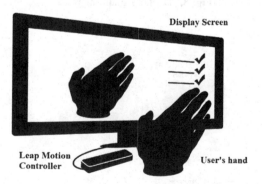

Fig. 2. Prototype apparatus

5.2   System Design

This rehabilitation system has special designs for patients with hand afunction to help them with hand rehabilitation and communicate with their doctors.

As the start of the whole rehabilitation process, doctor check patient's hand situation and have a basic diagnosis. Then instead of writing a prescription and teaching patients how to exercise, doctor log on his or her account and add a new patient's document under his account. (Of course, if this patient is come for a return visit, doctor can open his or her existing document and work on that instead of creating a new one.) Doctor needs to fill in patient's basic information and diagnosis before he gives prescription. He can choose among all the exercise motions, which have been recorded by Leap Motion and saved in the system, for patients to exercise with instructions about frequency and duration, etc., like prescriptions about taking medicine. After all these operations end, doctor will generate an account for patient, with a unique username and password, and rent a Leap Motion controller to patients. The main interface is shown in Fig. 3, where doctors can add new patients and enter certain patient's record. As for the patient's record, the interface arranges as shown in Fig. 4 with patient's basic information, diagnose, prescription and score for each exercise. Here, doctor can add comments as well.

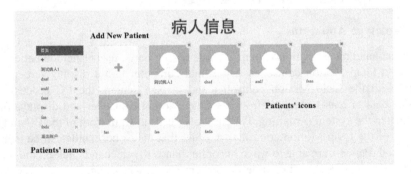

Fig. 3. Doctor's main interface

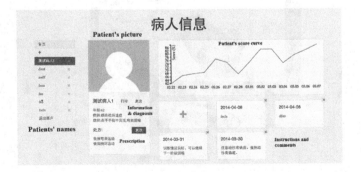

Fig. 4. Patient's record interface

Then comes to the patient's self-exercise. Patients can open the website and login with the username and password which is given by their doctors. After a basic calibration with Leap Motion, patients enter their homepage, as shown in Fig. 5 where they can choose to exercise with standard motion, view their score and play interactive games which encourage them to move their finger and wrist. When entering into the exercise part, as shown in Fig. 6, patients can see the standard motion, prescribed by their doctor, presents on the left for them to follow and at the same time, their real motion will present on the right with feedbacks showing where to improve. Moreover, a score based on the similarity between the standard motion and real one will appear on the left, for patients themselves and their doctor to estimate their rehabilitation situation.

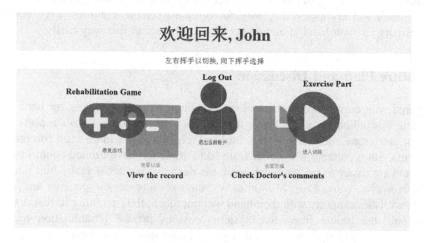

Fig. 5. Patients' homepage

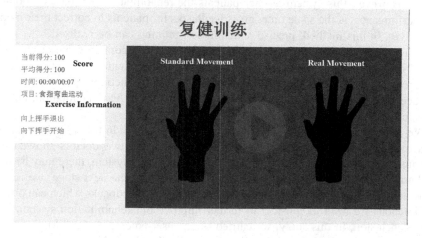

Fig. 6. Patients' exercise page

6 Prototype Evaluation: An Interview

In order to check whether this online system can satisfy patients' and doctors' demand and improve hand rehabilitation's efficiency, a prototype system was developed and evaluated by 2 doctors in June 2014.

The evaluation interview consisted of three steps: a brief introduction to the usage and design of the system, a short operation trial for doctors and a follow-up interview to collect their feedback. Since we don't have enough time to recruit more patients, this evaluation was carried out only with doctors.

According to doctors' feedback, they both acknowledged that the system met their demand and they believed it to be useful for hand rehabilitation. Also, they liked the interface and structure of the website. Besides, they mentioned that the interaction with Leap Motion and computer was easy for ordinary person, but they were not sure whether patients with hand afunction could also interact in this way easily.

7 Future Plan and Discussion

Compared with current wearable devices and interactive video games for hand rehabilitation, this online system is better for patients in the following three aspects.

First, the online interactive system for hand rehabilitation add no extra compression to patients. Since patients who suffer from hand afunction have limited control to their finger and are easier to be wounded, wearable devices may accidentally hurt patients' hands. However, using Leap Motion as a distant sensing device, patients are free to interact with the computer with their hand without touch, thus avoiding further damage.

Second, the online interactive system provides precise rehabilitation training, comparing with existing hand interactive game. Those task oriented game, for example, Fruit Ninja, usually set a task for players to finish, and the game only focuses on the whether the task is finished instead of how to finish it, thus cannot instruct accurate motion. However, this system teaches patients the rehabilitation motion and monitors their performance, at the same time, gives feedbacks for patients to correct their motion themselves. In this method, precise rehabilitation training can be realized.

Third, via the online system, doctors and patients can communicate at any time, instead of only during weekly visit back to the hospital. Patients' video and score will be shared with their doctors and doctors' comments and instructions appear on patients' interface as well. This has not only increased efficiency of the rehabilitation, but also make full use of patients' time at home.

We have to admit that because of time limitation, we didn't carry out evaluation experiment with patients for long term test. Although the two doctors showed their great interest in this system after a brief introduction to this system, there may be some problems we cannot find until the patients try this. So for the next stage, we need to cooperate with some local hospitals and get more detailed feedbacks which can point to the directions we need to consider to further improve our rehabilitation system.

In conclusion, in this study, we carried out a "user-entered design" for patients in developing a Leap-Motion-based online interactive hand rehabilitation system. User requirements were collected from an interview with both doctors in hand rehabilitation and patients who need rehabilitation. Based on these requirements, a prototype system has been designed and developed with Leap Motion sensor. We briefly evaluated the system with an introduction and presentation to two relevant doctors, and furthermore, a more detailed experiment with patients need to be carried out. Compared with the existing wearable devices and interactive games, this online system performs better in safety, accuracy, efficiency in assisting patients with hand afunction in rehabilitation training.

References

1. World Health Statistics (2014). http://apps.who.int/iris/bitstream/10665/112738/1/9789240692671_eng.pdf?ua=1
2. Mackin, E., Callahan, A.D.: Rehabilitation of the Hand, pp. 312–317. Mosby, Miles (1978)
3. Boian, R., Sharma, A., Han, C., Merians, A., Burdea, G., Adamovich, S., Poizner, H.: Virtual reality-based post-stroke hand rehabilitation. Stud. Health Technol. Inform. **85**, 64–70 (2002)
4. Cruz, E.G., Waldinger, H.C., Kamper, D.G.: Kinetic and kinematic workspaces of the index finger following stroke. Brain **128**(5), 1112–1121 (2005)
5. Seo, N.J., Rymer, W.Z., Kamper, D.G.: Altered digit force direction during pinch grip following stroke. Exp. Brain Res. **202**(4), 891–901 (2010)
6. Khademi, M., Mousavi Hondori, H., McKenzie, A., Dodakian, L., Lopes, C.V., Cramer, S.C.: Free-hand interaction with leap motion controller for stroke rehabilitation. In: CHI 2014 Extended Abstracts on Human Factors in Computing Systems, pp. 1663–1668. ACM, April 2014
7. Grünert-Plüss, N., Hufschmid, U., Santschi, L., Grünert, J.: Mirror therapy in hand rehabilitation: a review of the literature, the St Gallen protocol for mirror therapy and evaluation of a case series of 52 patients. Brit. J. Hand Ther. **13**(1), 4–11 (2008)
8. Boulanger, C., Boulanger, A., de Greef, L., Kearney, A., Sobel, K., Transue, R., Sweedyk, Z., Dietz, P.H., Bathiche, S.: Stroke rehabilitation with a sensing surface. In: Proceedings of the SIGCHI Conference on Human Factors in Computing Systems, New York, NY, USA, pp. 1243–1246 (2013)
9. Hallam, J., Whiteley, V.: Interactive therapy gloves: reconnecting partners after a stroke. In: CHI 2011 Extended Abstracts on Human Factors in Computing Systems, New York, NY, USA, pp. 989–994 (2011)
10. Eli Carmeli, S.P.: HandTutorTM enhanced hand rehabilitation after stroke. Physiother. Res. Int. J. Res. Clin. Phys. Ther. **16**(4), 191–200 (2011)
11. Gloreha – Hand rehabilitation glove. http://www.gloreha.com/index.php/en/gloreha-en
12. MusicGlove by Flint Rehabilitation Devices LLC: Home. https://www.flintrehabilitation.com/
13. Leap Motion | Mac & PC Motion Controller for Games, Designs, & More. https://www.leapmotion.com/

From Dechnology to Humart

A Case Study of Applying Nature User Interface to the Interactive Rehabilitation Design

Jui Ping Ma[1(✉)], Na Ling Huang[2], Miao Hsien Chuang[3],
and Rungtai Lin[1]

[1] Graduate School of Creative Industry Design, National Taiwan
University of Arts, New Taipei City, Taiwan
rupm08@gmail.com, rtlin@mail.ntua.edu.tw
[2] Graduate School of Crafts and Design,
National Taiwan University of Arts, New Taipei City, Taiwan
naling6@gmail.com
[3] Department of Visual Communication Design,
Ming Chi University of Technology, New Taipei City, Taiwan
joyceblog@gmail.com

Abstract. Some elderly with reduced mobility usually stay their own familiar environments and watch TV or do nothing. In addition, due to the lack of exchanges or proper physical activities, their physical and psychological status tends to imperceptibly become unhealthy. This study applies natural user interface and ceramic crafts regarding the integration of sensing technology with a multimodal interactive components, proposes the design of an interactive rehabilitation device based on video and audio context, and performs an on-site inspection, in order to assist subjects in alleviating negative emotions, promoting physical and psychological health, and reducing the home care stress of nursing personnel, as well as to establish a demonstration model for the use of digital aids in home care environments.

Keywords: Natural user interface · Interactive device · Rehabilitation

1 Introduction

Since the coming of an aging society, the issue of elderly home care has been concerning gradually in various countries around the world. Some experiments have been verifying that, the environmental factors established in the healing process, such as color, light, sound, material, and structural design appearance of other facilities, are found to be beneficial to health recovery [1]. With pleasant, user-friendly facilities will attract the elderly and improve their satisfaction with health care, which has become the approach advocated by the healthcare industry in marketing [2, 3]. Coyle [4] recommended that, to strengthen the collaboration between health professionals and computer science research provides a solution to the development of software and hardware for mental health treatment. Since the novel development of numerous care tools through

© Springer International Publishing Switzerland 2015
P.L.P. Rau (Ed.): CCD 2015, Part II, LNCS 9181, pp. 348–360, 2015.
DOI: 10.1007/978-3-319-20934-0_33

information technology, as based on information technology set up around the arena of elderly home care, have certainly become the necessary facilities of relevant home care or nursing sites. Furthermore, some studies highlighted that, it is necessary to proactively participate in the initiatives of stakeholders according to various aspects, such as design, development, implementation, and assessment, which can help understand the needs and behaviors of the groups involved [5–7]. Many allegedly interactive technologies developed based on user-centered concepts have been innovatively spread to medical and nursing fields. However, a study found that, it is difficult for general users to learn to operate computer-based human-computer interactive control systems. Moreover, it is difficult to overcome relatively mediocre operating skills [8]. Therefore, an increasing number of interactive systems with simplified operation have been continually developed. Some studies intended to investigate the fulfillment of "user-sensitive response generation systems (USRGS)" [9–11].

Caregivers can obtain information feedback regarding cognitive status of the elderly to further develop appropriate healing programs through the operation of user-sensitive response generation systems (USRGS). To the elderly, the information of physical, psychological, and cognitive impairment and degradation is sensed, but they must still undergo rehabilitation through the occupational therapist's arrangement of physical activities. Many healing and care facilities are either deficient in the staffing of occupational therapist or employ too few occupational therapists to take care numerous the elderly. As a result, they cannot fully take care of the elderly. Therefore, healing and care facilities have an urgent need for a series of simple and effective interactive rehabilitation systems, where the elderly is not required to learn anything in particular, in order to assist the elderly in self-healing and improve their participation in rehabilitation activities. In recent years, the "postural control system using a natural user interface (NUI)" has been widely applied to daily life [12, 13]. Consequently, an increasing number of developers have applied the NUI concept to the human-computer interaction of rehabilitation systems. Although healing systems that integrate sensors with NUI development have been available, to date, the development of an interactive device that considers the spirit of the elderly and uses some images to assist in healing has not been observed. Therefore, this study developed an interactive rehabilitation device integrating plants images with NUI and somatosensory technology to investigate three types of the elderly that require occupational therapy: the elderly with reduced mobility, the elderly admitted to ER, and bedridden the elderly, in order to respond to sensory perception, spiritual healing, and limb sensitivity, as well as to meet the needs of healing and recovery.

2   Literature Review

2.1   Natural User Interface

Natural user interface (NUI) is a general term used by human-computer interface designers and developers, and refers to the effective hiding and maintenance of the invisible parts of a user interface, which facilitates users to naturally and continually become familiar with gradually complicated interactive methods during operation processes. The word "natural" is contrary to most computer interfaces, as most inter-faces use artificial control devices, and users must intentionally learn to operate them [14]. Past studies in experimental psychology verified that, physical actions, including gestures, can exert functions in problem solving when promoting information transfer [15–17]. Kaushik and Jain [18] mentioned that NUI has three trends: multi-touch, voice, and gesture interaction. In an information system, users most frequently use their hands to implement human-computer interaction. Many researchers suggest that, in order to strengthen the intuition of a user interface, it is necessary to use a new user interface pattern, which enables users to use natural gestures to choose, operate, and convey a target [19–22]. With the development of the NUI concept, human-computer interactions involving hands are more inclined to the development of easy and natural learning, where complicated memory is not required. Hsieh et al. [23] and Fan et al. [24] advocated the use of a gesture recognition system to detect the actions and directions of users' hands in order to achieve the purpose of complicated human-computer interactions. The study by Bragdon et al. [25] verified that, touch gestures significantly improve the availability of mobile devices; however, not all touch gestures are intuitive and easy to use, as such operation usually requires detailed learning – similar to the hand dexterity training of normal people [26].

With the advance of sensory technology, the development potential of NUI is expected to provide space thinking that involves interactive design [27]. As NUI initially does not frequently provide specific guidance or instruction, Thomas and Lleras [17] found that the participants in a space are unwittingly guided to engage in physical action. Even though NUI endows users with highly instinctive convenience, Norman [28] mentioned that, NUI is different from the GUI used in the past – i.e. all actions can be achieved through a visualization menu. On the contrary, the NUI interface includes so many possibilities that it is difficult to determine all the possibilities and implement their actions. However, this study suggests that, if NUI can be used in combination with suggestive video messaging, this difficulty can be over-come.

2.2   Interactive Devices and Somatosensory Interactive Medicine

Interactive Devices. Interactive devices are mostly applied to human-computer interface systems to complete the objectives of information transfer and communication with users. During the design of an interactive human-computer system, the most important issue is to understand the relationship model between users and system in interactive fields. In addition, from the perspective of an interactive designer, an interactive designer not only has to understand the possibilities to be achieved by technologies, but also properly use suitable technologies to solve problems according to different occasions and environments for designing a good interactive device. In order to use the most suitable technology in a specific field, it is necessary to assess the operating model and procedures adopted by interactive users. Although some technological creations developed using assistive technology can meet need the elderly' for interactions, in terms of users' psychology, the latest idea suggests that it is necessary to assist the elderly in developing socialized self-acceptance [5, 29], and enable users to participate in the creation or use of cultural knowledge to support therapeutic experts in planning interactive software games [30–32], in order to improve the elderly' self-identity and confidence.

Somatosensory Interactions and Medicine. Ever since the Kinect 3D camera developed by Microsoft Corporation was used as a peripheral of Microsoft Xbox360, after becoming commercially available in 2010, the creations and studies concerning somatosensory technology have increased year by year. Kinect is a webcam that enables users to use NUI, body postures, voice, or image interaction to control a game, and a remote control or body sensor is not required [33, 34]. The Kinect camera has been integrated with the personal computer, and has a potential that even designers cannot predict – from helping children with autism to assisting surgeons in the operating room [35]. Recently, many studies involving this device in academia have focused on the classification of an instant postures and action recognition system [36, 37]. Some studies also investigated the application of somatosensory interactive technology to medicine. For example, Chang, Chen, and Chuang [38] used Kinect to train individuals with past cognitive impairment in order to enable their limbs to complete basic tasks, and then developed a Kinect-based rehabilitation system for adults [39]. Lange et al. used Kinect to develop a game-based recovery tool to provide adults with nerve damage with balance training [40].

3   Research Design

This study attached importance to both theories and practices. In the initial stage of this study, the researcher proactively asked about healing and care facilities willing to participate in the subsequent field survey. After a series of comparisons, the researcher eventually contacted the Suao Branch of the Taipei Veterans General Hospital. In addition to the general outpatient clinics of the general hospital, Suao Branch, Taipei Veterans General Hospital has a nursing home, where many elderly the elderly requiring long-term care are hospitalized. Therefore, opinions from health professionals of this facility could be obtained, and this study could conduct a field survey on elderly the elderly living in a nursing home for a long period of time. This study used the "Double Diamond Design Process (4D)" advocated by the UK Design Council [41]. Firstly, this study reviewed the studies concerning ceramics crafts, NUI, and interactive design, observed the healing facility, had discussions with the caregivers at the facility in order to preliminarily understand the elderly' needs, and applied the summarized principles to the prototype design of an interactive device. Secondly, this study conducted a field survey of the interactive device on professional caregivers and the elderly, and then interviewed users regarding their user experience. Lastly, this study adjusted and summarized the interactive design to meet the needs of users for this research purpose.

3.1   Research Process and Method

Research Process. In the research process, and according to the 4D method, the user-centered service design meets users' needs, and includes 4 steps - Discover - > Define - > Develop - > Deliver. The explanations are given, as follows:

Discover – the beginning stage of the double diamond model, and marks the beginning of a project. Initially, ideas and inspirations are obtained from the exploration of the identifiable needs of users. The implementation content includes: environmental research, user research, management information, and a design research group. Upon completion of this stage, a "feasibility review" is applied at the both ends of the diamond in order to explore possible solutions to the issues. Define – stage 2 explains and adjusts the content to meet the needs of the project and its objectives. The critical activities at this stage include: project development, project management, and project approval. Upon completion of this stage, both ends of the diamond converge to a "Brief" to facilitate the precise determination of the details of project, as expected to be implemented at the development stage. Develop – stage 3, at which the design-led solution is developed and retested in an organization, such as visual management, the development method, and project testing. The "Concept review" is used to confirm the final project to be adopted by a service provider. Deliver – the last stage, at which an effective product or a service-related market is confirmed and initiated. The critical activities and objects are: final test, approval, proposal of service project, objective assessment, and feedback reply. Through a series of defining service objects, content, questions, and conversion processes, the interactive effect between a healing provider and a care receiver was gradually revised to further develop the overall healing care service design project, as shown in Fig. 1.

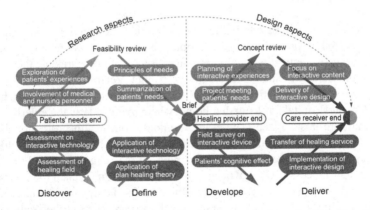

Fig. 1. Double Diamond Design Process (4D) (Source: Design Council, 2005. Compiled by this study).

Research Method. Prior to the formal design being put into practice, this study invited experts in fields of art therapy, video design, interactive engineering, and system design to participate in Stage 1 focus group meetings. The discussions focused on the corresponding estimated lines of art therapy perspectives, as well as the design of interactive content. The reason this study applied this method is that, past studies showed that the purpose of the assembly of these members to engage in group discussions is to reach consensuses on healing environments, facilities, and approaches, through communications and coordination regarding healing procedures and details. Focus groups have long been applied to develop research methodologies and standardized questionnaire items [42, 43], while open interviews and Q and A sessions can be used to generate subjects' qualitative data, such as attitudes, viewpoints, and opinions. Based on the discussion results of the focus group meetings in Stage 1, this study designed the interactive content, and further developed a semi-structured questionnaire for the subjects to conduct interviews. According to experts, the suggestions of interactive design are as shown in Table 1.

Table 1. Summary of focuses from art therapy expert meeting

Interactive content of plant images	Perspectives of art therapy
Garden interactive environment (a certain tree)	Garden environments are featured by higher accessibility and tolerance. Open spaces and bright lines create more safety, as well as the willingness and possibility of exploration. In addition, interactors' acceptance of visual colors, object abundance, and psychological control over environment is higher.
Leaves "falling from top to bottom" or "rolled up from bottom"	1. Leaves falling from "top to bottom" represent that people change from head to toe and throw away troubles.
	2. Leaves "rolled up from the bottom:" represent an upward force, obtainment of assistance, recall, memory, and re-obtainment of the lost.
Leaves "falling" or "bouncing"	1. Leaves "falling:" convey the meanings of loss, missing, and separation, and is the passage and change of time.
	2. Leaves "bouncing" enable viewers or interactors to perceive the signs of timing of self-maturation, to throw away everything that is old, shabby, negative, and inappropriate, and accept new things.
Leaves "shining or changing their color" when touched	"Leaves shining or changing their color" when touched signifies the energy of warmth and softness, enabling interactors to be covered by energy, perceive support, empower themselves, heal themselves, and purify themselves.
"Waving" of the elderly during interaction	"Waving" is the expectation towards attention from other people and environmental interaction, as well as the need for assistance or help.
Leaves "sounding" when touched	Touch, in combination with visual image stimulation and audio stimulation (sounds), can better deepen and internalize individual external experiences and trigger deep emotions and feelings.
A sprouting tree or fallen leaves returning to a tree	Represents self-recovery, rebirth, gradual exuberance, and recovery of existing vigor and feelings of regeneration

(Compiled by this study)

3.2   Design Case- Design of Interactive Rehabilitation Device

According to the preliminary testing of medical and nursing professionals, as well as the above mentioned literature review, this study initiated the advanced corrections and development of the design of interactive devices, including three parts: (1) image design; (2) sound design; (3) sensing design. The design process is briefly described, as follows:

(1) *Image design:* Based on the aforementioned studies investigating the positive effects of plants on users' cognition, this study mainly used a common arbor as the material. According to the survey, this study chose the tree shape of the birch, as it is featured by gentility and tenderness [44]. Moreover, relevant studies on tree shapes indicated that, users' visual preference is round shaped leaves. Therefore, this study mainly referred to the tree shape drawn by Booth [45] to select the shape display. Moreover, according to existing studies on preference for the visual shape of a tree, this study further simplified the shape to the final shape for the case according to the visual subject of interactive design, as shown in Figs. 2 and 3.

(2) *Sound design*: As humans rely on all things in nature to earn a living, when faced with natural elements, such as plants, water, and rocks, they usually develop positive responses, as well as naturally peaceful behaviors in their emotions [46, 47]. Throughout time, people have used natural elements to obtain actual effects. The sounds in the nature enable listeners to imagine that they are in a natural environment. The preset garden environment in this study was integrated with pure birdsong.

(3) *Sensing design:* This study mainly used computers in combination with Kinect somatosensory devices, as well as the program syntax of processing software, to form the content of movement and spatial depth framework of users for detection. As the principle for the use of NUI mainly focuses on limbs (especially gestures), many researchers advised some changes to guide users to use specific gestures to implement human-computer interactions, and priority should be given to such changes during the initial system design [48]. This study developed a type of interactive designs according to the elderly undergoing physical rehabilitation, as shown in Fig. 4.

3.3   Subjects and Limitations

The subjects were divided into two types. Upon completion of the initial interactive prototype design, this study performed testing on caregiving professionals at a healing

Fig. 2. The shape of tree in the case

Fig. 3 The shape of leaf in the case

Fig. 4. Interactive design proposals for three types of patients (From A to C: patients undergoing rehabilitation, bedridden patients, and patients with acute illness).

and care facility, as well as ordinary people, in order to provide professional assessment and assessments of various needs. The prototype design was corrected and adjusted according to professional opinions from various fields. Afterwards, the design was installed in a healing and care environment for the three types of the elderly that were the expected targets to use the design. The researcher observed the elderly, maintained records, and interviewed them about their feelings.

3.4   Experimental Process

As stated above, this experimental study was divided into two parts: Firstly, this study invited occupational therapist, head nurses, and medical administrative personnel to try out the design on their own (Fig. 5). Secondly, this study encouraged the elderly at the healing and care facility to try out the design (Fig. 6). Upon termination of the trial, the subjects were interviewed one by one (Fig. 7).

Fig. 5. Pre-test

Fig. 6. Test on a patient

Fig. 7. Interview

Table 2. Experimental results of the subjects using the interactive design

Samples	M07601	F08401	M08901	F05701	F09001	F07101	F08701	F08402
Gender	M	F	M	F	F	F	F	F
Age	76	84	89	57	90	71	87	84
Status	b	c	c	c	a	a	c	c
Number of days of hospitalization	180	365	1095	210	60	365	30	730
Emotion	e	e	e	e	e	e	e	f
Plants have a healing effect	Y	Y	NA	Y	N	Y	N	Y
Virtual plants can replace actual plants	N	Y	NA	NA	NA	NA	NA	NA
Aware of technological art	N	N	N	Y	N	N	N	N
Music in the interaction	e	e	e	i	i	i	i	i
Feeling after the interactive experience	e	i	e	e	e	e	e	e
Functions to be added	Dancing	Flower planting						

Gender: F: Female M: Male
Status: a: normal/b: crutch/c: wheelchair/d: others
Emotion: e: pleasant/f: sad/g: relaxed/h: Others/i: no feeling
Yes: Y /No: N /No idea: NA

4   Results and Discussion

This study used the participant observation method, and 8 subjects were enrolled (2 male and 6 female the elderly). The oldest subject was 90 years old, while the youngest one was 57 years old; 2 of the subjects were mobile, 5 were in wheelchairs, and 1 used crutches. The experimental results are as shown in Table 2: Among the 8 subjects trying out the interactive design, although none were aware of professional terms, such as interactive technology or art therapy, most of them agreed that the interactive experience of the interactive design created a pleasant feeling, and only 1 claimed not to feel anything. In terms of plant healing, as many as 5 subjects believed that plants have a healing effect, and only 1 agreed that virtual plants can replace actual plants and have a healing effect. Moreover, the music in the interactive design was usually ignored by the subjects, and only 3 of them had a vague impression of background music.

5   Conclusion

5.1   Interactive Design and the Elderly' Rehabilitation

This study used the interactive device planned and developed in this study to perform testing. The interactive device design provided by this study won the recognition of most of the elderly, as well as the healing and care facility. Most of the elderly participated in the test with an attitude of attempting a game or taking exercise. In addition, caregivers had to remind most of them to move their hands and feet to enable them to continue implementing dynamic video interactions. Therefore, it is important to build an initial sense of trust when the elderly are exposed to the interactive device interface. Some of the elderly that were older and could walk autonomously could better focus on the operational procedures of the interactive device. Apparently, healthy and mobile the elderly are more interested in, and are more willing to engage in, interactive behaviors. Moreover, this study found that, because the study site is located in a remote area and the hospital scale is small, it only has several outpatient clinics. During the test, this study found that some of the wards were not used, suggesting that there were only a few the elderly in the facility. In addition, medical and nursing staffing was more simplified, and most of the elderly were not those with critical illness. Therefore, the device developed in this study may meet the needs of this type of healing and care facility in the future.

5.2   Interactive Design and Rehabilitation Healing

Rehabilitation healing focuses on the recovery of past physical and psychological health and functions. Therefore, it is necessary to use a device that has been verified as effective by professionals and experiments. The focus of this study was not on the effectiveness of the developed aids or healing device, but on the use of visual and psychological healing of the plant images themselves, in combination with NUI, which has no particular learned requirements. This study intended to use a more simple and effective method to popularize professional interactive devices to assist in improving medical devices. Firstly, this study designed the interactive device based on the observations of the needs of elderly the elderly. According to the tests of healing professionals and the elderly, several principles for corrections of the interactive design were summarized. Although this creation is not a medical aid or device, it is not a pure video game. However, from the perspective of the elderly, the healing effect of this device still can be expected.

The development direction of subsequent devices should be intricate and abundant interactive forms. Future devices should better grasp the healing needs of the elderly of different levels of healing needs. Interactive devices or systems of various levels of difficulties should be designed through closer cooperation with professional scientists, anthropologists, professional doctors, therapists, and rehabilitation units. Moreover, it is necessary to develop a mechanism for testing the healing effect of the interactive device, integrated with plant images, in order to precisely grasp the healing effect of the elderly and develop a database of actual application cases. In this way, the seemingly simple but versatile interactive device, when integrated with humanity and patient-centered design, can be used as equipment for analyzing and determining the mechanism of people facing physical and psychological disability.

Acknowledgements. The assistance in the participation in the interviews and experiments of this study of medical and nursing professionals and the elderly in the Suao Branch, Taipei Veterans General Hospital, and affiliated nursing home in Suao Township, Yilan County, Taiwan, is highly appreciated.

References

1. Ulrich, R.S.: Effects of interior design on wellness: theory and recent scientific research. J. Health Care Inter. Des. **3**, 97–109 (1991)
2. Egger, E.: Designing facilities to be patient focused. Health Care Strateg. Manage. **17**, 19–22 (1999)
3. Hutton, J.D., Richardson, L.D.: Healthscapes: the role of the facility and physical environment on consumer attitudes, satisfaction, quality assessments, and behaviors. Health Care Manage. Rev. **20**, 48–61 (1995)
4. Coyle, D.: Computers in talk-based mental health interventions. Interact. Comput. **19**(4), 545–562 (2007)
5. Doherty, G., Coyle, D., Matthews, M.: Design and evaluation guidelines for mental health technologies. Interact. Comput. **22**(4), 243–252 (2010)
6. Assay, T.P., Lambert, M.J.: The empirical case for the common factors in therapy: qualitative findings. In: Duncan, B.L. (ed.) The Hearth and Soul of Change: What Works in Therapy. American Psychological Association, Massachusetts (1999)
7. Bath, P.A.: Health informatics: current issues and challenges. J. Inf. Sci. **34**(4), 501–518 (2008)
8. Carroli, J.M., McKendree, J.: Interface design issues for advice-giving expert systems. Commun. ACM **30**(1), 14–31 (1987)
9. Rich, E.: Users are individuals: individualizing user models. Int. J Man-Mach Study **18**, 199–214 (1983)

10. Schuster, E.: Custom-made responses: maintaining and updating the user model. Technical report of the Moore School, University of Pennsylvania, MS-CIS-83-13 (1983)

11. Paris, C.: Tailoring object descriptions to user's level of expertise. Technical report, Columbia University CS department (1986)

12. Mitra, S., Acharya, T.: Gesture recognition: a survey. IEEE Trans. Syst. Man Cybernet. Part C: Appl. Rev. **37**(3), 311–312 (2007)

13. Wachs, J.P.J., Kölsch, M., Stern, H., Edan, Y.: Vision-based hand-gesture applications. Commun. ACM **54**(2), 60–71 (2011)

14. Natural user interface. http://en.wikipedia.org/wiki/Natural_user_interface. Accessed October 2014

15. Cook, S.W., Tanenhaus, M.K.: Embodied communication: speakers' gestures affect listeners' actions. Cogn. **113**(1), 98–104 (2009)

16. Goldin-Meadow, S., Wagner, S.M.: How our hands help us learn. Trends Cogn. Sci. **9**(5), 234–241 (2005)

17. Thomas, L.E., Lleras, A.: Swinging into thought: directed movement guides insight in problem solving. Psychonom. Bull. Rev. **16**(4), 719–723 (2009)

18. Kaushik, M., Jain, R.: Natural user interfaces trend in virtual interaction. Int. J. Latest Technol. Eng. Manage. Appl. Sci. **3**(4), 141–143 (2014)

19. Lu, G., Shark, L.K., Hall, G., Zeshan, U.: Dynamic hand gesture tracking and recognition for real-time immersive virtual object manipulation. In: Proceedings of the CW 2009, pp. 29–35. IEEE (2009)

20. Scheible, J., Ojala, T., Coulton, P.: MobiToss: a novel gesture based interface for creating and sharing mobile multimedia art on large public displays. In: Proceedings of MM 2008, pp. 957–960. ACM Press (2008)

21. Yatani, K., Tamura, K., Hiroki, K., Sugimoto, M., Hashizume, H.: Toss-it: intuitive information transfer techniques for mobile devices. In: Proceedings of Extended Abstracts of CHI 2005, pp. 1881–1884. ACM Press (2005)

22. Yoo, B, Han, J.J., Choi, C., Yi, K., Suh, S., Park, D., Kim, C.: 3D User interface combining gaze and hand gestures for large-scale display. In: Proceedings of CHI 2010, pp. 3709–3714. ACM Press (2010)

23. Hsieh, C.C., Liou, D.H., Lee, D.: A real time hand gesture recognition system using motion history image. In: International Conference on Signal Processing Systems (ICSPS), vol. 2, pp. 394-398, Dalian, China, 5–7 July 2010

24. Fan, Y.C., Ting, W.C., Huang, P.K.: Three dimensional interactive video system based on the DTHI technology. In: International Symposium on Computer, Consumer and Control, pp. 161–164 (2012)

25. Bragdon, A., Nelson, E., Li, Y., Hinckely, K.: Experimental analysis of touch-screen gesture designs in mobile environments. In: Proceedings of CHI 2011, pp. 403-412. ACM Press (2011)

26. Bragdon, A., Uguray, A., Wigdor, D., Anagnostopoulos, S., Zeleznik, R., Feman, R.: Gesture play: motivating online gesture learning with fun, positive reinforcement and physical Metaphors. In: Proceedings of ITS 2010, pp. 39–48. ACM Press (2010)

27. Chao, K.J., Huang, H.W., Fang, W.C., Chen, N.S.: Embodied play to learn: exploring kinect-facilitated memory performance. Br. J. Edu. Technol. **44**(5), 15–155 (2013)

28. Norman, D.A.: Natural user interfaces are not natural. Interact. **17**(3), 6–10 (2010)

29. Doherty, G., Sharry, J., Bang, M., Alcañiz, M., Baños, R.: Technology in mental health. In ACM SIGCHI 2008 EA, pp. 3965–3968 (2008)

30. Anacleto, J.C., de Carvalho A.F.P.: Improving human-computer interaction by developing culture-sensitive applications based on common sense knowledge. arXiv preprint arXiv:1001.0418, 2010

31. Anacleto, J.C., Fels, S., Villena. J.: MR. Design of a web-based therapist tool to promote emotional closeness. In: ACM SIGCHI 2010 EA, pp. 3565–3570 (2010)
32. Silva, M.A.R., Anacleto, J.C.: Promoting collaboration through a culturally contextualized narrative game. In: Filipe, J., Cordeiro, J. (eds.) Enterprise Information Systems. LNBIP, vol. 24, pp. 870–881. Springer, Heidelberg (2009)
33. Pham A. E3: Microsoft shows off Gesture Control Technology for Xbox 360. http://latimesblogs.latimes.com/technology/2009/06/microsofte3.html. Accessed August 2014
34. Microsoft, E3 2009: Microsoft at E3 Several Metric Tons of Press Releaseapal-loza (2009). http://blog.seattlepi.com/digitaljoystick/2009/06/01/e3-2009-microsoft-at-e3-several-metric-tons-of-press-releaseapalloza. Accessed January 2014
35. Microsoft Research: Kinect Effect Magic pushes beyond the Living Room (2011). http://www.microsoft.com/Presspass/Features/2011/oct11/10-31KinectEffect.mspx. Accessed January 2014
36. Alexiadis, D.S., Kelly, P., Daras, P., O'Connor, N.E., Boubekeur, T., Moussa, M.B.: Evaluating a dancer's performance using Kinect-based skeleton trajectorying. In: Proceedings of the ACM International Conference on Multimedia, pp. 659–662 (2011)
37. Raptis, M,, Kirovski, D., Hoppe, H.: Real-time classification of dance gesturesfrom skeleton animation. In: Proceedings of the Eurographics/ACM SIGGRAPH Symposium on Computer Animation, pp. 147–156 (2011)
38. Chang, Y.J., Chen, S.F., Chuang, A.F.: A gesture recognition system to transition autonomously through vocational tasks for individuals with cognitive impair-ments. Res. developmental Disabil. 32(6), 2064–2068 (2011)
39. Benyon, D., Turner, P., Turner, S.: Designing Interactive Systems: People, Activities, Contexts, Technologies. Addison Wesley, Boston (2005)
40. Lange, B, Chang, C.Y., Suma. E., Newman. B., Rizzo, A.S., Bolas. M.: Development and evaluation of low cost game-based balance rehabilitation tool using the Microsoft Kinect sensor. In: Proceedings of the 33rd Annual International Conference of the IEEE EMBS, Boston, pp. 1831–1834 (2011)
41. Design Council.: The design process (2005). http://www.designcouncil.org.uk/designprocess. Accessed 10 November 2013
42. Fowler Jr., F.J.: Improving Survey Questions: Design And Evaluation. Sage, Thousand Oaks (1995)
43. Sudman, S., Bradburn, N.M., Schwarz, N.: Thinking About Answers: The Application Of Cognitive Processes To Survey Methodology. Jossey-Bass, San Francisco (1996)
44. Bouchardon, P.: Healing Energies of Trees. Journey Editions, North Clarendon (1999)
45. Booth, N.K.: Basic Elements of Landscape of Architectural Design. Waveland press, Long Grove (1990). pp. 94–95
46. Stoneham, J.A., Kendle, A.D., Thoday, P.R.: Horticultural therapy: horticulture's contribution to the quality of life of disabled people. Acta Hortic. 391, 67–75 (1995)
47. Strauss, D., Gabaldo, M.: Traumatic brain injury and horticultural therapy practice. In: Simson, S.P., Straus, M.C. (eds.) Horticulture as Therapy Principles and Practice, pp. 105–129. Haworth Press, New York (1995)
48. Kela, J., Korpipää, P., Mäntyjärvi, J., Kallio, S., Savino, G., Jozzo, L., Di Marca, S.: Accelerometer-based gesture control for a design environment. Person. Ubiquit. Comput. 10 (5), 285–299 (2006)

Physician Communication Behaviors that Predict Patient Trust in Outpatient Departments

Manrong She[✉], Zhizhong Li, and Pei-Luen Patrick Rau

Department of Industrial Engineering, Tsinghua University, Beijing 100084,
People's Republic of China
shemanrong@163.com, zzli@tsinghua.edu.cn,
rpl@mail.tsinghua.edu.cn

Abstract. This study aimed to provide a reliable instrument for evaluating the physicians' communication behaviors and to find out what communication behaviors could elicit patient trust. Questionnaires were distributed to patients and they were asked to evaluate the physician's communication behaviors he/she just visited and his/her level of trust in the physician. Through factor analysis, a three-factor physician communication behavior scale with good internal consistency was provided. The three factors were respect and caring, competence and thoroughness, patience and honesty. Through correlation analysis, all the behaviors identified in the scale were significantly associated with patient trust. Physicians' behaviors related to competence and thoroughness were regarded as most important to patient trust. Privacy, eye contact and necessary tests and procedures were not considered very important. Moreover, within different gender groups and age groups, patients' opinions about what behaviors had the strongest (least) association with patient trust were a little bit different.

Keywords: Physician-patient relationship · Physician communication behavior · Patient trust · Scale

1 Introduction

In recent years, the strained relationship between physicians and patients and the frequent medical disputes have become a common problem in Chinese society. With the reform of the health care system, the problem has not yet been well solved. Actually, the physician-patient relationship is probably one of the most complex interpersonal relationships (Ong et al., 1995). The physicians and patients are often in non-equal positions, deal with issues of vital importance, are therefore emotionally laden and in need for close cooperation (Chaitchik et al., 1992). Patient trust is a key feature in physician-patient relationship, with potential benefits such as increased satisfaction, adherence to treatment, and continuity of care (Thom et al., 1999). Communication is the tool by which physicians and patients exchange information in the health care process (Street, 1991). Good communication behaviors can increase the patient trust in the physician (Thom, 2001). Then here comes the question that what

P.L.P. Rau (Ed.): CCD 2015, Part II, LNCS 9181, pp. 361–373, 2015.
DOI: 10.1007/978-3-319-20934-0_34

communication behaviors are "good" enough to elicit patient trust? Most previous studies focused on either communication behaviors or patient trust, which did not involve the association between them. Several studies did focus on the rapport between communication behaviors and patient trust. Take the Stanford Trust Study (Thom, 2001) as an example. It provided a physician behavior scale and assessed the relative strength of the associations between physician behaviors and patient trust. The reliability of the physician behavior scale, however, is unknown. What's more, the research subjects in Stanford Trust Study were American individuals, and the conclusions might not be fully applicable for Chinese due to the difference in population, medical policy, medical institution, medical insurance, etc.

The objective of this study was to provide a reliable physician communication behavior scale, and to find out what physician communication behaviors have an impact on patient trust.

2 Literature Review

2.1 Physician Communication Behavior

Communication was defined as "the transmission of information, thoughts, and feelings so that they are satisfactorily received and understood" (Gerteis et al., 1993). Effective communication is beneficial to enhance patient trust, establish positive relationship and improve the patient's health care (Fong Ha and Longnecker, 2010). The purposes of communication were creating a good interpersonal relationship, exchanging information and making treatment related decisions (Ong et al., 1995).

Physician communication behaviors can be categorized as *(a) instrumental (task focused) or affective (emotion focused)*, in which instrumental communication behaviors include asking questions, giving information, providing treatment, counselling, etc. and affective communication behaviors include showing concern, giving reassurance, encouraging, etc. (Buller et al., 1987) *(b) verbal or nonverbal*, in which nonverbal communication behaviors include tone of voice, gaze, posture, expressions, etc. (Ong et al., 1995) *(c) high controlling or low controlling*, in which high controlling communication behaviors include dominating conversations, being very argumentative, constantly making gestures when communicating, etc. (Ong et al., 1995) *(d) private or non-private*, indicating how private the conversation between the physician and the patient is. *(e) medical or everyday language vocabulary*, indicating the extent to which a physician switches between medical and everyday language to maximize the communicative effectiveness.

Using focus groups, Thom and Compbell (1997) identified seven categories of physician communication behaviors related to patient trust, which were thoroughness in evaluation, communicating clearly and completely, providing appropriate and effective treatment, understanding patient's experience, expressing caring, building partnership and demonstrating honesty and respect.

The American Board of International Medicine (ABIM) developed a 25-item Physician Humanistic Behaviors Questionnaire (PHBQ) as an instrument for patients to assess the humanistic behaviors of their physicians (Weaver et al., 1993). Most items in

PHBQ can be partitioned into the seven categories identified by Thom and Compbell (Thom and Campbell 1997). For example, the item "including me in decisions and choices about my care" in PHBQ belongs to the category of "building partnership", and the item "asking me how I feel about my problem" belongs to the category of "expressing caring". Although the ABIM provided a useful instrument to evaluate physician humanistic behavior, it didn't build the rapport between physician behaviors and patient trust.

2.2 Patient Trust

Trust can be viewed as an expectation about the behavior of others in transactions (Lewicki and Bunker, 1995). Patient trust is the degree of confidence that his/her physician will work towards the best health outcome for him/her (Bambino, 2006). Leisen and Hyman (2004) pointed out that patient trust was essential to successful medical care. Several scholars have put forward instruments to evaluate patient trust in the physician (such as Anderson and Dedrick et al., 1990; Safran, 1998; Kao et al., 1998; Hall et al., 2002). These instruments were compared in terms of content, number of items, sample size, mean, standard deviation, reliability and Kurtosis/skewness in Hall's study(Hall et al., 2002), which was not detailed in this paper.

Among these instruments, the 10-item Kao's trust scale (Kao et al., 1998) and the 10-item Wake Forest trust scale (Hall et al., 2002) had good internal consistencies. Several items in Kao's trust scale, however, were not applicable for Chinese individuals. Take the item "to keep your health and well-being above keeping down the health plan's cost" for instance. With the health care reform in the United States, most Americans, including working families and small businesses, have health insurance or are eligible to have health insurance, meaning that they only afford a very small portion of medical cost. Thus, what they care about is whether the physician will put their medical needs above the consideration of health plan's cost. In China, however, many people have to pay a relative large portion of their medical cost. They cares more about how much they should pay for the medical treatment instead of the concern on keeping down the health plan's cost. Since the items in Wake Forest's trust scale seem applicable for Chinese individual, it was used in this study.

2.3 The Relationship Between Communication and Trust

The Stanford Trust Study (Thom, 2001) is famous for its focusing on the association of physician communication behaviors and patient trust. Patients from 20 family physicians rated physician behaviors and their trust in physicians (Anderson and Dedrick et al., 1990) after their visits. The five physician communication behaviors most strongly associated with patient trust were being comforting and caring, demonstrating competency, encouraging and answering questions, explaining what they were doing and referring to a specialist if needed (Thom, 2001). Still, the conclusions in this study might not be suitable for Chinese patients. In the United States, the patient often first goes to the family physician for medical care who is capable of most common diseases. When needed, the patient will be recommended to a specialist. Whereas in China, most patients go to the hospital directly for a specialist. Therefore, the physician behavior of referring to a specialist when needed might not be what Chinese individuals care about.

Other studies adopted various methods such as discourse analysis through the analysis of videotapes at the hospital (Manning and Ray, 2002) and trust survey with each item gauging patient's perception of a specific physician communication behavior (Bambino, 2006), but didn't measure the relationship between communication and trust.

3 Methodology

Questionnaires were distributed to obtain the patient's evaluation on the physician's behaviors and his/her trust in the physician he/she has just visited. To examine the structure of the physician communication behavior scale, the factor analysis was carried out. To find out what physician communication behaviors influence patient trust, correlation analyses were conducted.

3.1 Questionnaire Construction

The questionnaire was composed of three parts: demographic information, physician communication behavior scale and patient trust scale.

The demographic information included the subject's gender, age, education background, health status and whether living in Beijing. For the second part, 25 items indicating physician communication behaviors were adapted from existing studies—ten items adapted from the PHBQ, four from the Stanford Trust Study, three from Safran's, one from Anderson and Dedrick's, one from Kao's, and the other six from brainstorm with partners. The subjects were asked to rate each item on a 5-point Likert scale from 1 (strongly disagree) to 5 (strongly agree). For the third part, the 10-item Wake Forest trust scale was adopted and the subjects rated each item on a 5-point Likert scale from 1 (strongly disagree) to 5 (strongly agree). The average score of the 10 items was computed as the measure of patient trust in the physician he/she just visited. The paper-based questionnaire was used in this survey.

3.2 Subject and Data Collection

For the sample size, since a factor analysis would be conducted for the 25-item physician communication behavior scale, a subject-to-item ratio larger than 5 would be acceptable (Gorsuch, 1983). In this study, 220 subjects were recruited from the waiting room of pharmacies in Peking Union Medical College Hospital and Peking University Third Hospital. Most patients in the waiting room of the pharmacy had just finished seeing a physician and were waiting to take medicine. The subject was firstly asked whether he/she had just visited a physician. The one whose answer was yes was given a questionnaire to evaluate the physician's communication behaviors and his/her trust in the physician he/she just visited.

207 of the 220 questionnaires were valid. The demographic information of the 207 subjects were summarized in Table 1. There were 93 male and 114 female subjects. Their mean age was 43.6 with the standard deviation (SD) 15.89. The youngest subject was 14 years old and the oldest one was 82 years old. 11.6% subjects had junior high school or below education, 18.0% had senior high school education, 55.3% had bachelor degrees and 15.0% had master or PhD degrees. 85.0% subjects thought his/her health status was not very good. 82.0% subjects lived in Beijing while the others didn't.

Table 1. Demographic information of subjects

Item	Level	Number	Percentage
Gender	Male	93	44.9%
	Female	114	55.1%
Age	Age<=45	119	57.5%
	Age>45	88	42.5%
Education level	Junior high school or below	24	11.6%
	Senior high school	37	18.0%
	Bachelor degree	114	55.3%
	Master or PhD degree	31	15.0%
Health status	Very good	31	15.0%
	Good	84	40.8%
	General	81	39.3%
	Poor	10	4.9%
	Very poor	0	0.0%
Whether living in Beijing	Yes	169	82.0%
	No	37	18.0%

4 Data Analysis

4.1 Descriptive Statistics

The average score for most physician communication behaviors was between 3.50 and 4.00, with the negative items reversely coded. Among all the physician communication behaviors, the item with highest mean score was "asking questions about my symptoms thoroughly" and the item with lowest mean score was "being in a hurry". The average score of patient trust was 3.76 with SD of 1.00.

4.2 Factor Analysis

Exploratory factor analysis was carried out to examine the structure of the physician communication behavior scale. The Kaiser-Meyer-Olkin (KMO) measure was 0.942 and the Bartlett's test had the p-value less than 0.001, both indicating that factor analysis was proper. The extraction method was principal component analysis and factors with eigenvalue above 1.0 was extracted. The rotation method was Varimax rotation and a threshold of 0.50 loading was used when an item belonged to one factor. Item 13 (using terms I can understand, instead of many medical vocabularies) was excluded with a maximum loading of 0.305. A model with 24 items categorized into three factors was the best one. The loadings for each item to each factor were listed in Table 2. The three factors accounted for 62.4% of the total variance. The factors were named as respect and caring, competence and thoroughness, patience and honesty.

Table 2. Results of the factor analysis

		Factors		
N o.	Item	Respect and caring	Competence and thoroughness	Patience and honesty
15	Comforting or reassure me and my family	0.820	0.284	0.145
14	Expressing concern for my feelings and needs, not just my physical status	0.793	0.321	0.233
16	Encouraging me (that everything will be fine)	0.754	0.357	0.112
21	Discussing options for my treatment	0.745	0.261	0.155
19	Encouraging me to ask questions	0.712	0.312	0.192
22	Asking for my opinions about which options to take	0.686	0.242	0.197
23	Explaining why he/she recommends one treatment over another	0.671	0.414	0.137
13	Greeting me warmly	0.636	0.361	0.260
27	Looking in eye when I talk	0.582	0.217	0.196
20	Answering my questions clearly	0.506	0.454	0.374
9	Telling the expected effects of my treatment	0.416	0.717	0.062
6	Asking questions about my symptoms thoroughly	0.307	0.703	0.333
7	Explaining my problems in detail	0.385	0.664	0.309
24	Telling me the truth about my health, even if there were bad news	0.323	0.656	0.178
8	Asking me to perform necessary tests and procedures	0.261	0.634	0.020
10	Explaining side-effects of my treatments	0.467	0.626	0.075
30	Arranging for adequate privacy when examining or talking to me	0.176	0.614	0.201
29	Putting my medical needs above all other considerations	0.325	0.604	0.372
11	Listening patiently to my problems, worries and concerns	0.420	0.550	0.459
28	Being short-tempered or abrupt with me or my family	0.088	0.206	0.810
26	Trying to hide the mistake he/she has made in my treatment from me	0.134	0.159	0.806
25	Pretending to know things when he/she is really not sure	0.096	0.253	0.749
12	Making uncaring remarks	0.243	0.033	0.699
17	Being in a hurry	0.256	0.125	0.666

The internal consistency (Cronbach's alpha) within each factor was listed in Table 3. The overall internal consistency was 0.950, indicating the physician communication behavior scale was reliable. Moreover, the Cronbach's alpha for the Wake Forest's trust scale was 0.908, also indicating good internal consistency.

Table 3. Factors with corresponding percentage of variance explained and internal consistency

Factors	Initial eigenvalue	% of variance after rotation	Cumulative % after rotation	Cronbach's alpha
Respect and caring	11.580	48.250	48.250	0.932
Competence and thoroughness	2.200	9.168	57.417	0.912
Patience and honesty	1.197	4.987	62.404	0.833

4.3   Correlation Analysis

In order to find out what physician behaviors had an impact on the patient trust, the correlation analysis using Pearson coefficient was conducted for each specific physician communication behavior and patient trust. The results were shown in Table 4. At the 95% confidence level, all the behaviors significantly influenced patient trust ($p < 0.001$). The five behaviors most strongly associated with patient trust were listening patiently to my problems, worries and concerns, answering my questions clearly, explaining my problems in detail, asking questions about my symptoms thoroughly and greeting my warmly. According to the factor analysis results, three of the five behaviors belonged to the factor "competence and thoroughness" and the other two belonged to the factor "respect and caring". It seemed that patients attached the greatest importance to physician's competence and thoroughness in evaluation. Physician's respect and caring was also most important for patients to build trust. The five behaviors least strongly associated with patient trust were explaining side-effects of my treatments, looking in eye when I talk, making uncaring remarks, asking me to perform necessary tests and procedures, and arranging for adequate privacy when examining or talking to me. Patients did not seem to care about their privacy that much. It was a little bit surprising that eye contact and necessary tests and procedures weren't attached great importance to patient trust. Possible reasons would be discussed in the next part.

Did men and women take the same view about what behaviors elicit patient trust? The Pearson correlation was carried out for the male and female groups. The five communication behaviors that were most and least strongly associated with patient trust were listed in Tables 5 and 6. For the male group, physician's behavior of comforting or reassuring me and my family and encouraging me were among the top five behaviors associated with trust. For the female group, on the contrast, physician's behavior of discussing options for my treatment was regarded as important. Men seemed to need more caring, comfort and encouragement than women, while women seemed to be more rational than men. Possible explanations would be discussed in the next part.

Table 4. Pearson correlation between physician communication behavior and patient trust

Physician communication behavior	Pearson coefficient	P-value
Listening patiently to my problems, worries and concerns	0.746	<0.001
Answering my questions clearly	0.711	<0.001
Explaining my problems in detail	0.663	<0.001
Asking questions about my symptoms thoroughly	0.650	<0.001
Greeting me warmly	0.639	<0.001
Comforting or reassure me and my family	0.639	<0.001
Expressing concern for my feelings and needs, not just my physical status	0.637	<0.001
Discussing options for my treatment	0.619	<0.001
Explaining why he/she recommends one treatment over another	0.612	<0.001
Putting my medical needs above all other considerations	0.610	<0.001
Telling me the truth about my health, even if there were bad news	0.605	<0.001
Encouraging me (that everything will be fine)	0.602	<0.001
Telling the expected effects of my treatment	0.585	<0.001
Trying to hide the mistake he/she has made in my treatment from me[1]	0.584	<0.001
Encouraging me to ask questions	0.578	<0.001
Pretending to know things when he/she is really not sure	0.558	<0.001
Asking for my opinions about which options to take	0.555	<0.001
Being short-tempered or abrupt with me or my family	0.549	<0.001
Being in a hurry	0.528	<0.001
Explaining side-effects of my treatments	0.524	<0.001
Looking in eye when I talk	0.517	<0.001
Making uncaring remarks	0.508	<0.001
Asking me to perform necessary tests and procedures	0.429	<0.001
Arranging for adequate privacy when examining or talking to me	0.397	<0.001

[1]The negative item was coded reversely so that its Pearson coefficient was nonnegative.

Would patients with different ages take the same view about physician behaviors that elicit trust? The correlation analysis was conducted for younger (age<=45) and older (age>45) groups. The top and last five behaviors associated with patient trust were listed in Tables 5 and 6. Younger patients seemed to need more concerns about their feelings, not just their physical status. For older patients, telling them the truth about their health was important, even if there were bad news. Hiding the true health condition would make older people less likely to trust the physician. Another difference between younger and older groups was the behavior of putting medical needs above all other considerations. This behavior was in the top five for older group but in the last five for younger group. Older patients seemed to value their health very much and

Table 5. Five behaviors most strongly associated with patient trust for different subgroups

Subgroup	Physcian communication behaviors
Male	Listening patiently to my problems, worries and concerns
	Answering my questions clearly
	Comforting or reassuring me and my family
	Encouraging me (that everything will be fine)
	Explaining why he/she recommends one treatment over another
Female	Listening patiently to my problems, worries and concerns
	Answering my questions clearly
	Explaining my problems in detail
	Asking questions about my symptoms thoroughly
	Discussing options for my treatment
Younger (age<=45)	Listening patiently to my problems, worries and concerns
	Answering my questions clearly
	Explaining my problems in detail
	Comforting or reassure me and my family
	Expressing concern for my feelings and needs, not just my physical status
Older (age>45)	Listening patiently to my problems, worries and concerns
	Putting my medical needs above all other considerations
	Answering my questions clearly
	Telling me the truth about my health, even if there were bad news
	Asking questions about my symptoms thoroughly

extremely care about whether they can be cured, so they wanted their medical needs to be firstly considered. Younger patients did care about their medical needs since the behavior was significantly associated with patient trust. Besides the medical needs, in contrast with older ones, younger patients also had other concerns such as convenience, cost and side effects.

5 Discussion

Each specific behavior identified in the physician communication behavior scale was assessed to be significantly associated with patient trust. The behaviors indicating physician's competence and thoroughness were regarded as most important to enhance patient trust in the physician. The physician should listen to the patient's problems patiently, ask questions about symptoms and explain the problems in detail. Physician's caring and respect was also important for patients to build trust. A simple greeting would make the patient feel at ease and become more confident in his/her doctor.

According to the correlation analysis result, eye contact wasn't that important for trust, which was contrary to some previous studies on nonverbal behaviors (such as Griffith et al., 2003). In China, hospitals are often crowded with people. The outpatient

Table 6. Five behaviors least strongly associated with patient trust for differenct subgroups

Subgroup	Physcian communication behaviors
Male	Making uncaring remarks.
	Being in a hurry.
	Looking in eye when I talk.
	Asking me to perform necessary tests and procedures
	Arranging for adequate privacy when examining or talking to me.
Female	Pretending to know things when he/she is really not sure.
	Being short-tempered or abrupt with me or my family.
	Making uncaring remarks.
	Asking me to perform necessary tests and procedures
	Arranging for adequate privacy when examining or talking to me.
Younger (age<=45)	Putting my medical needs above all other considerations.
	Being in a hurry.
	Making uncaring remarks.
	Asking me to perform necessary tests and procedures
	Arranging for adequate privacy when examining or talking to me.
Older (age>45)	Telling the expected effects of my treatment.
	Explaining side-effects of my treatments
	Arranging for adequate privacy when examining or talking to me.
	Looking in eye when I talk.
	Asking me to perform necessary tests and procedures

amounts in both Peking Union Medical College Hospital and Peking University Third Hospital are over ten thousand a day. Often a physician has to finish seeing a patient within several minutes. This way, it may be acceptable for the patient if his/her doctor is busy inquiring symptoms and making prescriptions without much eye contact with him/her. Moreover, a previous study on nonverbal behavior and patient satisfaction showed that increased eye contact might lead to decreased satisfaction (Larsen and Smith, 1981), indicating eye contact might not be that necessary to build trust.

Another surprising result was that the physician behavior of asking me to perform necessary tests and procedures was not strongly associated with patient trust. During the interview, some patients said that his/her physician made prescriptions without asking them to perform any medical test and was perfunctory. Other patients said that his/her physician asked them to perform unnecessary tests just for his/her own benefit. It seems reasonable since in China many people have to pay a large portion of their medical costs and are not willing to waste money on those "unnecessary" tests. Whereas in the US in which most people owes high proportion of health insurances, what they care about is whether the physician asks them to perform necessary tests regardless of the health plan's cost.

As for the two gender groups, men seemed to need more comfort and encouragement than women. Men are always regarded as rational and strong, and how would they need more caring than women? A population-based study of spinal pain once found that when pain was at its worst, men took sick leave whereas women sought health care (Linton, Hellsing and Halldén, 1998). Despite often acting as the bread-winner, men are likely to become fragile when sick and need to be reassured. One cannot be strong or fragile all the time, no matter men or women.

Older people seemed to value their health more than younger ones. They wanted their medical needs to be firstly considered and would like to know the truth about their health status, even if there were bad news. Older people in this study were defined as those with ages above 45, which was the same as in Stanford Trust Study (Thom et al., 2001). Due to the relative small sample size of elder patients who were 65 years old or above, how elder adults associate physician communication behaviors with trust cannot be specified, which is a limitation of this study.

Another limitation of the study is in the design of the physician communication scale. In factor analysis, those negative items in the scale, though reversely coded, all belonged to one single factor called patience and honesty. Possible reason may be that the subjects could not switch freely between positive and negative items and tended to be a little conservative while rating the negative items.

In future studies, the Kano model developed by Noriaki Kano (1984) may be applied in health care and physician communication behaviors could be categorized as must-be, one-dimensional or attractive for patients to build trust. The must-be behaviors are basic and acting these behaviors will only lead to "not distrustful". For one-dimensional behaviors, patients' level of trust is proportional to the level of the behavior fulfillment. The higher level of fulfillment, the higher level of trust. For attractive behaviors, if fulfilled, patients' trust will increased and if not, patients' level of trust will not be lowered. Future studies can be conducted on finding what communication behaviors are must-be, one-dimensional or attractive, which can be used in physician communication training process.

6 Conclusion

Firstly, this study provided a reliable physician communication behavior scale which can be adopted for patients to assess the physician's communication behaviors he/she visited. The behaviors were categorized into three factors—respect and caring, competence and thoroughness, patience and honesty. Secondly, this study found out what behaviors could elicit patient trust and analyzed the relative strength of the associations between each specific communication behavior and patient trust. Since all the behaviors identified in the scale were significantly associated with patient trust, it will be better for physicians to fulfill as many of them as possible to enhance patient trust. Specifically,

- Physicians' competence and thoroughness was regarded as most important for patients to build trust. Physicians should take time to listen to the patient's problems patiently, ask questions about symptoms and explain the problems in detail.
- Men seemed to need more caring than women when sick. Giving a male patient some encouragement and comfort does not seem like a bad idea. Women were likely to be more rational when discussing about her treatment. Providing some options and giving detailed explanations may be a good way for a female patient to establish trust.

- Older people valued their health very much. While seeing an older patient, it will be better for the physician to put the patient's medical needs above all other considerations.

References

Anderson, L.A., Dedrick, R.F.: Development of the trust in physician scale: a measure to assess interpersonal trust in patient-physician relationships. Psychol. Rep. 67(3f), 1091–1100 (1990)

Bambino, L.E.: Physician Communication Behaviors That Elicit Patient Trust (2006)

Buller, M.K., Buller, D.B.: Physicians' communication style and patient satisfaction. J. Health Soc. Behav. 28, 375–388 (1987)

Chaitchik, S., Kreitler, S., Shared, S., et al.: Doctor-patient communication in a cancer ward. J. Cancer Educ. 7(1), 41–54 (1992)

Fong Ha, J., Longnecker, N.: Doctor patient communication: a review. Ochsner J. 10, 38–43 (2010)

Gerteis, M.: Through the Patient's Eyes: Understanding and Promoting Patient-Centered Care, vol. 531. Jossey-Bass, San Francisco (1993)

Gorsuch, R.L.: Factor analysis, 2nd ed. Hillsdale, Lawrence Erlbaum, New Jersy (1983)

Griffith, C.H., Wilson, J.F., Langer, S., Haist, S.A.: House staff nonverbal communication skills and standardized patient satisfaction. J. Gen. Intern. Med. 18(3), 170–174 (2003)

Hall, M.A., Zheng, B., Dugan, E., et al.: Measuring patients' trust in their primary care providers. Med. Care Res. Rev. 59(3), 293–318 (2002)

Kano, N., Seraku, N., Takahashi, F., et al.: Attractive quality and must-be quality. J. Japn. Soc. Qual. Control 14(2), 147–156 (1984)

Kao, A.C., Green, D.C., Zaslavsky, A.M., et al.: The relationship between method of physician payment and patient trust. JAMA 280(19), 1708–1714 (1998)

Larsen, K.M., Smith, C.K.: Assessment of nonverbal communication in the patient-physician interview. J. Family Pract. 12(3), 481–488 (1981)

Leisen, B., Hyman, M.R.: Antecedents and consequences of trust in a service provider. The case of primary physicians. J. Bus. Res. 57, 990–999 (2004)

Lewicki, R.J., Bunker, B.B.: Trust in Relationships: A Model of Development and Decline. Jossey-Bass, San Francisco (1995)

Linton, S.J., Hellsing, A.L., Halldén, K.: A population-based study of spinal pain among 35-45-year-old individuals: prevalence, sick leave, and health care use. Spine 23(13), 1457–1463 (1998)

Manning, P., Ray, G.B.: Setting the agenda: an analysis of negotiation strategies in clinical talk. Health Commun. 14(4), 451–473 (2002)

Ong, L.M., De Haes, J.C., Hoos, A.M., Lammes, F.B.: Doctor-patient communication: a review of the literature. Soc. Sci. Med. 40(7), 903–918 (1995)

Safran, D.G., Kosinski, M., Tarlov, A.R., et al.: The primary care assessment survey: tests of data quality and measurement performance. Med. Care 36(5), 728–739 (1998)

Street, R.L.: Information-giving in medical consultations: the influence of patients' communicative styles and personal characteristics. Soc. Sci. Med. 32(5), 541–548 (1991)

Thom, D.H., Ribisl, K.M., Stewart, A.L., Luke, D.A.: Further validation and reliability testing of the Trust in Physician Scale. Med. Care 37(5), 510–517 (1999)

Thom, D.H.: Physician behaviors that predict patient trust. J. Family Pract. 50(4), 323–328 (2001)

Thom, D.H., Campbell, B.: Patient-physician trust: an exploratory study. J. Family Pract. **44**(2), 169–176 (1997)

Weaver, M.J., Ow, C.L., Walker, D.J., Degenhardt, E.F.: A questionnaire for patients' evaluations of their physicians' humanistic behaviors. J. Gen. Intern. Med. **8**(3), 135–139 (1993)

Cultural Difference on Team Performance Between Chinese and Americans in Multiplayer Online Battle Arena Games

Huiwen Wang[1,2], Bang Xia[1,2], and Zhe Chen[1(✉)]

[1] School of Economics and Management, Beihang University, Beijing 100191, China
zhechen@buaa.edu.cn
[2] Beijing Key Laboratory of Emergency Support Simulation Technologies for City Operations, Beijing 100191, China

Abstract. This paper studies cultural difference on team performance in a multiplayer online battle arena game called Defense of the Ancient 2(DOTA2). 37 international competition replays are acquired from the game platform of DOTA2 between Chinese teams and American teams. Though observing the replays, seven variables are brought up and paired data for each variable is obtained. Non-parametric test methods have been used to analyze the data, such as Wlicoxon test and Mood test. The result indicates some cultural differences in online games between two countries' teams as following. Chinese teams are risk-avoiding while American teams are risk-taking. In addition, American teams show potential stronger masculinity than Chinese teams.

Keywords: Cultural difference · Multiplayer online battle arena game · Teamwork · Performance · Uncertainty avoidance

1 Introduction

Playing online game is a popular entertainment in recent years. Millions of people play online games every day and a variety of game-playing behaviors are produced in them. For instance, many guilds are set up in World of Warcraft(WOW), an massive multiplayer online role-playing game. It's interesting to study how guilds generate in online games and if every guild has its particular organizational culture. In addition, it is also meaningful to study whether the team performance is affected by the culture of the players in some real time strategy games like defense of the ancients 2(DOTA2) and whether different cultures will contribute to different results. The findings in online games can help to improve game design on one side. Meanwhile, they may be applied to organizations and enterprises in the real world to improve organization performance on the other side.

Thus cultural difference in online games is an important subject worth being studied, but few researches have been done in this field. While most of the cross-cultural studies focus on realistic society, there have been relatively few cultural researches into the virtual world like online games. And most of the

© Springer International Publishing Switzerland 2015
P.L.P. Rau (Ed.): CCD 2015, Part II, LNCS 9181, pp. 374–383, 2015.
DOI:10.1007/978-3-319-20934-0_35

studies on video games are carried out by questionnaire survey, which can't fully reflect reality. In a unique perspective, this paper compares the cultural difference between Chinese teams and American teams just using the data from a multiplayer online battle arena(MOBA) game called DOTA2 itself.

DOTA2 is a 5v5-player game which is in the dominant position of MOBA games together with another game named league of legends. It provides a platform for game players around the world to interact with each other and enjoy the games without boundaries. Each player controls an in-game avatar and the only victory condition is to conquer the opposite sides main building for each team. One game lasts about 40 min–60 min in common and includes many strategic elements, varying from teamwork to individual operation. In some sense, DOTA2 creates a simulated reality for the players. Every professional team has its unique characteristics in these strategic elements and shows a distinct style. Therefore it is an interesting scientific problem to examine how the performance of professional teams from different cultures shows in Hofstedes five cross-cultural dimensions [6]. According to his theory, cultural differences are elaborated from five different dimensions which are power distance, collectivism/individualism, masculinity/femininity, uncertainty avoidance and long-term/short-term orientation. Furthermore another motivation of this research is whether the result in online game is the same as the conclusions of realistic society.

This paper takes a case study using the combat data of the international DOTA2 championships held in Seattle, July 2014 (TI4). TI4 is one of the biggest electronic sports tournaments all over the world. Among all the matches in TI4, 37 matches between Chinese teams and American teams have been screened out and seven groups of paired observational data have been obtained. Using nonparametric methods, the test result indicates teams from the two countries show different behaviors in cross-cultural dimensions like uncertainty avoidance and collectivism.

The purpose of the research is to explore whether there are cultural differences on online game behaviors between teams from different countries. At the same moment, another purpose is to make clear of the cultural differences and examine whether the differences are the same both in the virtual and realistic world. This paper pioneers a new way to study cultural differences. The findings of this research is a supplement of the cultural research in realistic society. It stretches our attention of cultural differences into the virtual world and help us have a better cross-cultural understanding.

2 Literature Review

There are massive studies on cultural differences, but little research has been done from the viewpoint of online games. The previous research has tended to compare cultural differences between different organisations or nations in the realistic world [9,15]. Shane Scott studied uncertainty avoidance and the preference for innovation championing roles [14]. Zigang Zhang has made a comparison between America and China by applying the cultural dimensions of Hofstede in 2004 [20]. However, cultural differences in the virtual world like online games have not been deeply studied.

From the point of online games, research is also focused on aspects like influences of game addition, demographic factors of the players, game design and so on. There is also little research about cultural differences reflected by the performance of game players. Most of the early studies on online games have tended to concentrate on the more negative aspects such as excessive play and addiction, the medical and psychosocial consequences [1,2,10,18]. And research in this field continues as time goes on. An article verifies that gaming addiction is currently not a widespread phenomenon among adolescents and adults in Germany [3], which indicates people's understanding towards online games is becoming deep and mature. Then the research point turns to motivations, demographic factors and some playing variables of online game players [4,16,19]. An online questionnaire survey was used by Griffiths to examine basic demographic factors of online computer game players who played the popular online game Everquest. The result gave a detailed description of the game player on demographic aspects such as gender, age, frequency and so on. At the same year, a comparison of adolescent and adult gamers was made [5]. The researches above are focused on the influence of online games or the demographic factors of game players. Relatively little research has study the behaviors of the players in the game.

Latest research starts to examine aspects of organizational behaviours. The social life of guilds in world of Warcraft has been studied [17]. In keeping with current Internet research findings, players were found to use the game to extend reallife relationships, meet new people, form relationships of varying strength, and also use others merely as a backdrop. Tinnawat has taken a research of the leadership development in DOTA [12]. In the study, multinomial logistic regression and factor analyses have been done using questionnaire data. Based on the findings, it is concluded that players characterized as different game roles show different leadership styles. Ratan Rabindra has studied the gender embodiment in virtual spaces [13]. This article examines the pattern of behavior in League of Legends(LOL) which is another popular MOBA game similar to DOTA2. The results indicate that male players tend to focus more on combat activities while women focus on more social game activities. The general claim has also been supported that males tend to have an instrumental relationship with their avatars, while females tend to have an identity-relevant relationship. Social networks in multiplayer online games are also a hot area of research [11]. His research has addressed the problem of how to extract and analyse the implicit social structure in networked games such as DOTA and StarCraft series. Some interesting researches on online games also involve gender culture and collective culture [7,8]. Behaviors of players who choose the opposite gender in online games have been studied. The result shows men overcome their inhibition for help seeking when using female avatars.

In conclusion, more and more articles begin to study organizational culture in online games. But there are few researches conducted on cultural differences and cross-cultural factors. Besides studies on culture in online games are fragmentary lacking systematic carding.

3   Data and Method

3.1   Variables

As a real-time strategy game, DOTA2 contains massive equipment and props ranging from assault weapons to healing salve for avatars, which leads to a series of complicated attacking and defending performance. In the game, it is essential to have a good teamwork if one side wants to win the game. There are several items for the team in DOTA2 which are used almost in every game. For instance, smoke of deceit is an item used for a sneak attack. Upon activation, the user and all nearby allied player-controlled units gain invisibility and bonus movement speed for a brief time. Minimap icons will also be hidden. Upon moving within 1025 range of an enemy hero or tower, the invisibility is lost. The duration of smoke of deceit is 35 s. Due to the function of smoke of deceit, it can be concluded that one team will gain a greater chance to kill the enemy heros with this item. In some sense, a team is more aggressive and challenging if using smoke of deceit under a higher frequency than the other side. Thus the gender role of this kind of team is close to masculinity and the opposite team is relatively close to femininity applying the cultural dimensions of Hofstede. Another common item is ward. There are two kinds of ward, observer ward and sentry ward. Observer ward provides a broad perspective while sentry ward produces an invisible ward capable of spotting invisible enemy units, but lacking in vision. A team shows strong uncertainty avoidance if using observer wards and sentry wards frequently. In addition, runes are powerful items player can obtain with his avatar that vanish when they are picked up, and give the avatar a powerful effect for a limited amount of time. Every even numbered minute of game time, starting at the first creep spawn, a rune will spawn at one of the 2 rune spawning locations, if there is not already a rune at one of the spawning locations. Each spawning location is in the river, one of them is northwest of the middle of the map, and the other is southeast. Frequency of activating runes also shows uncertainty avoidance of a team.

According to the common items and common performance of the players in the game, seven variables have been brought up that can reflect cross-cultural dimensions. The first two variables are the frequency of kill by one player and the frequency of kill by multiplayer which show individualism and collectivism of a team. The following two variables are the frequency of picking fight and the frequency of using smoke of deceit which show the gender role of a team. The last three variables are the frequency of using observer ward, the frequency of using sentry ward and the frequency of activating runes, which reflect uncertainty avoidance of a team. Through making a comparison of two opposite teams upon these seven variables in each game, it can be tested whether cultural differences exist between teams from two different countries.

3.2   Procedure

From DOTA2 platform, 37 game replays have been acquired as our research sample between Chinese teams and American teams in the fourth international DOTA2 championship which is a top electronic sports tournament held every year from 2011. Observational data of seven variables is obtained in every replay. Table 1 shows the data observation standard. Each data is a cumulative value during one whole game.

Table 1. Data observation standard

Item	Observation standard
Frequency of kill by one player (KO)	Observe the death of each avatar. If the source of the damage is from one enemy avatar,frequency of the enemy side adds one
Frequency of kill by multiplayer (KM)	Observe the death of each avatar. If the source of the damage is from more than one enemy players, frequency of the enemy side adds one
Frequency of picking fight (PF)	Observe each fight. If avatars of one side launch attacks first, frequency of the corresponding team adds one
Frequency of using smoke of deceit(SD)	When one side uses smoke of deceit,frequency of the side adds one
Frequency of using observer ward (OW)	Count the times of using observer wards which are solid dots in minimap
Frequency of using sentry ward (SW)	Count the times of using sentry wards which are hollow dots in minimap
Frequency of activating runes (AR)	Observe rune spawning locations every even numbered minute of game time. If an avatar activates the rune, frequency of the corresponding team adds one

There were 16 top teams which consisted of five professional players in each team from all over the world attending TI4. Thus the performance of the players is representative of their own culture without the interference of inexperience. As the observation is completed, seven groups of paired data are acquired. Then median tests and scale tests have been conducted under each variable using non-parametric methods like Brown-Mood test, Wlicoxon test, Siegel-Turkey test and Mood test. The software we use is R language.

4   Results and Discussion

4.1   Basic Description of the Data

From 37 game replays, seven groups of paired data are acquired via observation. The basic statistic analysis of the data is as following in Table 2.

Table 2. Basic analysis of the data

Variable		Mean	Median	Std	Min	Max
KO	China	2.41	2	2.47	0	9
	USA	2.27	2	2.33	0	9
KM	China	16.57	16	8.45	4	42
	USA	16.70	19	10.43	1	42
PF	China	9.84	9	4.79	2	27
	USA	10.89	10	5.61	2	23
SD	China	3.57	3	1.97	1	9
	USA	3.30	3	2.12	0	7
OW	China	10.38	9	4.93	4	26
	USA	9.65	10	4.30	2	18
SW	China	7.49	6	5.92	0	23
	USA	4.46	3	4.39	0	18
AR	China	9.59	9	4.32	4	20
	USA	7.49	6	5.18	2	25

Basic statistic shows that Chinese teams and American teams have approximately same mean value of three variables which are KO, KM and SD. The remaining four variables especially SW and AR have unequal mean value between two countries' teams. From the viewpoint of median, the result is a little different from that of mean value. Median is the same of only two variables which are KO and SD. While median of KM exists relatively a large gap between Chinese teams and American teams, significantly different from the result of mean value. The reason of the difference is that mean value is sensitive to outliers while medium is relatively steady. Thus medium is a better index to explain the performance difference between two counties' teams. In addition, standard deviation has a relatively big difference in four variables which are KM, PF, SW and AR. The remaining three variables have nearly the same standard deviation.

To sum up, Chinese teams use more observer wards(OW) and sentry wards (SW) while American teams pick fights more than Chinese. These are preliminary conclusions. Further analysis should be done to test whether the differences above indeed exists. For each pair of observational data, median tests and scale tests will be conducted in the following. In the analysis process, non-parametric methods like Brown-Mood test, Wlicoxon test, Siegel-Turkey test and Mood test are used.

4.2 Non-parametric Test Result

Table 2 indicates that Chinese teams and American teams may have differences in some variables like PF, SW and AR. In this part each pair of observational data will be tested. Among the four test methods, Brown-Mood test and Wlicoxon test are used to examine whether the medians of paired data are the same. Siegel-Turkey test and Mood test are used to verify whether the scales of paired data are the same. Based on the test result comparison can be made of the team performance between Chinese and American teams. Table 3 shows the test result of each variable.

Table 3. Median test and scale test

Test method		KO	KM	PF	SD	OW	SW	AR
Median test	Brown-Mood	11	17	17	18	17	20	21
		(0.82)	(0.64)	(0.97)	(0.24)	(0.89)	(0.02**)	(0.03**)
	Wlicoxon	703.5	680.5	608.5	731.5	720	917	908
		(0.84)	(0.97)	(0.41)	(0.61)	(0.70)	(0.01**)	(0.02**)
Scale test	Siegel-Turkey	1437.3	1549.6	1549.2	1462.9	1345.3	1440.8	1558.6
		(0.62)	(0.08*)	(0.09*)	(0.38)	(0.69)	(0.59)	(0.06*)
	Mood	−0.226	−2.028	−1.876	−0.873	0.086	−0.524	−2.172
		(0.82)	(0.04**)	(0.06*)	(0.38)	(0.93)	(0.60)	(0.03**)

"*" indicates significant difference at 10 % level.
"**" indicates significant difference at 5 % level.

From the test result, Chinese teams and American teams are significantly different in the scale of KM and PF. The frequency of using sentry wards is also different between two countries teams at 5 % significant level. In other words, Chinese teams use more sentry wards than American teams. As for frequency of activating runes, median test and scale test are both significant. Chinese teams activate more runes than American teams in one game. Different from the preliminary conclusions, frequency of kill by multiplayer is not significantly different in median. To make a visualization of the test result, probability density plots of seven groups of data are drawn in Fig. 1.

Graphical results back up the median test and scale test. In Fig. 1, the red solid lines are probability density distributions of Chinese teams, while the blue dashed line are probability density distributions of American teams. It is obvious that scale difference exists in the second, third and last sub-figures, because the steepness of the two lines are not the same among which one is steep while the other is relatively gentle. In addition, position difference exists in the sixth and last sub-figures, because peaks of the two lines are stagger. Due to these results, cultural differences can be concluded in relative cross-cultural dimensions, which will be discussed in the last part of the paper.

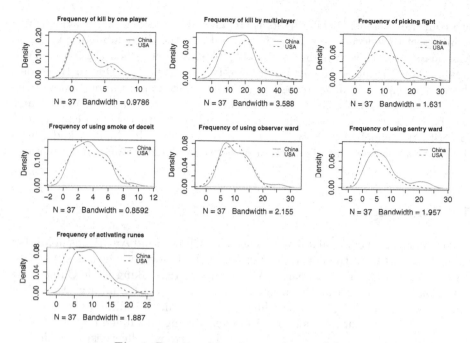

Fig. 1. Density plots of seven groups of data

4.3 Discussion

Through analyzing the data, there are mainly two conclusions of this research. Firstly, in the cross-cultural dimension of uncertainty avoidance, Chinese teams show stronger uncertainty avoidance than American teams which is clarified by the test results of SW and AR. It shows that Chinese teams activate more runes and use more sentry wards which is used to spot invisible enemy units. These performance can help the team reduce risk of a sudden attack from the enemy side. But American teams activate relatively fewer runes and use fewer sentry wards. Thus it can be seen that Chinese and Americans hold different attitude towards uncertainty in DOTA2. Chinese teams are of risk aversion and take measures like using sentry wards to avoid uncertainty. On the contrary, American teams show relatively weak uncertainty avoidance.

As for frequency of using observer wards, it is also a target to reflect uncertainty avoidance. But neither the median test nor the scale test is significant, which seems in conflict with the test results of SW and AR. Actually this phenomenon is reasonable. Because the observer ward is an item that can prevent sudden attacks on one side, on the other side it can be used for detecting the enemy avatars and making an active attack. So frequency of using observer wards is an aggregative variable of several cultural factors. This is why it's not significant in median test and scale test.

Secondly, American teams show potential stronger masculinity than Chinese teams. The test result indicates that scale of PF is significantly different between two countries' teams. Picking fights is a challenge and offensive behavior which is an aspect to reflect masculinity of a team. From the third sub-figure in Fig. 1, American teams have a higher probability to pick fights when the frequency is greater than 15, though median difference is not significant. Due to Hofstede's theory, challenge, earnings, recognition, and competition are important in masculine societies. The result in the third sub-figure means that American teams may be relatively more competitive and masculine. Further studies can be done to verify this conclusion. Lastly, in the dimension of individualism and collectivism, there are not any big differences between Chinese teams and American teams.

5   Conclusions

The conclusions of cultural differences between Chinese and Americans in MOBA games are similar to the conclusions in the realistic society which is studied by Zigang Zhang [20]. In his research, Americans are risk-taking while Chinese are risk-avoiding. And in the dimension of masculinity and femininity, Americans show medium masculinity while Chinese show medium femininity. These conclusions are consistent in this paper. However, Zigang concluded that Americans show strong individualism while Chinese show strong collectivism which isn't embodied in our research of DOTA2. This paper compares cultural difference in an online game called DOTA2 which comes up with a new perspective to study cultural difference. It stretches our attention of cultural differences into the virtual world and help us have a better cross-cultural understanding between Chinese and Americans. Besides, the research findings can be taken into account in game design and development to provide the game players with better game experience. Further research can be done to find out more variables and conduct a test of the remaining two dimensions of cultural difference which are power distance and long-term orientation.

Acknowledgement. This research is financially supported by National Natural Science Foundation of China (Grant No. 71420107025) and the National High Technology Research and Development Program of China (863 Program) (SS2014AA012303).

References

1. Anderson, C.A., Shibuya, A., Ihori, N., Swing, E.L., Bushman, B.J., Sakamoto, A., Rothstein, H.R., Saleem, M.: Violent video game effects on aggression, empathy, and prosocial behavior in eastern and Western Countries: a meta-analytic review. Psychol. Bull. **136**(2), 151 (2010)
2. Desai, R.A., Krishnan-Sarin, S., Cavallo, D., Potenza, M.N.: Video-gaming among high school students: health correlates, gender differences, and problematic gaming. Pediatrics **126**(6), e1414–e1424 (2010)
3. Festl, R., Scharkow, M., Quandt, T.: Problematic computer game use among adolescents, younger and older adults. Addiction **108**(3), 592–599 (2013)

4. Griffiths, M.D., Davies, M.N., Chappell, D.: Demographic factors and playing variables in online computer gaming. CyberPsychol. Behav. **7**(4), 479–487 (2004)
5. Griffiths, M.D., Davies, M.N., Chappell, D.: Online computer gaming: a comparison of adolescent and adult gamers. J. Adolesc. **27**(1), 87–96 (2004)
6. Hofstede, G.: Cultures and Organizations. McGraw-Hill, London (1991)
7. Lee, Y.H., Wohn, D.Y.: Are there cultural differences in how we play? Examining cultural effects on playing social network games. Comput. Hum. Behav. **28**(4), 1307–1314 (2012)
8. Lehdonvirta, M., Nagashima, Y., Lehdonvirta, V., Baba, A.: The stoic male how avatar gender affects help-seeking behavior in an online game. Game. Cult. **7**(1), 29–47 (2012)
9. Litvin, S.W., Crotts, J.C., Hefner, F.L.: Cross-cultural tourist behaviour: a replication and extension involving Hofstede's uncertainty avoidance dimension. Int. J. Tourism Res. **6**(1), 29–37 (2004)
10. Lo, S.K., Wang, C.C., Fang, W.: Physical interpersonal relationships and social anxiety among online game players. CyberPsychol. Behav. **8**(1), 15–20 (2005)
11. Losup, A., van de Bovenkamp, R., Shen, S., Jia, A.L., Kuipers, F.: Analyzing implicit social networks in multiplayer online games. IEEE Internet Comput. **18**(3), 36–44 (2014)
12. Nuangjumnonga, T., Mitomo, H.: Leadership development through online gaming (2012)
13. Ratan, R., Kennedy, T., Williams, D.: League of gendered game play behaviors: examining instrumental vs identity-relevant avatar choices. Meaningful Play **13** (2012)
14. Shane, S.: Uncertainty avoidance and the preference for innovation championing roles. J. Int. Bus. Stud. **26**, 47–68 (1995)
15. De Luque, M.S., Javidan, M.: Uncertainty avoidance. In: House, R.J., Hanges, P.J., Javidan, M., Dorfman, P.W., Gupta, V. (eds.) Culture, Leadership, and Organizations: The GLOBE Study of 62 Societies, pp. 602–653. Sage, Thousand Oaks (2004)
16. Teng, C.I.: Personality differences between online game players and nonplayers in a student sample. CyberPsychol. Behav. **11**(2), 232–234 (2008)
17. Williams, D., Ducheneaut, N., Xiong, L., Zhang, Y., Yee, N., Nickell, E.: From tree house to barracks the social life of guilds in World of Warcraft. Game. Cult. **1**(4), 338–361 (2006)
18. Williams, D., Yee, N., Caplan, S.E.: Who plays, how much, and why? Debunking the stereotypical gamer profile. J. Comput. Mediated Commun. **13**(4), 993–1018 (2008)
19. Yee, N.: Motivations for play in online games. CyberPsychol. Behav. **9**(6), 772–775 (2006)
20. Zigang, Z., Fan, P.: Cross-cultural challenges when doing business in China. Singap. Manage. Rev. **38**(3), 61–73 (2004)

Defining Design Opportunities of Healthcare in the Perspective of Digital Social Innovation

Dongjuan Xiao[✉], Miaosen Gong, and Xueliang Li

School of Design, Jiangnan University,
No.1800, Lihu Road, Binhu District, Wuxi 214122, Jiangsu Province, China
dj.xiao@yahoo.com, miaosen.gong@gmail.com,
1185110176@qq.com

Abstract. Digital Social Innovation is a relative new term, which describes new IT-enabled solutions that simultaneously meet a social need and enhance capacity to act. It includes the challenge of giving a clear identity to the digital essence that assist our way of knowing, and living. It is an emergent stream of social innovation research and a response to growing social, environmental and demographic challenges. There is great potential to exploit digital network effects both in social innovation activity and in new services and approaches that generate social value. By the development of the internet, especially the popular of social media, such as face book, twitter, Wechat, QQ and so on, the way of people interact is changed a lot. And this kind of platform is a new way of social innovation in healthcare field, but we still need to do more research on this field to make it more reasonable. In order to explore and define design opportunities related to healthcare field, an interdisciplinary course "Smart Healthcare" and workshops which combined the smart technology with social innovation were carried out. The sub-topic of the workshops related to the aged community, medical system. The paper addresses the result of the course and workshops by analyzing the case studies and defining design opportunities in the healthcare field. This could be a very preliminary step to understand how the social problems can be unbarred by digital social innovation approach.

Keywords: Digital social innovation · Healthcare · Service design · Social media

1 Introduction

Along with the rapidly developing of internet, the world we are living is changed remarkably. And the capacity of internet for generating societal and economic value is relatively well understood, and a number of innovative services are developed. Consequently, Digital Social Innovation (DSI) is an emerging field of study, with little existing knowledge on who the digital social innovators are, which organizations and activities support them and how they use digital tools to change the world to be better.

Digital social innovations (DSI) in this study refers to "a type of social and collaborative innovation in which innovators, users and communities collaborate using digital technologies to co-create knowledge and solutions for a wide range of social

P.L.P. Rau (Ed.): CCD 2015, Part II, LNCS 9181, pp. 384–393, 2015.
DOI: 10.1007/978-3-319-20934-0_36

needs and at a scale that was unimaginable before the rise of the Internet". This definition is derived from DSI interim report by Bria (2014) [1].

With the high diffusion in practice there has been a similar increase in ways of understanding social innovation enabled by collaborative digital technologies. However, definitions are certainly controversial and cannot capture the entire dimensions of the observed phenomena which are complicated and diverse. Social innovation is here considered in relation to the initiatives that are based on "meaningful discontinuities" in the way involved participants behave and interact collaboratively leveraging the power of collective intelligence through open digital technologies. This means that changes can be seen as a step towards social and environmental sustainability, for which the implementation and outcome would depend significantly on people's behavioral change and interactive effect. And where the "involved participants" are both the "user/co-producers" and all the other participants to the initiative, taking into account the transformation of the role of the consumer into active users as co-creators and their motivations to participate in the innovation process.

The paper describes the result of the course and workshops by analyzing the case studies and defining design opportunities in the healthcare field. This could be a very preliminary step to understand how the social problems can be unbarred by digital social innovation approach.

2 Smart Healthcare in the Context of Digital Social Innovation

Design challenges are inherently complex – and every client has their own particular knots to untie, especially in the complicated healthcare system. In recent years, service-oriented solutions are emerging as a response to the complicated aspects referring to environmental and social crisis, such as healthcare system. In order to improve the patient experience, create smooth dialogue between patient and doctors, ease the job burden of hospital staff, many new innovative methods were used. This collaborative mindset generates a mutually-shared sense of dedication to discovering solutions, and an optimism about making them work. This is exhilarating to experience, of course, but more importantly, it creates tangible results [2].

By the development of the internet, especially the popular of social media, such as Facebook, twitter, Wechat, QQ and so on, the way of people interact is changed a lot. It is so easy for people to share different kinds of information. Beside this, there are many special platform and smart phone APP for patients and doctors to communicate with each other. These kinds of networks provide a free patient platform where people can connect with each other to better understand their diseases, share condition and treatment information, and get support from peers to improve their health condition. It is also a research platform. As patients report on their disease experiences, they provide real-world insight into diseases and long term conditions. Those insights are shared with companies, government organizations and others who use them to continuously develop more effective products, pharmaceuticals, services and care. This kind of platform is a new way of social innovation in healthcare field, but we still need to do more research on this field to make it more reasonable. Moreover, aging population, the stiff relationship between patients and doctors are typical national social problems in China, even in the world. We believe that some serve social problems can be eased down by design.

2.1 The Value of Social Media in Healthcare

The role of the Internet in communication and information management has been becoming increasingly important for the last few years not only in medicine and healthcare, but it has been changing how we do shopping, interact with friends or organize events. The use of the Internet to search for health-related information has even become a common practice worldwide. Almost everyone online is doing search queries, but actually 80 % of Internet users have looked specifically for information about health topics such as diagnosis or treatment [3].

However, before social media became popular, hospitals approached communicating and marketing traditionally through one-way messages, for example by the broadcast. And the patients and community were forced to accept the messages passively [4]. This approach wasn't natural. Health is personal, something in which each of us is individually invested. We patients were scared of our health statuses, unprepared for hospital experiences, and lost in the confusion of healthcare, grasping at the information healthcare marketers pushed at us. Traditional marketing doesn't fit in healthcare. Fortunately, social media has leveled the playing field. Social media often can help bring people together. This is evident in the use of social media by both patients and healthcare providers. People will talk about anything on Facebook - even their surgery or their doctor. Patients are also most likely to share information about their health through social media with doctors and hospitals more than other groups or people. Now patients can communicate about health at any time. They can share fears about diagnoses with distant friends and families. They can connect with people across the world who struggle with similar health conditions, finding support and companionship. They can question whether the doctor gave the right diagnosis or express displeasure with a recent emergency room visit.

With the introduction of social media within hospitals, new networks and channels are opened up for the hospital. Anyone who has permissions to post to the social media can push out messages through a downward channel; in turn, patients can begin a dialog with a physician, recruiter, or event planner and deliver upward communication. The network that begins with this simple form of communication allows patients and those outside of the organization to communicate the needs of the surrounding communities. The introduction of social networking and social media for a hospital or healthcare facility plays an integral role in strengthening the communication between the provider and consumer. Social media is an important issue for hospitals and organizational communication alike because is it expanding on the backbones of interpersonal communication and new technologies in the work place [5].

Several studies explored the impacts of social media on healthcare organizations, clinicians, and patients. These studies found that healthcare organizations, clinicians and patients can benefit from the use of social media. For healthcare organizations, social media can be used primarily for community engagement activities such as fundraising, customer service and support, the provision of news and information, patient education, and advertising new services. These studies also found that the most widely used social media venues for physicians were online communities where physicians can read news articles, listen to experts, research new medical developments, network, and communicate with colleagues regarding patient issues. Patients can benefit from the use of social media through education, obtaining information, networking, performing research, receiving support, goal setting, and tracking personal progress. Future research should further examine other financial, technological, informational, ethical, legal, and privacy issues surrounding the use of social media in healthcare [6–8].

2.2   Review of Social Media and Digital Platform for Healthcare

Some of the most popular social media outlets include blogs for patients and personal blogs, healthcare-specific blogs (WebMD, New York Times' Well blog), social networking sites (Facebook, MySpace and LinkedIn), healthcare-specific websites (PatientsLikeMe and Organized Wisdom), social sharing websites such as YouTube, forums (Google Health Groups and Revolution Health Groups), and online networking groups. There are hundreds of websites to access social media but the main competitors include blogs, Facebook, LinkedIn, Twitter and YouTube. Each social site has a different look and feel and consumers go to each website looking for a different message. There are many concerns when beginning a new social media campaign for a hospital or social media websites, what information should be pushed out to audiences, and how to avoid violating patient privacy laws. The top social media websites chosen for hospital practice will include: blogs, Facebook, LinkedIn, Twitter and YouTube.

When people think of social media, they automatically think of Facebook. With over 600 million people logged into Facebook, hospitals can post timely videos, educate patients and reduce embarrassment around sensitive subject matters [6, 9]. With so many people already tuned into Facebook, many hospitals and healthcare organizations should strive to participate on Facebook. Hospital Facebook profile pages should be updated at least once a week to show that the organization is actively participating.

Twitter is a great resource to push out links and short messages to patients. Users can follow trusted colleagues, health organizations or journals to stay up to date with information without having to crowd an e-mail inbox. This form of social media has been used by hospitals and clinics to publicize health screening, fairs, and to acknowledge information from other health organizations.

YouTube is one social media where the user does not have to be a member to watch the videos posted. With over 48 h of video uploaded every minute, YouTube is a growing social media and getting the company's videos viewed by the proper patient involves selecting the correct keywords [10]. To add content to the hospitals official YouTube page start by repurposing videos that have already been made [11]. YouTube is the perfect outlet to place patient testimonials, education materials or recaps from past events.

PatientsLikeMe launched its first online community for amyotrophic lateral sclerosis patients in 2006. From there, the company began adding communities for other life-changing conditions, including multiple scleroses, Parkinson's disease, fibromyalgia, HIV, and many others. By October 2009, the number of registered users had grown to more than 45,000. In April 2011, the company expanded its scope and opened its doors to any patient with any condition. By June 2011, PatientsLikeMe had hit a new milestone of 100,000 members. The primary service provided by PatientsLikeMe is a social network for people living with a long term health condition. Once they have created a profile, PatientsLikeMe allows members to input real-world data on their conditions, treatment history, side effects, hospitalizations, symptoms, disease-specific functional scores, weight, mood, quality of life and more on an ongoing basis. The result is a detailed longitudinal record – organized into charts and graphs – that allows patients to gain insight and identify patterns. Answers come in the form of shared longitudinal data from other patients with the same condition(s), thus allowing members to place their experiences in context and see what treatments have helped other patients like them [1].

In China, there are also many kinds of social media, such as RenRen,TencentQQ, Wechat and so on. And these social media are using for healthcare related communication. Besides that, there are also special App and digital platform for healthcare, such as good doctor online, Ding xiang yuan, Chunyu doctor and so on. For instance, Chunyu Doctor seeks to rebuild the relationship between patients and doctors, by improving the process of health inquiry online with recording tools for daily activities related to people's physical condition.

The role of social media and social networks in healthcare can be classified into five categories based on interactions: patient-patient, clinician-patient, public health-health consumer, researcher-patient, and corporate/hospital-patient interactions [12].

3   Case Study

In order to explore and define design opportunities related to healthcare field, an interdisciplinary course "Smart Healthcare" and workshops which combined the smart technology with social innovation were carried out. The sub-topic of the workshops related to the self-management of chronic disease, community for the new pregnant woman (Baby Plan), self-management for preserve one's health, dealing with sub-health for college student, and service design for elderly. The paper addresses the result of the course and workshops by analyzing two case studies and defining design opportunities in the healthcare field. This could be a very preliminary step to understand how the social problems can be unbarred by digital social innovation approach.

3.1   Case Study 1- Service Design for Elderly

This case study was designed to motivate elderly do more outdoor activities.

Figure 1 shows the daily routine of most elderly people in China. Most of them have different kinds of chronic disease; reasonable amount of sports is good for their health. Although they do daily sports, such as square dance, tai chis, jogging and so on, most of them have no proper guidance and measurement for their amount of sports. Moreover, most of the elderly have no motivation to do outdoor activities.

Old user journery

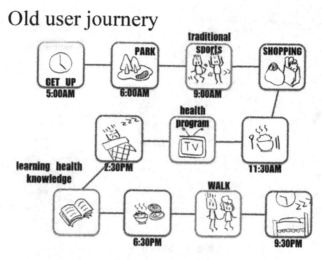

Fig. 1. Daily routine of elderly

Based on user research, we interviewed several elderly communities and elderly home; we think we can solve several problems by service design approach. Aging population is facing by all over the world; the government also put a lot of effort to tackle this problem.

Figure 2 shows a system map of the service system, the stakeholders are including hospitals, health center, government, dealers, and elderly people. The health center is located in every community, which can provide facilities, healthcare knowledge and advices for the elderly people, and they also provide the service of recording body data for free. Later they can share these body data to the hospital or to the elder's family member. The government can give the health center some finance support. Then the health center can cooperate with supermarket dealers by distribute the supermarket coupons to the elderly who took the activities in the health center. The more activities elderly took part in the health center, the more supermarket coupon they can get. So the coupon could be a motivation for elderly to take part in more exercise and activities.

Based on the system map, we came out of the new user journey as shown in Fig. 3.

3.2 Case Study 2-Baby Plan

Recently, Chinese government loosens the only one child policy, and more and more couple wants to have their second child. In the near future, China will have another baby booming. Pregnant women are a very important group, who deserved more attention, and they need more care during pregnancy. Pregnant women during pregnancy tend to be very focused on the status of the fetus to timely to check. How to connect the family, hospital, and the community effectively to improve the pregnant experience? What kind of form can reduce the unpleasant mood, and thus to add more pleasurable experience during pregnancy?

System map

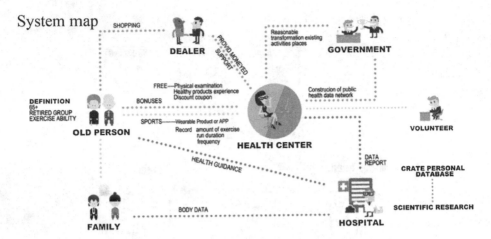

Fig. 2. System map

New user journey

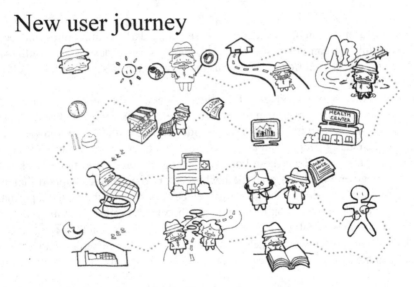

Fig. 3. New user journey

Several pregnant women were interviewed, and several hospitals were investigated. Based on the user research, the daily routine of pregnant woman was formulated as Fig. 4. The daily routine listed some difficult problems, such as can not bend over, travel issues, keep balance diet, movement, sleep difficulties, and emotion issues. From the interview and user research, we found that pregnant woman is easy to feel lonely and helpless, and they really need to share their feelings with family members or friends. Also they need more information and experience from others to relief their fear. Then the concept "Baby plan" came out. The system map of "Baby plan" is showed in Fig. 5.

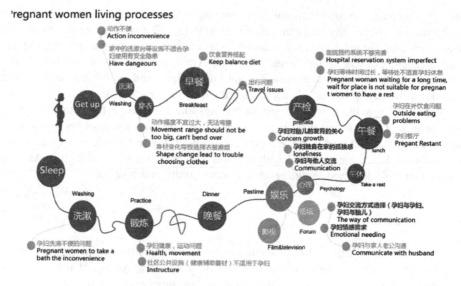

Fig. 4. Daily routine of pregnant woman

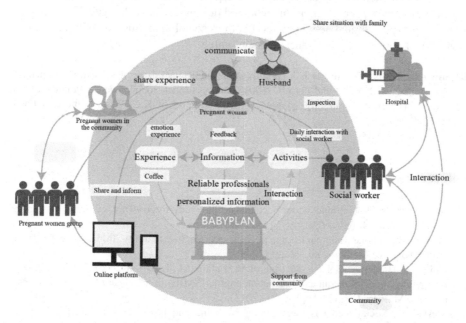

Fig. 5. System map of baby plan

Baby plan is a service proposal based on an online platform and a solid place in the community, defined as "an supporting network for pregnant women to deliver a healthy baby", whose purpose is to engage new mothers, the pregnant women their family member, social worker and the hospital into a collaborative community, where the pregnant women can share information, communicate with each other. The online platform can provide any pregnant related information. The solid place can provide a special location for the pregnant woman and new mothers to communicate face to face. And the new mothers are endowed with a new role: the adviser or assistant of the pregnant with their personal experience and knowledge. And as the pregnant women turn out to be new mothers, it's natural for them to switch the role.

Baby plan provide a better access to the personal knowledge for young pregnant women especially who have no such experience before and normally get themselves supported through internet or directly going to hospital. It also helps to relieve their fear and anxiety when communicating with the ones who have just went through it. And the "Baby plan" is supported by the residential community and hospital.

4   Conclusion

The communication capabilities of social media and social networks have the potential to improve healthcare. This kind of platform is a new way of social innovation in healthcare field. As technology grows and more consumers are comfortably using the new technology, the healthcare industry can be improved and changed remarkably by using of social media. It is an emergent stream of social innovation research and a response to growing social, environmental and demographic challenges. There is great potential to exploit digital network effects both in social innovation activity and in new services and approaches that generate social value.

Acknowledgements. The research is partially supported by Ministry of Education Humanities and Social Science Youth Fund (11YJC760018) and National Social Science Foundation-Art (12BG055). The author gratefully acknowledges the support of K.C. Wong Education Foundation, Hong Kong.

References

1. Bria, F.: Digital social innovation: Second Interim Study Report (rev. edition). Armstrong, K., Casebourne, J. (eds.) (2014)
2. Manzini E.: Service design in the age of networks and sustainability. In: Designing Services with Innovative Methods, pp. 44–59 (2009)
3. Fatima, I., Halder, S., Saleem, M., Batool, R., Fahim, M., Lee, Y.-K., Lee, S.: Smart CDSS: integration of social media and interaction engine (SMIE) in healthcare for chronic disease patients. Multimed. Tools Appl. 1–21 (2013)
4. Meskó, B.: Social media is transforming medicine and healthcare. In: Meskó, B. (eds.) Social Media in Clinical Practice, pp. 1–12. Springer, London (2013)
5. Weaver, B., Lindsay, B., Gitelman, B.F., Gitelman, B.: Communication technology and social media: opportunities and implications for healthcare systems. Online J. issues nurs. **17**(3), 3 (2012)
6. Essary, A.: The impact of social media and technology on professionalism in medical education. J. Physician Assistant Educ. **22**(4), 50–53 (2011)

7. Joregensen, G.: Social media basics for orthodontists. Am. J. Orthod. Dentofac. Orthop. **141** (4), 510–515 (2012)
8. Ressler, P.: Legislative: nursing's engagement in health policy and healthcare through social media. Online J. issues nurs. **16**(1), 1–10 (2011)
9. Verkamp, J.: Social media – as a way to connect with patients. Med. Gr. Manag. Assoc. Connect. **10**(6), 46–49 (2010)
10. Joregensen, G.: Social media basics for orthodontists. Am. J. Orthod. Dentofac. Orthop. **141** (4), 510–515 (2012)
11. Morarity, L.D.: Whisper to a scream – healthcare enters the brave new world of social media. Mark. Health Serv. **29**(2), 9–13 (2009)
12. Steele, R.: Social media, mobile devices and sensors: categorizing new techniques for health. In: Fifth International Conference on Sensing Technology (2011)

The Service System Study on Children's Hospital-Bed Nursing Based on Multi-level Experience

Linghao Zhang[✉], Chang Zhang, Sheng Huang, and Sichun Xiao

Jiangnan University, No.1800, Lihu Road, Binhu District,
Wuxi, Jiangsu Province, China
wowo.zlh@163.com,
{784734848,878447859,597724074}@qq.com

Abstract. Presently, there are rarely children's hospital-beds aiming at children patients' various demand level in the field of medical treatment, which results in children patients' emotional repression and psychological burden in the life of rehabilitation and even affects the state of the children patients' illness. And during the experience economy the integrated innovation with nursing system of children's hospital-beds through experience has become the key factor for children patients' medical treatment. In the whole process of monitoring process, the integrated innovation will contribute to the rapid deployment of nursing service and help the children patients take part in the treatment process happily, which will also meet the parents, children patients and nurses' needs. So based on the theory of multi-experience characteristics of children patients, what we study is trying to collect the pains during the medical service and analyze the opportunity point by taking the Wuxi hospital as an example and using the relative research method of user experience and service process to create new user model and a number of service situation. In the end, trying to create the new service model and multi-level experience touch point by the thought of integration. The paper provides new and effective solution to the traditional children's hospital-beds with the method of system integration from the angle of service design.

Keywords: Children's hospital-bed nursing system · Multi-level experience · Service system · Design strategy

1 Introduction

With the rapid development of economy, science and technology, our health care facilities and medical environment for children are also upgrading. However, in essence, the majority of replacement is only about the expansion of function and the updating of technology. Facing with the altering of consumption process, experience economy and medical culture, the replacement that stays in the change of function-oriented level requires large investment but the effect is not as expected. As people's emotional needs' expanding, the concerns of medical treatment process nowadays are not only about the physical rehabilitation, but also the field of emotional, educational and psychological

© Springer International Publishing Switzerland 2015
P.L.P. Rau (Ed.): CCD 2015, Part II, LNCS 9181, pp. 394–406, 2015.
DOI: 10.1007/978-3-319-20934-0_37

care. Thus the essence of medical products and service design has changed dramatically. The paper applies the concept of experience and service system to children's hospital bed design and discovers the methods of relatives' deeper involvement throughout the whole process of children's medical care service by means of the innovation of humanized children's health care system experience. In addition, the paper discusses the methods of promoting the communication between patients and medical staffs and improving the staffs' working efficiently.

2   Children's Hospital Bed Nursing System and Service Experience Research Method

2.1   Children's Hospital Bed Nursing System and Design Problems

Children's hospital bed is the most significant medical devices in the children's wards since it is not only a place for receiving the treatment, but also for taking various activities such as eating, playing, talking, relaxing, speaking, writing, etc. With the improvement of medical condition, the original furniture form of the hospital bed transformed into medical device form. Basically, children's hospital bed in china is steel welded flat bed with hand crank that can only apply to the general wards with single function. Currently, pediatric intensive care unit in China usually uses adult monitoring hospital bed for children patient or reduce the size to fit for children. Developed countries use more advanced ABS multi-function electric bed as it contains complex structure and all the functions of other types of bed which some of the functions are innovative and prospective like Eleganza Smart Junior, made by LINET like the Fig. 1, the Germany hospital beds Manufacturing company which has object-oriented control panels, plug adapters, etc.

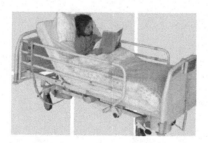

Fig. 1. Eleganza smart junior

However, for children's rehabilitation in experience economy era, children's bed should not only contain basic functions to satisfy the treatment, relaxation and daily activities for children patients, but also humanistic care and self-adaptability for unexpected problems. Moreover, it can be a suitable carrier for the doctor-patient communication and connection in the Internet age. Therefore, children's hospital bed can be developed into a system product to resolve complex problems and to adjust to the rapid development of medical care technology nowadays.

In nursing system perspective, children's health care process is gradually becoming a nursing system service platform with various experience shared by many users. The following contents will be discussed specifically: pediatric beds (size, functions and components, color and model, material and technology), pediatric wards, space environment, cultural environment, admission process, daily nursing process, discharge process, the relative care products, etc. Thus in nursing system design, not only the children's medical care, but also the psychological elements of children patients and relatives, the main contradiction and problem in the nursing process should be taken into consideration. Senior children hospital beds in market are function-oriented and design only aims at the function of bed without any improvement of experience so that obsession appears.

2.2 Service Experience Concept of Children's Hospital Bed Nursing System

Experience design is the research about user experience. The user experience is the psychological feeling set up by users during the process of using products (including material products and nonmaterial products) or enjoying the service, referring to all the aspects of interaction between people and products, programs or system (Tullis and Albert, 2008). Forlizzi and Ford (2000) defined experience from the perspective of the human-computer interaction of products, considering experience as the way users perceive products, including: the process users understand the way using a product; the mood and feeling when users use products; the humanization of products; the capability about whether the product can meet diversity of demands or not. Among them, in terms of the specific model of experience design, after the research of consumer psychology from the perspective of social psychology theory and the human brain module, Bernd Schmitt presented the experience model which contained sense, thinking, emotion, behavior and association [1] (Fig. 2).

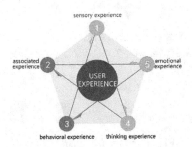

Fig. 2. Experience system presented by Bernd Schmit

Experience design brings entirely new vision and new method to create value for foreign medical treatment service, and people-oriented theory of experience design has taken positive impact on numbers of medical service design fields. For instance, the patient-nursing staff integration service system built by IDEO for Mayo Clinic in the U.S. is an innovation of behavioral and emotional experience. IDEO turned the internal medicine hall of the clinic into a lab to improve the experience of patient-nursing staff. They observed how the patients influenced each other in waiting area and laboratory and how they cooperated with doctors, nurses and other staff to finish their treatment. Kaiser Permanente and IDEO developed activities to promote the nurses' knowledge communication in wards which resolved the problem brought by working shift of nurses and increased the continuity of nursing between different nurses (Fig. 3).

Fig. 3. IDEO'S design cases with Mayo clinic and Kaiser permanente

Looking at the nursing system of children's hospital bed with the multi-level service experience model, the sensory experience, behavioral experience and emotional experience which are related to children's cognition need to be highlighted.

1. Sensory experience: by stimulating children's sensory system, hospital bed makes a direct experience for children. Although the stimulation won't last long, it is possible to become a deeper experience [2].
2. User experience based on behavior: Users operate products by their parts of body. As for child, the research needs to focus on the usability, durability, playability, edutainment brought by hospital bed. As for relatives and nurses, it includes further information interaction and medical activities support and etc.
3. User experience based on emotional demand level: The emotional feedback simulated by sense and interaction after using the products, including not only the emotional experience of behavior level, but also the emotional experience of communication level. It focuses on children' emotion and psychology. During hospitalization, many situations can lead to children's emotional repression such as reduction of playing space, decreasing of playmates, shortage of game, fear and aversion when faced of treatment, lacking of company of other relation and etc. which will obsess the medical treatment process. Meanwhile, during relatives' accompanying, many situations may cause passive waiting which leads to relatives' anxiety and misunderstanding. However, nurses also need more understanding in this process.

Therefore, for the hospital bed, related environment and information of children's nursing system, it is necessary to carry out investigation and analysis for the existing problems of users' needs and nursing services from the sensory part, behavior part and emotion part. Then establish new strategies to improve the existing service system and provide new solutions to avoid inappropriate behavioral and emotional feedback.

3 The Research Process

3.1 The Research Problems and Methods

Children's hospital bed design need to undertake the experience design focusing on position in sensory, behavioral and emotional experience of three macroscopic level. However, the content of experience is relatively emotional. It need to sort out by the multidimensional method about the relationship and problems between multi-users and related facilities, the environment and the service. Research will be carried out by two parts.

1. Based on the users and the environment research of nursing system, the urgent problem can be obtained from ward nursing process and space environment of participation of children patients, accompanying relatives and medical staffs. This part is mainly adopted qualitative interview analysis mainly in the children's hospital of Wuxi and the third hospital of Wuxi. At the same time, choosing typical children patients, accompanying relatives, medical staffs of different ages as a research object by observing, interviewing and recording to study the interaction in nursing service situations and problems. Interview questions explore the insufficient of hospital bed nursing space product and service experience mainly from the subjective user experience feeling. First is the background of the problem, which mainly refers to the basic situation of accompanying relatives, medical staffs, including gender, occupation, age, income, education, the disease characteristics of children patients; Second is the objective problem, which includes accompanying relatives and medical staffs' specific work in the nursing process and the nursing content associated with hospital bed use. Subjective problems is mainly referring to the emotions, attitudes, expectations and other problems of the subjective world of accompanying relatives, medical staffs. At the same time, what we need to understand is interactive information between users and hospital beds by observing behavior map to understand and trace children patients in this hospital bed space with the change of time and location. The related background information, interviews, conclusion should be intensively recorded format table (Fig. 4).

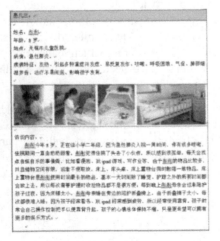 

Fig. 4. The user interview is recorded by the format table

2. The survey is conducted aiming to multi-role user behavior and emotional needs. Because children's hospital beds involve too many stakeholders and every party has different levels of needs as well as different needs can be divided into different sub-needs, these needs have the characteristic of diversity, ambiguity, dynamics, priority and etc. So in the process of this questionnaire survey the Kano model is introduced. Kano model was proposed in 1984 by a Professor named Noriaki Kano in Japan, which is based on products, objective performance of services and users' subjective feelings. Kano model make the quality attributes of product and service divide into five categories [3]. Multiple roles aiming to each hospital bed function through this method can be divided into attractive quality, one-dimensional quality, must-be quality, indifferent quality and Reverse quality. Then by the classification, sorting, statistical processing of user needs from the survey, we will use Kano model again to analyze the satisfaction and dissatisfaction of hospital bed nursing system. During the questionnaire design, the first one we need to do is clustering with KJ method. For children patients and accompanying relatives, the user needs of children hospital bed can be divided into emotional care, learning and entertainment, security, meeting the aesthetic needs, etc. Then the 4 parts will further subdivided to the children patients' psychology, emotional care, clinical psychology, behavior modification (facing treatment positively), patient communication assistance, medical expense information and so forth to 14 third level. On this base, what we get is personalized accompanying product design, accompanying manual design, evaluating services design and so forth to 14 design elements. When designing a questionnaire, you need to understand the pros and cons to every question that you want to detect (Fig. 5). They will include the users' evaluation whether or not the tool have such functions [4]. In addition, considering accompanying relatives and nurses having different subjective initiatives and needs, different Kano questionnaires will be compiled for them. The entire questionnaire survey collects 98 KANO questionnaires written by accompanying relatives and nurses, 77 of which are effective.

How do you feel if the hospital beds use electricity to adjust?	1 Like 2 Must do 3 Whatever 4 Acceptable 5 Dissatisfied
How do you feel if the hospital beds do not use electricity to adjust?	1 Like 2 Must do 3 Whatever 4 Acceptable 5 Dissatisfied

Fig. 5. The settings of forward-backward questionnaire questions

3.2 Research Process and Results Analysis

1. Children patient with emotional repression. Although the children patients' fear caused by disease is not obvious, the pain caused by the disease will lead to emotional changes. And children patients' living environment changing, lifestyle changing, disease impact, space and entertainment reduction will lead to emotional repression, resistance, eccentric psychology, which will indirectly affect their rehabilitation

condition. In the aspect of accompanying relatives' behavior, the learning materials will be taken to the hospital for homework tutoring by their parents. And with the use of mobile phones, iPad and other digital products, the attention of children patients can be transferred in the games and cute cartoon animation to bring joy to them to moderately reduce the disease caused by depression and frustration. So by creating a relaxing atmosphere through facilities and environmental improvement, the strategies called "psychology - society" should be encouraged.

2. Accompanying relatives could not timely access to accurate information. Although relatives and children patient always stay together, many cases they encountered is still passively waiting around with anxiety and even seeking treatment advice all around the hospital. Children with inpatient rehabilitation need to experience a process like injection, medicines, diagnosis, inspections and so on. And the accompanying relatives are fuzzy about the project like children prognosis, progression of the disease, treatment projects that require to be treat, which will easily lead to the increasing pressure for accompanying relatives. In the end, the whole process will result in the negative emotions, which is easy to cause disputes between doctors and patients.

3. Medical staffs around the hospital bed function and nursing service have similar problems. Because the hospital beds have low regional function expansion, entertainment, security, and other sensory experience requirements are difficult to meet. And because the spaces of hospital beds and surrounding areas are divided unreasonable, it will have a very low utilization. Then the hospital beds have the barriers with the accompanying facilities. And although the nursing service process is complete and clear, they can't answer every individual's question and can't talk too long and in time, which will result in misunderstanding like that checking the condition and testing results are not promptly informed or no detailed explanation. Research found that through the hospital bed nursing system it will establish effective communication mechanism to help relatives to establish effective communication with medical staff under the premise of information.

4. From analysis of the Kano questionnaire emotional care of children patients, the five sub-needs are parent-children psychological and emotional care, clinical psychology and behavior modification, communication assistance, medical financial aid and accessing to information. Among them the charismatic quality requirements include parent-children psychological and emotional care and medical financial aid. With that accompanying relatives will feel humanization thinking from the hospital and will increase the satisfaction. Other three dimensional types belongs to One-dimensional quality requirement. These are the situation that most hospitals have not achieved or not achieved accompanying relatives' expectations. So in order to enhance the experience, the group demand is bound to be solved. To analyze the demand by introducing the Better-worse coefficient, it is necessary to functionally design aiming at doctor-patient communication and information acquisition (Table 1).

5. Needs weight sorting and overall analysis of children patients and relatives. By Better-Worse coefficient coordinates analyzing emotional care, learning and entertainment, security, aesthetic satisfaction, what they do is meeting the relationship between every sub-need and system design, as the table showed. Through

Table 1. The better-worse coefficient table of emotional care

Needs	Kano sorts	Satisfaction degree when improving	Dissatisfaction degree when removing
Psychology care	A	0.75	−0.38
Behavior correction	O	0.74	−0.35
Communication	O	0.80*	−0.44*
Financial aid	A	0.83	−0.31
Information acquisition	O	0.81*	−0.45*

comparative analysis, the highest demand factor of the system design is putting teaching at medical, personal information not easy to leak, information acquisition, children patients in clinical psychology and behavior modification coordinating −0.9 × 0.9 to −1 × 1 region. The higher demand factor is setting private space, medical financial aid to meet the children mental game(A), parent-child psychology and emotional care in personally coordinating −0.8 × 0.8 to −0.9 × 0.9 area. In addition, the lower demand factor is out of bed with alarming, color (A/I), patterns, shapes (A/I), providing learning assistance and other demand factors in the coordinating −0.8 × 0.8 lines to 0 coordinate area (Fig. 6).

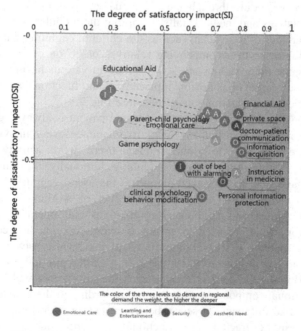

Fig. 6. Weight sorting coordinate of hospital bed needs

3.3   The Experiential Conclusion and Opportunity Analysis of User Needs

Through questionnaires and the results of the analysis, the whole process verifies the accuracy of the conclusion through the qualitative research and provides a large number of data to support. At the same time, the process also gets a high correlation demand list and defines the relationship between experience level and system need (Table 2).

4   Improved Strategy of Children's Hospital Bed Service System Experience

Based on the pain points from the survey and weight ranging from experience system problems and combining the theory and thought of emotion, behavior and sense as well as cognitive differences, environmental factors and requirement definitions, you can improve the children hospital bed nursing system from the following four aspects.

4.1   Based on Caring User's Individual Psychology, Creating Functional Hospital Bed Partition Through Modular Concept

Considering humanistic care through basic characteristic of individual element, trying to divide functional module through the individual motivation of children patients, accompanying relatives and medical staffs. Adopting the modular concept is based on different characteristics of individual, such as the children cognition difference of ages and appealing difference of accompanying relatives based on diverse cultural background. At the same time, various needs will result in various hospital bed functionalities. So what we need to do is flexible replacement and functional module reduction, which will enhance the utilization rate of resource Fig. 7.

Firstly, because the dispute between doctor and patient is always occurred during the process of subtle relationships. In order to guarantee every individual patients' psychological need, we need to ensure different users' work, activity and rest area according to the planning of functional module. Additionally, the function of every partition must make sure it is designed aiming to the users' cognition characteristic.

Secondly, in consideration of interaction effect of working and activity area between doctor, patient and accompanying relatives and operating motivation of intersection region, what we need to ensure is every function list, component and module position meeting design ergonomic. And meanwhile each user must have certain private and sharing space, which can't be meddled and influenced by others.

Lastly, by adopting the concept of module to design the hospital bed, we mainly peel off the functional component and collection according to the individual difference to design. Individual difference of sense, behavior and emotion from the same target determines the design characteristic of functional component and collection Fig. 8.

Table 2. System elements and experience conclusion of needs

	Experience level	Demand level	List of demand
Accom com- panyin g Rela- tives	A C	a b c d e	01.It brings fun entertainment experience features
	B	c d e	02.Actively promote children patients receiving treatment and reduce stress
	A	c d	03.Establish network of information management platform to access integrated information
	A	c d e	04. Establish an effective communication mechanism between the medical staff
	A	c d e	05. Establish feedback mechanism for health care workers
Doc- tors and Nurses	C	a e	01.The form of children patient's beds should be met the prefer- ences of most patients
	A	a	02.It should have more entertainment features without consider- ing the cost of hospital procurement
	A	a b	03.Clearly functional areas, random variations to meet the com- mon needs of the patients and relatives
	A	c d	04.Establish and improve the accompanying cognitive learning media
	A	c d e	05.By accompanying learning help relatives promote understand- ing the work of medical staff
	A B	a b c d e	06.Provide a wealth of recreational activities better for children patients
	A	c d	07.Correction the children patient's behavior by strategies
	A B C	c d e	08.Make patients maintain a pleasant mood
	A C	c d e	09.Make the humanistic care concept into physical care
	A B	a b c d e	10.Bed system of humanized design to reduce nurses' working strength
	A	c d e	11.Low level of technology professionals, they expect to get more support
	A	c d e	12. Through the bed nursing system to establish effective com- munication mechanisms and medium. Ensure that relatives, detailed understanding of the relevant information to establish communication with medical staff.
	A B	c d e	13. Establish a persuasive sickbed its system, which makes the patient's relatives understand the social law system of bed nursing system.
	A	a b	14.Ensure the safety of the receive space
	A	c d	15.Provide real-time nursing staff to assist function

Notes	
A-*behavioral experience*	a-*functional component*
B-*emotional experience*	b-*equipment escort*
C-*sensory experience*	c-*information content*
	d-*capability of information/ Propagation medium*
	e-*Individual subscriptions*

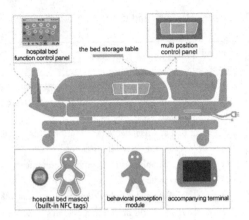

Fig. 7. Module formation of hospital bed

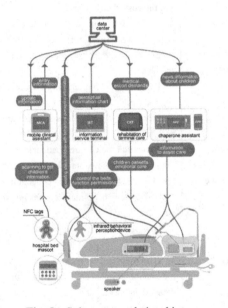

Fig. 8. Sub-system relationship map

4.2 Establishing Hospital Bed Cooperative Information System Oriented by the Real-Time Interaction Between Doctor, Patient and Accompanying Relative

Mainly behavior characteristic resulted from the psychological demands between doctor and patient creates a care experience of information collaboration. System element relationship will be established by the following 3 steps.

Firstly, the basic information system element is accessing and publishing of information. First of all, the nursing relevant information should be provided by the hospital to let accompanying relative, children patient and medical staff consult. Then the information of medical staff and accompanying relative should be easily announced and recorded. And the key impact of information system element lies on solving the accompanying relative's questions in time and improving the nursing cognition.

Secondly, the targeted information system element is developing real-time communication platform. First of all, the suggestion between the doctor and patient is easy to be conveyed friendly, which includes interaction and emotional communication between children patients and their relatives after nursing, as well as transformation the psychological intervention information to virtual one that are easily received by the children patient. In addition, we can establish the relationship between relatives and medical staffs, which will improve the harmony between them.

Thirdly, the persuasive information system element is setting up effective task cycling mode. The system through information technology can automatically analyze the behavior and psychology of the children patient and information concerned by the relatives. Meanwhile, the system will push high relevant information and suggestions and convey the typical psychology of relatives and expected appeals to the medical staffs. So what they do above is making the medical staffs be ready, persuading the accompanying relatives correcting anxiety and letting the children' behavior be collected, which will promote the virtuous circle of nursing service.

4.3   The Experience Level Partition of Children Hospital Nursing System

The experience of children hospital bed nursing system is decided by the condition of meeting the target, difficulty and complexity during the nursing process. According to the different users' process experience, we will make the subsystem product and service of hospital bed nursing system.

To the children patient, the cyclic process can be divided by four parts. They are overall orientation process to promote the recovery of children patients, periodical cyclic process to please the children patients, to correct the behavior and psychology and to make the teaching into the treatment. On account of the close function of task flow collection, the three subsystems include the hospital basic functions like treatment, rest, security protection and daily activities needs, rehabilitation care terminal to pay attention to the psychology, behavior perception function.

To the accompanying relatives, the process can be divided by five parts. They are orientation process to follow up the nursing process, to do daily accompanying tasks, to get the information and communicate, to care the emotion of the children patient and to escort the knowledge learning. The subsystem aiming at task collection is mainly about the hospital bed control interface that can be connected with the cell phone and information service terminal. These two subsystems have a strong expandability and majority of experiencing function exists by software and the hardware architecture of subsystem will not change by the changing of the function.

To the medical staffs, the process can be divided by four parts. They are orientation process to follow up nursing service, to do the daily nursing task, to care the psychology of children patients and relatives and to promote the communication between doctors and patients. The subsystem aiming at the task collection mainly includes information service terminal, hospital bed mascot (NFC label), hospital bed control interface and basic control parts.

5 Conclusion

Using the multi-field knowledge integration design to solve the complex medical service problem is a general trend. In this case, we integrate some parts like the multi-level experience design concept, medical technology, system innovation management and so on. In the system of children hospital bed nursing, to start with the stakeholders of multi-level experience and nursing service, we want to use the various research tools to embody the needs and redesign the experience footprint around different processes, which will satisfy the needs of children patients, accompanying relatives and medical staffs. Especially applying new information technology to the specific hospital bed creates a new solution to the traditional hospital bed design. It provides not only effective media for the service connection and communication between doctors and patients but also provides a new perspective for the manufacturer in this information and innovation era.

References

1. Juan, W.: Internet Product Interface Design Study Based on User Experience. Zhejiang Foresty and Farming University, Hangzhou (2012)
2. Xiaoyu, Y.: User Experience Level Study on Product Design. Guangdong University of Technology, Guangzhou (2011)
3. Kano, N.: Attractive quality and must-be quality. Jpn. Soc. Qual. Control 14(2), 147–156 (1984)
4. Juanli, W.: Concept Design Method Study Based on QFD. Zhejiang University, Hangzhou (2011)

Field Study on College Students' Uses and Gratifications of Multitasking Interaction with Multiple Smart Devices

Yubo Zhang and Pei-Luen Patrick Rau[✉]

Institute of Human Factors and Ergonomics, Tsinghua University, Beijing, China
yubo-zhang@outlook.com, rpl@mail.tsinghua.edu.cn

Abstract. In order to deeply understand college students' multitasking inter-action with multiple smart devices, we conducted a field study with the experience sampling method. We tracked 25 college students for 14 days about their multitasking activities and the dynamic characteristics of behavior motivations and feelings from the perspective of Uses and Gratifications. The participants reported their multitasking activities according to the designated format via WeChat. The researchers coded the qualitative data and classified multitasking activities into three types. It was found that multitasking with relevant content on different devices outperformed the other multitasking types in gratifying cognitive need. To the opposite, multitasking with irrelevant content on different devices was found to serve better at gratifying emotional need than the other multitasking types. The implications for designing cross-platform collaborative user experience in the era of smart computing were discussed.

Keywords: Multitasking · Uses and gratifications · Experience sampling · User needs

1 Introduction

1.1 Research Significance and Objective

Benefiting from the development of emerging interactive techniques and computing technology, people are able to interact with multiple smart devices simultaneously and pervasively. It is described that people's life and work are engaged in a smart environment. It is common and popular that a person who owns multiple smart devices such as tablet, smartphone, laptop interacts with these devices in a multitasking way. Based on a survey by Nielsen Company, roughly 40 percent of tablet and smartphone owners in the United States used their devices daily while watching TV [1]. One survey by the Hollywood Reporter showed that 79 % of the respondents said that they always or sometimes visited Facebook while watching TV and 41 % tweeted about the show they were watching and three quarters said that they posted about TV while watching live shows [2]. Another survey focusing on multi-screen users in the US found that in 2011 there were about 34 % of four-screen users, 32 % of three-screen users and 28 % of two-screen users above 18 years old who were prone to using devices such as PC, smartphone and tablet while watching TV. Besides, 47 % of the four-screen users

© Springer International Publishing Switzerland 2015
P.L.P. Rau (Ed.): CCD 2015, Part II, LNCS 9181, pp. 407–416, 2015.
DOI: 10.1007/978-3-319-20934-0_38

would vote and purchase online with their mobile devices when seeing promotions on TV [3]. These activities, referred to as "a person's consumption of more than one item or stream of content at the same time", are called media multitasking [4].

In contrast to the prevalence of media multitasking, research evidence has confirmed the negative impact of multitasking on individuals' performance [5], memory [6] and learning abilities [7]. It is surprising that heavy media multitaskers' ability of task switching is even worse than light media multitaskers' [4]. If multitasking has such negative impacts, why do people increasingly get involved in multitasking activities? Figuring out the answer to this question can shed light on the causality between multitasking activities and the corresponding motivations, and facilitate designing appropriate interventions to reduce the negative impact of multitasking in the environment surrounded by various media.

As indicated by [8], American teenagers from 8 to 18 years old spend 29 % of the media use time in using two or more media concurrently. It is found that among American young people who engage in media multitasking activities, they devote about a quarter of their media time to more than one medium [9]. Young people tend to have paradoxical experiences of media multitasking, with both positive and negative experience mixed [10]. Hence, in this study we selected young people as the research subjects of multitasking behaviors.

We define both simultaneously conducted activities and switching between activities as multitasking [11]. Further, we focus on multitasking interaction with multiple smart devices including personal computers, tablets and smartphones, as people's interaction activities with various smart devices have been more and more ubiquitous and fragmented [12]. Researchers have tried to yield the motivations behind people's multitasking behaviors. The theory of Uses and Gratifications (U&G) is frequently adopted as the framework to examine media choice and the underlying motivation [13]. However, previous studies from the perspective of U&G lack in focus on emerging situations where people interact with multiple smart devices. They concentrate on multitasking combining a media task and a non-media task [13, 14], or merely interruption-driven multitasking [15]. Besides, these studies consider media multitasking just as a whole group of behaviors, without further typology. Hence, it is necessary to investigate the motivations behind individuals' multitasking behaviors concerning interaction with multiple smart devices, and how different types of multitasking behaviors gratify different user needs.

1.2 Related Work

Theory of Uses and Gratifications. The theory of U&G was first adopted in mass communication research in the 1940s, and it was later systematically organized and proposed by Katz et al. [16] in 1973. According to the basic assumptions in U&G, audience are active and their media use behaviors are goal oriented, meaning that audience have the initiative in linking need gratification and media choice, but not the media. Since audience vary in their need gratifications, media that differ (or are similar) in attributes are more likely to serve different (similar) needs. This theory successfully explains audience's behaviors to adopt traditional mass media such as television, broadcasting, newspaper, books and movies [16] and it is also used to explain how people are motivated to consume new media like social media [17] or online games [18].

In U&G, needs and gratifications are two core concepts. Needs are "the combined product of psychological dispositions, sociological factors, and environmental conditions" [19] which motivate media uses. Gratifications are the "perceived fulfillment" [20] of the needs through media uses. Needs, uses and gratifications are mutually influenced. Needs drive multitasking media uses and media uses generate gratifications. Multitasking uses may deliver none of, some or all of the gratifications sought and those gratifications obtained in turn can influence user needs. User gratifications are determined by what needs exist and how the needs are fulfilled by multitasking uses. What's more, needs, uses and gratifications have dynamic reciprocal causality, meaning that needs, uses and gratifications provide feedback for subsequent needs, uses and gratifications [14].

Typology of User Needs. Previous studies accumulated various typologies of user needs in media multitasking. Katz et al. [16] raised a classification of media-related needs. Their classification scheme consists of three facets including mode, connection and referent. Mode includes: (1) to strengthen; (2) to weaken; (3) to acquire. Connection includes: (1) information, knowledge, understanding; (2) gratification, emotional experience; (3) credibility, confidence, stability, status; (4) contact. Referent includes: (1) self; (2) family; (3) friends; (4) state, society; (5) tradition, culture; (6) world; (7) others, negative reference group. Each possible and reasonable product of the items in the three facets form a type of user needs, such as to strengthen the understanding with my friends or to strengthen my confidence in the society. Under this scheme, considering the real media-consuming situations, Katz et al. [16] formed five meaningful user needs. Later on in this field, there were many typologies classifying user needs of media-consuming behaviors in different situations. They are summarized in Table 1.

U&G and Media Multitasking. One conclusion concerning media multitasking and U&G is that media multitasking is "emotionally satisfying but cognitively unproductive" [13]. It indicates that people conduct media multitasking activities motivated by their cognitive needs, but media multitasking actually cannot bring them improved efficiency. However, emotional gratifications are obtained despite not being actively sought. Thus, people will form the circle of continuous media multitasking.

The conclusion made by Wang and Tchernev [13] is largely based on multitasking with media and non-media activities mixed. However, it warrants questioning whether all media multitasking activities can gratify emotional needs but not cognitive needs. Zhang and Zhang [22] find that the relationship between need gratifications and multitasking behaviors is influenced by situational factors. Specifically, convenience needs are strong predictors of work-related type of computer multitasking, but not interaction type of multitasking like communication with IM while playing online games. Jeong et al. [24] state that in multitasking with media and non-media activities mixed, media use is usually the secondary activity. This pattern has important influence on media effect, or the gratifications brought by media use. However, in the era of multitasking with smart devices, users' multiple tasks can be all related to media. Users' needs and gratifications should be studied in caution with different multitasking types into consideration.

Table 1. Typology of user needs in different media-consuming situations

Source	User needs	Situation
[16]	• Cognitive needs to strengthen information, knowledge and understanding • Affective needs to strengthen aesthetic, pleasurable and emotional experience • Integrative needs to strengthen credibility, confidence, stability and status • Integrative needs to contact with others • Escaping or tension-release needs	Mass media use
[13, 14]	• Emotional needs • Cognitive needs • Social needs • Habitual needs	Media and non-media mixed multi-tasking activities; social media and other media use
[21]	• Recognition needs to establish personal identity, gain respect, build confidence and publicize expertise • Cognitive needs • Social needs • Entertainment needs	User-generated content on the Internet
[22]	• Convenient/easy/instant • Control/habitual • Social/affective/relaxation	Multitasking with computers
[23]	• Information processing • Enjoyment experience	Media multitasking

In this study, we aimed to investigate whether different types of media multitasking differ in gratifying users' different types of needs, especially the two types of needs: emotional needs and cognitive needs. The former one is related to relaxation and entertainment while the latter one is related to productivity, convenience and efficiency. Hence, the two core research questions were:

Research question I: Which type of media multitasking has the advantage of gratifying users' emotional needs?

Research question II: Which type of media multitasking has the advantage of gratifying users' cognitive needs?

2   Method

In order to deeply understand young people's needs and gratifications concerning media multitasking, we conducted a field study among college students. We adopted an experience sampling method to track their daily media multitasking activities and their dynamic state of needs and gratifications. Experience sampling is an effective method to gain insight into what people are experiencing during a particular period and it has been used a lot in the study concerning multitasking [13, 25, 26].

We recruited 25 college students in a 14-day experience sampling ethnographic study. All the participants owned at least 3 types of smart devices including a personal computer, a smartphone and a tablet computer. They all had the habit of multitasking interaction with multiple smart devices. During the study period, each participant received one message via WeChat at fixed time to remind him/her to report media multitasking activities in the past four hours. One experimenter sent messages three times at 12:30, 16:00 and 22:00. Upon receiving the message, the participant should reply in 1.5 h, otherwise the reply would be regarded invalid. They were also allowed to actively report their media multitasking activities anytime they were willing to. Each report of media multitasking should contain information on location, people involved, devices, content on each device, motivations and feelings. If a participant left out a particular detail, the experimenter would send a message asking for supplement. Before the formal field study, the experimenter gave participants instructions in a training section about how to reply to messages to report. In the training section, the experimenter also provided two examples as the report templates. One template is as follows:

I by myself (**people**) *used my computer* (**device**) *to watch The Voice of China* (**content**) *in my dorm* (**location**), *meanwhile used my smartphone* (**device**) *to tweet about the singers' performance* (**content**) *because it is very interesting* (**motivation**). *Then I was very happy to communicate with my buddies* (**feeling**).

After the 14-day field study, each participant filled in a questionnaire about demographic information. We provided three options of electronic devices as the incentive: a set of wireless keyboard and mouse, a mobile power and a Bluetooth earphone. Participants reported their choice at the end of the questionnaire.

Since most data were qualitative, they were coded into frequency of each type of gratifications. We categorized multitasking activities into three types. The first type (called type A) indicated those multitasking activities in which there were data communications between different devices. The second type (called type B) indicated those multitasking activities in which there was no data communication between devices but the content on different devices was relevant. The third type (called type C) indicated those multitasking activities in which there was no data communication between devices and the content on different devices had no relevancy. Based on the typology of user needs in Table 1, we chose cognitive need, emotional need, information need, social need and recognition need as the types of user gratifications in the analysis.

For each item of report, the researcher first recognized its multitasking type and added the frequency value of the corresponding gratifications by one point if the participant reported that his/her need was gratified. Then the points for all the five types of user gratifications were summed up. The ratios of the five types of gratifications were calculated by dividing the sums for each type of gratifications by the total frequency points. ANOVA was used to analyze the relationship between the ratio of the corresponding gratifications and multitasking types.

3 Results

3.1 Descriptive Statistics

Among the 25 participants, 14 (56.0 %) were males and 11 (44.0 %) were females. The average age was 21.8 (SD = 2.0). The education level of the sample was: 11 undergraduate students (44.0 %), 7 master students (28.0 %) and 7 PhD students (28.0 %).

Their experience of smart device use is shown in Table 2. It can be seen that most of them had a rich experience of using smart devices including computers, tablets and smartphones. As screened in the recruitment phase, participants all had the habit of multitasking interaction with multiple smart devices.

Table 2. Participants' smart device use experience (N = 25)

Item	N	Mean	SD
Computer use time length (years)		10.7	4.0
4–6	2		
6–10	12		
11–15	7		
15–18	4		
Tablet use time length (years)		2.1	1.2
<1	3		
1–2	12		
3–4	10		
Smartphone use time length (years)		3.2	1.2
<3	9		
3–4	14		
5–7	2		
Computer use frequency (hours per day)		7.1	3.8
<6	11		
6–9	6		
10–12	6		
13–15	2		
Tablet use frequency (hours per day)		1.2	1.6
<.5	3		
.5–1	17		
>1	5		
Smartphone use frequency (hours per day)		4.5	4.9
<2	6		
2–4	13		
5–8	1		
>8	5		

The ratios of gratifications among three multitasking types are shown in Table 3. It can be found that cognitive need of type B tended to be better gratified than that of the other two types, and that emotional need of type C tended to be better gratified than that of the other two types. These two differences were further tested via ANOVA in the next sub-section. As for the other three types of user needs, the data fluctuated too much among individuals and the differences between different types of multitasking were not obvious.

Table 3. Ratios of gratifications among three multitasking types (percentage)

User needs	Type A		Type B		Type C	
	Mean	SD	Mean	SD	Mean	SD
Cognitive need	15.14	27.24	52.63	38.09	21.90	19.10
Emotional need	9.59	23.84	14.25	28.82	38.20	20.90
Information need	4.00	20.00	8.27	14.19	3.72	6.56
Social need	1.33	5.20	11.64	23.77	6.68	9.50
Recognition need	19.74	37.09	7.99	21.62	2.06	3.33

3.2 Variance Analysis

The results of ANOVA test of multitasking types for cognitive need and emotional need are shown in Table 4. It can be seen that there exist significant differences between different types of multitasking concerning either cognitive need or emotional need. Pairwise comparisons between types of multitasking for the two needs are shown in Fig. 1. Participants' cognitive need was significantly more gratified when they conducted the second type of multitasking activities than when they conducted the other two types of multitasking activities. The first and the third types of multitasking did not differ in gratifying participants' cognitive need.

Table 4. ANOVA test of multitasking types for cognitive need and emotional need

Variables	df	F	p	Partial η^2	Cohen's f^2
Cognitive need	2	13.599	<.001	.362	.567
Emotional need	2	14.576	<.001	.378	.608

In order to investigate if the two needs differ in the extent of being gratified within each type of multitasking, we conducted the ANOVA test of cognitive need and emotional need within each type of multitasking, the result of which is shown in Table 5. At the significant level of 0.05, the two needs showed significant differences in the extent of being gratified within type B and type C. Type B had the advantage of gratifying cognitive need over emotional need, while the situation for type C was the opposite.

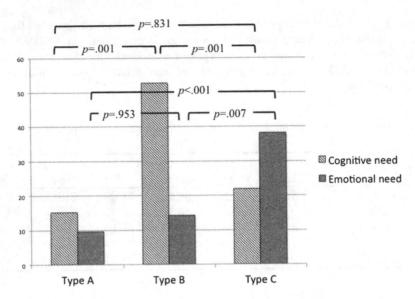

Fig. 1. Pairwise comparison between types of multitasking for cognitive need and emotional need.

Table 5. ANOVA test of cognitive need and emotional need within each multitasking type

Variables	df	F	p	Partial η^2	Cohen's f^2
Type A	1	.578	.455	.024	.025
Type B	1	10.954	.003	.313	.456
Type C	1	7.652	.011	.242	.319

4 Discussion

The core finding of this study is that multitasking activities are not necessarily "emotionally satisfying but cognitively unproductive" [13]. Whether a certain user need is gratified or not may depend on the multitasking type, to be specific, whether the content on each device has relevancy. Relevant content on different devices can improve the collaborative works and activities, resulting in higher perceived productivity and higher perceived efficiency. A typical use scenario is as depicted by the following report:

[No. 8, female] *"I forgot to print out the lecture slides, so I used the laptop to do my homework and referred to the lecture slides on the iPad in my dormitory. I felt it very convenient."*

To the opposite, irrelevant content on different devices can aggravate the interruptions caused by multitasking, resulting in lower perceived productivity, as described in the words below:

[No. 24, female] *"I was in my lab searching for some literature, while I received text messages on my mobile phone. I had to reply to it. The coming messages disturbed my work and I felt very anxious."*

In this case, her social need was gratified while the negative effect was the reduced productivity. A more extreme example to gratify emotional need in the third type of multitasking is as follows:

[No. 23, male] *"I was in my dormitory watching the cartoon Initial D on my computer. Since the plot of the cartoon was very slow, I meanwhile read the book On Top of Tides on the tablet. I felt it very comfortable and I didn't miss either."*

The finding can provide implications for designing collaborative applications or services based on multiple platforms. In the era of smart computing, the collaboration and communication between devices are becoming more and more popular. For application designers, the goal should be enhancing the whole user experience provided, but rather user experience on a single device. Thus, the content relevancy on different devices is not ignorable. Reducing the interruptions between devices and maximally improving the cooperation and consistency between devices are beyond all doubt beneficial for providing excellent whole user experience across platforms. From the results of the study, we can see that multitasking activities with data communication between devices are still insufficient for gratifying either cognitive need or emotional need. The fact that type B multitasking outperforms type A multitasking implies that humans are still better at coordinating and managing different devices than technology itself. In other words, humans are smarter at choosing the work for each device in a multitasking setting. In this direction, more research needs to be done to exploit the capacity of each device and explore the possible collaborative work patterns for multitasking contexts.

Acknowledgments. This study was funded by a National Natural Science Foundation of China grant 71188001.

References

1. Nielsen. http://blog.nielsen.com/nielsenwire/online_mobile/40-of-tablet-and-smartphone-owners-use-them-while-watching-tv/
2. Hollywood Reporter. http://www.hollywoodreporter.com/gallery/facebook-twitter-social-media-study-302273-3
3. iResearch. http://wireless.iresearch.cn/88/20120719/177001.shtml
4. Ophir, E., Nass, C., Wagner, A.D.: Cognitive control in media multitaskers. Proc. Nat. Acad. Sci. U.S.A. **106**, 15583–15587 (2009)
5. Bowman, L.L., Levine, L.E., Waite, B.M., Gendron, M.: Can students really multitask? An experimental study of instant messaging while reading. Comput. Educ. **54**, 927–931 (2010)
6. Van Winsum, W., de Waard, D., Brookhuis, K.A.: Lane change manoeuvres and safety margins. Transp. Res. Part F: Psychol. Behav. **2**, 139–149 (1999)
7. Wei, F.-Y.F., Wang, Y.K., Fass, W.: An experimental study of online chatting and notetaking techniques on college students' cognitive learning from a lecture. Comput. Hum. Behav. **34**, 148–156 (2014)

8. Rideout, V.J., Foehr, U.G., Roberts, D.F.: Generation M2: Media in the Lives of 8-to 18-Year-Olds. Kaiser Family Foundation, Menlo Park (2010)
9. Foehr, U.G.: Media Multitasking Among American Youth: Prevalence Predictors and Pairings. Kaiser Family Foundation, Menlo Park (2006)
10. Bardhi, F., Rohm, A.J., Sultan, F.: Tuning in and tuning out: media multitasking among young consumers. J. Consum. Behav. **9**, 316–332 (2010)
11. Circella, G., Mokhtarian, P.L., Poff, L.K.: A conceptual typology of multitasking behavior and polychronicity preferences. Electron. Int. J. Time Use Res. **9**, 59–107 (2012)
12. eMarketer. http://www.emarketer.com/Article/UK-More-Screens-Mean-More-Fragmented-Viewing-Behavior/1009708
13. Wang, Z., Tchernev, J.M.: The "myth" of media multitasking: reciprocal dynamics of media multitasking, personal needs, and gratifications. J. Commun. **62**, 493–513 (2012)
14. Wang, Z., Tchernev, J.M., Solloway, T.: A dynamic longitudinal examination of social media use, needs, and gratifications among college students. Comput. Hum. Behav. **28**, 1829–1839 (2012)
15. Rosen, L.D., Carrier, L.M., Cheever, N.A.: Facebook and texting made me do it: media-induced task-switching while studying. Comput. Hum. Behav. **29**, 948–958 (2013)
16. Katz, E., Haas, H., Gurevitch, M.: On the use of the mass media for important things. Am. Sociol. Rev. **38**, 164–181 (1973)
17. Quan-Haase, A., Young, A.L.: Uses and gratifications of social media: a comparison of facebook and instant messaging. Bull. Sci. Technol. Soc. **30**, 350–361 (2010)
18. Chang, B.-H., Lee, S.-E., Kim, B.-S.: Exploring factors affecting the adoption and continuance of online games among college students in South Korea integrating uses and gratification and diffusion of innovation approaches. New Media Soc. **8**, 295–319 (2006)
19. Katz, E., Blumler, J.G., Gurevitch, M.: Uses and gratifications research. Public Opin. Q. **37**, 509–523 (1973)
20. Palmgreen, P.: Uses and gratifications: a theoretical perspective. In: Communication Yearbook, vol. 8, pp. 20–55 (1984)
21. Leung, L.: User-generated content on the internet: an examination of gratifications, civic engagement and psychological empowerment. New Media Soc. **11**, 1327–1347 (2009)
22. Zhang, W., Zhang, L.: Explicating multitasking with computers: gratifications and situations. Comput. Hum. Behav. **28**, 1883–1891 (2012)
23. Jeong, S.-H., Fishbein, M.: Predictors of multitasking with media: media factors and audience factors. Media Psychol. **10**, 364–384 (2007)
24. Jeong, S.-H., Hwang, Y., Fishbein, M.: Effects of exposure to sexual content in the media on adolescent sexual behaviors: the moderating role of multitasking with media. Media Psychol. **13**, 222–242 (2010)
25. Mark, G., Iqbal, S.T., Czerwinski, M., Johns, P.: Bored mondays and focused afternoons: the rhythm of attention and online activity in the workplace. In: The 32nd Annual ACM Conference on Human Factors in Computing Systems, pp. 3025–3034. ACM, New York (2014)
26. Mark, G., Iqbal, S., Czerwinski, M., Johns, P.: Capturing the mood: facebook and face-to-face encounters in the workplace. In: The 17th ACM Conference on Computer Supported Cooperative Work and Social Computing, pp. 1082–1094. ACM, New York (2014)

Author Index

Printed in the United States
By Bookmasters